POWER
PLAY

POWER PLAY

PROFESSIONAL HOCKEY AND THE POLITICS OF URBAN DEVELOPMENT

JAY SCHERER, DAVID MILLS & LINDA SLOAN MCCULLOCH

UNIVERSITY of ALBERTA PRESS

Published by

The University of Alberta Press
Ring House 2
Edmonton, Alberta, Canada T6G 2E1
www.uap.ualberta.ca

LIBRARY AND ARCHIVES CANADA
CATALOGUING IN PUBLICATION

Title: Power play : professional hockey and
　　　the politics of urban development /
　　　Jay Scherer, David Mills, and Linda Sloan
　　　McCulloch.
Names: Scherer, Jay, 1975- author. | Mills,
　　　David, 1952- author. | McCulloch, Linda
　　　Sloan, 1960- author.
Description: Includes bibliographical
　　　references and index.
Identifiers: Canadiana (print) 20190174730 |
　　　Canadiana (ebook) 20190174749 |
　　　ISBN 9781772124934 (softcover) |
　　　ISBN 9781772124941 (EPUB) |
　　　ISBN 9781772124958 (Kindle) |
　　　ISBN 9781772124965 (PDF)
Subjects: LCSH: Arenas—Alberta—
　　　Edmonton—Finance. | LCSH: Arenas—
　　　Economic aspects—Alberta—Edmonton. |
　　　LCSH: City planning—Alberta—
　　　Edmonton. | LCSH: Public-private sector
　　　cooperation—Alberta—Edmonton.
Classification: LCC GV418.R64 S34 2019 |
　　　DDC 796.06/8712334—dc23

First edition, first printing, 2019.
First printed and bound in Canada by
Houghton Boston Printers, Saskatoon,
Saskatchewan.
Copyediting and proofreading by
Angela Pietrobon.
Indexing by Stephen Ullstrom.

University of Alberta Press supports copyright. Copyright fuels creativity, encourages
diverse voices, promotes free speech, and
creates a vibrant culture. Thank you for buying an authorized edition of this book and for
complying with the copyright laws by not re-
producing, scanning, or distributing any part
of it in any form without permission. You are
supporting writers and allowing University of
Alberta Press to continue to publish books for
every reader.

University of Alberta Press is committed to
protecting our natural environment. As part
of our efforts, this book is printed on Enviro
Paper: it contains 100% post-consumer recycled fibres and is acid- and chlorine-free.

University of Alberta Press gratefully acknowl-
edges the support received for its publishing
program from the Government of Canada,
the Canada Council for the Arts, and the
Government of Alberta through the Alberta
Media Fund.

Every effort has been made to identify copyright holders and obtain permission for
the use of copyright material. Please notify
University of Alberta Press of any additions
or corrections that should be incorporated in
future reprints or editions of this book.

This work is published with the assistance
of the Western Canadiana Publications
Endowment.

For citizens of Edmonton: Past, present, and future

Rogers Place was built on Treaty 6 territory, a traditional gathering place for diverse Indigenous peoples including the Cree, Blackfoot, Métis, Nakota Sioux, Iroquois, Dene, Ojibway/Saulteaux/Anishinaabe, Inuit and many others. Discussions of Rogers Place, therefore, necessitate an acknowledgement of the broader history of our presence on Indigenous lands.

CONTENTS

FOREWORD

NEARLY THIRTY YEARS AGO, the iconic Canadian literary critic Northrop Frye commented on Toronto's aspirations to be a "world-class" city. If Toronto is a world-class city, Frye suggested, "it is not because it bids for the Olympics or builds follies like the Skydome, but because of the tolerated variety of people in its streets."[1] For Frye, world-class cities are characterized by their diversity and cosmo-politanism and it is only here where Toronto might stake its claim to world-class status. In Frye's optimistic vision, truly world-class cities celebrate human variety rather than ignoring it, condemning it, or pushing it to the urban periphery.

I think this argument is more compelling than ever when you consider how increasing gentrification has been pushing major Canadian downtowns toward greater socioeconomic uniformity. It is also an advance warning against the renewed visibility of reactionary populist racial and ethnic prejudice in recent years. Having said this, it is important to consider the subtext of Frye's remarks, that ambitions for major sporting events, spectacular new stadiums, or arenas should not be written off simply as economic follies or barriers to progressive models of urban development. The difficulty is that the issues in question here are extremely complex, vary over time, and differ from city to city. A blanket view of *all* supposedly world-class urban spectacles and projects as financial losers, bread and circuses, or as pathways to racial or ethnic one dimensionality is no substitute for serious thinking on the matter.

Still, it is undoubtedly true that boosters and promoters in Canada's major cities over the past 40 years have understood the phrase "world class" in a much different way from Northrop Frye. For them, a world-class city is a site for magnificent architecture, exclusive hotels, upmarket shopping experiences, major league sports teams, and internationally prominent events. In this view, being world class means securing a privileged place on national and international circuits of capital investment, advertising, consumption, and tourism. Proponents have argued that zoning and tax concessions or public subsidies to support a city's world-class aspirations are in the public interest. This is because they are said to create employment and attract private capital, as well as affluent immigrants, and tourists.

Since the 1980s, in particular, major Canadian cities have engaged in national and global competition for world-class status through strategic linkages between mega-projects, real estate development, place branding, and imagined world-class entertainments. The rising tide of investments in the pursuit of such things is supposed to lift everyone up, to float all boats, as the popular saying goes. A project-driven and event-based model of urban development is not only presented by proponents as something positive, it is also typically represented as a necessary, even inevitable, response to pressures and opportunities deriving from the mobile nature of capital in the globalized, highly mediated, consumption-oriented world of the twenty-first century.

Focusing on relationships between NHL hockey, urban boosterism, and the changing politics of city building in Edmonton, this remarkable book by Jay Scherer, David Mills, and Linda Sloan McCulloch analyzes and dissects the promotional spin that so often accompanies this vision of urban development. Faced with what the authors refer to as the "haunting spectre" of losing the Oilers to another city, an influential power bloc of civic boosters and local politicians, along with Edmonton's billionaire team owner Daryl Katz, responded with an elaborate public–private partnership involving a new state-of-the-art arena and surrounding entertainment and residential area known as "Ice District." Direct financing costs for the arena were well over $600 million, requiring an innovative financing scheme, arguably with negative tax implications for the city, and draining resources from other infrastructure needs and social services. There has yet to be a thorough and full accounting of costs from the city, while critics have suggested that the arena development represents a public gift to the Katz Group in excess of a billion dollars.

In recent years, there have been several books about how owners of major league sports franchises have used the threat of leaving cities to leverage concessions from governments for new, publicly-funded stadiums and arenas. The best of these books situate their consideration of contemporary urban politics and stadium funding in an integrated analysis of the rapidly changing nature of the professional sport industry and pressures on city governments arising from the growing importance of the tourist, media, and entertainment industries. As these industries have become more central to North American urban economies, city governments have felt increased pressure to accede to demands for public subsidies made by team owners looking to find new revenue streams.

Through a combination of interviews and exhaustive documentary research, Scherer, Mills, and McCulloch discuss brilliantly how all of this has played out in Edmonton. But, for me, their analysis of contemporary events is made even more convincing by an extensive historical discussion of the long and shifting relationships between hockey in Edmonton and boosterism as a "corporate–civic project." The narrative reveals sometimes-subtle changes in the control and ownership of hockey and the differing ways hockey has been connected to shifting coalitions of Edmonton's business and professional elites. It is all here: from the earliest teams and founding of the Edmonton Exhibition Association, through to Western Hockey League teams in the 1920s, and the WHL and NHL Oilers teams in the 1970s and 1980s, including changes in arenas, team ownerships, and various debates about arena funding. The authors provide a nuanced longitudinal case study of the politics, history, and political economy of a major sports team, sports arenas, and their combined role in the

development of a North American city. They have written a book that
will not only be of interest to sport scholars, hockey fans, and followers
of Edmonton's civic politics, but also to anyone struggling to understand both the rhetoric and reality of what it means for cities to be
world class in the twenty-first century.

RICHARD GRUNEAU
Co-author of Hockey Night in Canada
Bowen Island, 2018

PREFACE

DR. JAY SCHERER is a Professor of Sociology of Sport in the Faculty
of Kinesiology, Sport, and Recreation at the University of Alberta. He
has researched and published for two decades on political debates
over the use of public funds to build urban infrastructure for major
league sports franchises. Jay first became involved in the arena debate
in Edmonton as a member of Voices For Democracy, a grassroots
group organized to oppose the use of public funds for the development
of Rogers Place. He grew up in Winnipeg and was a fan of the Winnipeg
Jets until the franchise relocated to Phoenix in the mid-1990s. He
has played recreational hockey for most of his life.

Linda McCulloch's (then Linda Sloan) involvement began during
her time on city council in Edmonton from 2004 to 2013 (after acting
as a Member of Alberta's Legislative Assembly from 1997 to 2001).
She was active in Edmonton Minor Hockey, including elected terms
on the Edmonton Girls Hockey Association and volunteering with
the Knights of Columbus, Whitemud West, and Canadian Athletic
Hockey Clubs. During her nine years on council, two public issues
captured and divided the electorate: closing the Edmonton City
Centre Airport and building the downtown arena. She voted against
both the closure of the airport and the arena financing agreement.
Many in Edmonton characterized her opposition to the arena financing
agreement as opposition to the Oilers—a standard approach to

critics in these types of debates. Linda really voted against the arena financing agreement because she thought that most of the benefits of the deal fell to the Katz Group, while the city of Edmonton took on most of the risks and costs. She had also become increasingly skeptical of the secretive and restrictive political process associated with the arena debate, which was conducted very differently from other deliberations over the expenditure of public money. Jay and Linda met after the culmination of the arena debate in 2013, after Linda had announced that she was retiring from public life and would not seek re-election in the upcoming municipal election. They agreed that a fuller account of the arena debate—especially an account of the negotiations and discussions behind closed doors— needed to be published.

Dr. David Mills, a recently retired professor who taught Canadian history and sports history in the Department of History and Classics at the University of Alberta for over 30 years, and who has written on the business of hockey in Edmonton, especially during the Pocklington era, then joined the team. Although David grew up as a Toronto Maple Leafs fan, he transferred his allegiance to the Oilers during the club's glory years of the 1980s after he moved to Edmonton. Now he is a long-suffering Edmonton Oilers season ticket holder. He was a goalie for old-timer's hockey teams in and around Edmonton for almost 35 years, until injuries ended a less-than-stellar career.

This book does not provide the definitive account of the arena debate. Certainly, our own biases and assumptions have shaped and coloured our analysis. We simply have a different vision for the city and for the use of scarce public resources than the influential growth coalition of boosters who supported the $613.7-million, publicly-financed arena development for the Edmonton Oilers. However, we have tried to provide a balanced and richly detailed account of the debate, its political processes, and its historical antecedents. In so doing, we have accessed numerous historical reports and relied heavily on the arena-related documents and materials that Linda retained from her time on city council, including her own detailed personal notes on the political proceedings and, in particular, the in-camera meetings, of which there are limited records and no audio recordings. She kept her copies of council reports and her personal notes from the arena debate precisely precisely because of her concern with how the political process was being manipulated. Frequently, when council's agenda indicated that councillors would receive an update on the arena debate from the city manager, what they were presented with behind closed doors was much different; often, motions were made to provide direction to administration in the next steps of negotiations with the Katz Group without any public discussion. This strategy limited transparency and democratic accountability for a volatile political issue. Over time, Linda became increasingly concerned that city administration had abandoned its traditional remit to provide disinterested and objective analyses about arena-related issues and had simply become a broker, mediator, and booster of the deal.

That Linda retained a significant collection of files and well-kept notes was fortunate, as we continually encountered obstacles in our attempts to obtain public information about the arena debate from the city of Edmonton through Freedom of Information requests. We experienced some lengthy delays that went well beyond the stated 30-day time limit of the *Freedom of Information and Protection of Privacy Act* (FOIP) for public bodies to provide requested information. We were routinely quoted exorbitant fee estimates to access public information, sometimes even tens of thousands of dollars. Most troubling, though, was the sheer number of times that we were denied access to public information. Often, municipal officials had redacted public reports, documents, and communication to such an extent that they were virtually incomprehensible. On another occasion, we were informed by the Office of the City Clerk that crucial information—including foundational arena-related reports—could not be located. Then, in response to a request for all communication between Mayor Mandel and Daryl Katz, we were informed by the city clerk's office that not a single email message existed—a claim that the Office of the Information and Privacy Commissioner of Alberta (OIPC) disputed. Even when municipal officials were able to retrieve information, municipal bureaucrats withheld numerous documents and communications. In one instance, the city clerk's office refused to release a single document from over 1,000 pages of written communications between municipal officials and the NHL, including the NHL commissioner, Gary Bettman.

We eventually obtained some of the information we asked for, but only after requesting a number of reviews by the OIPC. These appeals take time, and public bodies can effectively delay the release of information for years, if they want to. For critics, the institutional obstacles that restrict access to public information across Alberta underscore the need for reform to the FOIP Act (1994), including the establishment of protocols to ensure minimal fees and shortened timelines, as well as meaningful penalties to eliminate political interference.[1]

We would like to extend our sincere gratitude to Councillor Mike Nickel, who made enquiries on our behalf and who personally called for a probe into the secrecy at city hall and the misapplication of FOIP rules and policies by municipal officials. In response to these concerns, and others raised by citizens, including Elise Stolte, a journalist at the *Edmonton Journal*, the city of Edmonton has introduced new rules and regulations to improve transparency and to ensure that documents and reports are not kept secret in perpetuity. Still, as we discovered in later attempts to access information, problems remain, as the city of Edmonton, the Katz Group, and the Edmonton Economic Development Corporation have continued to restrict access to documents and information pertaining to the city-owned facility in question by claiming that releasing this information would prove harmful to the business interests of the Katz Group (Section 16 of the FOIP Act). All of these issues, of course, point to the substantive democratic limitations that inevitably accompany these types of public–private partnerships and restrict the ability of citizens to be involved in municipal affairs.

On the other hand, many people involved in the arena debate were extraordinarily generous with their time and made themselves available to be interviewed for the book. We would like to thank Bryan Anderson, Jerry Bouma, Tony Caterina, Rick Daviss, Neil deMause, Kerry Diotte, Simon Farbrother, Max Fawcett, Ed Gibbons,

Andy Grabia, Doug Griffiths, Fish Griwkowsky, Scott Hennig, Brad Humphreys, Lorne Humphreys, Andy Huntley, Gordon Kent, Ken Knowles, Patrick LaForge, Gary Lamphier, Karen Leibovici, John MacKinnon, Wayne MacDonald, Stephen Mandel, Al Maurer, Scott McKeen, Cec Purves, Jan Reimer, Paula Simons, David Staples, Mimi Williams, and Andrew Zimbalist.

The following people were contacted, but either did not respond or did not wish to be interviewed: Richard Andersen, who signed a non-disclosure agreement upon his departure from Northlands, Margaret Bateman, Bob Black (Katz Group), Don Iveson, Dr. Dan Mason, Naheed Nenshi, Cal Nichols, Lorna Rosen, and Tim Shipton (Katz Group).

ACKNOWLEDGEMENTS

WE WOULD LIKE TO THANK the following individuals who read
parts of the book and offered constructive feedback and helpful
comments: Ziad Fazel, Rylan Kafara, Michael Leskow, Robert
McCulloch, Brian Soebbing, Kevin Taft, Paul Voisey, and David
Whitson. We are grateful to Andy Grabia, who not only reviewed a
number of chapters of the book, but also generously shared with us
his own research on the arena debate. A special thanks to Rick
Gruneau for his comments on the book, and for contributing the
Foreword. We would also like to thank the Faculty of Kinesiology,
Sport, and Recreation for its support of this project, as well as Dan
Rose of the Edmonton Heritage Council and Terry O'Riordan of the
Provincial Archives of Alberta for their assistance.

Thanks, as well, to Douglas Hildebrand, Cathie Crooks, Duncan
Turner, Alan Brownoff, and the rest of the staff at University of
Alberta Press, and to Leslie Robertson and Angela Pietrobon for
their editorial assistance. An enormous debt is owed to Peter
Midgley, who has supported this project since our first meeting,
and who has provided sage advice over the course of many years of
research and writing.

Jay would like to extend his gratitude to his friends at Boyle Street
Community Services.

Finally, we would like to thank our respective families—Heather, Emma, and Christopher Scherer; Janice Mills; and Bill McCulloch—who have gone above and beyond in supporting our work on this project.

XXII

ACKNOWLEDGEMENTS

IMPORTANT TERMS

The Arena Financing Agreement

The $613.7-million financing agreement between the city of Edmonton and the Katz Group (Edmonton Arena Corporation, or EAC) is complex and expansive. It includes a range of financing mechanisms to cover the costs of the arena development and related infrastructure for the next 35 years, which are recorded in Table 1.[1] Other significant expenses—including the city of Edmonton's interest and other borrowing costs—are not included in the table.

TABLE 1. Breakdown of Financing for Arena Development Project (Figures in Millions)

Element	Estimated Cost	CRL (Community Revitalization Levy)	General City Funding	EAC Lease Funding	EAC Cash	Ticket Surcharge	Other
Rogers Place (the arena)	$483.5	$145.0	$81.0	$112.8	$19.7	$125.0	
Winter Garden	$56.8	$25.0	$0.1	$25.0	$6.7		
Pedestrian Corridor	$15.0	$15.0					
LRT Connection	$7.0	$7.0					
Community Downtown Arena	$24.9	$14.0	$0.1		$0.3·		$10.5
Arena Land	$26.5	$25.0	$0.5		$1.0		
TOTAL	*$613.7*	*$231.0*	*$81.7*	*$137.8*	*$27.7*	*$125.0*	*$10.5*

Source: Adapted from City of Edmonton, "The Agreement," 2019, https://www.edmonton.ca/attractions_events/rogers_place/the-agreement.aspx.

The EAC Cash funding shown in Table 1 came from the EAC and ICE Joint Venture—the Katz Group holds an ownership interest in both. The total $10.5 million shown in the final column ("Other"), includes funds provided by the federal government ($7 million), notably through the Federal Gas Tax, and MacEwan University ($3.5 million).

Community Revitalization Levy

A Community Revitalization Levy (CRL) is a funding mechanism created by the Alberta government in 2005 to help municipalities revitalize underdeveloped areas within their boundaries. It grants a municipality the power to freeze the assessed tax base for a defined geographic area (the CRL boundary) at a specific point in time for up to 20 years. After this baseline assessment, all of the *new* tax revenue within the CRL boundary—the lift in revenue that occurs from new development and from the increased value of real estate—is redirected to support the development and servicing of amenities and infrastructure within the boundary. This includes the city's portion of property tax, which is diverted away from general revenues, as well as the education property tax collected on behalf of the province. The Capital City Downtown CRL was approved by the government of Alberta in 2014, and activated by the city of Edmonton in December 2014 after setting a baseline for assessed property values. The Capital City Downtown CRL was originally intended to contribute $231 million to the cost of Rogers Place. It expires in 2034.

General City Funding

Annual principal and interest payments on $81.7 million of self-supporting, tax-guaranteed debt was intended to be funded over 20 years with a combination of downtown parking revenue, property taxes from the downtown arena parkade, and a reallocation of the Northlands arena subsidy.

Ticket Surcharge

A ticket surcharge has been one of the central mechanisms for raising money for renovations at the Northlands Coliseum and for the construction of Rogers Place. It is a tax added to the price of tickets for events in the facilities and is paid for by the users—the spectators attending hockey games or concerts. A similar tax was introduced by the city in the mid-1990s, when the former owner of the Oilers, Peter Pocklington, demanded another source of revenue; this tax also provided revenue to Northlands from non-hockey events.

The ticket surcharge is now to be collected by the Katz Group and set annually, subject to approval by the city manager. When Rogers Place opened in 2016, the initial surcharge was set at 9.5 percent. Every three months, the Katz Group is required to remit the proceeds from the ticket surcharge to the city to cover the principal and interest payments for the $125 million that was borrowed over a 35-year term, plus provide a $1.5 million annual contribution to the city to create a fund for ongoing major capital expenditures. If the ticket surcharge exceeds the amount required to cover these costs for a three-month period, the Katz Group is entitled to retain this surplus. This surplus, therefore, will not be used to pay down the city's loan faster. Nor will it carry forward to future years when the market may not accept a ticket tax on a 20 to 35-year-old arena.

A ticket surcharge on admissions at the Coliseum has also been levied by the city to the same rate as the ticket surcharge on non-hockey events at Rogers Place, to a maximum of 7 percent. The proceeds of this surcharge go to the city. At the time of writing, the Coliseum remains unused, sits empty, and faces future demolition.

1

INTRODUCTION

IN SEPTEMBER 2016, amidst much fanfare and celebration, Rogers
Place—Edmonton's $613.7-million,[1] publicly-financed arena and the
new home of the National Hockey League's (NHL) Oilers—opened
for business. To mark the occasion, the city's most influential political, business, and cultural leaders, plus the media, were in attendance
to show their support for the facility and for the public–private partnership between the city and the Katz Group in the civic–corporate
project of transforming Edmonton in the new millennium. In a fitting
and symbolic gesture, Daryl Katz, the Oilers' billionaire owner, and
Mayor Don Iveson, once a vocal opponent of the arena's public financing agreement, were photographed together on the red carpet at
the reception. In their celebratory remarks, both Katz and Iveson
heralded the arena and its surrounding entertainment area, known
as Ice District, for revitalizing the downtown and announcing
Edmonton's arrival on the world stage.

Certainly, for its main proponents, as well as its main beneficiaries, the new arena development represented a success story for
both public and private interests. The Edmonton Oilers would be
financially sustainable for decades to come and committed to a
35-year location agreement, putting to rest longstanding concerns
about the viability of NHL hockey in a peripheral Western Canadian
city. For boosters and hockey fans alike, the prospect of losing the

Edmonton Oilers owner Daryl Katz (right) and Edmonton Mayor Don Iveson celebrate during the opening ceremony at Rogers Place Arena, the new home of the Edmonton Oilers, on September 8, 2016. [Canadian Press/Jason Franson]

club remained a haunting spectre, especially after the turbulent years of the 1990s, when the team's former owner, Peter Pocklington, threatened to move the Oilers first to Hamilton, then to Minneapolis, then to Oklahoma City, and finally to Houston, unless he was granted more and more concessions and additional public subsidies at the team's former home, the Northlands Coliseum—a facility that had opened in 1974 to similar fanfare. The success of Pocklington's threats was not lost on the current owner of the Oilers, who, in September 2012, had flirted with the idea of moving his team to Seattle if he didn't get the deal he wanted.

Rogers Place was built on time and on budget, and, according to its supporters, has since attracted more than $2 billion in investment to Edmonton's central core, where large blocks of undeveloped land had been assembled by the Katz Group and other powerful property developers. Significant caveats must accompany the claims about "new" investment downtown; for one thing, as investment, spending, and jobs have been relocated and centralized in a small part of the downtown, other areas and neighbourhoods—especially around the abandoned Coliseum—have declined. It is also necessary to acknowledge that Edmonton's central core has been enjoying a period of substantive growth and redevelopment since the turn of the new millennium, and that this pattern was set to continue, with or without a new arena.[2] Still, Rogers Place has undeniably played a major, though not primary, role in the transformation of Edmonton's downtown and in the expansion of leisure and residential choices—and income opportunities—for the city's business and professional elites, for whom living in a "world-class city" matters. And, as both Katz and Iveson suggested, the new arena and entertainment district has created, especially for young people, a sense of vibrancy, atmosphere, and pride in the city that has, for local boosters, sometimes been in short supply, especially in light of the range of unflattering caricatures applied to Edmonton, like "Canada's boiler room" or "Deadmonton."

However, even in the midst of the celebration, and before the Oilers hit the ice for their first regular-season game at Rogers Place, the arena also represented controversy and division. Hundreds of millions of dollars of scarce public resources had been spent to support the business interests of a billionaire at the expense of other infrastructure needs and social services. Not every Edmontonian can participate equally in this world-class development. Just before the new arena opened, for example, some downtown residents appeared at city hall to protest the absence of a meaningful community benefits agreement (CBA) and the far-reaching effects of the development on people, including the city centre's homeless community—most of whom are Indigenous—as well as on many pre-existing businesses that were struggling with increased property tax payments and parking issues.[3] The protestors painted a radically different picture of life in Edmonton's gentrifying downtown core. They spoke, too, about the social issues that have received less attention and considerably fewer public resources from city hall than its economic growth agenda, and they questioned the oft-cited, but rarely demonstrated, claim that subsidizing professional sports teams benefits "the community as a whole." They weren't the only Edmontonians with such concerns. On the day the arena officially opened, a poll was released indicating that nearly 40 percent of the city's residents still disapproved of public financing for the arena; only 44 percent of the respondents indicated that they supported the development. Strikingly, less than 40 percent of Edmontonians aged 35–49—a demographic that had been targeted by the aspirational rhetoric of the project's boosters—said they endorsed the project.[4]

There was also considerable residual unhappiness with the terms of the 35-year arena financing/subsidy agreement that had been nego-tiated mostly in private and signed by the city of Edmonton and the Katz Group in 2013 *without a plebiscite*. The agreement was the culmi-nation of a nearly decade-long political debate that included threats by the Katz Group to relocate the Oilers unless they were granted enormous concessions and subsidies, not only for the arena but also for ancillary developments around Rogers Place. The financing agree-ment also marked a significant break from the private funding models for other Canadian arenas built in Vancouver (1995), Ottawa (1996), Montreal (1996), and Toronto (1999).

Unlike these and facilities in other cities,[5] the city of Edmonton owns the arena. It debt-financed nearly all of the total cost of Rogers Place, and agreed to pay down the debt and interest expenses through a complex public and private funding model over the course of 35 years. The city also agreed to cede all revenues from the city-owned facility— hundreds of millions of dollars including all liquor sales, all non-hockey revenue including concerts, concessions, parking, advertising, and the lucrative naming rights, which were sold to Rogers Communications and Ford and worth tens of millions of dollars alone, as well as full operational control of the arena—to the Katz Group in exchange for a 35-year location agreement. The Katz Group is responsible for operating and maintenance expenses at Rogers Place and will make annual lease payments of $5.5 million for the duration of the agreement, in lieu of a significant upfront contribu-tion to the cost of the arena. However, the city agreed to offset these payments for the next 10 years by providing the Katz Group with an annual subsidy of $2 million in the form of a "marketing partnership."

The new arena, as intended, has already dramatically increased both the franchise's valuation and its revenue streams. According to *Forbes*' 2017 franchise valuation, after the Oilers' first season at Rogers Place (2016/17), the team's value was estimated at US$520 million, up 17 percent from the previous year and far more than the US$200 million that Daryl Katz paid for it in 2008. The team also enjoyed an estimated 23 percent increase in revenue over what it had earned at Rexall Place (as of summer 2016, called Northlands Coliseum once again). Operating income had jumped to an estimated US$24 million, up from an estimated US$15.4 million in the 2015/16 season. In the 2017/18 season, the team's value had increased again to US$540 million, although revenue and operating income had declined slightly; unlike the previous season, the Oilers failed to make the playoffs in 2018 and missed the opportunity to accumulate playoff revenue. Still, revenue remained high because the Katz Group had secured a non-compete clause at the expense of the Northlands organization, the longstanding non-profit operator of the Coliseum and a once-dominant civic institution, thus giving the Oilers Entertainment Group total control over NHL/WHL hockey played at Rogers Place and a virtual monopoly of major concerts scheduled in Edmonton.

Perhaps most important, though, is that the arena is the anchor of a much larger real estate play on the downtown land that the Katz Group assembled to build condominiums, hotels, and an office tower. Over the course of the arena negotiations, the Katz Group demanded that the city lease space in the new office building. The city initiated a request for proposals for leased office accommodation in downtown Edmonton, but ultimately awarded the contract to the Katz Group and entered into a 20-year lease *at increasing rates* to centralize two-thirds of city staff in the new Katz-owned Edmonton Tower, just across from the new arena.[6] We do not suggest that this arrangement involved deception; Mayor Iveson has said that all of the proposals were evaluated by independent advisors. However, it does signal the extent to which the city's interests have been aligned with those of the Katz Group on multiple levels

TABLE 2. *Value of The Edmonton Oilers Franchise from 1997/98–2017/18*
(Figures in Millions USS)

Season	Revenue	Operating Income	Valuation	Forbes Ranking
2017/18	$145	$21	$540	13th, of 31 teams
2016/17	$151	$24	$520	12th, of 30 teams
2015/16	$117	$15.4	$445	14th, of 30 teams
2014/15	$119	$17.2	$455	12th, of 30 teams
2013/14	$119	$25.3	$475	12th, of 30 teams
2012/13	$80	$10.3	$400	14th, of 30 teams
2011/12	$106	$16.2	$225	14th, of 30 teams
2010/11	$96	$17.3	$212	15th, of 30 teams
2009/10	$87	$8.2	$183	20th, of 30 teams
2008/09	$83	$9.4	$166	24th, of 30 teams
2007/08	$85	$11.8	$175	20th, of 30 teams
2006/07	$71	$9.9	$157	20th, of 30 teams
2005/06*	$75	$10.7	$146	18th, of 30 teams
2003/04	$55	$3	$104	29th, of 30 teams
2002/03	$48	$-0.1	$91	30th, of 30 teams
2001/02	$43	$-0.8	$86	30th, of 30 teams
2000/01	$43	$3	$81	29th, of 30 teams
1999/2000	$40	$4	$77	28th, of 28 teams
1998/99	$36	$3	$72	26th, of 27 teams
1997/98	$34	$2	$67	26th, of 26 teams

Source: *Forbes'* annual list of franchise valuations, which can be found at Forbes.com by year.
*Figures for 2004/05 are not included because the NHL had locked out the players for the
whole season.

for the next 20–35 years, ensuring for the Katz Group, at least, a sizeable return on many of its investments in the downtown core, with
minimized risk. In 2018, the Katz Group sold the Edmonton Tower
to the Alberta Investment Management Corporation for a reported
$400 million.[7]

The value of all of these landholdings has skyrocketed in recent
years—a fact that underlines the dramatic changes to the business
model of professional sport over the past two decades. As Howard
Shubert has noted in *Architecture on Ice*, contemporary hockey

arenas must now be understood as the centrepieces of much larger land development opportunities, and as the hubs of integrated and expansive corporate-entertainment complexes. Even the changes in the names of facilities—from Gardens, Forum, and Coliseum to Centre and Place—underline the extent to which the hockey arena now serves as a component of a much broader commercial spectacle to allow owners to accumulate as much of the sports/entertainment dollar as possible, including money from the upmarket restaurants, bars, and casinos often located within the facility itself.[8]

The appeal of these types of projects for a city like Edmonton is obvious: large tracts of underdeveloped land in the hollowed-out urban core have been redeveloped, and increases in municipal tax revenue in the downtown are being dedicated to paying off the cost of the arena through the Capital City Downtown Community Revitalization Levy (CRL).[9] Still, there are always risks to such bargains, and important questions must be asked about the use of scarce public funds to subsidize not only the operations of professional sports franchises, but also the broader business interests of team owners like Daryl Katz, whose personal wealth is unimaginable to most Edmontonians. This point was reinforced in 2018 when news emerged that, since the end of the arena debate five years earlier, Katz had added to his already sizeable asset portfolio by investing just shy of US$140 million (over CA$180 million in 2018 dollars) in the Los Angeles property market alone, including the purchase of a single property in Malibu for US$85 million. Of course, Edmontonians had been told repeatedly that private financing of the new arena was impossible, and that it was unrealistic to expect the Katz Group to bear the burden of paying for and operating it.

Moreover, while the upfront cost of the arena development appears to be $613.7 million, like most publicly financed major league sports facilities, the actual price tag is far higher and includes a host of uncounted public costs. In light of the closure of the Northlands Coliseum, the city had to forgive over $47 million in debt owed by Northlands for the construction of a new Exhibition Centre and a remaining debt of over $500,000 for the old scoreboard at the

Coliseum. Demolishing the Coliseum may cost another estimated $20–25 million. The city is also on the hook for an annual expense of $4 million for additional policing around the downtown arena ($140 million over 35 years). The city has foregone tens of millions of dollars[10] by agreeing to receive a fixed annual amount of $250,000 from the Katz Group in lieu of municipal property taxes for the arena for the next 35 years; likewise, the Katz Group's lease payments have been capped for the duration of the agreement with no escalator clause to address inflation. Meanwhile, there is no way of knowing how much public funding may be required to redevelop the city-owned grounds at Northlands to prevent the further deterioration of its surrounding neighbourhoods.

While money and investment are being concentrated in the arena and entertainment district—and around the Katz Group's proper-ties—condominium sales prices in the city dropped 8.8 percent in 2017, and assessments fell by another 4.5 percent in 2018; office vacancy rates remain high, and other parts of the city are stagnating. Even in the downtown core, office vacancy rates hovered around 18 percent[11] in 2017, thanks, in part, to the opening of the Edmonton Tower a year earlier—a development that may have consequences for the Capital City Downtown CRL financing mechanism and associated arena debt repayment; and some downtown businesses are not doing as well as expected.

Some have suggested that when the total cost of the new arena is added up—in addition to the hundreds of millions of dollars of fore-gone revenue over 35 years, coupled with the dramatic increases in the value of the Oilers franchise and the Katz Group's surrounding land holdings—Rogers Place represents a public gift to the Katz Group that is *conservatively estimated* at $1.5 billion.[12]

Rinks of Schemes?
The debate over the publicly-financed arena development in Edmonton was always about competing visions and political priorities for the city. It's a dramatic and compelling story involving powerful people and institutions operating at the intersections between money,

sport, local politics, and real estate development. It's also a story about Edmonton's longstanding aspiration to attract major league hockey to the city and keep it there.

At the turn of the twentieth century, local politicians, prominent business leaders, and land developers, as well as powerful institutions like Northlands—then called the Edmonton Exhibition Association— were already building the first indoor rinks and using sports, especially men's professional hockey, to boost and promote both the city and their own interests.[13] Proposals to build new arenas in Edmonton have often invited controversy, and for many of the same reasons as today's Rogers Place. In the 1960s, for example, there were a number of contentious proposals to build new arenas to attract an NHL franchise and to revitalize Edmonton's downtown core. The most ambitious (if not fantastic) proposal was the Omniplex, a city-financed multi-purpose sports facility that was voted down by citizens in a plebiscite in 1970. Only four years later, after receiving funding from senior levels of government for the 1978 Commonwealth Games (a summer event), Northlands Coliseum opened—not downtown, but further to the east on the Edmonton Exhibition Association grounds—becoming the home of the WHA's (World Hockey Association) Edmonton Oilers, which became in 1979 the long-sought NHL franchise.

While some of these historical factors are unique to Edmonton, much about the story of Rogers Place will be familiar to readers across North America who have seen similar stories play out in their own cities. Indeed, many readers will be all too familiar with the well-worn playbook deployed so often in recent years by the commissioners of professional sports leagues and the owners of major league sports franchises intent on extracting billions of dollars of concessions for the construction of increasingly costly and spectacular sports facilities and entertainment districts. Between 1990 and 2010, over 100 new facilities were built across North America—a replacement rate of more than 90 percent. Nearly all of these facilities were funded by taxpayers at an estimated cost of US$20 billion. To this we can add an estimated US$10 billion in uncounted public costs—land and infrastructure expenses, foregone property taxes, municipal services, operations, and capital improvements—that often go underreported. In the United States, where the majority of these facilities have been built, it is estimated that the loans used to pay for facility construction—tax-exempt municipal bonds—will cost the federal government over US$4 billion in taxpayer subsidies to bondholders.[14] While the average public cost of a new building in the 1990s was estimated at US$142 million, by the end of the first decade of the new millennium, it had risen to US$241 million—an increase of 70 percent (in 2010 dollars)—and it continues to go up.[15] In perhaps the most startling of these examples, after accumulating a debt of US$18–20 billion and filing for Chapter 9 bankruptcy in 2013, the city of Detroit committed over US$350 million in public funds toward the construction of a new US$862-million arena for the Detroit Red Wings and the Detroit Pistons as part of a downtown revitalization strategy.

The political strategies of franchise owners to secure new publicly financed arenas and stadiums have been thoroughly explored by Neil deMause and Joanna Cagan in their influential book *Field of Schemes*.[16] These strategies have not changed much over the past three decades, despite heightened public opposition to the escalating demands of owners for concessions and subsidies:

> It's just always the same demands and the same strategies; it's threaten to move; it's claiming that there's an economic boon from investing in these things; it's talking about how the team can't be competitive without a new arena; and you cycle through the same things until you get the result you want. There are sometimes new twists on it, like state-of-the-art clauses, but mostly it's the same old shtick and it's remarkable how well it's held up.[17]

The central and intentionally dramatic threat to relocate a franchise continues to be used by leagues and team owners because it's usually successful, not just for the owners, but also for municipal officials who need emotional reasons to justify financing new arena and stadium developments. As sports economist Brad Humphreys says:

These threats really work for elected officials who want to have some plausible deniability about what they're doing because they can say "well, I didn't have any choice, we might have lost the team." And it's something that's often completely un-checkable, and it often ends the questioning. It's something too big to risk, and it's a dynamic that's survived because it works both for the team owners trying to get money and for public officials. They don't want the team owners to be mad at them; they don't want the constituents to be mad at them; so if they can come away with something that at least gives them some sort of cover for their decision and, unfortunately, they're happier with that than with actually making whatever is the best decision for taxpayers and residents and sports fans.[18]

Other strategies have also remained unaltered: the claims that a facility is obsolete and unprofitable, even if it's only two or three decades old; the refusal of franchise owners to disclose financial records to provide concrete evidence that a team is losing money; and, the hiring of a cast of like-minded and sympathetic consultants to support these claims in reports that often inflate economic benefits, while also downplaying costs and risks. Crucially, the promotion of the economic benefits of a new arena or stadium needs to align with the dominant municipal growth agenda—one that in recent years has almost exclusively focused on the gentrification of a city's downtown core. As Richard Gruneau and David Whitson have remarked, "It is simply through the negotiation of the financial interests of team owners (that is, in maximizing the profitability of their franchises) and the co-ordination of these interests with the growth strategies of local political and business elites that new arenas are built or not, and that teams come to and threaten to leave cities like Edmonton."[19] Finally, owners exert continuous pressure on municipalities through the announcement of arbitrary deadlines—a tactic that prevents proper assessment and public debate—and through the use of bait and switch tactics to secure additional concessions and subsidies. As negotiations drag on, often for years, such tactics ensure that they usually go the owners' way.

If the owners of major league sports franchises follow such a predictable pattern, why do cities like Edmonton keep falling for it? Why do cities habitually subsidize major league sports franchises that are now owned almost exclusively by billionaires and deep-pocketed corporations? Why do municipalities regularly invest in these developments when the overwhelming consensus of disinterested research shows that building them, or even having a professional sports team in the first place, creates no net increase to employment, investment, and spending?[20] Why have so many municipalities across North America prioritized the construction of increasingly expensive publicly financed sport and entertainment districts when other urgent social issues and other infrastructure deficits remain unaddressed? The spending of hundreds of millions of scarce public dollars always leaves fewer resources for social services, cultural activities, and infrastructure. How do elected officials and bureaucrats structure the political processes associated with these types of debates to secure preferred outcomes, despite public opposition? Finally, why have citizens who oppose the use of public funds to finance new arenas and stadiums largely been unsuccessful in their efforts to stop these developments? This book explores these interrelated questions as they played out in Edmonton.

Readers from outside of Edmonton—a city of about a million people in Alberta—might wonder why a detailed case study of this arena debate matters to them and to their cities. Even in Edmonton, many argue that it's no longer an issue—Rogers Place has been built and is open; the Oilers are financially secure for the foreseeable future; and tremendous development has occurred in the downtown core. Let's move on, they say. Our answer is that these questions and political debates will recur in cities across North America. Understanding what happened in Edmonton can provide insight into the tactics, claims, and templates that will be used in future negotiations between cities and owners. The arena agreement in Edmonton will also, quite frankly, affect every other city involved in the NHL, as well as aspirant cities like Quebec City, simply because it has set another costly precedent of public subsidy—one that the cities of Calgary and Ottawa were quickly "invited" to follow in their negotiations with the owners of the Flames and the Senators. Rogers Place, and the broader debate over subsidies given to Daryl Katz and the Katz Group, will thus cast a long shadow not only in Edmonton, but throughout Canada and the United States, and the stakes are only getting higher.

The long, complex, and divisive arena debate in Edmonton offers a fascinating story about public pressure and backroom negotiations over one of the most powerful symbols of the city's identity, the Edmonton Oilers, and over billions of dollars in land development opportunities. It is both revealing and sobering, precisely because it exposes how power is exercised in municipal politics, and how those who hold power are able to push through their agendas, whether citizens like it or not.

2

BOOSTING EDMONTON

Hockey and the Promotion of the City, 1894–1977

EDMONTON HAS BEEN CALLED "The Heartland of Hockey."[1] The first Stanley Cup game played by an Edmonton team was not in May 1983 against the New York Islanders, but in December 1908 against the Montreal Wanderers—Edmonton lost. Edmonton challenged for the Cup again in 1910 and in 1923, but by 1926 professional hockey was gone, as players left for the greener pastures of National Hockey League teams in the east.

The NHL was far away—read about in the local press, and heard and, eventually, seen Saturdays on *Hockey Night in Canada*—but Edmonton had teams in amateur and minor professional leagues from the 1920s into the 1960s. The World Hockey Association came in 1972 and, finally, in 1979, the NHL. Since then there have been highs and lows. The "Boys on the Bus" won five Stanley Cups between 1984 and 1990, but since the Stanley Cup run in 2006, the Oilers have made the playoffs only once. Yet Edmonton fans remain loyal. They may reminisce about "the good old days," but they are also quick to debate the latest coaching decision, trade, or free-agent signing on sports call-in radio—"the world's cheapest therapy"[2]—and, increasingly, on social media. They drive on Wayne Gretzky Drive and the Mark Messier Trail. Edmonton is a hockey town, and hockey has shaped the identity of the city.

Over time, hockey became an expression of boosterism, a way to promote Edmonton, and the facilities where hockey was played were part of the vision of what Edmonton could be. The construction of Rogers Place and the development of an entertainment area downtown, Ice District, together are just one more example of the old desire to make Edmonton "a world-class city."

Edmonton's Early Days, 1894–1913: *A Corporate–Civic Project*

From its beginnings, Edmonton has been dominated by a small, but influential, group of largely Anglo-Protestant businessmen and professionals who have pursued economic success, shared political affinities, and embraced the ideology of boosterism, the "view that the active encouragement of growth and business enterprise [is] the primary concern of a municipal corporation." These boosters saw big things ahead. They understood that the city was in constant competition with other communities for economic and political advantage, as well as civic prestige. They promoted it aggressively to sell prospective investors, businesses, and settlers on the advantages of locating in Edmonton rather than somewhere else.[3] It was in this spirit that Frank Oliver, Edmonton's principal booster, pronounced in 1892, the year Edmonton was incorporated as a town, that "there is no reason that Edmonton should not be, in a very few years, as nature plainly intended, the leading city in the Northwest."[4]

Boosterism, then and now, equates the interests of the business community and the ideology of expansion and economic development with the interests of the city as a whole. Public funds in Edmonton's early days were used "to promote urban growth by luring railways, factories, and government institutions with promises of free land, property tax exemptions, and cash bonuses. Often, too, governments acquired the ownership of utilities in order to offer free connections and cheap rates."[5] As the city expanded, large areas were annexed, thanks to political pressure exerted by real estate interests on city council, raising the value of real estate holdings and increasing both the tax revenue and the borrowing power needed to counter the rapid growth of city expenses and, inevitably, debt. Historian Carl Betke has referred to this as a "corporate–civic

A detail of Mundy's map of Edmonton and Strathcona (1911), showing the Exhibition Grounds where the Edmonton Stock Pavilion was built in 1913.

project."[6] Edmonton relied on property taxes as its main source of revenue. City council encouraged development and the valorization of land, while reducing the need for other forms of taxation. Likewise, high land assessments and low property tax levies could boost Edmonton and attract even more investment, and, hence, increase the limits of civic borrowing.[7]

Not to be a booster—not to be part of the team—showed a lack of community spirit. There's no place for critics or "knockers" of the dominant political/economic growth agenda, and boosters regularly and effectively use the idea of community solidarity to discredit opposition, "by successfully promoting the notion that all classes and groups could be united on the basis of faith in the city, belief in its destiny, and commitment to its growth."[8] The reality of early Edmonton, though, did not reflect this ideal. Rapid growth and substantial immigration brought significant social change, and the city was sharply divided along class and ethnic lines. Moreover, although they promoted a unified vision of the city, the "attitude of boosters toward organized labour and the poor and disadvantaged was one of scorn." Far less was spent on social services, health, and welfare than was spent on promoting growth.[9]

City leaders wanted to establish political, social, and cultural institutions that would bring order and stability to the city, including cultural, recreational, and leisure activities. They "vigorously promoted any sporting event or other leisure attraction that promised to draw their town to the attention of potential investors and visitors."[10] They promoted a wide range of British sports such as cricket, soccer, and horse racing, as well as other increasingly popular North American sports, like baseball, hockey, and football.[11] Sports, especially hockey, provided citizens with recreation and spectatorship, as well as opportunities for social interaction, including the establishment of common bonds with their new neighbours.[12]

As hockey became more commercialized, it began to attract audiences with money and leisure time. In the early twentieth century, therefore, hockey was increasingly governed by commercial exchange as the value of mass audiences increased. Against this backdrop, Edmonton's early civic leaders created the hockey teams and built the first arenas, which became popular civic institutions and sites for some of the most memorable events in the city's history. They also came to recognize that state-of-the-art facilities were valuable amenities that could boost the profile of the young city and encourage even greater growth. Thus, the broader corporate–civic project and the promotion of hockey were, from the earliest days "all inextricably linked."[13]

Hockey in Early Edmonton and the Thistle Rink

Hockey, then, served social, cultural, and economic purposes.[14] Edmonton had outdoor rinks and one small enclosed facility, but many games were still played on the North Saskatchewan River. The Thistle Club, made up largely of members of prominent local families, was formed in 1894. Hockey, for them, represented Edmonton's aspirations, spirit, and pride, based on close personal connections with the players:

> It could be credibly claimed that the quality of a team's performance actually said something about the community that produced it—not only about the skill levels of its players, but also about the character of its people. When local athletes or community teams began to represent their communities, the significance of winning or losing increased dramatically.[15]

Long before the "Battle of Alberta"—coined for the historic battle between the NHL's Oilers and Flames that began in the 1980s—there were meaningful games between Edmonton and Calgary teams. But the most important rivalry was between neighbouring Edmonton and Strathcona. On Christmas Day 1905, for example, a game between the two at the new Thistle Arena drew more than a thousand people.[16]

It was the business and professional elite, "with the skills, resources, and inclination to create sporting recreations that organized leisure in new ways," who exploited the economic possibilities of hockey.[17] They saw the growing population as a lucrative market for hockey games. Seeing the sport's commercial potential, early promoters wanted to present the highest calibre of hockey possible, so they increasingly, though controversially, used professional players who were paid to play hockey and to represent Edmonton, even if they did not live there. As these practices became more normal, a growing labour market for professionals emerged and Edmonton teams regularly hired players from other communities to represent the city. Winning trumped any organic sense of community, and fans became consumers. Hockey was sold as a product.[18]

But if hockey was to succeed in Edmonton, a new commercial facility was needed. Large arenas could hold more spectators, thus increasing the revenue streams for local promoters. The first arena that fulfilled these aspirations was the Thistle Rink, which could hold more than 1000 spectators[19] and opened in December 1902 on what is now 102 Avenue and 102 Street, just north of Jasper Avenue—only a block or so away from the current site of Rogers

Edmonton's first downtown arena—the Thistle Rink (1902–13).

Place in downtown Edmonton. An influential local businessman, land developer, and booster, Richard Secord, put up $13,000 to build the wooden structure on land that he owned; it was announced as "a credit to the town as well as to the public spirit and enterprise of the proprietor."[20]

Hockey could now be played indoors, rather than on the frozen North Saskatchewan River or outdoor rinks, and it became more market-driven. "With an enclosed arena...promoters could schedule a game 'in advance', promote it heavily, and be certain that the event would take place. This meant that investments would pay off."[21] The rink was built near Secord's other businesses and would provide him with even greater commercial opportunities. It would also stimulate economic growth and downtown development for Edmonton. "One thing common to sport at all levels was money...For entrepreneurs, it was the raison d'etre for building facilities and promoting competition."[22]

Secord had some expectations of civic officials, though. In September 1903, he wrote to city council demanding "water and sewer connections with my hockey and curling rinks...I may say that this request was made last fall. If possible I should like you to have these connections made by the 1st November." The connections were made, and by his deadline. Secord did cover the expenses of the rink's operation; in 1906, his expenditures were $30,784.71. He was also willing to spend his own money on renovations.[23]

Boosterism was good for Secord's bottom line as well as for the development of Edmonton. Until he built the Thistle Rink, the community had no significant meeting hall or covered rink for skating and curling. Had Secord built his arena a century later, it would have been marketed as a multi-purpose facility that would optimize and maximize hockey and non-hockey revenue streams and increase the value of the owner's land holdings. Secord enjoyed a monopoly, and because his initial capital investment was high, he wanted to attract as many events as possible to his rink—concerts, community meetings, exhibitions, receptions—so he could make money by renting it out. It became a popular gathering place that contributed immensely to the social fabric of early Edmonton.

Challenging for the Stanley Cup and Boosting Edmonton

In 1908, four years after Edmonton was incorporated as a city, the Edmonton Thistles, now called the Edmonton Hockey Club and run by local businessman and booster James A. MacKinnon, officially challenged for the Stanley Cup.[24] The goal was not simply to win the trophy, but also to promote Edmonton. In September, there had been an appeal to "[a]ny person interested in Edmonton, its advancement, glorification and extension" to support the club; "a million dollars of good publicity" would follow.[25] The city's business community, led by Joseph H. Morris, who owned a wholesale grocery store, provided the money to send the team to Montreal.

The local media were eager boosters of the city and promoters of hockey. The sporting activities of Edmontonians were reported in the recently established *Journal*,[26] in a regular column called "The Sporting Life." Although the *Journal* concentrated on local contests,

The Edmonton Hockey Club practices at the Thistle Rink for the 1910 Stanley Cup challenge. [Provincial Archives of Alberta B6528]

it included items about sporting events elsewhere. Edmonton was thus part of an increasingly unified "world of sport" created by the mass media, which included amateur and professional sports at the local, regional, national, and international levels.[27] Boosters relied on the media to put Edmonton "on the map." In 1907, for example, the *Edmonton Bulletin* assured its readers that a benefit hockey game at the Thistle Rink would offer "a superior class of hockey, and incidentally...give the city itself prominence in the athletic arena."[28]

The Edmonton Hockey Club had won the Senior A league championships in 1907 with mostly local players. When the team's challenge to the Montreal Wanderers was accepted, the club added imported professionals, like Lester Patrick, and dropped the Edmonton players. The signings were controversial because the players had been poached before they could play for the club's competition. As one

Montreal newspaper reported, the practice of paying for ringers was unethical, but this time Edmonton's actions were even worse: "It's time for the Stanley Cup trustees to intervene in the dickerings which are making a huge joke of the championship emblem. The right of such a team to play for the championship is questionable in the extreme. If the team ever goes back to Edmonton, its chances for filthy lucre will disappear."[29] Some of the players never even skated in Edmonton; Patrick joined the team for the first time in Winnipeg when he met the train taking the team to Montreal. The city did garner national attention, but not for the reasons that the boosters had hoped. Edmonton was accused of trying to "buy" the Stanley Cup. The *Manitoba Free Press* wrote, "It is no longer a question of local pride and ambition but a matter of the club that has the most money."[30]

There was much excitement in Edmonton about the series, with a local newspaper reporting, "Till the result is known, we must expect the wheels of business, and almost everything else, to clog."[31] Unfortunately, Edmonton lost the two-game series to the Wanderers 13–10 on total goals. Another Edmonton team, still just called the Hockey Club, challenged for the Stanley Cup in 1910, but was unable to add imports and so lost to the Ottawa Silver Sevens. While one team owner in the east railed against Edmonton's "lunacy and profligate spending" that would "ruin hockey," local boosters had a different complaint—the Eastern-based Stanley Cup trustees had discriminated against the team from Western Canada.[32]

After World War I, the trustees of the Stanley Cup decided that only teams in the NHL and the Pacific Coast Hockey League (PCHL) were eligible to play for the trophy. After the formation of the Western Canada Hockey League (WCHL) in 1921, with teams in Calgary, Edmonton, Regina, and Saskatoon, the new league could also play for the Stanley Cup. The Edmonton Eskimos, with "Duke" Keats and "Bullet" Joe Simpson, finished first in the WCHL regular season in 1922–23, and defeated Regina in the playoffs for the championship. Boosters were elated; the *Edmonton Journal* of March 17, 1923 reported that "seven thousand Edmonton citizens will tell their children and their children's children that it was on this night the

Eskimos emblazoned their names large on the pages of hockey history by winning the championship of the WCHL in the most thrilling contest in the annals of the game in Western Canada."[33] Edmonton played Ottawa, which had defeated Vancouver in the first series, for the Stanley Cup, and lost both games.[34]

Francis Nelson, writing in the *Toronto Globe* in this period, argued that "The Stanley Cup provides a fine spectacle and makes money for the teams and the rink proprietors, but the competition does not advance the interests of the national sport."[35] Some NHL teams in Eastern Canada in larger and more prosperous markets may have been making money, but not all of them, and cities in Western Canada weren't making much, either. For the 1924–25 season, the PCHL and the WCHL were forced to merge, creating the Western Hockey League (WHL). Promoters quickly claimed major league status for the emergent league, and some even predicted that the WHL would "overshadow the present NHL."[36] The economic limits of professional hockey in Western Canada were, however, quickly becoming apparent; the smaller communities simply could not compete for the services of professional players, while cities like Edmonton didn't even have artificial ice plants in their arenas. The WHL cities in the Prairies "had populations of less than 100,000; club revenues ranged from $44,000–$65,000, compared to over $200,000 for most NHL teams."[37] Lester Patrick (one of the paid ringers who had played for Edmonton in its first Stanley Cup challenge) said the WHL lacked the "exuberance" of the East for hockey; there was no "desire of American financiers to get in on the ground floor" or meet "the big increase in salaries paid by the National Hockey League." As the *Edmonton Journal* acknowledged, "New York pro hockey outdrew the combined attendance of any four cities in the Western League."[38]

Under these circumstances, the WHL collapsed within two years, and, in 1926, the NHL purchased the reorganized WHL and dispersed its players, including "Duke" Keats and Eddie Shore ("the Edmonton Express"); "Bullet" Joe Simpson had left the year before. WHL team owners were happy to sell their players to the NHL, and major league hockey shifted from Western Canada back to Eastern

Canada and south to the larger markets in the United States. As historians John Thompson and Allen Seager have noted, "Canadian hockey was revolutionized by American money."[39] Carl Betke has argued that "the cities of the west were able to enjoy top-class professional hockey for a few years in the 1920s only because there was a short time lag before the potential of promoting the game in the much larger American centers was seen and acted upon."[40]

After the WHL collapsed in 1926, professional hockey left Edmonton for almost 30 years, but boosters worked hard to keep the city on the hockey map. Local teams continued to play in senior amateur leagues, and the Edmonton Flyers, sponsored by the Edmonton Exhibition Association (EEA), won the Allan Cup (awarded annually to Canada's best senior amateur team) in 1948. Just three years later, the Flyers became a farm club in the Detroit organization. The Red Wings eventually took over direct operation of the Flyers, thanks to a lease payment of $1 per season to the EEA. The Flyers won WHL titles in 1953, 1955, and 1962. The Red Wings, however, eventually withdrew support for the club, and the Flyers folded in 1963. This was another sharp reminder that the hockey club had never really belonged to the fans—it was controlled by a profit-driven NHL club. The junior Oil Kings were established in 1951 and competed in every Memorial Cup final from 1960 to 1966, winning the trophy in 1963 and 1966. Occasionally, an Edmonton team was also successful at the international level, but even when an Edmonton team won the World Hockey Championship, as the Superiors did in 1932, or the Olympics, as the Mercurys did in 1952, the victory brought little change to the city's hockey status. Edmonton was a minor-league city.

Edmontonians still followed NHL hockey—on the radio, and, beginning in 1952, on Saturday night television broadcasts of *Hockey Night in Canada*. Interest in the NHL was also sustained because Edmonton players like Johnny Bucyk, Bruce MacGregor, Eddie Joyal, and Gerry Melnyk played in the NHL. So, Edmonton was still part of the wider world of hockey, and, in the decades to come, as capital and people came west, boosters pursued major league status through the acquisition of a professional hockey franchise and the construction of a modern hockey arena. By the end of the 1970s, Edmonton finally had its own NHL franchise, thanks in no small part to the role and influence of the EEA.

The Edmonton Exhibition Association and Hockey Arenas

Despite Edmonton's growth, Winnipeg remained the dominant regional metropolis and Edmonton could not compete with it, much less with Montreal or Toronto. While "the vision of a northern commercial empire continued to fuel Edmonton's aspirations," growth slowed after 1918. "Booster campaigns no longer yielded results," and it became difficult for the city to raise capital. Edmonton, which had vigorously promoted and expanded municipally-owned utilities and services, now had to pay for them. Land speculators could not sell their properties, nor could they pay taxes, so the city acquired land banks that generated no revenue. "As early as 1917 Edmonton's per capita debt soared beyond the level of any major city in Canada," yet the boosters continued to promote various plans to stimulate the city's growth.[41]

The Thistle Rink had burned down on October 31, 1913. With the beginning of the hockey season less than two months away, teams looked to the brand-new Edmonton Stock Pavilion in the city's east end, built by the EEA. It was never intended to be a hockey arena, but, under the circumstances, it was decided that the floor could be flooded to make an ice surface.

The EEA (later renamed Northlands), Edmonton's most powerful corporate–civic institution, was founded in 1879. Leading residents and businessmen were on the board, and when it was reorganized in 1899, its goal was to boost the community: "Edmonton was not merely a town but a cause."[42] By 1905, business partners John A. McDougall and Richard Secord (who had financed the Thistle Rink) were the leaders of the EEA. Its fairgrounds were in Rossdale in the river valley, and it offered to lease them to the city for $3,000 for one year, with an option to purchase the land for $60,000. Although the city was willing to support the EEA, which was having financial difficulties, the asking price was too high, and the city council had its eye on 140 acres east of the city for the new fairgrounds. But

The Edmonton Stock Pavilion on the Northlands Grounds, circa 1914. This was a multi-use facility built by the Edmonton Exhibition Association and used from 1913 to 1974. [City of Edmonton Archives EB-3-12/Byron May Co.]

acquiring parkland outside the city limits required a plebiscite. In a closed meeting in January 1906, the mayor and the councillors decided to buy the land in their own names and sell it back to the city. A plebiscite was then scheduled for December 1906. Although the location was remote and swampy, and the secrecy of the deal was criticized, the measure passed with a small majority.[43] Making such deals in secret has a long history in Edmonton.

The EEA had built the Stock Pavilion as a venue large enough to attract indoor events and attractions that would boost the city's profile. It was located well away from the city centre so that the noise and smell of the animals would not bother downtown residents. Its promoters claimed that it was the foremost arena in Western Canada, "larger than Madison Square Garden in New York," and could seat 6,000 spectators "as comfortably as in a modern theatre." Not even in Eastern Canada, exulted the *Edmonton Journal*, was there "[s]uch a handsome pavilion as can be seen on the Exhibition grounds of Alberta's Queen City."[44] The building and the atmosphere it created made a statement about the city's drive and

Top: The "Old Barn." The Edmonton Flyers play the Calgary Stampeders at the
Edmonton Gardens on March 3, 1950. [City of Edmonton Archives EA-45-1134/Alfred Blyth Studios]
Bottom: Edmonton Gardens after postwar renovations, circa 1950.

[City of Edmonton Archives EA-356-1]

boldness of vision, and local boosters believed they could use it to promote Edmonton.

The Eskimos, the Flyers, and later the Oil Kings all played there. In the 1930s came calls to build a new arena downtown because the old facility still relied on natural ice.[45] So, in 1937, the EEA installed the first artificial ice plant, which cost about $30,000 and added about 10 weeks to the hockey season. Renovations after World War II, costing more than $170,000, increased seating to 7,700, and it was renamed the Edmonton Gardens. But, as one fan remembered, watching games there was not a happy experience:

The Edmonton Gardens did not coddle its patrons. This was a building that made you work for the privilege of seeing what you'd come to see... From the nosebleed seats at the south end of the building, fully half the ice surface was obscured by the overhanging lights. Even the wealthier citizens further down were obliged to contort themselves in order to see around the many diagonal support posts holding the great building up.[46]

In the 1960s, there were further renovations in response to complaints about the appearance of the building, the poor sight lines, and the uncomfortable seating. There were problems with the roof, and water regularly dripped onto the ice. Another $60,000 was poured into improvements, but there were safety concerns, and the *Journal* considered the building "a disaster waiting to happen. The old house, with its obsolete lighting fixtures, oily wooden floors, and sordid washrooms, is an eyesore to hockey fans."[47] In May 1966, the Fire Chief officially condemned it as a fire trap and ordered it closed. After another $670,000 in renovations, the Gardens remained in use until 1974 and was demolished in 1982.[48]

Revitalizing Downtown Edmonton: *Take 1*

The Gardens had done little in 50 years to boost the city's status— nor had it brought professional hockey back to Edmonton. Although Edmonton was the largest city in Alberta and a booming centre of the new oil and gas industry, local promoters continued to celebrate its rural roots by supporting annual agricultural fairs at the Exhibition grounds. As the population grew from 94,000 in 1941 to 496,000 in 1971, a new urban identity that could be shared by the local community and projected onto the national and continental stage was needed.

Edmonton's city council was still dominated by a civic elite "primarily responsible to the business community."[49] The municipal bureaucracy was focused on economic development (the city's motto, after all, is "Industry, Integrity, Progress"), providing Edmonton with business-like management of public services in order to attract investment and population and to enhance the city's prestige. The boosterism of the city government continued to be supported by the *Edmonton Journal*.[50]

The boom/bust cycle of the oil-based economy created unemployment and other social problems. Social service providers recognized that the downtown was in decline, especially in the Boyle Street neighbourhood (bounded by 82 Street to the east, Jasper Avenue and Rossdale to the south, 97 Street to the west, and 104 Avenue to the north), where various social issues—poverty, homelessness, prostitution, and alcohol and drug abuse—abounded. In 1963, a city commission concluded that these problems were a "contagious disease [causing] delinquency and immorality."[51] But the city did little to address them. The area was a "discard."[52]

Still, the boosters on the council and in the business community had a vision to revitalize Edmonton's downtown through economic development. The Planning Department recognized that,

> Downtown...is the symbol of the city. It contains the highest and generally the costliest buildings. Land values are the most extreme. Transportation facilities serving it represent the greatest public investment. Offices and stores are larger, more specialized, and more varied. It is administration, government, recreation, protection. It is wealth; it is power. The greater the development, the more this is so, for with increasing concentration downtown becomes more and more attractive as an environment in which to conduct the city's major business.[53]

The CN Tower (10004-104 Avenue), Edmonton's first "skyscraper," was finished in 1966; it had just 26 storeys because higher buildings would interfere with flights to and from the City Centre Airport. By the end of the 1970s, six more office towers and a hotel had been built downtown. Edmonton's boosters fully expected that these developments, centred on Jasper Avenue, would attract people to live there. The *Journal* announced in 1967 that the proposed Edmonton House (a 45-storey building at 10205-100 Avenue that opened in 1971), with 304 units that could house as many as 700 people, would be the largest residential apartment building in the city and reverse the flight to the suburbs. It reported: "The apartment way of life, rather than fighting traffic daily in drives from the suburbs, seems to be in for people with good salaries" and that "Edmonton could supply enough of the jet-set crowd to fill a high-priced but luxurious apartment building."[54] As it turned out, Edmonton was not so much a jet-set city with a dynamic downtown as it was a station-wagon community with decentralized suburbs characterized by single-family homes, car-centred mobility, and neighbourhood schools, parks, churches, leisure activities, and shopping.[55]

In the 1970s, when oil prices spiked, money flowed into the hands of governments, both provincial and municipal, and businesses. By 1981, Edmonton's population had increased to 521,205. Local political and business leaders believed that the city was on the verge of becoming a centre of "commerce and culture, from which ambitious people would no longer have to move to central Canada in order to be 'movers and shakers' on the national stage."[56] Edmonton was becoming a "big-league city" and was set to enter a new stage "in civic competition in which newly wealthy cities...sought to redefine themselves not only in relation to each other but also in relation to the traditionally dominant metropolitan centers."[57] The attraction of major league sports franchises and high-profile international sporting events was understood to be important in these campaigns, and in the broader competition among cities to be seen as centres of culture and consumption. The result, as it had been for decades, was close cooperation between boosters and local government to ensure success, and politicians at all levels of government were prepared to put significant amounts of public money into new sports facilities to attract, or retain, major league franchises, and to offer "a variety of other concessions and tax breaks that [would] provide further opportunities for profitability for franchise owners."[58] For both Calgary and Edmonton, the construction of new arenas, the attraction of NHL franchises, and the hosting of hallmark sports events like the 1978 Edmonton Commonwealth Games and the 1988 Calgary Winter Olympics would be at the forefront of their respective civic agendas, despite the emergence of public opposition to many of these aspirations.

Neo-boosterism, Civic Ambition, and the Pursuit of National Status

Boosterism in the postwar television era continued to depend on promotion. In Edmonton in the 1970s, the civic elite aggressively boosted the municipal "brand" to market the city as a modern urban centre full of cultural and shopping attractions. Historian Paul Voisey has argued that, "Aside from the immediate economic gains, the idea...was to generate 'free' publicity that would continue to attract investors, conventioneers, and tourists; to erect striking monuments that would forever identify the city; and to acquire new infrastructure and other civic improvements at the expense of other competitors." Voisey calls this neo-boosterism. Whitson and Macintosh have also argued that this "strategy for urban revaluation" and increased property values led to "investment in image building (in the arts, sports, etc.)...Hence, the succession of spectacular stadiums and concert halls, and the striving...to forge an image that would attract 'capital and people of the right sort.'"[59] Neo-boosters were prepared, in other words, to support public spending on major league facilities to attract increasingly mobile private investment and to stimulate economic growth and development. They were far less likely to support public spending on low-cost housing or social services to address problems detracting from the image of Edmonton as a "world-class city."[60]

Like the boosters before them, neo-boosters conflated their self-interest with the interests of the city as a whole; what was good for Edmonton was also good for the neo-boosters. After the publication of the *Urban Renewal Concept Report* (1967), suggestions for renewing the downtown core and increasing the value of downtown land holdings included the construction of a convention centre or a new arena. Cec Purves, a member of the city council in this period (and later mayor), remarked that Edmonton "had the old arena and... we had hockey in the Western Canada Hockey League. The hockey people were always talking about getting a new building because they said we couldn't get a National Hockey League team unless we [got] a new building."[61]

As early as August 1962, there was a meeting between city officials and representatives from the EEA about building a new, publicly-funded arena. A report published in 1964 explored two proposed sites—one beside the Exhibition grounds, and the second in the river valley. The first site offered

> *no serious problems with regard to additional site development costs, public transportation, parking or cramped location. It is well located in relation to the Exhibition Grounds and the possible relocation of Clarke Stadium. Moreover, its position is convenient to the most densely populated sector of the city, to continued residential growth in the North East and to the Southside residents by way of an East End Bridge...and it will not compromise the development of a downtown coliseum at some future date.*[62]

A downtown location for a new arena, though, would "discourage many suburban or out-of-town visitors unless ample parking is made available and unless the site is immediately accessible from existing traffic arteries and proposed freeways." Plus, as the Edmonton Gardens clearly illustrated, an arena, in itself, did not "stimulate or advance urban renewal, roadway improvements, rapid transit, parks and recreational development, or the replacement of obsolescent commercial buildings or schools"[63]—a fact apparently forgotten in the twenty-first-century debate about the building of a new downtown arena.

Just four years later, another municipal planning report recommended a multi-purpose facility with a trade centre, a convention centrc, and a hockey arena to regenerate the downtown core and "improve the city's image."[64] The city preferred a location near the current Ice District, near 104 Avenue and 104 Street, although another possible site was at the corner of Jasper Avenue and 98 Street (close to where Citadel Theatre is now). Clarence Campbell, then president of the NHL and a former Edmontonian, came to the city and recommended to local boosters that a new building have "no more than 7000 seats for hockey."[65] Despite the optimism of council and the downtown business community, in a plebiscite, citizens rejected proposals to borrow $4 million to buy the land and an additional $10.25 million to build the facility.[66]

The failure to secure popular support for a new, publicly-financed downtown arena did not deter the neo-boosters, who kept the proposed convention centre/arena development at the forefront of municipal politics until 1970. In another plebiscite in 1968, almost 72 percent of citizens voted in favour of spending $23 million for a new "Trade, Convention and Sports Complex," setting the stage for yet another proposal to make Edmonton a "world-class city" by building a multi-function venue called the Omniplex. It was to be a 14-storey facility located between 96 and 97 Streets, and between 103 A Avenue and the railway tracks at 105 Avenue (just over two blocks away from the current location of Rogers Place).

The Omniplex was promoted as "a downtown sports arena that would act as an economic catalyst, spurring an economic boom, capturing millions of tourist dollars, and boosting civic pride." It would have an NHL-sized arena, a domed football field, a convention centre, a concert hall, and several restaurants.[67] Prominent supporters of the Omniplex, predictably, included the most influential players in the city's sports scene and business community. Bill Henning, president of the EEA, which was expecting to operate the Omniplex, was chairman of Citizens for the Omniplex. Bill Hunter, owner of the Oil Kings and another member of that committee, declared that the Omniplex, "centred in the downtown area of Edmonton, the heart of Edmonton, will revitalize the whole economy of the city, and bring into our city untold millions of dollars through service industries such as hotels, restaurants, theatres." It would be

Drawing of the futuristic Omniplex, 1970.

[Edmonton Heritage Council and the City of Edmonton Archives]

enjoyed by all Edmontonians and attract tourists, and as many as four new hotels would be built. One developer enthused, "Edmonton has a unique opportunity to dramatize and anchor its core area, arrest the further dissipation of downtown development, attract new and needed structures that could yield valuable tax assessment and create an urban environment that would be second to none."[68]

Cec Purves, then a councillor, was initially supportive of the Omniplex: "I thought: Hey! That makes sense and then as I dug into it I said, it won't work. You can't have football and hockey in the same...building."[69] He wasn't alone in his opposition, especially in light of the escalating price tag. In November 1970, the proposal went to Edmonton voters in another plebiscite; council wanted to spend over $26.4 million to build the Omniplex, but 54 percent of the electorate said no.

The rejection of another proposal taught civic leaders and neo-boosters a number of lessons that would inform their later strategy. First, rather than relying solely on municipal property taxes, thus alienating local residents, they had to secure funding from other levels of government. This door had been opened in 1970 when Montreal was awarded the 1976 Summer Olympic Games and "established a precedent of substantial federal and provincial funds for

vote YES for Omniplex

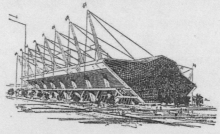

MAKE EDMONTON THE MAJOR CENTRE OF THE GREAT NORTHWEST!

When you vote on the principle of a trade, convention and sports complex on October 16th, you will be approving or rejecting much more than the amenities of a downtown centre.

YOU WILL BE APPROVING OR REJECTING 'NEW MONEY' injected into Edmonton's economy by convention delegates and trade-show exhibitors. 10,000 delegates spend $1-million which in turn generates an additional $450,000 in new jobs and recirculated money.

YOU WILL BE APPROVING OR REJECTING NEW INDUSTRY. Statistics show that one major trade show generates two new industries for the community — new job opportunities, new tax resources.

YOU WILL BE APPROVING OR REJECTING THE SPEED-UP OF CITY-CORE REVITALIZATION. One revitalized block can mean $1-million additional tax assessment — to ease the burden on the homeowner.

YOU WILL BE APPROVING OR REJECTING EDMONTON'S ECONOM-IC DEVELOPMENT. Omniplex would assure the major conventions and trade shows for Edmonton, new industries, increased tourism and international events of stature. Edmonton would become the major centre of the great northwest.

Give the City the go-ahead to look at final designs, final costs and feasibility. Omniplex won't cost you more than two mills for financing and operating. It will surely cost you less . . . and it might cost you nothing at all!

On October 16th, "Vote YES" for Omniplex

Sponsored by the CITIZEN'S COMMITTEE FOR Omniplex

W. J. M. HENNING ● BILL HUNTER ● DURWOOD ASHCROFT ●
MATT BALDWIN ● DR. MAURY VAN VLIET ● ZANE FELDMAN ●
E. K. UPSTONE ● E. A. CHRISTIANSON ● BRYAN ELLIS ●
W. J. CONNELLY ● MRS. JANIE BODNER ● W. ROY WATSON ●
R. W. CHAPMAN ● A. R. McBAIN ● ● BRUCE MATHEW ●
HON. GEORGE PRUDHAM ● C. A. KOSOWAN, Q.C. ●
NORM KIMBALL

facilities that would be attractive to major league franchises."[70] City
officials in Edmonton included a new arena (as well as a new football stadium for the Edmonton Eskimos) in the bid to host the 1978
Commonwealth Games. Second, neo-boosters had to be prepared
to mount a highly organized campaign to overcome public opposition. And third—the biggest lesson of all—such important decisions
should remain firmly in the hands of elected officials and municipal
administrators, not in those of the electorate, unless the right decision could be guaranteed.

NHL Dreams, WHA Realities: *Edmonton and the Oilers*

Many boosters believed that the Omniplex vote had damaged the
city's hopes for both an NHL team and a revitalized downtown. But
"Wild Bill" Hunter, along with Dr. Charles Allard,[71] his business
partner, and Norm Kimball, the general manager of the Edmonton
Eskimos football team, were prepared to buy the Pittsburgh
Penguins and relocate the franchise to Edmonton. NHL President
Clarence Campbell, though, who had supported an earlier arena
plan, told Hunter, "you must be smoking something to think that
Edmonton could support a National League team...It'll never
happen." Hunter was undeterred: "It isn't the size of the city—it's
the size of the heart of the city."[72] Dr. Allard, prominent in local television ownership and land development, was also a booster and his
"commitment to hockey was not as much about business as it was
about establishing a new hockey franchise which would benefit the
local community."[73]

"Wild Bill" acquired a franchise in the new WHA when that
league was incorporated in 1971.[74] The Alberta Oilers, renamed
the Edmonton Oilers the following season, played their first game
in the decrepit Edmonton Gardens in October 1972. Hunter and
Allard considered building an arena privately on a property at 101
Street and 45 Avenue (close to where the Labatts Brewery is now,
on Edmonton's south side). Allard's boosterism didn't distract him

< *The Omniplex proposal was an expression of boosterism.*
[*Edmonton Heritage Council and the City of Edmonton Archives*]

from the bottom line. The Oilers' ownership group demanded that the city forego taxes, provide without charge the land upon which the facility would be built, and construct related infrastructure. Council balked at the expense and wanted the EEA, which had experience running an arena, involved. The EEA, likewise, was prepared to defend its interests and its broader historical status in pursuit of a new facility.

In September 1971, the city announced plans to bid for the Commonwealth Games. A new arena was to be part of the project, and the EEA pressed to have it built on its grounds, lobbying both the provincial and the federal governments for funding.[75] As Jack Bailey, president of the EEA, recalled, "If Edmonton was going to grow and be the kind of community that you wanted to live in, we had to have a facility of that kind."[76] Still, not all Edmontonians were prepared to embrace this agenda, and grassroots citizen groups opposed to funding the Commonwealth Games, and concerned about the impact on surrounding communities, collected enough votes to force a plebiscite.

Drawing upon familiar rhetoric, proponents argued that the Games would put Edmonton on the map and create a legacy of sporting infrastructure that would benefit the city as a whole. These boosters "enjoyed free coverage of their arguments in the local media (themselves ardent Games boosters), where the pro-Games views of public figures were presented *as news*."[77] Opponents of the bid, on the other hand, were reviled as knockers, despite legitimate concerns about the cost of the event and the effects of the construction of the Coliseum and Commonwealth Stadium on the surrounding communities of Boyle Street, McCauley, Norwood, Parkdale, Cromdale, and Bellevue, which were working class, ethnically diverse, and less affluent. In the case of the stadium, for example, hundreds of residents were at risk of displacement. But on this occasion, the main boosters and beneficiaries of the Games—the Edmonton Oilers, the Edmonton Eskimos, the EEA, and various downtown business interests (hotels, restaurants, the construction industry, and the entertainment industry)—would prevail. On March 20, 1974, 76 percent of Edmonton voters approved a proposal in a plebiscite to authorize the city to borrow $11.6 million to purchase the land and pay a portion of the

costs of constructing facilities for the Commonwealth Games. But
the federal and provincial governments had already committed to
providing $20.5 million. Drawing upon a familiar refrain, the *Edmonton
Journal* pronounced, "Had the vote not carried, Edmonton would
have been branded a 'loser' by fellow Canadians. There can be no
doubt now that Edmontonians are set to show that their city is a
modern, alive city of world class."[78]

The city bought land north of 118 Avenue and turned it over to the
EEA for a new arena. Cec Purves confirmed that the process "wasn't
in isolation of City Hall" because the city commissioner, the mayor,
and one or two aldermen were on the board of the EEA.[79] The new
facility, to be named the Northlands Coliseum, was projected to cost
$10 million (although the total would rise to roughly $18 million). The
federal government provided a $10-million loan, and the province
contributed $3.7 million; there was no private money for the arena.

The Coliseum would be owned by the city and administered by
the EEA, which had further entrenched its role in Edmonton's sports
culture. "Northlands can get something done a darn sight easier and
more efficiently than a lot of other people can," according to then-
director Harry Hole, who was chair of its building committee.[80] Of
course, the other side of the coin was that the EEA, later Northlands,
had power and influence in Edmonton and was not afraid to use them,
whether by distributing perks, such as hockey tickets, or withholding
information from council. As Bob Westbury, former president of the
organization, remembered, "You never wanted to tick Northlands off
and you always wanted to be on the side of Northlands."[81] When the
"Big, Beautiful, Best" Northlands Coliseum officially opened on July 1,
1975, the EEA had no doubt who was responsible: "The Coliseum
didn't come about by luck or accident. Credit for it coming about at
all belongs to the Exhibition Association." Earlier attempts to build
an arena had "floundered on the shoals of timidity." Edmonton was
about to enter the world stage because of the efforts of its biggest
boosters. The fact that big profits could be made in a new facility
was not mentioned.[82] The EEA would "manage and operate the new
arena...help with its financing, and eventually own the facility."[83]
The first game was played on November 10, 1974, months before the

official opening, and the spectators, used to the old Gardens, "were astounded by its size and brilliance, with comfortable sightlines from all seats, wide walkways for meeting friends between periods, even the radiating roof supports which glittered high overhead like the Aurora Borealis."[84]

Northlands Coliseum was modelled on Vancouver's Pacific Coliseum. Sports facilities built in this era have been criticized for their "architectural blandness and indistinguishability"; their design was "similar to other interchangeable, utilitarian places such as airport lounges, motels and convention halls...They are meant to be judged as 'facilities', pragmatically conceived containers of entertainment functions."[85] Arenas were often built in the suburbs, where the population was growing, land was cheaper, parking was plentiful, and there were good roadway connections to move cars and people. Edmonton's focus had shifted away from the downtown core and back to the suburbs, something twenty-first-century proponents of the new arena sought to reverse.

Neo-boosters routinely argued that if a new arena was built on the Exhibition grounds, development would follow, thus justifying public financing; it would be an economic engine that would attract hotels and stimulate existing businesses, while increasing tourism by attracting conventions and entertainment. And, of course, they argued that the Coliseum would generate millions in revenues for the city, thus reducing the burden on Edmonton taxpayers. City officials, the EEA, and neo-boosters in the business community also assured the public that a new arena was "an investment in the city's cultural life for the enjoyment of its citizens and the possible generation of civic pride."[86] Northlands Coliseum thus became a civic symbol; public support for it could be rationalized as "the necessary cost of membership in the select club of big-time cities" in an "increasingly competitive market for sports franchises."[87] Paul Voisey, among many others, has argued that facilities like Northlands Coliseum "make a statement about the city's progress and boldness of vision, even though these new buildings were expensive to build and maintain." In supporting the Coliseum, council "justif[ied] their actions on economic grounds, but perhaps [this] speaks more to a psychological need to fuse personal identity with place...[While] neo-boosterism frequently costs cities dearly, its actual economic benefits, both short and long term, [have] often proved disappointing."[88]

In the Northlands Coliseum, Edmonton finally had a state-of-the-art facility, but the ultimate goal for the neo-boosters remained an NHL franchise, which would surely announce Edmonton's arrival as a "world-class" city. They were supported in this endeavour by hockey fans who identified with the local product—the "community symbol"—and also wanted to be entertained by "an elite brand of skilled hockey that could only be provided by a league of 'national' scope and status."[89] Enter Peter Pocklington—who had quite different ideas about the purpose of a professional hockey franchise.

THE BLUE LINE AND THE BOTTOM LINE

Peter Pocklington, the EIGLP, and the Business of Hockey in Edmonton, 1977–2005

Peter Puck Buys the Oilers

Hockey teams in Edmonton are both popular cultural institutions for the fans and representative community symbols for boosters. For owners like Charles Allard or Peter Pocklington, clubs are luxury toys that give them local status. But they are also businesses, and owners are motivated by self-interest more than by concern for the community or the fans. Owners control the only game in town, so they can extract "bucks from the rest of us."[1] They may talk about the benefits of capitalism and free enterprise, but they really don't want competition for limited entertainment dollars. They want cost certainty and reliable revenues. They are not generally risk-takers, and, for the most part, don't want to invest their own money in facilities, preferring to use funds from taxpayers. In the game of negotiating with cities, they are ruthless, and their goal is to win— by getting every dollar, every subsidy, every tax break, and every concession that governments are prepared to grant.[2]

Fans generally do not begrudge owners a profit, as long as they have a local team to cheer for—and as long as the team is winning. But the Edmonton Oilers in the mid-1970s were not winning. They were also losing money, according to the owners, despite having just moved into the new Northlands Coliseum, and despite a booming provincial economy.[3] Dr. Allard was also upset by rising player salaries and negative coverage in the *Edmonton Journal.* He bought out his partners and then sold the team for $300,000 to Nelson Skalbania, a Vancouver real estate promoter who also bought and sold sports franchises.[4] In March 1977, Skalbania sold a 40 percent interest in the Oilers, plus the assumption of half the debt, to Peter Pocklington, a car dealer and real estate promoter, whose long-term ambition was to own an NHL team.[5]

Pocklington had come to Edmonton from Ontario in 1971 and so was an outsider, not part of the city's small, tight business community. Nor was he linked to the old establishment families who controlled the EEA. He made his money in the car business first, and then in the rapidly growing economy of the 1970s, fuelled by the oil boom that stimulated property speculation, real estate development, and business investment.[6] His goal was to get rich, and he said that he did it on his own terms: "I prefer to own what I'm doing instead of getting the world in bed with me."[7] But he also bragged that his financial empire was built on borrowed capital: "To create wealth you must utilize other people's money and other people's labour."[8] A federal tax judge was blunter in his assessment of him. Pocklington, he said, "was ready to sell anything, except his wife."[9]

Edmonton, led by teenage sensation Wayne Gretzky, was one of four WHA teams to join the NHL in 1979. The Oilers faced a stiff initiation. The entry fee was set at $6 million, and another $1.7 million was reserved to meet possible legal challenges presented by WHA teams left out of the expansion. The Oilers also could not expect to share national television revenue for five years. Still, local fans were eager to see NHL hockey, and, in their first year, the Oilers sold 14,000 season tickets, played in front of sellout crowds, and generated gross gate revenues of about $6.14 million, second only to the New York Rangers. The average ticket price of $10.12 was the highest in the league. Pocklington (soon nicknamed "Peter Puck" by the local media) was able to negotiate a lucrative local television deal with Molson Breweries for exclusive advertising and promotional rights. The franchise had an estimated profit of $1.4 million in its first year of operation, although Pocklington claimed he had lost around $750,000.[10] By 1981, the young Oilers were one of the most exciting teams in the NHL, generating revenues of approximately $10 million and an estimated profit of $1.6 million.[11]

Profiting in Hard Times: *A "New" Downtown Agenda?*

After the boom of the 1970s, though, Canada fell into recession in the 1980s, and business borrowing became more expensive. Then the energy sector collapsed, devastating the Alberta economy. Edmonton faced economic disaster as its debt exploded, and civic employees, including police and firefighters, were laid off. For the downtown, "the general downturn was compounded by massive suburban expansion. Between September 1981 and March 1982, more than 500 new stores opened in shopping malls, inflicting an economic blow on the city core."[12] The iconic Hotel Macdonald, for example, closed in the 1980s, while the opening of the West Edmonton Mall in 1981 further heralded the expansion of the suburbs.

Canadian author Mordecai Richler described Edmonton in unflattering terms in this period:

> *The capital of Alberta is a city you come from, not a place to visit, unless you happen to have relatives there or an interest in an oil well nearby. On first glance, and even on third, it seems not so much a city as a jumble of a used-building lot, where the spare office towers and box-shaped apartment buildings and cinder-block motels discarded in the construction of real cities have been abandoned to waste away in the cruel prairie winter.*
>
> *If Canada were not a country, however fragmented, but, instead, a house, Edmonton [would be] the boiler room. There is hardly a tree to be seen downtown, nothing to delight the eye on Jasper Avenue.*[13]

His critique provoked howls of protest, and local boosters demanded an apology. The *Journal* called Richler's story "a deadly blow...Can you imagine the impact that article will have on the decision makers of large corporations considering a branch operation in our town?" Mayor Laurence Decore attacked "the haughty easterner making some rather fraudulent, foolish statements." Publisher Mel Hurtig called Richler a "rude little wimp," a writer who "jealously guards his position in the U.S. by denigrating his fellow citizens."[14]

The real decline of downtown, though, had profound implications. Council, still dominated by businessmen, remained susceptible to proposals promising to develop the core and increase property values. In 1980, the Triple Five Corporation, owned by the Ghermezian family, who, incidentally, built the West Edmonton Mall, proposed a $500-million development of property adjacent to the City Centre complex. With the Eaton Centre project, which promised a hotel, apartment-hotel, recreation centre, 20 theatres, a parkade, and more retail space, Triple Five "offered themselves as a solution to the problem of suburban commercial expansion that they were helping to create."[15] Their proposal was enthusiastically received by the boosters on council, even with the proviso that Triple Five receive concessions from the city. Despite objections from municipal planners—including concerns about road and air traffic, policing, transit, and the need for new infrastructure—an agreement was signed in October 1980. However, Triple Five pulled a bait and switch, appearing before city council only two months later to demand a host of additional concessions, without which they would cancel the project. Council capitulated, and, by 1984, after another round of negotiations, had provided an estimated $30.4 million for a project that was only a fraction of the originally planned development and no longer included a residential component. In 1990, just a few years later, Edmonton's auditor general would conclude that the city had lost on the deal, swallowed "broken promises," and made "concessions in return for new promises."[16]

Against this background, municipal politics began to change, and council adopted a more cautious approach to development. Administration produced a new Downtown Area Redevelopment Plan (DARP) "requiring developers to adhere to design guidelines and offering incentives for the development of downtown housing and the preservation of older buildings."[17] Its effect was short lived because of the recession, and boosters pressured council to support new development proposals. The most egregious example occurred when the Bank of Montreal sought to demolish the Tegler Building, Edmonton's oldest downtown office building, to build a regional headquarters. Council had initially designated it a historical site, but, in February 1982, the designation was withdrawn because of pressure from the bank. Edmonton's nagging inferiority complex has provided "a fertile ground for the promises and threats of developers, and some of them have become practised in the art of gaining public compliance for unpopular developments by a deft combination of promises of investment, threats to go elsewhere, and high estimates of the cost of alternative proposals."[18]

In 1983, Mayor Cec Purves appointed a Task Force on the Heart of the City, chaired by Joe Shoctor, an influential lawyer and booster. It reported that the DARP bylaw would have to be revised to provide "freedom for developers" and eliminate limits on downtown growth.[19] But Mayor Purves, who believed that development should take place with little direction from city council, was tarred by the Triple Five debacle and defeated in the fall municipal election by Laurence Decore. Decore was a pro-business lawyer, but he understood that the city had an important role to play in managing development. Plans began for a public square downtown, a concert hall, a new campus for Grant MacEwan Community College (now MacEwan University), a park, and a retail complex to be shaped by the new business-controlled Edmonton Downtown Development Corporation. The latter's establishment provided another marker of the continued influence of boosterish business interests in both political affairs and downtown development. In 1986, the Downtown Business Association of Edmonton was created to facilitate further private-sector leadership in downtown development and in municipal politics.

Success On the Ice, But Failure Off It

The continued economic problems in this period had significant consequences for Peter Pocklington, who had borrowed heavily to finance his failed campaign to become leader of the federal Progressive Conservative Party in 1983, and to support his businesses. The energy bust depleted his oil and real estate holdings, and interest rates skyrocketed. Tensions further increased between Pocklington and his landlord, Northlands (the EEA's name from 1983). The Oilers were the main tenant and an important source of revenue for the organization, but "Northlands needed other events and activities to generate funds to keep the facility financially viable." Pocklington, though, acted as if he personally owned the arena, and "Northlands occasionally had to remind both Pocklington and Glen Sather, former coach and now president and general manager (GM) of the Oilers, that Northlands owned and operated the Coliseum." In 1979, for example, the EEA had wanted its logo at centre ice, but Pocklington wanted the Oilers' logo, and when the EEA's logo was unveiled for the first NHL game, the crowd booed.[20]

Northlands always wanted to make sure that Pocklington knew his place in Edmonton. Its leadership believed that his business empire was built on a shaky economic foundation that was likely to collapse in the near future. "And if Pocklington lost control of the Oilers, Northlands wanted to take over ownership."[21] Pocklington was, however, unwilling to sell the Oilers at this time—"the hockey team is sacred to me," he said—and he transformed himself into a booster: "You don't own a professional sports franchise. You hold it in trust for the community."[22] Hyperbole aside, the Oilers provided the foundation for Pocklington's economic recovery; he used the franchise and the players' contracts as security to borrow $31 million from the banks to finance new business deals. Pocklington became increasingly dependent on government subsidies and borrowed money to finance the expansion of his businesses, while proclaiming that he was a free enterpriser. He said that, in a perfect economic world, "individuals should be free to create wealth by operating for their own gain within a system of private property and unencumbered by rules or confiscatory taxation by the state." But in "an imperfect world, where the state demands taxes from its corporate citizens, then the state must be willing to offer offsetting grants to help these corporations prosper."[23]

Of course, the Oilers were "sacred" to Pocklington mostly because they made money, even as his other businesses were faltering. After the team won its first Stanley Cup in 1984, ticket prices went up to offset higher player salary demands and higher rents at Northlands Coliseum.[24] Northlands was not above pressuring Pocklington in its effort to gain control of the team. In the 1978/79 season, its last in the WHA, the team paid an annual rent of $200,000; by the 1983/84 season, rent was $1,200,000. Although Pocklington wanted a better deal, the new 5-year agreement he signed on September 15, 1984 still favoured Northlands, which received revenues from concerts and non-hockey events, parking, and concessions. Moreover, the owner could not sell the team without Northlands' "prior written consent."[25]

But even in the midst of a devastating recession, the Oilers continued to be profitable—earning an estimated $5.7 million from December 1984 to August 1985, and another estimated $3.2 million in fiscal 1986.[26] Documents presented to the NHL's Board of Governors break down the Oilers' operations in that year. Revenues were $17,701,000, mostly from admissions ($13,116,000) and broadcasting ($2,292,000). Expenses were $14,169,000, mostly from team and hockey costs, including the minor league team ($10,893,000) and administration ($2,194,000). Income was $3,532,000, with another $2,234,000 from the playoffs. Total revenue was $5,766,000, minus the $1,109,000 amortization of the franchise and $120,000 for the WHA settlement, leaving income before taxes at $4,533,700.[27]

While Pocklington certainly profited from the team, he remained a tenant of Northlands. He did not own the arena or the surrounding property. And, while Northlands promoted itself as "a great happy service club banded together to serve the public" and boost the city, many Edmontonians believed it to be "a private club beholden to nobody."[28] It was public knowledge, for example, that Northlands paid no taxes, although its revenues in 1983 totalled more than $33 million from events like horse racing, Klondike Days, and the Canadian Finals Rodeo (which had arrived in 1974), as well as the arena rental. The Northlands board assured citizens that there was "no direct cost to the city arising from its operations, but that did not diminish public hostility."[29]

Boosters continued to believe that Edmonton was on the cusp of becoming a "world-class city," despite the recession. The Oilers' first Stanley Cup in 1984 became a triumph for the city, as well as for the team. One councillor enthused that the team "put us on the world-wide map."[30] Likewise, the general manager of the Edmonton Chamber of Commerce said the win was "worth millions" to the city in terms of promotional value and benefits to local businesses, including the hospitality and tourism sectors.[31] Former vice president of public relations for the Oilers, Bill Tuele, later noted that the success of the Oilers made Edmonton "feel like a major-league city."[32] In a climate of intense competition among cities, the idea of being "world class" took on increasing importance, and Edmonton's boosters had to counter the perception that the city was in decline and unable to retain its best and brightest young people.

The Oilers continued to be successful, winning four more Stanley Cups between 1985 and 1990. Pocklington said the business of hockey was "simple, as long as you're winning and creating excitement. A winning team can make a lot of money."[33] He also became more hands-on in the running of the hockey team, negotiating contracts with players and trading Wayne Gretzky in August 1988 for two players, three draft choices, and a reported US$15 million in cash. Despite a huge uproar in Edmonton, which prompted several local businesses and Oilers fans to boycott products from Pocklington-owned companies like Gainers and Palm Dairies, and made the owner a target on the cartoon page, Pocklington insisted that the deal made hockey sense and, more important, it made business sense. Gretzky was getting older, and his points total had been declining.[34] Moreover, he would become a free agent without compensation in 1992; he was "an asset worth zero in four years." There were also tax advantages in shedding a large contract that could no longer be depreciated for two smaller ones that could. Fans, however, did not see it as a business deal. The best player on the team—a national hero—had been sold, and many felt as though Pocklington had betrayed them personally.[35]

The Oilers had a disappointing 1988/89 season, but still made money. While average paid attendance declined from 16,957 to 16,780

Edmonton Oilers owner Peter Pocklington shakes hands with L.A. Kings centre Wayne Gretzky after a press conference in Edmonton, on October 15, 1989.

[Canadian Press/Dave Buston]

per game, ticket sales yielded an estimated $14,520,000, and broad-casting revenues were over $3 million. With total expenses of about $13.7 million, Pocklington admitted that, even without Gretzky, "our bottom line will be almost identical to last year" (a profit of about $3–4 million).[36] Pocklington's obsession with the bottom line was further illustrated by his comment that if the Oilers lost the Stanley Cup, profits would go up: "You can make as much as $1.8 million if you get to the final and lose."[37] The team, which didn't have to pay players during the playoffs, wouldn't have to pay bonuses for winning the Cup or buy Stanley Cup rings.

Revenues from the Oilers continued to support Pocklington's other business ventures. The team was his cash cow. The support of the Government of Alberta and its Treasury Branch also reduced financial pressure. This relationship, cemented by Pocklington's political donations to the provincial Conservative Party, though, would have disastrous consequences for Alberta's taxpayers.[38] On October 1, 1989, after Gainers defaulted on an interest payment, the ATB foreclosed on the company, then deeply in debt. But Pocklington was again able to walk away without further financial damage to himself.[39] When the hockey club won its fifth Stanley Cup in the spring of 1990, the team generated an estimated profit of $3.7 million.[40] Ticket prices went up again, and, in 1991, *Financial World* estimated the value of the franchise at $52 million, tying it for fourth in a league whose teams had an average value of $44 million.[41]

Yet trouble was brewing, not just for Pocklington, but also for Northlands. Don Clarke, a shareholder with Northlands, would say later, "What the Coliseum became, in my mind, was nothing more than a cash cow to Northlands and to Pocklington, which they could use to fund outside activities."[42] Fans doubted that Northlands' focus was public service because of the perks enjoyed by its members, including free tickets to hockey games and other events. There was considerable unhappiness with Northlands' perceived arrogance when the organization bristled at having to pay city taxes; in 1989, though, it signed a new 30-year lease agreement, and agreed to pay taxes on licensed premises and on private homes in return for the rights to the fairgrounds and buildings. The city, though, still

Exterior of Northlands Coliseum, circa 1974. [City of Edmonton Archives EA-340-31]

owned the Coliseum, prompting the general manager of Northlands to grouse, "If the city owns the building, why the hell are we still paying the mortgage?"[43]

Game Over

By the early 1990s, though, the glory days of the Oilers were over. After winning the Stanley Cup for the last time in 1990, the team's few remaining stars were traded away or sold because it was cheaper to shed expensive contracts and use younger and less costly players, even if the team lost more games. Success in the playoffs came less often, and the club missed the playoffs for the first time in 1993; by the 1997 season, it had missed them four years in a row. Attendance fell—from 14,797 per game in 1992/93 to 12,335 in 1995/96 (less than 75 percent of capacity)—and gate receipts declined to about $12.7 million, one-third below the league average; stadium revenues totalled only about US$1 million, less than 10 percent of that generated by the wealthiest franchise, the Detroit Red Wings. Regional television revenues were low, and there were few opportunities to increase revenues from merchandise or corporate boxes.[44] Likewise, new expansion fees dried up after five more teams were added by 1993.[45] In that year, Gary Bettman was hired as commissioner of the NHL, and he favoured adding more teams in the United States, increasing television revenue, and controlling escalating player costs, even if those actions meant the cancellation of entire NHL seasons, or large portions thereof.[46] He also insisted on a league-wide cycle of facility renewal to increase the revenues and valuations of individual franchises—a strategy with enormous consequences for Edmonton.

The Oilers began to lose money—an estimated $2.3 million in 1993, after an estimated profit of $1.3 million in the previous season, although Pocklington insisted that the team had been losing money since 1988:

> we were losing $3 million to $4 million a year. And then it really got serious. The losses reached as high as $10 million a year. The payroll was to blame. By 1993–94, the cost of the players was 105 percent of my gate...So, what are you supposed to do? Do you suck every nickel out of every other business you own to run the Oilers? No. You start selling off your more expensive players.[47]

In addition to cutting expenses, Pocklington also tried to increase revenues, once again raising ticket prices—from an average of $24.51 to $30.41. Attendance, however, continued to fall, and Bill Tuele, the club's publicity director, remarked, "We have to get away from the mindset that [prices] are geared for a family of four." Tickets had become primarily "a corporate thing."[48] Many fans were unhappy with the segregation of Northlands Coliseum into the haves—in the $60 gold seats near the ice—and the have-nots—in the nose-bleed sections at the top of the arena. Pocklington apologized for "disrupting the culture" of Edmonton hockey fans, but would not change the situation.[49]

He also threatened to relocate the Oilers to Hamilton or Minneapolis, if he didn't get a better deal from Northlands. Meanwhile, he created a new company, Pocklington Sports Marketing, to build up season-ticket sales for the Oilers from the low base of just 8,000, and to capitalize on new advertising opportunities in the increasingly com-modified arena. As the head of Pocklington's marketing company noted, "Priority No. 1 is advertising. Signage in the Coliseum and on the boards and on the clock [is worth] $3 million...I'm also working on selling the names of both the new ball park and the Coliseum" (at 10 years for $10 million).[50] Pocklington also hired an arena consul-tant who claimed that Northlands was "in the bottom 10 percent of major North American arenas."[51] The Coliseum was just two decades old, and a costly, new, publicly-funded arena was a political non-starter for left-leaning Mayor Jan Reimer, elected in 1989. As she noted, these types of claims on public resources were becoming increasingly common:

> Well, back then it was very strong. And the Ghermezians were in that mix at the time as well—tax concessions were a bit of a mantra back then, and I campaigned against that quite strongly...If you really believe in the free market then it should be able to stand the test of economic performance, right? I remember one developer coming in and showing me plans and saying "these are the numbers, I really need this help." And then, "Oh no, those are the ones for the bank, look at these ones."...It was the same type of thing [with Pocklington]. The bluster that we're going to take the team away to get everyone all whipped up and concerned about municipal identity, and then the sports writers converge on that and the tension around it, and it never ends.[52]

Instead, for now, the Oilers' owner demanded new luxury boxes and sky suites to increase his revenues. Even Northlands criticized this blatant attempt to divide the fans further. Harry Hole said that the arena "was built for the people in this area, and they can't carry lunch buckets all day and go and pay $100 for a hockey game at night." While Northlands portrayed itself as a "partner of the city" and defender of the hockey fan, it remained "an exclusive club financed by the public."[53] Bob Westbury of Northlands later agreed: "There was a degree of arrogance around Northlands at that time, like we're bigger than the city itself."[54]

The Oilers were not just losing money, they were losing value—
from US$51 million in 1991 to US$46 million in 1994. One analyst
suggested that this was the result of an unfavourable lease and the
lack of new revenue-generating amenities, and Pocklington himself
publicly deplored his existing lease agreement with Northlands,
which he had signed in 1986 and which ran until June 1999.[55]
The lease required Pocklington to pay $2.3 million annually to

Northlands, and he received no share of parking or concessions.
Thus, for Pocklington, breaking an enforceable lease and gaining
control of a newly renovated Coliseum, rather than achieving
success on the ice, became the key to increasing revenues. This
strategy also reflected the new corporate mentality of the NHL.
So, Pocklington demanded better lease terms from Northlands,
plus the revenues from parking and concessions. He also offered
to sell the team to Northlands for $105 million, which would have
cleared his debt with ATB. Knowing that Pocklington's financial
empire was collapsing, Northlands rejected this offer. In response,
Pocklington once again threatened to move the team. Colin Forbes,
general manager of Northlands, balked: "The clear-thinking people
of this city have to say 'At what cost do we succumb to the demands
that have been placed upon the city?' I don't think anyone should
attempt to hold a city hostage."[56] Pocklington later said of his threat
to leave: "I wasn't going to do it, I wasn't going to move the team.
I was using it for leverage to get people to come to the table...I was
committed to dear Edmonton."[57]

Under the circumstances, though, the threat was enough. Bob
Westbury remembered, "The fear of losing that team was palpable,
just palpable. I was in this huge dilemma. On the one hand, I lose
the building and Northlands goes bankrupt, and Northlands hates
me...Or I could lose the Oilers and then the whole city is going
to feel the same way."[58] The fans certainly believed the threats to
leave were real, and as Mayor Reimer noted, "Pocklington was very
good at playing to the sports media...who boosted the idea that a
professional sports team should get everything it wanted."[59] In fact,
375 people contacted the Citizens Action Centre concerned about
the Oilers leaving, and more called the mayor directly.[60] Under

pressure from Pocklington, Oilers fans, and Northlands, Reimer finally relented and agreed that it was in the best interest of the city to provide public funding because of the civic importance of the hockey club to Edmonton. She later reflected on the difficulty of balancing the competing interests of the Oilers, Northlands, and the city:

> *Both of those were very male-dominated organizations at the time. And I remember actually going to a Northlands meeting around this time because they were being very difficult as well in trying to work something out, and not even being allowed to speak. Part of it was the position that I took, and I think part of it was gender. They [Northlands] were exceedingly difficult on just about any little issue that came up. So, on the one hand, you were dealing with Peter Pocklington, which was a whole other story, and then with Northlands, and then the provincial government was there in the backdrop, and the city. So, it was very challenging...I think we actually had a press conference almost every day to take on Northlands.[61]*

Edmonton's boosters now sprang into action. In 1994, Rick LeLacheur, president of the newly formed, non-profit, Economic Development Edmonton (EDE), brokered a deal that gave Pocklington full control of the Coliseum. The total came to $9 million and included all arena revenues, concessions, and the newly constructed luxury boxes.[62] The rent to Northlands was set at $2.8 million annually, and, crucially, Pocklington accepted a location agreement stipulating that the Oilers would remain in Edmonton until 2004 and could not be sold without the approval of the EDE and Northlands. He also agreed that local ownership would be the first priority if the team was ever sold, and a sale price was anchored at US$70 million.[63]

To help with the rent, the city of Edmonton introduced a ticket tax, which the Oilers collected for hockey games and Northlands collected for non-hockey events.[64] The city also received about $2.8 million from the ticket surcharge per season. In the end, the renovations of the Coliseum were funded by a combination of city financing, a $15-million federal grant originally intended for urban infrastructure, and money from Pocklington himself via a loan from the ATB; a new baseball park for Pocklington's Triple-A club, the Edmonton Trappers, also became part of the deal.[65] With the infrastructure money going to the arena, little was left to improve roads and sewers, social programs had to be cut, and outdoor neighbourhood rinks closed. The result was especially galling to Mayor Reimer, who had campaigned on ending handouts to businesses and on shifting limited city resources to social services. Indeed, as she reflected, the Oilers' saga in the 1990s hijacked scarce public resources and tremendous amounts of political capital:

> It just dominated...This took so much energy and time and certainly it was not something that anyone campaigned on. So, when you have these things come forward, it's a detriment to the other issues that really need to be attended to at a municipal level that have a much broader impact in terms of community well-being.[66]

With public money being spent to upgrade and build facilities for his teams, Pocklington, who only a couple of years before had labelled Edmonton a second-class city, once again became an old-fashioned booster, with all the usual rhetoric. Helping him was a good deal for the city, he said, because, "First of all, the sports teams give the city international recognition....All the studies I've seen [suggest that] a major-league franchise brings in roughly $100 million in economic activity."[67] He praised Edmonton as "a great spot" where "I can get things done." The city has "a lot to offer" because of its "heart and spirit."[68]

The deal raised questions about the value of the Oilers to Edmonton. Was the team worth millions of tax dollars? It has been argued that "local boosters, media and politicians are all responsible for promoting the idea that a pro franchise is crucial to the welfare of a city...[that] the modern city's alleged dependency on pro sports is one of the biggest shams of the 20th century...[and that] sports teams don't contribute much, if anything, to a local economy." And the argument that a sports franchise improves the "quality of life" is "absurd on its face."[69] Yet, boosters continued to argue the opposite—Edmonton needed the Oilers, and the use of public funds to keep them was entirely justifiable and in the city's interest, economically, socially, and culturally. Businessman Cal Nichols (who later was part of the group that bought the Oilers) said that, if the team left, corporations "could decide they want to live in major-league status towns, [and] pick up and leave."[70] Boosters also assumed that support for the hockey team and the pursuit of "world-class status" for Edmonton was shared by everyone within the community.[71]

Not everyone liked the deal. Some in the business community objected to pumping additional money into the Coliseum and supporting Northlands' interests. As Mayor Reimer later noted, "even the downtown business owners were saying why put all that money out there? And at the time, too, Northlands [was] building the Agricom and competing with the convention centre, which was also drawing people away from the downtown."[72] But in 1995, Reimer was defeated by Edmonton booster and businessman Bill Smith, who promised a return to the agenda of economic development, and, in particular, the hosting of mega-sporting events to showcase the city. He wanted to bring the 2008 Olympics to Edmonton, for example, but that bid failed. As mayor, he believed his job was to sell Edmonton and constantly promote it: "Edmonton is the best city in the best province in the best country in the world."[73]

Edmonton, though, continued to endure a recession. Real estate prices had fallen, and the city lost a number of corporate head offices to Calgary, notably Canada Safeway and Shaw Communications, among others. Meanwhile, the downtown core was a "disaster," at least according to several prominent civic boosters, including Jim Taylor, the long-time director of the Downtown Business Association, who recalled: "It was just black hole after black hole."[74] Mayor Smith was subsequently presented with yet another downtown plan in 1997, which shifted the focus from "previous efforts which placed a priority on building new projects" to a recognition that "buildings alone do not revitalize a downtown. People do."[75] While promoting economic development, attracting new business and investment, and increasing tax revenues remained important, the goal was to draw more people into the city core. This would be done by building more housing, making the area more accessible, improving the physical environment, encouraging arts, culture, and entertainment, and linking downtown to the river valley. In this way, Edmonton could showcase its role as the capital city. Mega-projects were out, and small projects were in. And, with the Northlands Coliseum recently renovated, there was no mention of a downtown arena.[76]

Although their facility had improved, the Oilers had not. They continued to lose, and as ticket prices spiralled upwards and hockey seasons were disrupted by a strike and a lockout, fans stayed away from the Coliseum in greater and greater numbers. The franchise continued to lose money, at least according to Pocklington. But, even more important, the ATB called in its loan because he could no longer pay even the interest on his debts, which had been secured using the Oilers—and, once again, he looked to the city for support.

In 1995/96, the Oilers also sought financial assistance from the NHL. Pocklington, like other owners of Canadian teams, took his cue from the NHL, which blamed franchises' financial problems on the lack of a salary cap and a league-wide revenue sharing plan, as well as the low value of the Canadian dollar.[77] Spearheaded by Gary Bettman, the NHL created the Canadian Currency Assistance Plan to assist small-market Canadian teams affected by the low Canadian dollar. It would provide $2.5 million to teams that sold 13,000 season tickets and 90 percent of its corporate boxes, and a subsidy to help Canadian teams sign free agents. Edmonton received about $3 million annually under this plan.[78] Still, two teams, the Winnipeg Jets and the Quebec Nordiques, left Canada for larger US markets with newer facilities.

With the Oilers facing yet another crisis, local boosters rose to the occasion. Cal Nichols created a group called the Friends of the Oilers, whose goal was to sell tickets and keep the team in Edmonton: "I guess I saw, in the community at that time, the will to go to the wall.

The common goal was to keep the team, because this is Edmonton, and this is the roots of hockey, and it's where the game is best understood."[79] EDE concluded that the Oilers had a net impact of $74.7 million in Alberta overall, and $62.9 million in the Edmonton region alone. According to these boosters, the team generated 1200 full-time jobs locally and another 160 regionally. Total wages were $44,075,127, with $38,682,368 staying in Edmonton. The EDE report also suggested that the Oilers paid $19.5 million in taxes (mostly income taxes, which came in at $8.6 million; property and business taxes paid to the city came to $2.1 million).[80] Boosters in the media quickly jumped on board, and the *Journal* argued: "The ultimate winners are the people who will keep their jobs in the restaurants, the bakeries, the hotels and establishments that rely on all of the tangible and intangible benefits [that] Oilers hockey has brought and will bring to our town."[81] The team also brought intangible benefits, it was said. According to Bill Tuele, the Oilers had a "special relationship" with the city because they were "active members of the cultural and charitable lives of Edmontonians. The team strengthens community spirit." Even when the team was losing, he said, "the fact remains that [we] stay connected to the community and they [the fans] will still care."[82]

By this time, Pocklington's financial empire had finally collapsed. He claimed that the Oilers had lost $45 million since 1990, although his businesses were so intertwined that it was impossible to ascertain the true amount. He later conceded that, "The ATB was charging 19 percent interest on the Oilers' overdraft—and, well, the whole thing was the overdraft. So, they nailed me for $20 million, $25 million in interest every year." Pocklington owed the ATB more than $120 million; the bank called in his loan and forced him to sell his personal and corporate assets.[83] In June 1997, he announced that he was selling the team for US$70 million to Les Alexander from Houston, the owner of the NBA's Rockets. Alexander, though, walked away because of the location agreement. He returned in February 1998, after increasing his offer to US$82.5 million and committing to keep the team in Edmonton for another three years. Pocklington was desperate for

Alexander to buy the team, but the ATB, as per the 1994 agreement, instructed the EDE and Northlands to find local buyers within 30 days.[84]

A group of prominent local boosters, the Edmonton Investors Group Limited Partnership (EIGLP), stepped up. They raised $60 million and borrowed the remainder. Cal Nichols contributed $1 million (later $3 million) and Bruce Saville contributed $7 million, but Nichols had experienced little success with Edmonton's old elite, which preferred private philanthropy to buying a hockey team, so he approached younger operators in the oil patch who were also Oilers fans—a group Nichols called the "blue-collar millionaires"—and raised the money by selling shares for $1 million.[85] The EIGLP, with 38 members altogether, including the *Edmonton Journal*, took control of the team on May 5, 1998. The Pocklington era in Edmonton was officially over, and he left the city in October 1998.[86]

The EIGLP Era

Cal Nichols said that his group bought the Oilers not for the profits, but because "I saw in the community...the will...to keep the team because *this is Edmonton*." Nichols was praised as "the man most responsible for keeping the National Hockey League in Edmonton and for ensuring its future." He acted as "the ultimate community worker" to better Edmonton: "I believe in being rewarded for superior effort, harder work. You should benefit from that, but in the process of benefiting, you should never forget where you came from, and how can I use my good fortune to help those who are less fortunate."[87] Nichols was a classic booster seeking to foster "local pride and civic spirit."[88] He was also a tough negotiator who defended the interests of the new ownership group in an era of financial uncertainty.

The initial goal of the EIGLP was to keep the Oilers in Edmonton. Patrick LaForge, president of the team from 2000 to 2015, would later say that,

> Cal's group...had a single purpose—support and stabilize the Oilers
> in a successful mode until the NHL completed their new labour agree
> ment. And that labour agreement by promise of the owners and Gary

*[Bettman] would have a salary cap. So, the cost certainty to run a
franchise would have been clear...They committed to get it to that
labour agreement which came to the table in 2004.*[89]

Some in the ownership group were involved individually with
Northlands, but that organization wanted to maintain as much
control as possible in its relationship with the new owners, especially as it regained control of the Coliseum and non-hockey events.
And the city wanted Northlands involved and was willing to provide
additional subsidy to ensure the viability of both organizations
and of professional hockey in Edmonton. Nichols was unsure of
Northlands' role, but understood that the organization wanted
revenue from the Coliseum for its other activities. Northlands, in
turn, provided a generous new lease to ensure the Oilers' viability.[90]
The EIGLP would pay only a nominal rent of $1 annually, and would
receive all suite revenue and naming rights to the arena, a portion of
concessions from hockey events, a share of parking revenue, and
$2.2 million from the ticket surcharge from the city. Northlands
would regain revenues from non-hockey events, approximately $12
million, and would receive $1 million annually from the EIGLP to
cover the Coliseum's operating costs, which now fell to the non-profit
organization—roughly $17 million. Importantly, the city would also
kick in $2.5 million annually to Northlands to cover part of the short-
fall of its costs, as well as $600,000 of the ticket surcharge revenue
that had once only flowed to the municipal coffers. According to
Nichols, "We got what we wanted, they got what they wanted."[91]

When the deal went to city council, the debate was contentious.
Some councillors feared that another precedent had been established
for both organizations to receive continued public assistance. "They'll
be back," predicted Councillor Brian Mason, "and we'll have to dig
into our wallets once more."[92] He was right.

A new lease agreement, however, did nothing to address the continued growth of salaries and the decline of the value of the Canadian
dollar. The owners of franchises across the country began to pressure the Canadian government for federal subsidies. With the recent
relocation of the Jets and the Nordiques to US cities fresh in fans'

minds, Minister of Industry John Manley said that he was looking into a long-term national solution to help all the Canadian teams. In January 2000, he announced that Ottawa would pay up to $3 million annually to each of Canada's six NHL teams to help keep them competitive. The Oilers were only too happy to take the money. Although they had sold 13,000 season tickets to qualify for NHL assistance, average attendance was about 2,000 below capacity, and corporate support remained minimal.[93] Public reaction to the subsidies across the country was, however, both swift and loud. The Canadian Taxpayers Federation called on Canadians to send pucks to Prime Minister Jean Chrétien to show their disgust with the bailout. Few Canadians supported giving money to billionaire owners and millionaire players. Others objected to spending public money on professional sports, while

programs intended to address urgent social needs remained chronically underfunded. It was obvious, though, that a significant segment of the Canadian public did not want to subsidize NHL hockey, even if it meant Canada losing more of its NHL teams. Although many Canadians still professed to care about hockey, the game simply did not have the same mythological hold on Canadians that it had in the past. Put a little differently, NHL hockey was no longer regarded by most Canadians as a "priceless" part of our heritage, something to be saved at any cost.[94]

After just three days, with much embarrassment, the federal government rescinded its offer.

The EIGLP seemed to struggle through crisis after crisis. The ownership group was not cohesive, and its interference led to Glen Sather's resignation as Oilers president and GM in May 2000. Sather had wanted to spend more on salaries than the budget allocated. Gary Gregg, a member of the ownership group, later said on the matter: "The [management] group that was in place at the time had no control over costs and no attitude to try and control costs. There was a mindset that: 'This is hockey. It's going to lose money. Accept

The still perfectly serviceable Rexall Place, interior, 2003. [City of Edmonton]

it.' And, of course, that doesn't work."[95] Two prominent members of the group, Jim Hole and Bruce Saville, were pushed off the board because they supported Sather's position, and Cal Nichols ended up as chair and spokesperson for the EIGLP.

The Oilers continued to be represented as an important city resource and an integral part of community life. Patrick LaForge, the new president of the Oilers, said, "I think that sports and entertainment is a unique industry and it adds value to a city...You can't replace it with a refinery or a pulp mill. They might have similar economic impact, but it's not a substitute for entertainment for the masses." Without an NHL franchise, "money would fly out of the city, as people sought world-class entertainment elsewhere, going to shows in cities such as Las Vegas, or NHL hockey in Calgary or Vancouver."[96] The local media remained similarly boosterish. When *Forbes* reported in its annual valuations that the Oilers had the lowest franchise value in the NHL during the 2002/03 season, Dan

Barnes, writing in the *Journal*, asserted: "Edmonton and the Oilers have a whole different balance sheet, one that has way more to do with the intensity of interest and support for NHL hockey and the value the Oilers provide to the image of the City of Edmonton. Both the city and the team look to other measures to determine the value of the club to Edmontonians."[97]

The economic value of the club, though, continued to decline. Edmonton was a small-market team that had to pay player salaries in US dollars at a time when the Canadian dollar was low, but generated revenue in Canadian funds.[98] The owners wanted a limit on the amount of hockey revenue paid to the players; when the NHL Players' Association (NHLPA) rejected any sort of salary cap, they were locked out. Nichols strongly favoured a salary cap, even though the issue cost the NHL its 2004/05 season.[99] There had been a $14-million cash call for the EIGLP investors in the summer of 2003, and Nichols wanted to avoid further calls by achieving "cost certainty" for the Oilers. The EIGLP would support the lockout for as long as it took to force the NHLPA to accept a smaller proportion of the League's revenues (even though the team lost an estimated $9 million during the lockout).

He also threatened to sell and move the team: "We are just not prepared to carry on with an open chequebook. I don't see Edmonton in the cards."[100] Later, he would double down: "These weren't idle threats. I was deadly serious about our needs in Edmonton and I wanted to make no misrepresentation or have no misunderstanding of what we had to have."[101] It should not be forgotten, as Peter Pocklington never did and as the EIGLP quickly learned, that owning the Edmonton Oilers was about making as much money as possible: "a hockey team is a business, after all," said Pocklington.[102] However, following the turmoil of the 1990s and the uncertainty of the first five years of the new millennium, a vastly more profitable era—one that included the prospect of a new downtown arena and associated land development opportunities—was on the horizon.

4

PREPARING THE POLITICAL TERRAIN

FOR OVER A CENTURY, urban boosterism and the corporate–civic project of building the city through hockey and arena developments have worked together in Edmonton. In 2005—after months, if not years of private discussions—executives from the Edmonton Oilers first cautiously began to publicize their desire for a new arena through trusted allies in the local media. Rexall Place (then called Northlands Coliseum) had opened in 1974 at a cost of roughly $18 million ($83.7 million in 2016 dollars) and had been extensively upgraded in the 1990s. As recently as 2001, the city of Edmonton had loaned Northlands $3.1 million to purchase a new scoreboard, payable over a 20-year term at an interest rate of 6.5 percent—a debt that the city would never fully recover with the opening of Rogers Place and the shuttering of the Northlands Coliseum (as it was now called once again). Even as political momentum was gathering for a new downtown arena, the government of Alberta would spend $10 million to renovate the home and visiting team dressing rooms in Rexall Place.[1]

Despite these public investments—upgrades made to ensure the Oilers remained financially viable and competitive with teams playing in newer arenas—the Oilers regarded Rexall Place as an antiquated facility that damaged their business interests. The claim of facility obsolescence typically marks the beginning of a public relations campaign for a new, publicly subsidized facility that is equivalent in both size and revenue-generating potential to those recently built elsewhere.[2] In Edmonton, as in countless other cities, the facility obsolescence claim would be used to counter an obvious obstacle to the Oilers' demands for a new, publicly-financed arena: a profitable one already existed, and it was only 30 years old.

The orchestrated cycle of arena and stadium renewal has only intensified in recent years, a point underlining the astonishingly brief lifecycle of major league facilities in North America, which now "erode" at unparalleled rates compared to other buildings and infrastructure, whether public or private. Unlike the replacement of the dismal "Edwardian" infrastructure of English football—a long overdue change insisted upon by the British government after 96 football fans died at the Hillsborough football stadium in Sheffield in April 1989, and only made possible by "very considerable public subsidy"[3]—municipalities across North America have replaced fully functional and safe facilities simply to accommodate the ever-increasing revenue demands of team owners and the changing business model of major league sport. By the new millennium, a wave of costly and sizeable stadium and arena developments with an expansive range of premium amenities for affluent fans and corporate customers, as well as substantive ancillary land development opportunities, had emerged as standard elements of the new business model for major league franchises in North America, including the NHL.

Beginning in the 1990s, under the leadership of NHL commissioner Gary Bettman, former senior vice president of the National Basketball Association, new hockey arenas were built to improve the value and revenue-generating capacity of clubs in cities like Anaheim and San Jose (1993), St. Louis and Chicago (1994), Boston and Vancouver (1995), Buffalo, Ottawa, Tampa, Nashville, and Montreal (1996), Washington and Philadelphia (1997), Miami (1998), Denver, Raleigh, Toronto, Atlanta, and Los Angeles (1999), St. Paul and Columbus (2000), Dallas (2001), and Phoenix (2003). Revenue from luxury suites and corporate boxes in these increasingly spectacular facilities—as well as from the sale of local television rights—is not subject to league-wide revenue-sharing agreements and has buttressed the financial fortunes of franchises in larger, more prosperous urban markets, where new stadiums and arenas can "translate into millions more a year in team profits."[4]

The political economy of major league sport in the new millennium is radically different from that of earlier eras and is based on a much broader and more integrated business model. Increasingly wealthy franchise owners—billionaires like Stan Kroenke, owner of Kroenke Sports & Entertainment, which includes stakes in the NHL's Colorado Avalanche, NBA's Denver Nuggets, and NFL's Los Angeles Rams, and Philip Anschutz, owner of Anschutz Entertainment Group, the world's largest owner of sports teams, including stakes in the NHL's Los Angeles Kings and NBA's Los Angeles Lakers, as well as venues like the Staples Center in Los Angeles—and deep-pocketed corporations like Maple Leaf Sports and Entertainment have radically diversified their sports empires in ways that would have been unimaginable only two or three decades ago. Deep-pocketed owners and powerful corporations have acquired multiple sports franchises as key components of vertically integrated entertainment companies. They also own, or at least fully control, the arenas and stadiums where their franchises play (and hence accumulate revenue from all events that occur in these facilities), as well as various digital distribution networks for their sports properties.

These companies increasingly aspire to capitalize on lucrative land development deals—with condos, shopping areas, hotels, restaurants, bars, and office towers—in upmarket sports and entertainment districts connected to the growth agendas of cities wanting to revitalize their downtown cores. The construction of a new arena or stadium is intended to trigger massive land development deals and to revalourize underdeveloped land, all to the benefit of team owners who have purchased surrounding properties, and of those in the land development industry who are well-positioned to capitalize on these trends.

The aspiration of the Oilers to replace Rexall Place with a more modern NHL facility had little, if anything, to do with the actual condition of the profitable, safe, and well-used facility that, in addition to hosting Oilers games and other sporting events, ranked as *the third-busiest concert venue in Canada, 12th in the world.*[5] Still, by 2005, Rexall Place was one of the oldest NHL buildings, and out of sync with the new business model of major league sport and the revenue-generating standards set by other recently constructed facilities. At the time, the average NHL rink had 94 luxury suites, while Rexall Place had only 62 (Canadian NHL facilities averaged 106 suites). Unlike ordinary fans who purchase individual tickets or season ticket packages, corporations can claim a 50 percent business and entertainment tax deduction for the total price of their suite. Team owners can therefore charge more for their corporate boxes, "knowing that corporations will happily pay higher rates if the purchase is tax deductible."[6] These deductions are thus another form of subsidy that can amount to sizeable lost tax revenue for governments (in this case, the government of Canada).[7] Rexall Place was also comparably smaller than newer facilities, especially in terms of concourse space for the sale of concessions and other amenities—another important source of revenue for NHL franchises.

In Edmonton, then, a new, publicly-financed facility represented a chance to boost the franchise's already significant arena-related revenue—NHL clubs enjoy an average increase in arena revenue of 52 percent from playing in a new facility[8]—and increase its valuation. A new and publicly-financed arena would also benefit the NHL, by setting another precedent for other owners preparing to enter into negotiations with municipalities to replace facilities in the continuous cycle of league-wide facility renewal (e.g., Calgary and Ottawa). In Edmonton, a host of recently constructed, publicly-financed arena developments—in Newark, New Jersey, and Pittsburgh, Pennsylvania, among others—would be held up by boosters as state-of-the-art, revenue-generating archetypes that the Oilers expected the city of Edmonton to emulate in order to ensure a competitive balance throughout the NHL.

The main effect of all of these developments has been to drive up the construction cost of new facilities that now require considerably more space for luxury suites, premium seats, and concourse space with a range of upmarket concessions and shopping opportunities. The typical North American major league baseball stadium, for example, now has "double the footprint of an older ballpark," while construction costs have risen from "as low as $25 million in the late 1960s to $300 million and up today."[9] The cost of a new, single-use, publicly-financed arena development in Edmonton would grow to over $600 million.

Making the Pitch

In 2005, Cal Nichols, chairman of the EIGLP, remarked at the conclusion of a lengthy feature piece by David Staples in the *Edmonton Journal* that the team needed a new arena with more amenities and seats to generate more revenue.[10] For members of the EIGLP, who had bought the club just a few years earlier from Peter Pocklington, a new facility would secure its long-term future in Edmonton. A generation of Oilers fans, including Staples, was well aware of the financial uncertainties affecting the club and its ownership in the 1990s, and of the stigma of being a "small-market" franchise that competes against the NHL's larger and more prosperous cities.

Staples was, at the time, undertaking his own research for a book on the EIGLP and had access to Oilers executives to tell the group's story.[11] In the years to come, as both a sports and city hall columnist who was well connected to sources in the Oilers, the local business community, and city administration, Staples would emerge as the chief media booster for the arena development. As one of the main contributors to *Cult of Hockey*, a blog from the *Edmonton Journal*, he would also make the case for a new arena on this website, while discrediting critics of the public financing proposal. The *Edmonton Journal* was itself a shareholder in the EIGLP and relied on coverage of the Oilers to secure an audience, largely of male readers, that could in turn be sold to local advertisers. Even at this stage, then, the *Journal*'s interests were aligned with those of the Oilers' ownership group, and as a prominent civic booster, the paper's coverage of the arena debate would largely reproduce the optimistic narratives associated with the arena development and downtown revitalization.

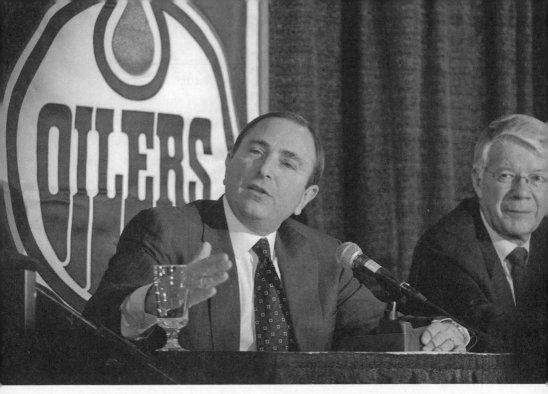

A new arena on the horizon. NHL Commissioner Gary Bettman (left) speaks to reporters with Edmonton Oilers Chairman Cal Nichols in Edmonton, on November 30, 2004. [Canadian Press/John Ulan]

Having visited several of the newer and larger NHL arenas recently built across North America in his travels as chairman of the Oilers, Nichols considered Rexall Place a dated facility that lacked the most profitable, contemporary, revenue-generating amenities that benefitted other franchises, despite having been extensively renovated in the 1990s. As Nichols would later acknowledge, these discrepancies as well as the broader, league-wide, orchestrated cycle of facility obsolescence—of which NHL commissioner Gary Bettman was the main promoter—were frequent topics of discussion among the owners of NHL franchises: "Every time we would meet at governors' meetings there was also discussion about upgrading buildings and building revenues to deal with salaries. Everyone was always trying to get ahead of each other."[12]

Although most of the new generation of NHL arenas had been built in downtown locations, Nichols initially refrained from publicly stating that a new facility in Edmonton should be located downtown, in order to avoid spurring land speculation on potential development sites and inflaming the relationship with Northlands during negotiations over the Oilers' lease renewal. Still, behind closed doors, discussions between members of the EIGLP and other interest groups about the need for a new downtown arena had already begun. As Patrick LaForge has acknowledged: "It wasn't difficult for us to get to that point; within half an hour of our first conversations in 2003 and 2004 when we were heading into renewing our lease, behind closed doors we were already talking about a new building and what we needed…and we were within 12 square blocks of where it is today fairly early in the conversation."[13]

While the EIGLP would ultimately decline to pursue Nichols' vision, this agenda was soon embraced by both Mayor Stephen Mandel—himself a prominent Edmonton booster and former developer, who had defeated three-term Mayor Bill Smith after a well-organized campaign in October 2004[14]—and, eventually, Daryl Katz, the future owner of the Edmonton Oilers. By October 2005, Mayor Mandel had publicly acknowledged that discussion of a new downtown arena was already occurring in private, as part of a much broader growth agenda to redevelop downtown, including the expansion of MacEwan University, the creation of the University of Alberta's Enterprise Square, and the construction of the Art Gallery and a new home for the Royal Alberta Museum. As Cal Nichols reflected, the mayor was an early supporter of the plan for a new downtown arena: "The mayor, he kind of bought into the whole notion. He was good. He just saw the wisdom of it."[15]

Throughout the 2005/06 NHL season, while the wheels of a new, publicly-subsidized, downtown growth agenda were turning behind closed doors, the Oilers continued to prepare the political terrain for a new arena by citing facility obsolescence, competitive disadvantage, and the need for a "level playing field" with other NHL teams that were playing in newer facilities. This promotional work was enthusiastically performed by then-CEO and President of the Edmonton Oilers Patrick LaForge, who had accompanied Nichols on a number of business trips to other arenas. "We'd walk into the same place together and say, 'Holy man, imagine having something like this to work with,'" Nichols recalled.[16] Without providing financial evidence to support his argument, LaForge claimed that Rexall Place simply did not generate enough revenue for the Oilers.[17]

After an economic decline in Edmonton in the 1990s, the millennium promised new growth, and the Oilers wanted a new, publicly-financed arena to tap into those opportunities—one over which they had full control. Their ambition aligned with the NHL's new business model, and signalled the Oilers' intent to remove Northlands, the longstanding non-profit operator of Rexall Place, from the business of NHL hockey and from arena management in Edmonton altogether. As Mayor Mandel recalled, these were the crucial dynamics at play in the earliest discussions of a new arena:

> *The Oilers and Northlands never got along so there was a fundamental conflict between the two of them...and they were constantly butting heads. And so Cal and Patrick LaForge had travelled all over the place to look for ideas about building a new arena, and I think they progressed more in their heads but they hadn't really approached the city at all. I had a meeting with them once, maybe twice, about looking at what they were doing. But they never approached the city to do much because they needed to get their group of people organized. I think at some point if they would have gotten all of the ownership group together, they would have approached the city. But they didn't. At least to my knowledge they didn't. Or to my memory they didn't. But they were definitely keen about building a new arena. They saw that they couldn't get along with Northlands but also that the facility wasn't state of the art in order to be successful and that's really one of the challenges that everyone had faced. So that was the beginning.[18]*

As Patrick LaForge noted, Mayor Mandel was very influential in these early discussions, and he ultimately supported the Oilers' aspirations. He was also well connected to people who had supported him politically and who had a vested interest in the club, including many important developers:

So, we knew him well, the Butler boys [notably Bill Butler, a property developer and member of the EIGLP], who were part owners of the Oilers, were significant supporters of Stephen. So, we did a lot of things together, and he came to the games and the suite and were very good socially together on different things and then we were talking about the airport, we were talking about all kinds of things and trying to contribute in our own way...We had lots of time with the mayor and certainly he was aware of our interest in re-housing the Oilers somewhere. The idea of downtown was well put together.[19]

According to LaForge, these early conversations included preliminary plans for a public–private funding model and an initial estimated cost, albeit one that was drawn from thin air:

[R]ight from our first conversations, we were bouncing it back and forth. Yeah, we're watching a hockey game saying there's a four-sided way of paying for a building: the owner, the city, the province, and the fans...We had the model done probably in the first month of conversations. By we, I mean collectively, not just the Oilers; a ticket tax, a Community Revitalization Levy (CRL)...The cost and value of the building, somebody invented $400 million. It wasn't the number, and nobody ever took it as the number, but it just kind of came out of the clouds and dropped on the table.[20]

By 2005, then, the main proponents and beneficiaries of a new downtown arena development had already agreed behind closed doors on the importance of building a new, publicly-subsidized arena to support the interests of the Oilers, and on a range of financing mechanisms, including a CRL. The Oilers had already secured the full support of the mayor, the mayor's office, and civic administration—but without the knowledge or participation of the city council or citizens of Edmonton.

A Matter of Timing

The idea made its first public appearance in 2005, once three crucial economic factors were in place. The first—which secured the economic foundation of the Oilers—was the signing in 2004 of a 10-year lease extension with Northlands and the city. Like the 1998 agreement that had been designed to ensure the sustainability of the Oilers in the post-Pocklington era, the new lease agreement had Northlands continue to manage the operations of Rexall Place and be responsible for building operations and capital costs, including event costs associated with professional hockey games—another subsidy for the Oilers. The agreement continued to cap the Oilers' rent payments at $1 per year and absolved the franchise from contributing to facility or game-day expenses, even though the general trend in the industry at that time was for franchises to pay rent and to cover all expenses in return for collecting all NHL-related revenue.[21]

The Oilers got all hockey-related revenue from Rexall Place, including food, beverage, and merchandise revenue, 50 percent of parking revenue, and all building advertising and sponsorship revenues, including naming rights,[22] plus all suite rental revenue from *every* event held in the arena, including concerts. As Jerry Bouma (former chair of the board of directors for Northlands) noted, the non-profit organization had willingly ceded the Oilers an enormous amount of revenue:

> Now of course the suites have value for two reasons. One for hockey games, and the other for the concerts—we had a real revival in the concert business thanks to Northlands and a transition in the concert business and increased touring, because that's the way musicians made money. Now, when I sell you a suite...I can charge you $250,000 because you'll receive 80 hockey games [Oilers and Oil Kings] as well as 60 concerts. If I only have 80 hockey games and a couple of concerts, you might only be willing to pay $150,000. But now that you have 60 high quality concerts, you're willing to pay more. That's how they capitalize the value of the suite. That all went to the Oilers. They got every penny of that, and that was done in the spirit of community and the original lease agreement.[23]

The only revenue stream that Northlands withheld from the Oilers was from events unrelated to hockey, such as concerts and the Canadian Finals Rodeo, which helped cover the non-profit organization's expenses.

All of these developments—in particular, the combination of lower-than-average arena contributions and favourable lease terms—underline the extent to which the Oilers have been subsidized by the non-profit organization and by taxpayers, through "one of the more financially advantageous" lease agreements "compared to other NHL franchises."[24] The lease agreement also continued the ticket surcharge and the $2.5-million contribution from the city to Northlands to assist with the operation of Rexall Place. As Andy Huntley, Northlands' former chairman, noted, this contribution essentially went straight to the Oilers:

> ANDY HUNTLEY (AH): It's a strict flow-through to subsidize the operation of the Edmonton Oilers. It's nothing to help Northlands, and it should be stated on their financial statement as a subsidy for the Edmonton Oilers.
>
> JAY SCHERER: Why did the city of Edmonton put it through Northlands—just because they didn't want to give it directly to the Oilers?
>
> AH: That's exactly right.[25]

Despite the generous terms of their lease agreement with Northlands, though, the Oilers coveted the revenue from non-hockey events at Rexall Place, too—a source of income that the EIGLP had abandoned when it purchased the hockey club in 1998, but that had become central to the NHL's new business model. In the years to come, Oilers executives would aggressively pursue this revenue stream by repeatedly claiming a $15–18-million competitive disadvantage compared to other NHL franchises that either owned their own facilities or had been able to extract concert revenue as a further concession from the local government or third-party, not-for-profit agency that owned or operated the building, including the club's provincial rival, the Calgary Flames.[26] The larger prize for the Oilers, though, was always a new arena, and, according to Patrick LaForge, executives from the Oilers had made it clear during the negotiations with Northlands and the city that they had no desire to stay at Rexall Place after the lease expired in 2014: "We were negotiating the new lease [with Northlands] and the city was involved—they had councillors on the board and the city manager was there, and we weren't shy about saying we don't expect to renew this lease [in 10 years]: we expect that we'll have a new facility."[27] Northlands, as we shall see, had its own expectations: that a similar lease arrangement would be struck with the Oilers in a new, city-owned, downtown facility, which the non-profit organization would operate.

A New CBA

The second factor was that the NHL had locked out its players for the whole of the 2004/05 NHL season, and it would have been politically imprudent for the Oilers, or any local booster for that matter, to have raised the prospect of a new, publicly-financed arena during an acrimonious labour dispute that alienated hockey fans. The resolution of the lockout and the ensuing collective bargaining agreement (CBA), however, provided NHL owners with both the long-desired salary cap to limit players' rapidly growing salaries to 54–57 percent of league-wide, hockey-related revenue[28] and a revenue-sharing plan. These developments placed the Oilers' franchise on much firmer financial footing. Indeed, one of the main arguments made by NHL owners to justify the lockout to Canadian fans was that a new CBA would protect small-market teams. Hockey clubs like the Oilers would get cost certainty to protect them from the low value of the Canadian dollar, which usually traded considerably below that of the US dollar.

The importance of this agreement cannot be understated: if expenses in the form of player salaries paid in US dollars went down, or at least didn't keep spiralling upwards, and if revenues grew as a result of a new, publicly-financed facility, then profits for ownership and the value of the franchise would both increase significantly. Crucially, the new CBA also provided franchise owners with the opportunity to capture greater amounts of non-hockey revenue—

money that does not have to be shared with NHL players and cannot
be used by the owners to run their teams—through arena building
and ancillary land development opportunities. The new agreement
also granted owners a greater share of hockey-related revenue (shared
with players and used to operate the franchise) from luxury boxes/
suites/premium seating—another reason for the increased importance of these amenities in new facilities—and from fixed signage,
naming rights, and sponsorship sales. Finally, according to the new
CBA, significant amounts of revenue from non-hockey events, including
from parking and concessions, did not need to be shared with the
players, thus creating a powerful incentive for the owners of hockey
franchises to maximize revenue streams that don't count, or only
partially count, toward hockey-related revenue.[29]

Thus, by 2005, after getting the hard-fought financial security of a
new CBA and signing an extraordinarily generous 10 year lease with
Northlands, the Oilers were about to enter an era of unprecedented
profitability.[30] According to a report commissioned by Northlands
in 2009, the Oilers in this period generated $US70.3 million per year,
the third-highest net arena revenue among NHL franchises, despite
playing in one of the oldest facilities in the league, and despite not
accumulating non-hockey revenue.[31] Only the Toronto Maple Leafs
and the New York Rangers earned more in net arena revenue (and
both teams play in substantially larger markets than Edmonton).
This fact would never be made public during the arena debate
because it would have undermined the Oilers' obsolescence claim,
as well as the public perception of the franchise being a revenue-
poor, small-market team hurt by playing in a dated facility.

City-Building and Downtown Revitalization

This brings us to the third essential factor preparing the ground
for the proposal of a new arena: Edmonton's economy. Unlike in
the mid-1990s, by 2005 Edmonton was in the midst of a period of
profound growth, thanks to a resource-led economic boom and
the development of the oil sands in northern Alberta, "the second
largest oil reserve in the world, after Saudi Arabia."[32] The city was
thriving as the province's service and supply centre for the oil and

gas industry, and due to its being home to successful publicly traded companies like The Brick, Stantec, and Canadian Western Bank. Other large private firms were doing very well—the Katz Group, PCL, and WAM Development Group—all of which would soon become key players in the arena debate. By 2005, then, Alberta had become an important region in the continental political economy, and both Edmonton and Calgary had emerged as prosperous, arriviste urban centres. These themes were widely trumpeted by urban boosters over the course of the Oilers' remarkable 2006 playoff run as symbolic of Edmonton's return to financial fortune and as a player on the world stage.[33] Neo-boosterism aside, by the middle of the first decade in the new millennium, there were enough wealthy people in Edmonton to pay for the premium amenities targeted by the Oilers as an increasingly lucrative revenue source.

It was during this period of economic expansion that the Oilers and local political leaders—and their champions in the media— began aggressively promoting the need for a new, world-class arena as part of a broader image-building campaign for the city and its underdeveloped downtown core. Throughout the 1980s and 1990s, Edmonton's downtown, like that of so many other cities across North America, had continued to decline, a pattern exacerbated by the opening of West Edmonton Mall in 1981, as businesses relocated to the outskirts of the city to take advantage of cheaper rents, and as more middle-class families moved to the suburbs and nearby municipalities. Downtown swiftly hollowed out, becoming mostly a place to work without many of the popular entertainment and cultural features associated with a night-time economy. Crime and a visible homeless population, the majority Indigenous, contributed to perceptions of the area as derelict and helped to depress property values.

The key boosters and beneficiaries of a new downtown arena soon connected a new arena not only to the long-term prosperity of the Oilers, but to the revitalization of Edmonton's downtown core as a centre of culture and consumption. By this point, as Patrick LaForge of the Edmonton Oilers acknowledged, the Oilers had no interest whatsoever in even exploring the possibility of renovating

Rexall Place, and had already recognized the value of aligning their financial interests with the political momentum that was gathering to redevelop Edmonton's downtown core:

> *It says a lot about the need for a new building. You can see Edmonton's exploding and you need these component parts. You need a good airport, the Anthony Henday, a well-maintained and functioning downtown. All of us know the recipe for a good city and, in Canada's case, you need NHL hockey in a world-class building. In a 10-year horizon...we have to have a new arena.*[34]

The Oilers had a powerful ally in their pursuit of this agenda in Mayor Stephen Mandel, whose election marked a decisive turning point in the future of the city for a variety of reasons, including his well-publicized desire to transform Edmonton into a more cosmopolitan urban centre. This "new" vision of Edmonton, offering tremendous land development opportunities in the downtown core, was predicated upon many of the ideas of North American urban planning guru Richard Florida (now at the University of Toronto), who published his influential *The Rise of the Creative Class* in 2002. Florida's ideas—including a creativity index that assessed a city's economic potential—informed the revitalization strategies of cities seeking to gentrify their downtown cores, in order to appeal to creative workers who aspired to live in "edgy" and diverse neighbourhoods with cafes, galleries, and experimental music venues.[35] Still, even though many of Florida's insights were summoned in Edmonton to justify a new, publicly-subsidized arena development to re-image the city's downtown core, Florida himself has consistently opposed using public funds for arena and stadium developments—a position conveniently ignored by boosters in Edmonton.[36]

Nonetheless, civic leaders in Edmonton emphasized the importance of attracting and retaining people working in the creative knowledge economy through a host of new urban developments. In his state-of-the-city address in 2005, Mayor Mandel was lauded by prominent civic boosters when he declared his desire to see higher quality architectural developments throughout the city, especially in the downtown core, and a more cosmopolitan, urban aesthetic for the city overall. "No more crap!" he declared. As the mayor later reflected,

> People were unhappy about downtown. They didn't feel safe down-town, felt that there was nothing to do downtown...And, we had done a bunch of things on the external parts of the city, we built the 23rd Avenue overpass, the recreation centre in the southwest, so there was also a debt that was owed to downtown...Because, prior to the start of the construction of the arena, there was an equity issue. We'd spent $500 million here, $300 million there, and nothing was being spent downtown. And then things started to mushroom. I'd like to say I had this great vision but a lot of times it's one step, one step, one step. I also wanted to see a pretty city, a city that I'm proud of when I look at it.[37]

As former city manager Al Maurer recalled, there was a growing awareness at city hall that the downtown core had been neglected with respect to public investment, and that substantial amounts of underdeveloped land promised development opportunities that could eventually help fund an arena through a CRL:

> Well, Stephen really felt that our downtown lacked something and over the years we were having discussions with council about the fact that we were taking all the tax revenue out of downtown, but what were we doing for downtown? We also started looking at a development levy, where you take this loan and you get an area zoned by the province where you get all the increased tax revenue, including education tax revenue that would have gone to the province. We used this [CRL] concept for The Quarters, which was the east side of the downtown. The thought process was it's a hell of a way to generate money, and then as Mandel wanted to revitalize downtown this became more prominent in the sense of that it would be really difficult to do that around Northlands. So, I think this really pushed Stephen to visualize

that he could do something for downtown that was really going to be
unique as long as all these other things fell into place.[38]

Still, while coming to the position of promoting a new, publicly-
financed arena and entertainment district as the centrepiece of this
broader growth agenda for the downtown, the mayor knew that
Edmonton faced a range of financial pressures as a rapidly expanding
city, especially given the cuts to municipal grants. During the mayor's
first term, council budgeted nearly $1 billion for LRT expansion,
new recreation centres, and other neighbourhood upgrades to
address the infrastructure deficit associated with the growing suburbs,
while taking on an increasing amount of debt. As Mayor Mandel
himself noted, any potential arena development, therefore, would
need a substantial contribution from the provincial government of
Alberta, which was at the time awash in surpluses:

> *I can't say no to it [a request for provincial funding] at this point. But*
> *we also need recreation facilities for our kids and a number of other*
> *things. And the province has that big surplus in their coffers. So given*
> *the demands on our city and the tremendous dollars the province has*
> *right now, I think it's something that the province should take a look*
> *at. The city will support the project as much as we can, but we have*
> *limited capacity.*[39]

But despite the lobbying efforts of municipal leaders, (and later by
Daryl Katz), the provincial government repeatedly refused to make
any type of direct contribution to a new arena development downtown, especially once more challenging economic circumstances
arose. As former city manager Al Maurer reflected, past experiences
may also have tempered any enthusiasm about investing in a new
downtown arena: "There was always some initial hope that the province may come forth on the arena but they got burnt the last time
with Pocklington."[40]

Municipal officials and the Oilers also knew that any proposal for
a new arena underwritten by the city's money would meet strong

opposition. By the new millennium, Canadians across the country were more inclined than ever to voice their opposition to subsidizing major league sports franchises, including, in 2000, the federal government's modest proposal to support the six Canadian NHL franchises. Key arena proponents in Edmonton recognized from the outset that they would need to adjust their arguments to address opposition to the use of public funds, and they would get substantive ideological assistance from NHL commissioner Gary Bettman on how to extract concessions from municipalities for arena developments. The mayor's office and administration knew that the political process associated with the new arena would have to be strictly controlled to circumscribe public opposition and to secure the support of councillors.

Promoting the Plan

By the beginning of 2006, following an agenda set behind closed doors, a narrative championing a new, publicly-financed arena on an LRT line to revitalize the downtown core and cement the long-term financial security of the Oilers was being endorsed in the mainstream media, especially by the *Edmonton Journal*, whose sports columnist, John MacKinnon, was an early promoter of the scheme:

> *Imagine the powerful, positive jolt to downtown revitalization an NHL arena would provide, linked as it would be to the LRT system, within easy reach of hotels, restaurants, shops and close to the office towers where countless season ticket-holders work. The economic components all mesh together seamlessly and there are many successful models already up and running to learn from, like Montreal, Toronto, Nashville, St. Paul, Minn., and Denver. All places where people spill out of their workplaces into restaurants or bars, grab a bite and a beverage, then stroll to an arena...Now that the NHL's new economic model permits the Oilers to assemble a long-term strategic plan, the centrepiece of that plan, in concert with the city and the province, should be such an arena. That's not to disrespect sturdy, serviceable Rexall Place, where the Oilers' lease still has 8½ years to run. It's merely a recognition of the obvious—arenas, like collective bargaining*

agreements, expire or become inadequate to changing realities. Rexall
Place, the second-oldest building in the N H L next to Pittsburgh's
outdated Mellon Arena, will be overdue for replacement well before
the lease runs out. Such is life. The tradition-soaked Canadiens
moved out of the Montreal Forum. The Maple Leafs decamped from
legendary but tawdry Maple Leaf Gardens to the spiffy Air Canada
Centre. It's time to start thinking seriously about showcasing the
Oilers in Edmonton's front yard.[41]

Unlike both Maple Leaf Gardens (built in 1931) and the Montreal
Forum (built in 1924), though, Rexall Place was not old. It just lacked
some of the amenities designed to increase revenue streams in the
Air Canada Centre (now Scotiabank Arena), which opened in 1999,
and the Molson Centre (now the Bell Centre), which opened in 1996.
MacKinnon also ignored the fact that both of these new facilities—
like those in Ottawa and Vancouver—were entirely privately financed.

Similar arguments would be promoted by other enthusiastic
boosters in the *Journal* who early on supported the downtown arena
development. The media, as always, led the charge in favour of the
civic growth agenda, and the positions of pro-arena boosters and
public figures, like the mayor, were habitually presented as "news."
In an early commentary on the prospect of a new downtown arena,
the *Journal*'s business columnist, Gary Lamphier, wrote that a new
facility was needed as both a "driver of downtown redevelopment"
and a counter to the city's "coolness deficit." He even returned to
Mordecai Richler's comments from two decades earlier ridiculing
Edmonton as a city that is, as Lamphier put it, "remote, unat-
tractive, bland, cold and unsophisticated." Echoing Richard Florida,
Lamphier argued that the city's lack of upmarket facilities in the
downtown core made it difficult to "attract and keep the kind of
young, smart, skilled, energetic and talented people Edmonton's
booming economy so desperately needs."[42] Three months later,
Lamphier returned to this theme:

Edmonton doesn't look like a successful corporate town. And like it
or not, optics matter. Where other cities boast impressive downtown

skylines filled with gleaming office towers and corporate banners,
Edmonton's skyline remains stunted and gap-toothed. Too many
dusty, garbage-strewn parking lots still rim a downtown core that
desperately needs more density...To make matters worse, instead of an
iconic downtown sports palace like Vancouver's BC Place or Calgary's
Saddledome, Edmonton's aging Rexall Place is located in a seedy area
far from the heart of the city. If downtown is going to make a go of
it, Edmonton needs a splashy new arena—preferably east of the city
centre, near the Shaw Conference Centre.[43]

In 2006, Dr. Dan Mason, a sports management scholar at the University of Alberta, approached the city about working on a short-term contract to learn more about the nuts and bolts of civic administration. He quickly became involved in the arena debate and suggested that Dr. Mark Rosentraub, another sports management expert, be hired by city administration to provide an "assessment of the impacts of sport arenas on urban redevelopment in North America and the assessment of strategies that have *produced the most success*."[44] As a scholar who had earlier been a well-known critic of the subsidy of professional sport franchises, exemplified by the publication of his book *Major League Losers* in the late 1990s, Rosentraub would reverse his position a decade later with the publication of *Major League Winners*, and would work as a pro-development consultant in numerous cities, including those that would be cited as success stories for Edmonton to emulate. City councillors were not initially informed about the hiring of these consultants on sole-source contracts, whose remit also included an overview of various financial tools used in recent arena developments, such as a CRL or a TIF (Tax Increment Financing mechanism).

The city showed no interest in commissioning objective assessments of the political and social implications of such a costly development and its funding models. Nor did municipal officials look for the kind of disinterested analysis of the economic impacts and viability of a new arena development that could have been provided by economists, such as Dr. Brad Humphreys.[45] Administration sought, instead, support for a predetermined position. As the debate progressed, both Mason and Rosentraub were positioned as expert media sources providing favourable commentary about the value of a new, publicly-financed downtown arena and surrounding entertainment district. In short, they became boosters. Their role underlines the growing practice in cities across North America of employing consultants to provide selective information in campaigns to manage public opinion. In the years to come, the city of Edmonton made a practice of hiring like-minded consultants whose research and public statements could be used to promote its arena-related growth agenda, underscoring the erosion of the traditional distinction between administration and politicians, and the principle that city officials ought to provide objective and balanced, research-based advice.[46]

The momentum for a new downtown arena was now undeniable. In November 2006, *Journal* columnist Paula Simons, who would emerge as the most consistent critic of the deal, wrote that a new downtown arena development proposal had already gained powerful supporters in the business community who wished to "remain anonymous."[47] She raised a number of questions that she hoped would be addressed in any future political debate. How much new development could be anticipated from a new downtown arena, especially given the lack of it around both Rexall Place and Commonwealth Stadium? How could a new arena be developed in the downtown to promote meaningful and inclusive urban vibrancy? Who would pay for a new facility for an already profitable NHL franchise? What types of democratic mechanisms would enable citizens to decide collectively whether public investment in a new arena was warranted, especially given the powerful interest groups that had already committed to supporting it?

The prospect of a new downtown arena was given significant political traction in late 2006, only a year after the Oilers first publicly raised the idea, when Mayor Mandel formally endorsed it as part of a broader $1-billion downtown development plan, including a hotel, office buildings, condos, restaurants, and bars,[48] that had been "floated for several months" behind closed doors.[49] Who would pay for it all remained unclear, and he refused to speculate on any public contribution, insisting that a financing plan would need to be "creative and not burden the taxpayer."[50]

The significance of his endorsement of a new downtown arena and entertainment district cannot be understated. Mandel was a popular mayor, wielding tremendous influence on Edmonton's city council. He was also well connected to many of the key players in the land development sector and the provincial Progressive Conservative Party. Over the next few years, he and a loyal cadre of influential bureaucrats in the mayor's office and administration would manipulate the levers of bureaucratic power to surmount every political, legal, and financial obstacle that the arena project encountered.

Thus, by the end of 2006, an influential and united coalition of boosters, including the Oilers' ownership group, prominent downtown developers, Northlands, and powerful civic politicians, had joined together to promote a new arena to sustain the franchise and revitalize Edmonton's downtown. Much work had yet to be done to prepare the political terrain—and much of that work would be done in private, far away from public scrutiny. The prospect of a new downtown arena development would eventually raise pressing questions about the future of Rexall Place and about Northlands itself, especially with a change in the ownership of the Oilers and the ascendance of the NHL's new billionaire business model on the horizon. Within months, Northlands released a study promoting its role in the operations of a new facility, and Daryl Katz announced both his intention to buy the Oilers from the EIGLP and his desire to develop a new sports and entertainment district to be anchored by a publicly-financed arena.

5

MAKING THE TEAM

In 2006, following the mayor's endorsement of a $1-billion down-
town arena-centred development, as well as the much-publicized
desire of the Oilers to extract more revenue from a new, publicly-
financed facility, Northlands commissioned a report by global
architectural firm Hellmuth, Obata & Kassabaum (HOK), now called
Populous, to examine the potential cost of renovating Rexall Place.
HOK's remit was to determine if Rexall Place could be renovated
"into an arena that would be comparable to current NHL arenas
recently constructed or under construction,"[1] although it already
met NHL arena standards. In particular, another renovation of
Rexall Place would have to meet the Oilers' demands for a greater
number and variety of seats, especially luxury boxes and premium
seats, and wider concourses. HOK was also asked to estimate the
cost of renovation and to provide a schedule for doing the work
during the NHL off-season. As Andy Huntley recalled,

> We were always being reminded [by the Oilers and the NHL] that
> we were the second oldest, actually the third oldest until Madison
> Square Gardens was renovated, so something had to happen. So, I just
> thought, hey, can something be done with the existing location? We
> were constantly reminded that we lacked suites, and what was missing
> was concourse space, but how would they have known that in 1973?

*The building [Rexall Place] is built like a brick you-know-what, so it's
not a throwaway, it's still a very functional, useful building.*[2]

Because it had supported so many corporate–civic projects and
sustained and subsidized professional hockey in Edmonton for
decades, Northlands expected a role in the management of any new,
city-owned hockey facility, without which it would lose influence,
status, and enormous revenues. Northlands was therefore keen to
demonstrate its enthusiasm and its executives soon offered their
support for a new downtown facility, with two crucial caveats: the
development had to be both "financially viable and in the best
interest of all Edmontonians."[3]

HOK's *Rexall Renovation Study* came out in February 2007. It estimated that bringing the facility in line with other NHL arenas and
the Oilers' revenue-generating expectations would cost $225–250
million[4] (this figure was later revised to "under $200 million").
Other cities had built entire new arenas for what HOK estimated it
would cost to renovate Rexall Place, and sometimes even for less.[5]
The average cost of recently constructed NHL-only facilities was just
US$232 million in 2007 dollars.[6] HOK used the Prudential Center,
home of the New Jersey Devils, as the sole comparative benchmark
to calculate renovation costs. The Prudential Center is a multi-sport
facility (not an NHL-only building) owned by the City of Newark,
which opened in October 2007 at a cost of US$380 million. HOK was
the architect for the Prudential Center and had clearly chosen a
facility with which it was familiar, and one that set the latest precedent in terms of both amenities and cost; although it had designed
many other less expensive NHL facilities, too. While Rexall Place
fell short on a number of comparative markers, especially overall
spectator seating and total building area, the two facilities were not
completely dissimilar.[7] In fact, an un-renovated Rexall Place already
had more premium seating.

According to the estimates from *Forbes* for the 2005/06 NHL
season, the New Jersey franchise was valued at US$149 million, with
revenues of US$62 million and an operating loss of US$6.7 million.[8]
By 2007/08, according to *Forbes*, a year after the opening of the

TABLE 3. Comparative Numbers from HOK Report for Prudential Center, Existing Rexall Place Facilities, and Renovated Rexall Place

Arena	Premium Seats	Luxury Suites	Seating Capacity	Team Facilities (in net sq. ft)
Prudential Center	2,524	78	17,350	21,231
Existing Rexall Place	3,500	64	16,681	19,107
Renovated Rexall Place	5,500	92	15,789	22,219

Source: Adapted from HOK, *Rexall Renovation Study*, 2007, 3.

Note: Team facilities refers to the number of net square feet existing or recommended for players' (home and visitor) locker room suites, officials' locker rooms, and auxiliary locker facilities.

Prudential Center, the estimated value had increased to US$222 million, and the club had been able to capitalize on more non-hockey events, boosting its revenue to an estimated US$97 million with an operating income of US$1.9 million.

In the same year, *Forbes* estimated the Oilers' value at US$175 million (up from US$157 million in the previous season, a gain of 11 percent), with revenues of US$85 million and an operating income of US$11.8 million. In other words, when compared to the New Jersey Devils—a franchise that had clearly benefitted from playing in a new, publicly-funded, state-of-the-art arena—the Oilers were more profitable and had a greater operating income (including gate revenue), despite playing in one of the oldest facilities in the league, and without the benefit of non-hockey-related revenues.

TABLE 4. 2007/08 Forbes NHL Team Valuations (Figures are in Millions US$)

Valuation Breakdown	Edmonton	New Jersey
Franchise value	$175 (+11 percent)	$222 (+14 percent)
Revenue	$85	$97
Gate	$49	$44
Average ticket price	$62	$64
Operating income	$11.8	$1.9
Player expenses	$52	$53

Source: Adapted from the 2007/08 *Forbes* annual list of NHL team valuations, which can be found by year at forbes.com.

The estimated cost of renovating Rexall Place was based on conceptual drawings prepared by HOK and a preliminary "Order of Magnitude" budget developed by PCL Construction (eventually selected by the city of Edmonton as the construction manager for the new arena). However, the report provided no budget details, nor were budgetary and architectural estimates for the project put out to tender.

HOK had emerged as one of the go-to architectural/consulting firms for new professional sports facilities (and would later design Rogers Place in Edmonton).[9] In 1987, in the early stages of a debate about replacing Tiger Stadium, HOK was commissioned by the city of Detroit to create a report like the one it produced for Northlands two decades later. At that time, HOK estimated that renovating Tiger Stadium would cost up to US$245 million, recommending instead that a new, 56,000-seat stadium with 150 corporate boxes be built.[10] HOK was the architect for the publicly-financed Comerica Park, which opened in 2000 and promised to revitalize Detroit's downtown.[11] The close cooperation between firms like HOK and their clients represents a lucrative and "mutually beneficial relationship."[12] As one architect quoted in the book *Field of Schemes* explained,

> *The team owners say it has to be this way because the architect says it has to be this way; the architects say it has to be this way because the team owners tell them it has to be this way. That's another unrecognized scandal of the business. The corporate architects, the stadium architects, market their services to the tenants of these facilities rather than to...the people who pay for them.*[13]

The HOK *Rexall Renovation Study*, not released publicly by Northlands until 2011, anchored the potential cost of renovating Rexall Place at more than $225 million—a large sum, though far less than the final cost of Rogers Place. The main boosters of a new arena quickly framed the results of the study to support their own claims, including the mayor, who suggested that renovating Rexall Place was simply too expensive to contemplate:

Two-hundred-and-fifty million dollars is a fair chunk of change on a
renovation, and you end up with a renovated building versus some-
thing you build from scratch with new technologies and all the new
things that you have and need for a facility.[14]

At other times, he inflated the cost of renovating Rexall Place to $300
million to defend his vision of a substantially more expensive downtown arena project.[15]

Northlands might have anticipated these reactions before
commissioning a report that confirmed an expensive renovation
estimate, and might have also proposed some legitimate financing
mechanisms to minimize the use of public funds, including the
use of its own resources. For example, could a ticket tax raising
$125 million—the same amount dedicated to paying down the debt
for Rogers Place—and a small CRL have covered the entire cost
of a $200-million renovation?[16] Could other opportunities have
been suggested to genuinely integrate Rexall Place and Northlands
grounds with its surrounding communities? Should the Oilers have
been expected to pay more rent than $1/year to help pay for a reno-
vated facility that would increase the team's revenues and valuation?
And could Northlands have used its connections with other levels of
government to secure additional financial support for the renovation? These options were never publicly explored, and a convincing
argument that taxes would not have to be raised nor existing grants
used was never made.[17]

Still, the arguments against the renovation were significant:
the proposed renovation was expensive; construction would have
been disruptive over multiple years; a renovated facility would
have a reduced seating capacity; and a renovated Rexall Place
would do little to support the dominant downtown growth agenda.
Northlands was in a difficult position. The prospect of a new downtown arena and its land development opportunities had powerful
and influential supporters who had already endorsed the Oilers'
expectations of playing in a new facility when their lease ended, and
the club was eager to reap the financial rewards of the NHL's new
business model, including control of all of the revenue streams from

a new facility. Indeed, for the arena's main boosters, especially those in the land development sector who were already assembling parcels of land, a renovation of Rexall Place was never seriously considered. The mayor had already endorsed building a new arena and entertainment district in the city core, and there was little interest and even less political will to ensure the stability of Northlands or its surrounding neighbourhoods.

Beyond satisfying the interests of downtown developers, building a costly new sports facility instead of renovating an old one held enormous appeal for civic leaders and the team. The decision gave the mayor, administration, and the Oilers tremendous influence over the development, including the power to bestow lucrative sole-source contracts to familiar and dependable consulting companies; to determine which architects, developers, and construction companies would be hired to design and build the facility; and to rezone and revalourize substantial amounts of downtown land in support of projects worth billions. Ultimately, they would also have the power to determine who would operate the new arena. And Northlands, said the mayor, "would be an integral partner" in any new downtown arena development—at least for now.[18]

Playing the Game

In the same month as the renovation study (February 2007), another piece of commissioned research was presented to city administration that further prepared the political terrain for a new downtown arena. This one also was not released to the public. Written by Dr. Dan Mason of the University of Alberta, *Sports Development Projects: Current and Proposed in North America* provided "an overview of the current status of arenas used by NHL franchises" to assist the city of Edmonton in "understanding the expectations the Edmonton Oilers Hockey Club (Oilers) have expressed with regards to a new or updated facility."[19] It contained useful information about current NHL facilities and various arena financing and lease agreements, but reproduced without evidence the assumption of boosters that "A new or renovated arena will be required within the next 5–10 years."[20]

TABLE 5. Comparable Costs of North American Arenas, Adjusted to 2007 US$ (Figures in Millions)

Arenas	Year Opened	Cost
Sommet Center/Bridgestone, Nashville	1996	$275
Verizon Center/Capital One, Washington, DC	1997	$340
Air Canada Centre, Toronto	1999	$298
Pepsi Center, Denver	1999	$260
Philips Arena, Atlanta	1999	$280
Nationwide Arena, Columbus	2000	$290
Xcel Energy Center, St. Paul, MN	2000	$125
Jobing.com (Gila River Arena), Glendale	2003	$245
Toyota Center, Houston	2003	$260
Prudential Center, New Jersey	2007	$240
Sprint Center, Kansas City	2007	$200

Source: Adapted from HOK, *Rexall Renovation Study*, 2007, 118.

Mason estimated that a new facility would cost US$400 million—the first time an official cost estimate for a new facility in Edmonton entered the debate, though not publicly and without either a detailed cost breakdown or a concrete architectural estimate. The amount exceeded the cost of every single recently constructed NHL facility in North America (see Table 5).

The report also provided two case studies of recent arena developments—projects considerably cheaper than the estimated cost of a new arena in Edmonton—to give "new insights and benchmarks for a proposed arena in Edmonton."[21] The first, Nationwide Arena in Columbus, Ohio, was built entirely with private funds at a cost of US$175 million (US$290 million in 2007 dollars), after citizens voted five times against the use of public funds. Its boosters thought it had spurred new private and public investment and ultimately "revitalize[d] Columbus's downtown core," although these changes also benefitted from a 10-year residential property tax exemption in the city centre and other exemptions for commercial development. Nationwide Arena, however, proved to be unprofitable and required a bailout by taxpayers in 2011; in 2016, an editorial in *The Columbus*

Dispatch characterized it as a "money pit" for local taxpayers.
Nonetheless, Edmonton's arena boosters routinely cited it as the
archetypal arena/entertainment district success story that Edmonton
ought to emulate. The second case study, Glendale Arena (now called
Gila River Arena) in Glendale, Arizona, was a publicly-financed facility
that opened in 2003 at a cost of US$220 million (US$245 million in
2007 dollars) and was accompanied by a moderate level of development. Not only would the city of Glendale eventually have to bail out
the Coyotes—while laying off city workers, cutting services, and
raising taxes to close annual budget gaps—but by 2016, the franchise
was preparing to relocate to another new, publicly-financed arena.
Consequently, boosters ignored the example of Glendale.

From the beginning, then, there was never any real intention to
renovate Rexall Place—a facility only three decades old that had
been extensively upgraded over the years at considerable public
expense. What would happen to it if a new arena was built? No one
knew. Many proponents of a new downtown facility, who considered
themselves politically conservative and financially prudent, were
also not prepared to consider building a modestly priced facility.
Instead, boosters ignored any notion of fiscal responsibility by advo-
cating what would be, at the time, the most expensive single-use
NHL facility in North America.

Arena Leadership

The HOK *Rexall Renovation Study* recommended another study to
compare "the cost of and inconvenience of such an extensive renovation" of Rexall Place with "the feasibility of a new arena."[22] Given
Mayor Mandel's endorsement of a new downtown arena and the
discussions that had already occurred, such a comparison was point-
less, but the mayor did strike an Arena Leadership Committee (ALC)
on April 24, 2007, to "study the potential of constructing a new
sports/entertainment facility in the city of Edmonton."[23] The ALC's
remit, structured to support the broader downtown growth agenda,
was to identify the requirements for a new arena that would accelerate urban development; meet current and future NHL standards
and the needs of the Edmonton Oilers; and maximize non-hockey

opportunities (i.e., concerts and major events). The ALC was also instructed to provide an estimate of the total project costs associated with a new facility, including the identification of possible financing options. Of course, the answers to nearly all of these questions had already been decided.

Boosters knew that the cost of a new, publicly-financed arena would greatly exceed that of renovating Rexall Place, so they would have to manage public opinion, as the mayor was already starting to do:

> *I think there's many ways to look at how we can do this. I've several ideas but I don't want to talk about them yet until we get a little further down the road, but we're not going to burden our taxpayers with a $400-million or $300-million debt to have a new facility. That just won't happen.*[24]

He insisted in August 2007 to business columnist Gary Lamphier, "I've been very clear that the citizens of Edmonton—the taxpayers—are not going to foot the bill for a new arena," allowing Lamphier to conclude, "In other words, absolutely no residential or non-residential tax monies will be used to fund a downtown arena, he says. Full stop."[25] Only a month later, the mayor insisted again, "It's not going to impact your pocketbook. No taxes of yours will go into an arena."[26]

Within a year, though, he was making two altogether different promises: (1) municipal property taxes would not be raised to pay for a new arena development; and (2) existing funding for municipal infrastructure would not be reallocated to finance a new facility. Such promises are routinely made by public officials in their attempts to obfuscate the use of public funds to build new arena developments—but tax money is still tax money, whatever the source. The mayor's promise not to raise taxes or redirect existing grants also signalled the city's intent to debt-finance a significant amount of the cost of a new arena, while using *future property tax revenue* in the form of a CRL/TIF to pay down the debt. In other words, by 2007, all the strategies associated with the major league playbook that aligned a new, publicly-financed arena and its associated financing mechanisms with land development opportunities had been fully embraced in Edmonton. These strategies would guide the actions—and the conclusions—of the ALC, and would preclude any consideration of renovating Rexall Place or building a new arena at Northlands.

The mayor's protean commitments to minimize the dedication of existing public funds to any new development were politically astute in other ways. Many Oilers fans were probably prepared to support his vision at any cost, especially after almost losing the team in the 1990s. But a new, publicly-financed arena was bound to generate controversy, especially after the Pocklington era, and to have honestly acknowledged that hundreds of millions of dollars of public money would be used to enrich the Oilers and property developers would have provided substantial ammunition to critics of the project. By claiming that taxes would not be raised and that existing grants would not be redirected, the mayor blurred the role of debt financing in any future tax increases by not addressing the complexity of the city's mandate. Taxes could not be increased to directly finance the arena or future debt payments, although they could certainly be raised as a result of other expenses that were directly and indirectly incurred as a result of the new develop-ment, such as upgrading the old drainage system, LRT expansion, increasing the number of police officers around the arena, refur-bishing or tearing down Rexall Place, and so on. Likewise, any discussion of the opportunity costs associated with debt financing a new arena development and its effect on the city's ability to invest in other public projects, services, and infrastructure was carefully avoided. The challenge of attributing a tax increase to the arena becomes even more complex when one tries to track all the municipal resources—administrative time, salaries, consultant expenses—that would be dedicated to the arena but might have been used in other ways. The city would raise property taxes repeat-edly during the arena's discussion process and after Rogers Place was opened—and the arena is at least part of the reason for raising them.

The high-profile membership of the ALC was handpicked by Mayor Mandel himself, without approval from city council—an instructive example of the influence the mayor (and the mayor's office) would exercise over the course of the debate, as well as the democratic deficits that would accompany many key decisions. He appointed people with expertise in professional sport and arena management and with influence in the community. Many had been actively cultivating political support for a new, publicly-financed downtown arena for years. How could the main beneficiaries of the development reconcile their own interests with the broader public good and provide objective and balanced recommendations, especially in light of the pre-determined conclusions that had already been reached secretly?

Behind the scenes, the Oilers kept pushing for a new, publicly-financed arena. Their goals, Jerry Bouma of Northlands noted, were the dominant "underlying dynamic that was going on in the formation of the Arena Leadership Committee," and they had started to widen the already sizeable fissure between Northlands and the Oilers:

> It became pretty evident that there was a new business model that had emerged, and this was what I call the US billionaire model where you control everything and particularly the building. You control the building, you have two if not three professional teams in there. You have an entertainment company. You may even own the entertainment in the case of AEG, and you own everything around it in terms of the parking, office buildings, you make a real estate play and you use the arena as a leverage to really generate revenues from everything that's around the arena, plus in the arena. And if you can up that even further by challenging or inspiring the city to own the facility, well you have total control, it's even better for the billionaire. So, I think Cal Nichols and the Oilers and a few people around the Oilers saw that model and realized this is what they needed to do. So what happened then, the mayor struck this committee and of course the billionaire model was very much in the background.[27]

The ALC was chaired by Lyle Best, a former director of the Edmonton Oilers Community Foundation and the executive director of the Edmonton Oilers Alumni Association. Members included Patrick LaForge (president and CEO, Edmonton Oilers Hockey Club, and chair, Edmonton Chamber of Commerce); Cal Nichols (former chair, Edmonton Oilers Hockey Club, and current member of the EIGLP); Greg Christenson (past chair, Edmonton Chamber of Commerce, and owner, Christenson Developments Ltd.); Bob Normand (former president and CEO, ATB Financial, and board member, Capital Health Authority); Patricia Mackenzie (former city of Edmonton council member; former president, Alberta Urban Municipalities Association; board member, Law Enforcement Review Board); Al Maurer (city manager, City of Edmonton); Jerry Bouma (chair, Northlands Board of Directors); and Andrew Huntley (first vice chair, Northlands Board of Directors, and chair, Northlands Facilities Master Planning Committee).[28]

The ALC was supported by various subcommittees (finance, design, and community working groups) that included more familiar names and sympathetic stakeholders. Sport management scholars Dan Mason and Mark Rosentraub were influential contributors, and HOK Sports was commissioned to examine location options. The total cost for the ALC's work, including what it commissioned, would come to $250,000, a bill split equally among the city of Edmonton, Northlands, and the Oilers.

The crucial process of determining the feasibility and location of a new, publicly-subsidized arena would be handled by a coalition of influential public and private interest groups—including the Oilers, Northlands, and prominent businessmen, mostly land developers—with the full support of politicians and city bureaucrats, who would consistently direct resources, decisions, and actions in its support. Political decision-making and urban governance had, in other words, shifted to an appointed body rather than an elected one, creating an *ad hoc* political space not bound by the rules and obligations that applied to elected officials and less exposed to democratic scrutiny. The city of Edmonton had been captured by private interests aligned with boosterism, professional sport, and land development opportunities.

The formation of the ALC and the prospect of a "majestic modern arena...to symbolize our status as an emerging power-house" were largely supported by the mainstream media, although some pundits noted that a number of unanswered questions about the development remained.[29] Columnist Paula Simons, for example, invited readers and perhaps some of her colleagues at the *Journal* to "check our pompoms at the door," and asked a pressing question: "Who, after all, is paying for this project?"[30] Foreshadowing the fervent boosterism that would accompany the arena debate, as well as the opprobrium directed at arena critics, Simons got innumerable emails treating any expression of "the slightest doubt about the wonders of a new half-a-billion-dollar downtown arena...[as] an act of black heresy."[31] As Simons reflected in a later interview,

> *People could tell me in real time that I was a bitch and a fat bitch, as though my body mass index was somehow relevant to the debate. I got called many words for the female anatomy. There was a certain "bro" mentality that to question this was to question the manliness of Edmonton, that I was somehow emasculating them. It was as though to raise questions about whether a CRL was properly structured was literally cutting their balls off.[32]*

While supporters of the development used social media to voice their opinions, a number of local hockey bloggers in the "Oilogosphere," well-versed in analytics and the business of hockey, began investigating the merits of building a new, publicly-financed downtown arena for the Oilers.[33] The new terrain of social media would emerge as a significant ideological battleground in the arena debate, although these online skirmishes would have little effect on the political process.

Enter the Billionaire: *Daryl Katz*

In the spring of 2007, local billionaire Daryl Katz publicly put forward
an all-cash $145-million purchase offer for the Edmonton Oilers. Born
and raised in Edmonton, Katz had made his fortune in the pharmaceutical business; at the time, the Katz Group owned the seventh-
largest drugstore business in North America (with annual sales of $6
billion from 1800 outlets), and Katz's personal wealth was estimated
at nearly $2 billion. According to Patrick LaForge, though, Katz had
already begun moving into the entertainment industry before
buying the Oilers and getting involved in downtown land development opportunities.[34]

Katz's bid was greeted with enormous fanfare. He was represented by the local media as a hometown, reclusive Bruce Wayne
figure, and a long-time Oilers fan whose wealth would help stabi-
lize the franchise and return it to the Stanley Cup successes of the
"Boys on the Bus" in the 1980s—the team that Katz had grown up
watching, cheering, and eventually befriending. He may have been
largely unknown to Edmontonians, but he was familiar to many
in the existing ownership group: "Daryl was already close to us, he
was a sponsor of the building, Rexall had its name on the outside...
and most people knew him."[35] According to one report, in 2005,
shortly after Stephen Mandel had secured the mayoralty and around
the time the prospect of a new, publicly-financed arena was first
emerging as a public issue, Katz had started talking to some of the
members of EIGLP, including Bruce Saville, about purchasing
the Oilers.[36]

After his first offer was rejected by the EIGLP—board chair
Cal Nichols was especially vocal in his opposition to the takeover
bid—Katz announced that he had embraced the vision of a new
downtown arena and its associated land development opportunities. He would later say, in a 2015 interview, that he had originally
envisioned the arena as the centrepiece of a much broader downtown project before his original offer to buy the team in 2007
(roughly the same time the public debate began): "I would not have
bought the team without the challenge and opportunity to build

the arena and everything around it."[37] According to Patrick LaForge, Mayor Mandel was well-informed about these developments:

> [As early as] 2007, he [Katz] was negotiating. I know he was sharing
> his interests in the broad scope with Stephen and...everybody agreed
> in the beginning—the team stays, new building, long-term lease.
> What's a new building [require]? 17,500 to 18,500 plus or minus...It's
> got to have heated, underground parking; there's a list...What about
> the land? So there was land assembly, but at 4 million an acre...What
> did CN sell [its land] for?...probably $50,000 an acre. Just highway
> robbery. [So the question for Mayor Mandel was, are] you on side?
> Sure, I'm on side. You're on side, the team stays. What does the mayor
> want? He wants downtown redevelopment and a team. Loses the
> team, he's the mayor that lost the Oilers. So that's before Daryl prob-
> ably wrote a cheque. [Katz wanted to know] if I buy the team whatever
> the price is, can we work together to get a building done? Where?
> Somewhere in the city centre, what do you think? Well I've got to deal
> with Northlands. That's what Stephen's going to say. So what? So deal
> with them. That's over to you. I'm buying the team. What else [does
> Katz] want? Team and a building, downtown redevelopment. I just
> want a team and a building but...I need to make money after I buy the
> team. I've got to pay off whatever I paid for it. So it's got to be on top
> of an LRT line where I give good access to the million people that live
> here. That's it...everybody goes, yeah okay. Pick a spot, let's go, let's
> do it.[38]

LaForge said that Katz was the only serious bidder, although some members of EIGLP opposed his bid in an attempt to retain control of the team. Given the team's popularity, Oilers executives knew they had significant leverage over the mayor and council because they were the only game in town:

> I will say this, that when it came to sell[ing] the team, the lineup was
> one, just one. And for all the things people say about Daryl, he was the
> guy and he never backed off and when the EIGLP asked for more, he

put more on the table. It was a lineup of one. I had never seen Daryl
make a deal like that before, so emotions overtook him, I guess.[39]

According to Northlands' Jerry Bouma, most of the EIGLP wanted just to own the team, preferably with increased revenue streams and a higher valuation, but Daryl Katz envisioned a whole sports and entertainment district:

> *I think the EIGLP realized that they were going have to come up with*
> *more money to make this work or refinance this thing if they were*
> *going to run their own building. Some of them had been around. Some*
> *of them were older. They decided we're out and that sort of triggered*
> *the sale that Katz had started to negotiate. Now he clearly knew what*
> *the AEG integrated approach really offered and that was his model*
> *from the very beginning.*[40]

Former city manager Al Maurer concurred: "With the change of ownership, the whole thing escalated. The Katz Group wanted everything and they just trotted out these examples around the NHL of teams that had control of arenas."[41] Katz was eventually able to secure Cal Nichols' support but, according to Nichols, several members of the EIGLP weren't interested in financing a new arena and were generally satisfied with their profitable long-term arrangements with Northlands and the cost certainty provided by the NHL's salary cap: "They thought it was impossible. 'We got a pretty good building and the price is right (roughly $1 million a year for all rent and expenses).' They'd come back and say, 'It doesn't make sense to go to all this trouble to build a new building and have all this debt. What do you gain by it?'"[42] As Patrick LaForge explained,

> *In 2004 and then in 2005 and 2006, when the new building came*
> *on the table, Cal started to dimensionalize [sic] for people [EIGLP]*
> *various deals for new arenas, because we'd seen all the buildings,*
> *we've seen the Columbus deal, we've seen the LA deal, we'd seen*
> *Dallas' new deal for their arena, on and on and on; [we had] probably*
> *seen 20 new contracts [including] Pittsburgh's...The owners [EIGLP]*

have chipped in between 50 and 150 million...So Cal was saying, "You
know, we've all had good lives here, we're all in a certain state, we
should all throw in 10 million each to start the pool at 100 from the
ownership group and commit to a long-term lease and go from there."
And not everybody was as excited about that idea as Cal was. There
was a group, a middle group, who said, "I'm too old for that shit, I'm
out of here right away." Not rudely, and it didn't hurt anybody's feel-
ings. About 30 percent thought "Okay, more work to be done," and the
balance said, "Yeah, I'm probably done,"...There's always that exit
clause for folks, so they were interested, they're taking it and they were
having those conversations with Cal. So, he realized that...if you need
an arena, you have to participate at 100 plus million, and he didn't
have the guys in the room that were willing to do it. So, he worked
hard, months and months...reconstituting the balloon with a smaller
number of faces and wallets and I don't think he could get the kind of
resources he thought he needed. There were lots of billionaires in the
room, some of the people were richer than Daryl, but that was their
own choice. So, somebody said, "Well, why don't we put it up for sale,
and then do it that way?" This is months later...and somebody said
"I know this guy, he might be interested," and that sort of began the
conversation...So that's the way it kind of transitioned.[43]

In light of these dynamics, the EIGLP began to fracture. Katz drove
a further wedge into these divisions in July by making a second
purchase offer of $170 million, which now included a commitment
to invest capital in a new downtown arena and a new training facility
at the University of Alberta. This, and a subsequent offer of $185
million, were rejected by the EIGLP. In December 2007, Katz made
yet another purchase offer for $190 million—almost $50 million more
than his initial offer—plus an explicit commitment of $100 million
in cash for a new arena complex in the "heart of a revitalized
downtown"—a commitment reflecting the terms of the original deal
brokered behind closed doors a few years earlier. It was a commitment that would be radically amended during the course of the
negotiations with the city of Edmonton.

Despite continuing opposition from some of the EIGLP, several prominent shareholders—including Cal Nichols, Jim Hole, Bruce Saville, and Larry Makelki—were now prepared to sell their shares to Katz, who was aggressively selling himself as a "community-minded man" whose "entire focus was having an elite Oilers team playing in the heart of the city."[44] His offer was greeted with enthusiasm by many of the other key players in the arena project and in the media.

"It changed everything," said the mayor. "Now you have a different individual who has a specific vision of what he expects, what he wants...I was quite optimistic when I heard he was buying the team because he was a single owner who had an incredible history with the city."[45] He anticipated tough but fruitful negotiations with Katz:

> *I felt that we'd be able to strike up some kind of a deal that would be beneficial for both the city and for the Oilers because, at the end of the day, if the Oilers aren't successful they're going to be sold...billionaires aren't billionaires because they're stupid people. They'll only lose so much money for so long and then something has to break, and so given the competition within the world of hockey, something had to be done...You know he's a business guy; he wants to put up as little as possible.*[46]

Before beginning formal negotiations, though, the location of a new arena had to be decided. According to Patrick LaForge, the Katz Group's land acquisitions began long before the purchase of the team: "It was early in the process. Successful business guys don't show up late with a cheque book. They get into solutions pretty quickly. I don't think it's appropriate for me to share all that with you, but we didn't show up late."[47]

The Politics of City Shaping: *The Katz Era Begins*

Despite all this manoeuvring, the project was off the political radar in the October 2007 municipal election. Political leaders were still awaiting the release of the ALC's report and its recommendations, so they were reluctant to raise the issue prematurely and without full background information. Polls continued to show widespread opposition to the use of public money to build a new arena, which may have encouraged both incumbents and challengers to avoid the issue altogether. The right-wing Canadian Taxpayers Federation opposed it, too, and local hockey bloggers continued to challenge both the need for a new, publicly-financed arena and the boosterism of pro-arena columnists and consultants.

Mayoral incumbent Stephen Mandel captured 65.8 percent of the popular vote (his nearest challenger, Don Koziak, got only 25.3 percent) and was easily elected to another three-year term, thus ensuring that city business would continue to be guided by the chief proponent of the downtown arena project. Despite low voter turnout (27.2 percent of eligible voters), the mayor's supporters trumpeted his re-election as proof that Edmontonians had embraced "Mandel's big-city vision" and called his victory a "turning point in Edmonton's history...a shift away from historic nickel-and-dime civic politics."[48] Daryl Katz, who would be the main beneficiary of a new, publicly-financed arena, donated $15,000 to the mayor's re-election campaign via Katz Group Canada, and another $5,000 through Medicine Shoppe,[49] underscoring his support for Mandel's vision for both the city of Edmonton and the Oilers.[50]

Katz continued to be portrayed as a civic visionary and a major financial player with the resources to take both the Oilers and the city of Edmonton "to the next level." For his supporters in the media and at city hall, there was simply too much at stake in the proposed downtown arena development to rely on a "quasi-community owned operation" to transform Edmonton's image and its downtown core, especially after numerous failed attempts. These sentiments were echoed by Dr. Dan Mason, who, against the backdrop of Katz's attempts to purchase the Oilers, encouraged the city to make a new arena and a revitalized downtown a political priority, in order to propel Edmonton higher in the transnational economic and cultural urban hierarchy:

The city is at a [historical] turning point where it has to decide whether it wants to be a player or not. I honestly think these next couple of years will determine where Edmonton ends up in the global

urban food chain. This is the time where Edmonton needs to decide
whether it's a city that worries about potholes or a city that worries
about the vitality of its downtown and the way it's perceived on the
global stage.[51]

This theme—that Edmonton needed to reposition itself in the
"global urban food chain" with a vibrant downtown—would be
expounded by the main proponents of the new arena development
and promoted by the media in the years to come. Conversely, ordinary citizens who opposed the use of public funds to build a new
facility, or were more concerned with less glamorous issues like the
state of the city's infrastructure and the provision of social services,
would be routinely framed as small-minded naysayers who lacked
vision, community spirit, and business sense. The historical debate
between boosters and knockers was being played out once again in
the twenty-first century.

In February 2008, Katz increased his purchase offer to $200
million—a price that decisively ended the efforts of a small group
of EIGLP members who wanted to retain control of the Oilers. They
had purchased the team for only US$70 million in 1998, so they
stood to profit handsomely from the sale. The price was in the ballpark of the US$175 million valuation estimated by *Forbes* in 2008.[52]
The increased value of the franchise reflected a combination of
factors—the cost certainty provided by the 2005 CBA, Edmonton's
status as a growing urban centre and valuable hockey market, the
strengthening of the Canadian dollar, and, especially, the prospect
of a new, publicly-financed arena promising lucrative new land
development opportunities. As Rick Daviss, the city of Edmonton's
executive director for the new arena, reflected, "Really, I think from
his [Katz's] perspective, this was a real estate play. He didn't see this
as an arena, this was the opportunity to totally change Edmonton's
downtown and he could dominate it with his development."[53]

Daryl Katz was not unique in his ambition. From the early 2000s,
franchise owners had recognized the value of being involved in broader
land development schemes anchored by new, costly, publicly-financed
arenas or stadiums from which they received all the revenue, while

Daryl Katz uses money to silence critics of Edmonton Oilers purchase, February 6, 2008. [Malcolm Mayes/Artizans.com]

municipal governments wanted to attract mobile capital and white-collar workers to downtown cores. These types of development synergies promoted urban expansion, downtown development, and the growth of municipal tax revenues. It just took the construction of a sports and entertainment facility, as Rick Daviss pointed out:

> We were looking at this as a city arena: we're going to own this thing. We are making a play to rejuvenate our downtown. We want to generate tax dollars. We want to generate investment. And, in our analysis of what's happening in North America, we can do that if we build a proper entertainment district. If we brought the right pieces together, we could generate investment and we could get a return on that investment.[54]

The traditional arguments used by team owners and local boosters to justify public subsidies—that teams and arenas provide direct positive economic impacts and jobs—have been discredited by over three decades of disinterested academic scholarship, so a new argument was needed to justify public investment in major league facilities. Owners and boosters alike will now state categorically that a new, publicly-financed sports facility will benefit a municipality by stimulating downtown growth and expanding the municipal tax base. Of course, for municipal tax revenue to increase overall, a new arena development will have to avoid cannibalizing businesses (and tax revenues) from other areas of the city, and stimulate new growth and therefore new property tax revenue to pay down the accumulated debt. In Edmonton's case, the central financial mechanism would be the CRL. The Katz Group's deep pockets inspired confidence, too, as Rick Daviss noted:

> *I've seen three downtown plans come and go. None of them had an implementation plan...I think that's why this plan—when you have an owner with the financial ability to actually implement and you had the city with the CRL making a bet on the development occurring, and council having the courage to gamble on their own city—created the funding that enabled it all to happen.*[55]

David Staples promoted similar arguments in the *Journal*, including the merits of the public–private partnerships and creative funding models used in both Columbus, Ohio, and San Diego, California. Staples speculated that any investment by the Oilers' owner in the area surrounding the arena would not only reduce the controversy "about public money going into the venture," but would also ensure that the "interests of the city and team owner to create a vibrant area in the core...align[ed]."[56] Furthermore, the Katz Group's investment of private money in these developments would likely eliminate the possibility of the team leaving Edmonton—a threat that still haunted Oilers fans who remembered the dark days of the Pocklington era. Unlike Pocklington, though, Daryl Katz was a billionaire, so the question that should have been posed was this: Why was it necessary to use public money to build a new arena for a private corporation or to encourage private development in the downtown core?

TABLE 6. *Calder Bateman Arena-Related Contracts with City of Edmonton*

Year	Contracts	Amount
No date	Arena Report	$12,103
No date	Arena District Advisory Committee	$958
No date	Arena Tracking Survey	$12,391
2010	Arena Public Consultation	$195,300
2011	Arena Public Consultation and Communications	$74,760
2012	Arena Public Consultation (amending agreement to 2011 contract).	$246,750
2013	Edmonton Arena Tracking Survey	$48,016

Source: City of Edmonton.

It Has to be Downtown

The ALC's much-anticipated[57] *City Shaping* report was released in March 2008. Northlands' Andy Huntley didn't express much confidence in its preparation: "it [the ALC] felt like a few chaotic lunches and a couple trips to buildings, and a lot of whispering in the corner [about Katz's purchase offer] and then bada-bing, bada-boom, there's a report."[58] The *City Shaping* report, which enthusiastically confirmed the downtown pro-arena mandate, had been outsourced to and overseen by Margaret Bateman of the influential local consulting company Calder Bateman,[59] the "go-to consulting firm" for important clients like PCL and Epcor, in addition to government agencies, developers, and corporations; Bateman is well-connected to the most influential power brokers in the city and the province.[60] Between the beginning of the process and 2013, the company earned hundreds of thousands of dollars in contracts from the city of Edmonton. It would also be hired by city administration on sole-source contracts to do communications work and organize the public consultation process associated with the arena debate.

Bateman was also an important civic booster. In 2010, she joined Yes! For Edmonton, a lobby group created to support the re-election of Mayor Mandel and his vision to close and redevelop the City Centre Airport as a sustainable, mixed-use, urban community.[61] While Bateman would recuse herself from Yes! For Edmonton's lobbying for the downtown arena development, her association with powerful civic interest groups emphasizes the extent to which the key players from the public and private sectors were entangled from the outset in this debate.[62]

The *City Shaping* report was accompanied by a research paper by Mark Rosentraub entitled "Sports Facilities, A New Arena in Edmonton, And The Opportunities for Development and A City's Image: Lessons from Successful Experiences,"[63] commissioned by the city manager to provide scholarly support for the report's findings. Before writing it, Rosentraub talked to Patricia Mitsuka, Mayor Mandel's chief of staff, to ensure that he "hit the points wanted."[64]

Both documents fully endorsed the growth coalition's preference for an expensive, new, publicly-financed downtown arena and entertainment district and its integrated ancillary development opportunities to create a strong "brand" for Edmonton:

> *The right development, in the right place, will not only draw millions of visits to the city annually from far and wide; it will revitalize our downtown. A new sports/entertainment facility can capture and focus the city's projected growth, revitalize our downtown core and generate tax revenue through new housing, retail and office space, hotels, restaurants and additional facilities.*[65]

The *City Shaping* report also supported the Oilers' revenue-generating demands, particularly in its Key Findings and Recommendations section:

1. *A downtown sports/entertainment facility in Edmonton is clearly feasible.*
2. *It is not just feasible, it is desirable. It provides a unique opportunity to develop an urban sports/entertainment district downtown to the benefit of the citizens in the city, region and primary catchment areas, such as northern and central Alberta.*
3. *Based on the level of analysis and the stated assumptions, a downtown sports/entertainment facility is financially feasible.*

4. *Given the scale of investment required, and the potential impact a new downtown sport/entertainment facility would have on the community, the most appropriate funding structure involves both private and public participation.*

5. *No existing financial structure applies wholly to the Edmonton facility. A "made-in Edmonton" financing proposal should therefore be developed by project proponents and reviewed by the City.*[66]

Given the entanglements noted throughout this chapter, it is important to question whether the ALC performed due diligence when formulating its recommendations, especially in light of the conclusions already reached behind closed doors since at least 2004. Earlier city plans had suggested other locations, including near the Northlands grounds, for a new arena, but the *City Shaping* report simply endorsed boosters' well-known preference: "Why downtown? It has to be downtown."[67] No analysis was provided because none was needed. It was taken for granted that the arena had to be built downtown, so the report worked backwards to justify that assumption.

The ALC tried to assert its independence and objectivity by acknowledging the contribution of a number of now-familiar players: HOK Sport had been "hired to identify location issues and the criteria necessary for a successful facility development"; Convention, Sports & Leisure International (CSL) was "commissioned to evaluate the market potential for the proposed facility, assess comparable facilities, provide case studies and develop financial models to inform the evaluation of proposals put forward by project proponents"; and Dr. Mark Rosentraub was retained as "an acknowledged expert in the study of sports facilities and how they can be a catalyst to revitalize urban centres."[68] Much of the underlying work and analysis was not made public until after the arena debate ended in 2013. Although Rosentraub's promotional paper was released alongside the *City Shaping* report, the ALC carefully retained control over other publicly-commissioned information; neither the HOK Study, which ranked the top sites for a new arena development, nor the full version of the CSL report, which contained five-year revenue and expense projections for a new facility, were made public due "to the commercially competitive nature of their information on prospective facility sites and Oilers business information."[69]

The initial restriction of public access to the HOK study was perhaps understandable. To have disclosed the locations of the proposed sites for a new arena development would have encouraged land speculation and driven up the price of downtown land holdings. Of course, anyone in the property development sector could have guessed the potential sites, which is why the Katz Group faced some obstacles in assembling some of the land it wanted. But the *City Shaping* report's assumptions and lack of transparency were problematic, underlining the ease with which public scrutiny and independent analysis in public–private partnerships can be restricted in the interests of a corporation.

Another of the ALC's conclusions—that a public–private financing structure was necessary to build the development—was derived from financial analyses that were also never made public. Ignoring the fact that a number of the ALC's most prominent case studies were on arenas that were privately funded (as were most NHL arenas built in Canada), the *City Shaping* report concluded: "Major civic facilities such as these do not generate sufficient returns on investment to attract 100 percent private development capital. Incentives and participation from the public sector should be considered a necessary component of a financing plan."[70] The ALC rejected a total private financing option because it viewed "a new facility to be the centerpiece of [an] integrated downtown development plan, [and] a total *private* funding option would limit the ability of the municipality to influence the nature and concept of the development and its impact on downtown."[71] In other words, it was in the city's best interest to partially finance the new arena. But, as we shall see, the city of Edmonton had very little influence over the eventual location or design of the city-owned arena. Those would be determined by the Katz Group.

The report contained other important omissions. It suggested that a $450-million capital cost for an arena was a "reasonable basis to move forward with future discussions,"[72] but provided no information to show how the ALC came to that number. Even some members of the ALC who had signed off on the *City Shaping* report confided that they weren't sure where it came from. As one member who requested anonymity acknowledged, "I don't know. That number just came out and we never challenged it." The report also suggested that the arena would generate an annual surplus of $11 million, and that new residential and commercial development would probably generate another $20 million annually in new property taxes, which would then be levied via a CRL to pay for the arena. It provided no financial data to support these numbers, though it said they had been reviewed by the city's assessor, nor was there any acknowledgement of economists' well-known concerns about the CRL financing mechanism, including the likelihood that other areas of the city would decline as investment and spending shifted downtown.

The report recommended that at least 30 percent of capital costs (a minimum of $135 million) come from direct beneficiaries of the new arena, and said that "any increase in the final costs of the facility would result in a proportional increase in the expected equity contribution. It is, for example, possible to achieve additional private equity contributions through naming rights or pre-selling of corporate suites."[73] The *City Shaping* report broke down capital cost and debt financing as follows:

Capital Cost of Project: $450 million
$100 million commitment from prime tenant (Katz Group)
TBD: *Additional private equity contributors*
TBD: *Public sector equity contributions (all orders of government)*
TBD: *Corporate sector contributions (e.g., naming opportunities)*
$135 Million: One-time equity contribution
$315: Debt financing

Revenue Contributions to Finance Debt

$2.5 million: Redirection of existing city subsidy to Rexall Place

$3.0 million: Increase to ticket surcharge

$10 million: Potential Community Revitalization Levy (CRL)

$11 million: Surplus cash flow from facility operations

TBD: Rental/equity contributions through associated developments

TBD: Other user pay revenues (i.e., downtown parking and other surcharges)[74]

Neither the *City Shaping* report nor the Rosenstraub paper mentioned the Oilers' current profitability, the history of the team's public subsidies, or the amount of arena-related revenue already being generated at Rexall Place thanks to the Oilers' lease arrangement with Northlands. Nor did they provide data on average NHL attendance or ticket prices. The potential social impact of a new arena and entertainment district on inner-city residents didn't merit even a cursory discussion.

The ALC assumed that Rexall Place would not compete with a new downtown arena, although the "role of Northlands in any new sports/entertainment facility must be considered."[75] There was no discussion at this stage of what would happen to the Northlands grounds, although the report did say that the city and Northlands would have to "decide the best use of that land and facility," including redeveloping the site to "support the rejuvenation of the 118 Avenue area"[76]—another potentially significant expense for taxpayers. Northlands was still involved in the deliberations, and Mayor Mandel said that it would be "up to Northlands and the Oilers to see what they can put together."[77]

The *City Shaping* report was, predictably, greeted with much cheerleading by the usual boosters in the local media, including the editorial board of the *Journal* and many of its columnists. One of the *Journal*'s sports columnists underlined that without a downtown arena similar to the new Yankees Stadium in New York, "Edmonton becomes another Winnipeg."[78] Not all of the *Journal*'s columnists were convinced by the report. Paula Simons dryly noted that the "fix was in" and pointed out the "utter vacuousness of the so-called 'feasibility study.'"[79] She also criticized the departure from the mayor's earlier promises: "Initially, we were given the impression no city tax dollars would fund a new arena. Now we're getting a different spin. No existing tax dollars would be diverted but the committee proposes that any new businesses that develop within a certain radius of the arena would have to pay a 'community revitalization levy', a special business tax to subsidize the new arena."[80]

For all of its flaws, though, the *City Shaping* report did make some important recommendations: that the full amount of the $11-million operating surplus, the existing operating grants paid by the city to Northlands for Rexall Place, and the existing ticket surcharge all be directed toward debt servicing, and that higher contributions should be required from the Oilers than those in their existing lease agreement. Many of these recommendations, especially the dedication of any operating surplus to pay down public debt, would be ignored in the years to come as the city negotiated with the Katz Group.

The *City Shaping* report also noted the necessity of contributions from all levels of government for a new arena to be economically viable. This recommendation would also be ignored by the city in future negotiations, and Edmonton taxpayers would ultimately contribute virtually all of the upfront costs associated with the arena's debt financing. Finally, the report recommended that a detailed assessment of the potential arena sites identified by HOK be undertaken, including the estimated cost and timing of land acquisition—another recommendation that would be ignored, especially when it became clear that the Katz Group had already started to assemble land at Katz's preferred downtown location.

The creation of *ad hoc* political spaces like the ALC allows unelected interest groups and consultants to support pre-determined political decisions, which are often made behind closed doors, away from public scrutiny and away from traditional forms of democratic oversight, thus insulating politicians (and their supporters) from accountability and criticism. In their unwavering support of the arena development and its associated downtown growth agenda, officials in the mayor's office and in administration wanted reports that supported decisions made years earlier—and they got them.

Taking these processes out of the political realm has become increasingly common for cities like Edmonton, especially in their dealings with private interests trying to avoid public debate—and public accountability. It has also become normal for public authorities to deny citizens the opportunity to participate in the early stages of debates over the construction and funding of new sport and entertainment districts. This was certainly true in Edmonton, where secrecy prevailed. City council had minimal opportunity to debate the contents of the *City Shaping* report. The recommendations that the arena *had to be downtown* and that it had to be publicly financed were not critically examined by elected representatives. Instead, the report became a carefully orchestrated moment in the arena debate in Edmonton—one in which disinterested analysis, public consultation, and democratic input counted for nothing.

Thus, by March 2008, the political terrain for the construction of a costly, new, debt-financed arena development had been prepared, largely thanks to the publication of what was essentially a pro-arena "advocacy study"[81] produced by boosters and beneficiaries. Obstacles remained, including growing public criticism and the Oilers' insistence that Northlands be removed from the business of NHL hockey in Edmonton. This development would irreparably fracture the alignment of stakeholders that have historically dominated the city's politics, the local sports scene, and Edmonton's broader growth agenda.

6

POWER PLAYS

WHILE EXECUTIVES from the Oilers, much of the downtown
business community, local media, and fans of the team, especially
season-ticket holders, greeted the findings of the *City Shaping* report
with enthusiasm, most Edmontonians disagreed with its conclusions
and continued to be less than convinced of the merits of a new, publicly-
subsidized arena development. Scores of letters to the editor were
published in both the *Edmonton Journal* and the *Edmonton Sun* in the
following months, expressing opposition to using public money
for a new arena. A survey by the University of Alberta's Population
Research Group showed that a plebiscite about using public money
to build a new arena in Edmonton would certainly fail.[1]

Mayor Mandel, though, continued to spin his own financial
narratives through trusted media sources, claiming that the new,
publicly-financed arena "wouldn't cost the taxpayers any money"
thanks to the CRL mechanism:

> *If you have nothing there and you're going to build an arena, then
> that's new money, and you could maybe use that as a source of
> revenue through what is known as a community revitalization levy.
> If you asked people, "Do you want the old rink to pay $300 million
> on your taxes or the new rink to pay no money on your taxes?" what
> would they say?*[2]

The mayor thus continued to suggest that the accumulation of hundreds of millions of dollars in debt did not count as a public expense, and that taxes would not be raised to pay for the new arena or to service interest because the repayment mechanisms, such as the CRL, were "new money." Proponents of new arena and stadium developments often insist that taxes won't go up to pay for modern professional sports facilities, and so public money won't be given to billionaire owners and millionaire players. For critics, though, these assertions obfuscate both the use of public funds and subsequent opportunity costs to support the creative financing strategies developed to subsidize increasingly costly sport-related developments.

Despite these attempts to frame the construction of a new, publicly-financed arena as being virtually without cost for Edmontonians—especially compared to the immediate $300-million tax burden of renovating Rexall Place (a classic straw man argument)—opposition mounted. After the *City Shaping* report came out, the Canadian Taxpayers Federation submitted a number of FOIP requests to obtain the unreleased CSL and HOK reports, as well as a fuller account of the publicly-funded information circulated by the ALC behind closed doors, including earlier drafts of the *City Shaping* report. The documents that the city released in response to these requests were so heavily redacted by civic officials that they were largely unreadable. The Canadian Taxpayers Federation did, however, discover that early drafts had recommended taxi and hotel levies to raise revenue, and that at least 60 percent of the cost of a new arena should be borne by its primary beneficiary, the Oilers. That the ALC never seriously considered significant private financing was, for the Canadian Taxpayers Federation, "mind boggling."[3] Of course, a public–private financing structure that limited private investment to 25 percent of the total cost of a new facility had already been agreed upon behind closed doors.

Most revealing, though, was the discovery that the chair of the ALC, Lyle Best, had intentionally omitted any reference in the final version of the report to the fact that recent NHL arena developments in Toronto, Montreal, Ottawa, and Vancouver had been privately financed. When the Canadian Taxpayers Federation released the results of its FOIP request and emphasized this omission, city officials denied that citizens were being misled, while Best explained that he had "removed the reference to the other arenas because he didn't think it was needed and because he wasn't sure it was correct"[4]—a puzzling explanation given that the ALC had full access to the 2007 CSL report that had explicitly outlined the funding models of 26 North American arenas, including the four privately-funded Canadian rinks. Nonetheless, as Scott Hennig of the Canadian Taxpayers Federation reflected in our interview, arena boosters were caught off-guard by the revelations:

> *I released it and decided it was newsworthy, but then Lyle Best went on Global and CTV and said "I don't know why you're bothering with this guy who likes to dig through my garbage. That's what those drafts are, is our garbage, we were writing stuff and we weren't going to use it so we threw it in the garbage. But, you know, hey if the government ever needs someone to pick fly shit out of pepper, this is your guy."[5]*

The Canadian Taxpayers Federation had damaged boosters' credibility and their political claims. In response, public officials continued to manipulate the terms of the FOIP Act to control arena-related information and to shield themselves from criticism.[6]

In retrospect, it's easy to understand why the city restricted access to these reports during the course of the arena debate, and even long after the deliberations had ended. The 2007 CSL report made clear how much revenue the Oilers were generating, despite playing in one of the oldest facilities in the league. And, while the *City Shaping* report repeated some of the demographic information featured in the CSL report, other information—including the fact that the Oilers ranked second in the NHL for average ticket prices, despite playing in the second smallest market in the league—was omitted. The CSL report also pointed out that the Edmonton Oilers generated the 11th highest amount of premium seating revenue, well ahead of franchises playing in much newer facilities and in far larger markets, including Boston and Vancouver. All of these financial figures—numbers confirmed by the Edmonton Oilers as a result of their involvement in the ALC—demonstrated that claims that the Oilers could not make a profit playing in Rexall Place were simply untrue. Findings from the 2007 CSL report included the following:

NHL Arena Funding Case Studies
- *Average cost (in 2007 dollars) of NHL-only facilities: $232 million[7]*
- *Average breakdown of public/private contribution: 48 percent public, 52 percent private[8]*

Edmonton Market
- *NHL average ticket price: Edmonton Oilers ranked 2nd of 30 teams; annual average price increase of 18.0 percent over past five seasons[9]*
- *NHL attendance: Edmonton Oilers ranked 11 of 30 teams (five-year average: 16,894)[10]*
- *NHL annual premium seating revenue (luxury suites and club seats): Edmonton Oilers ranked 11 of 30 teams ($28,934,400)[11]*

This initial CSL report did point out, though, just how much more money the Oilers stood to make playing in a new, publicly-financed arena, especially if they got full control of it and all its revenue streams: an average increase in profitability of over $11.2 million per year for the first five years.[12] The average five-year income projections in a report that CSL produced for Northlands two years later, unlike CSL's initial analysis, included in its calculations an estimated $3 million in income per year from naming rights that would go to the Oilers, and showed that the franchise would be the beneficiary of an average increase in profitability of $16.6 million per year for the first five years. Using this latter figure, over the duration of a 35-year agreement, the Oilers would thus stand to gain $581 million in additional profit from a new facility.[13] These conservative income projections, it's safe to conclude, have only increased for the Oilers since CSL produced this final report for Northlands in 2009. Table 7 shows a comparison of the 2007 and 2009 figures.

TABLE 7. CSL Income Projections in 2007 and 2009 (Figures in Millions)

Year	Annual Average	35-Year Total
2007	$11.2	$392
2009	$16.6	$581

Source: CSL, *Proposed Edmonton Arena Feasibility Study—Preliminary Draft*, 2007, 47; CSL, *Report on the Potential New Arena in Edmonton*, 2009, 97.

The HOK Arena Site Report

The information in the HOK report was equally problematic, and to have disclosed the document and the site rankings at any point during the negotiations between the city of Edmonton and the Katz Group would have inflicted significant damage both to the arguments made in the *City Shaping* report and to the credibility of the ALC itself. HOK had examined and ranked seven potential downtown arena sites (inclusive of two sites at The Quarters), as well as the existing Northlands grounds—a total of eight potential sites for the new arena. Crucially, the inclusion of the Northlands site was never made public by the ALC and was entirely omitted from the *City Shaping* report, which insisted that a new arena "had to be downtown"—a conclusion that had already been reached before the ALC was formed. In contrast, the HOK report actually endorsed a credible alternative: building a new facility on the Northlands grounds. In support of this hitherto undisclosed option, HOK noted:

> Northlands offers perhaps the most expedient solution to the community's need for a new arena—parking and transit infrastructure are in place, arena patrons are accustomed to getting there, an exhibition/meeting complex is adjacent, and the massive site is owned and controlled by a single not-for-profit entity. It may be characterized as an island unto itself but it offers the potential to become a large-scale entertainment hub in its own right.[14]

Although the HOK report concluded that the construction of a new facility at Northlands would not directly affect the development of the downtown core, it emphasized the site's other positive attributes, such as its potential to revitalize the 118 Avenue corridor from NAIT to Northlands, a less affluent area of the city with high rates of crime. The HOK report invited the ALC to consider the potential of transforming the sizeable city-owned grounds at Northlands into a far greater sports and entertainment hub with ancillary land development opportunities near an existing LRT station, including residential development. For HOK, the sheer size and scale of the grounds at Northlands—exceeding the footprint of Disneyland and almost matching that of Edmonton's entire downtown core—represented an enormous civic asset, comparable to "the recent Kansas Speedway development that has spurred a major entertainment/retail destination in a previously unheralded and underdeveloped area of Metro Kansas City."[15]

Many of the advantages of the Northlands site noted by HOK—the parking, the land, the road network, and the LRT—were the reasons the Coliseum had been built there in the 1970s. For HOK, as Andy Huntley recalled, these characteristics meant that Northlands remained a favourable site for a new arena in the new millennium: "They [HOK] called it the million-dollar site. You can actually get an arena there on the footprint out beyond the Expo Centre, and you've got two freeways to drain everybody out after. And that ranked so highly on their report."[16] There would also be minimal land acquisition costs at Northlands and few difficulties with land assembly (i.e., having to negotiate with multiple land owners), because all of the land (170 acres) had been given to the city in return for a long-term lease and tax-exempt status. Given the existing infrastructure, there would also have been no need for the additional investments necessary to construct a new arena on the land owned by Daryl Katz, including $56.6 million for a "winter garden" to allow safe passage over 104 Avenue; $15 million for another pedestrian crossing; $7 million for an LRT connection (although the existing LRT station at Northlands would likely have had to be expanded); and $25 million for a new community rink (the Coliseum could have served that purpose). In other words, the Northlands site could have potentially reduced the final cost of the arena and entertainment district

($613.7 million) by over $125 million, and by far more if arena boosters had been prepared to consider a more modest facility.

There were other arguments in favour of building a new, city-owned arena on the grounds at Northlands—for example, it could have been operated by the non-profit organization, which still had longstanding relationships with both the provincial and federal governments. Plus, the city was represented on Northlands' board of directors by three members of city council, thus ensuring a continued level of oversight. Unlike the Katz Group, Northlands also provided audited annual financial statements to city council. A new arena development would also have ensured that the Northlands site would still be used, thus maintaining the stability of the surrounding community and its property values, while minimizing the cost to taxpayers of redeveloping, or discarding, the site in its entirety if a new facility was built downtown and operated solely by the Katz Group. Moreover, a new arena at Northlands would still have increased the profitability of the Oilers and the valuation of the franchise, thus securing the future of the club for decades to come. By this point in the debate, though, all these facts were largely irrelevant, and the only viewpoints that mattered were the ones that argued for a downtown facility, the downtown growth agenda, and its related financing mechanisms, especially the CRL.

From the city's perspective, the attraction of people and investment to the downtown core vastly outweighed any potential gains (and cost savings) associated with building a new arena at Northlands. The focus of current urban planning and the business model of arena development had both shifted considerably since the Northlands Coliseum was built in the 1970s. Revitalization of the downtown core had become the key to entrepreneurial growth agendas in Edmonton and other cities; as well, the owners of professional sport franchises wanted to capitalize on land development opportunities like those identified by the Katz Group, rather than rely solely on revenues from the arena. One of the arguments in favour of an arena-anchored downtown development, especially for the city, was that it would create a dynamic synergy with existing downtown businesses, spurring the kind of development that the

CRL financing mechanism depended on. Admittedly, as the HOK report pointed out, there were also land development opportunities at the Northlands site, but these didn't align with the dominant municipal growth agenda.

As a result, the option of building and financing a new facility at Northlands and all of the advantages outlined by HOK were never raised in the *City Shaping* report and were completely omitted from public discussion by the ALC, including by the representatives from Northlands. In retrospect, it's worth asking why Northlands was complicit in ignoring the credible and less expensive option of constructing a new facility on its grounds. For one thing, releasing this information would have violated the terms of reference of the ALC and its accompanying confidentiality agreement. It would also have been politically damaging to the aspirations of Northlands executives who believed that they would be anointed operators of a new downtown arena. However, by not demanding a more robust public debate or a thorough evaluation of all of the potential sites from the beginning, Northlands undermined its own position and strengthened that of the main beneficiary of the new project—the Katz Group.

The HOK report had identified seven additional potential locations for a new downtown arena: (1) North Post Office; (2) The Quarters North (2a) and South Sites (2b); (3) Post Office; (4) Casino; (5) Greyhound Depot; and (6) West Jasper Avenue.

Of these, HOK overwhelmingly endorsed the West Jasper Avenue site:

> *Of the downtown sites, we would judge West Jasper Avenue (at 106 Street) as richest in variety and offering the most immediate urban design opportunity. It best leverages current development trends and is surrounded by an inventory of buildings compatible with a mixed-use district. Thus it offers immediate private development potential with no substantial economic stimulus requirement.*[17]

HOK further explained the site's advantages:

Depending on the disposition of 106th Street, this site offers between
6.5 and 11 acres that are virtually surrounded by a fabric of desirable
and fertile mixed-use opportunities. It boasts a strong tie to Jasper
Avenue and excellent LRT access. The scale of the neighbourhood is
pedestrian friendly and rich in variety. The site comfortably reaches
to both the heart of the downtown and burgeoning warehouse district
neighbourhood redevelopment. These inherent strengths could be
expected to spur significant and immediate "organic" redevelopment
driven by the interests of many property owners.[18]

It identified the two sites at The Quarters as the next most favourable locations, as they offered "an ambitious opportunity to redefine
the eastern edge of the central business district."[19] Importantly, both
sites, like the Northlands option, also aligned with a pre-existing
city revitalization policy and a future CRL to encourage development in the area, then identified as the Downtown East Side. The
northern option also offered

an attractive and high impact gateway to the Quarters that could
provide an effective jumpstart to the eastern district and boost the east
Quarters armature. And with the closure of 103rd Avenue a 7.42-acre
site is created that is ample for the arena and ice sheet with adequate
service entry. The ice sheet and community uses could be helpful to the
transition of the neighbourhood. The LRT and Sir Winston Churchill
Square are within reasonable reach but synergistic development is
stymied on the north and west by large government buildings. The city
controls much of the site. Selectively preserv[ing] existing buildings on
the site's edges could add a desirable urban design element.[20]

The southern option, meanwhile, "would enjoy a synergistic link to
the convention centre" and an

environment that could prove more fertile for ancillary private devel-
opment. In combination with the convention centre, there exists
potential for an east Quarters entertainment district that would
extend downtown to the east along Jasper Avenue and would reinforce

connections with the river valley—one of Edmonton's defining
attributes.[21]

In contrast, the remaining sites, located north of the central business district, were reviewed less favourably by HOK because of the "issues of psychologically and physically bridging the wide span of 103rd/104th Avenue."[22] HOK discounted the North Post Office site, which was limited by size and access difficulties, but was more supportive of the sizeable Post Office site, which had the potential to spur a broader mixed-use development and could be a "transitional link to the north and west."[23] Still, HOK considered the Post Office site to be relatively isolated from downtown by the 104 Avenue corridor, while the nearby courthouse, jail, and city hall represented developmental barriers.

The HOK report provided a more supportive review of the Casino site in terms of compatibility and suitability for mixed-use development, but noted that it lacked an LRT connection—an issue that the city was soon to address with the Metro LRT Line. The real value of the Casino land, though, was to be found by the inclusion of the final site assessed by HOK: the Greyhound Bus Depot site, which at 4.53 acres was too small on its own for a new arena. As the report noted, the importance of the Greyhound Bus Depot would be "as an enhancement to the Casino site that could provide highly desirable linkage to the existing downtown fabric of shops, restaurants and entertainment."[24] In 2009, it became clear that these two options— the Casino and Greyhound sites—were the precise locations of the Katz Group's land holdings, and so, ultimately, the eventual location of the city-owned arena.

According to an HOK document provided by an anonymous source, the Katz Group's land holdings (Casino and Greyhound Bus Depot) never ranked highly in HOK's evaluation categories. In the category of Urban Design, which included rankings for "new development opportunities adjacent to arena," "potential to spur broader community renewal," and "image/visibility," the Katz Group's land holdings ranked 5th and 7th. In the category of Transportation ("on-site parking," "proximity to public transit," and "pedestrian

TABLE 8. HOK Arena Site Rankings and Evaluation Scores

Rank	Site Location	Total Score
1	West Jasper Avenue	115
2	Northlands	98
3	South Quarters	95
4	North Quarters	85
5	Casino[a]	83
6	Post Office	76
7	Greyhound Bus Depot[b]	64
8	North Post Office	30

Note. Information obtained from anonymously provided HOK document.

[a] Katz arena land.

[b] Katz arena land.

movement," among other factors), the Katz Group's land holdings ranked 4th and 7th. In the category of Site Factors ("site size," "displacement of existing users," "environmental issues," etc.), the Katz Group's land holdings ranked 3rd and 4th. In the crucial category of Costs ("land acquisition"), the Katz Group's land holdings ranked 3rd and tied for 4th with two other sites.

At no point did the city of Edmonton perform a comprehensive and comparative analysis of the merits of other potential arena sites, as the *City Shaping* report had recommended, including those ranked considerably higher in crucial categories than the Katz Group's land holdings that could have decreased the overall cost of the arena, including land acquisition costs (both the sites at Northlands and the South Quarters were cheaper) and pedestrian movement (the Katz Group's site necessitated the construction of a costly pedestrian plaza to cross 104 Avenue that would diminish street-level pedestrian activity). Still, as people close to the negotiations confided to us under the condition of anonymity, despite the high ranking of the West Jasper Avenue site—seriously considered by the ALC, which had privately discussed the closure of 106 Street to facilitate an arena development—deliberations were being directed by city administration in favour of the Katz Group's land holdings, regardless of its poor showing in the HOK report.

Playing for Keeps

In September 2008, the foundation of the global economy was profoundly shaken by the collapse of Wall Street financial services firm Lehman Brothers, triggering a credit crunch and the near-implosion of the world's financial system. While Canada was relatively insulated from the worst effects of the global recession, the economic downturn was an ominous sign for proponents of a debt-financed, speculative arena/land development project. The city of Edmonton itself was already facing a deficit of $29.7 million and was further asked to help finance Northlands' expansion of the Expo Centre, a project that had already received funding from both the provincial and federal governments. As Northlands' vice president Mark Bamford noted, the non-profit organization was required by its bank to approach the city to guarantee a loan, "given what has transpired in the financial markets the last few months, combined with the ongoing discussions around a new arena in downtown Edmonton and how this might affect Northlands financially."[25] As Andy Huntley explained, Northlands was eventually able to borrow the remaining funds for its expansion from the city as a result of its close ties to the upper echelons of city administration, and was supported directly by both the government of Alberta and the government of Canada, with which the organization maintained longstanding relationships:

> We thought we could do more with the site, with the Expo Centre, so I took the concept to the province, and I thought we could rebuild the whole site for $150 million...and the province said "here, you've got your first $50 million, now go to the other two orders of government."... We ultimately did get close to that from the federal government, but we never got any money from the city of Edmonton, so we knew there was going to be a debt piece and we were going to borrow it from the Bank of Montreal. That was in 2008 and we were going to get the loan in place. The Bank of Montreal changed the deal, and they said we need a city guarantee now. So, we told the city manager [Al Maurer] about this and he said, "I will borrow money from the Municipal Finance Corporation, and I've got to mark it up a little so that I can

get it through council and we'll make the fee but pay us back then." So
that's how it was arranged, and I've heard the spin that they had to
bail us out because we got in trouble on the project, but it's so far from
the truth it's absurd. Those are the facts around how that was put
together.[26]

In March 2009, the city of Edmonton officially borrowed $59 million
from the Alberta Capital Finance Authority and loaned Northlands
the funds under the same terms, further aligning municipal interests with the non-profit organization's long-term aspirations. This
development would have profound ramifications following the
conclusion of the arena agreement between the city and the Katz
Group, which excluded Northlands altogether and granted the Katz
Group a veto over the future use and redevelopment of Rexall Place
in any sport or entertainment capacity. The decision to build a
new conference centre at Northlands was puzzling because the city
already owned one downtown (the Edmonton Convention Centre).

Nonetheless, by December 2008, Northlands, officials from
the city, and the Katz Group had begun preliminary meetings to
discuss the next possible steps in the development process for a new
downtown arena. Councillors were generally not formally advised
that these early meetings were occurring; instead, the meetings
were mostly coordinated by the mayor's office and generated no
public reports. Yet within a matter of months, despite the mayor's
reassurances, Northlands would be officially excluded from the
negotiations.

As a result of widespread opposition to any public contribution
to the new arena, as well as the effect of the global economic downturn in Edmonton—oil prices closed the year at under $40 per barrel
after peaking at nearly $150 per barrel earlier in July—Mayor Mandel
ended the year with calming reassurances:

I think that when the vision for an arena comes forward, it will
be strong enough on its merits that citizens will see how it can be
supported. And it will be supported substantially across the board,
on council as well as in the public. The vision will sell itself. We

estimate the cost of the arena to now be substantially under $400
million—substantially.[27]

Meanwhile, both the Oilers and the NHL were undermining his
political strategy—an example of their solipsistic approach to the
arena debate. Only days later, during an Edmonton Chamber of
Commerce luncheon hosted by Patrick LaForge of the Edmonton
Oilers, NHL commissioner Gary Bettman insisted that a new
building was imperative for both the Oilers and the city of
Edmonton, recycling many of the widely used and repeatedly
discredited arguments promoted by professional sport leagues to
secure public funds:

> *It can become an economic engine. It can attract tourists. It is critical*
> *both for the future of the Oilers and the city. Yes, the team is in good*
> *shape, but you have to look into the future. This is a city and a team*
> *that vitally needs a new building. I think it's important that nobody*
> *lose sight of its importance and we continue to move the process along*
> *to get to the right place.*[28]

Despite Bettman's acknowledgement that the team was "in good
shape" (a fact confirmed by the *Forbes* NHL financial estimates), the
Oilers in 2010 painted quite a different picture as they intensified
their pleas for public subsidy by claiming that they were unprofitable and had been losing money, all the while refusing to open their
books to city council. For Bettman, getting to "the right place"—i.e.,
building a new arena from which the Oilers would receive all hockey
and non-hockey revenue—was only possible with public funding, an
assertion he delivered without any supporting evidence and without
reference to the other privately-financed NHL arenas in Canada:
"There's no way I believe a building can be built here without a
significant public element."[29] Bettman's commentary would mark
the first of several interventions by the NHL commissioner into the
arena debate, and he was enthusiastically supported by the local
media—especially the Oilers beat writers—in creating a false sense
of urgency on behalf of the team. As former city manager Al Maurer

reflected, Bettman was a skilled and determined lobbyist: "I can't remember when it was, but Kevin Lowe introduced me to Bettman and he was very aggressive with me about helping them to get a new rink. His whole strategy was getting in the room with the Katz Group and working at it, and he's kind of doing the same tactic in Calgary now."[30]

The interference of league commissioners in these debates is, of course, a well-known tactic in the manual of "sports welfare brinkmanship" to support owners' aspirations, but also to warn civic leaders of the political consequences of failure.[31] Bettman was already unpopular with Canadian hockey fans who were angered by his drive to expand the NHL into non-traditional US markets, and who held him responsible for the loss of the Winnipeg Jets and Quebec Nordiques in the 1990s (although he was also credited with playing a major role in keeping the Oilers in Edmonton in this era). Still, Bettman had demonstrated for years that he was more than willing to play the part of the US villain in the minds of Canadian hockey traditionalists—he unashamedly prioritized the expansion of NHL general revenues through expansion fees and the revenue streams of individual franchises by supporting their orchestrated claims of facility obsolescence. He was therefore fully prepared to interject his views at such an early stage in the arena debate on behalf of the Oilers and Daryl Katz, as he had done in Winnipeg in the 1990s, and as he would do in Quebec City later in 2009 by suggesting that a new, publicly-financed arena would facilitate the return of the Quebec Nordiques, and then, later still, in Calgary. It would have been ill-timed and counterproductive for Katz, still a new owner, to intervene so publicly at this point in the arena debate. Instead, he bided his time, letting boosterish journalists and politicians push his demands, all the while keeping alive the threat to relocate the team.

Building an Arena, Closing an Airport

The year 2008 ended with Bettman's inflammatory and patronizing intervention, but the arena debate remained off the public's radar as discussions continued behind closed doors, and, perhaps most important, as the Katz Group continued to assemble the land in the downtown core upon which the new arena would be built. Political energies were instead focused on another divisive debate: the closure of City Centre Airport, a project championed by Mayor Mandel to spur additional residential development in the city centre. Later, in March 2009, Cal Nichols, who opposed the mayor on this issue, stepped down as chairman of the Edmonton Oilers to focus on the Alberta Enterprise Group's campaign to save the airport.

The Katz Group had genuine concerns that Nichols' campaign would be held against them in the arena negotiations by political leaders, including the mayor, who had already committed to closing the airport. The Oilers and various downtown developers stood to benefit handsomely from the closure of City Centre Airport, which would result in the removal of the height restrictions that had hitherto prevented developers from building the tall office and condominium towers that would feature as value-added components of the proposed downtown arena and entertainment district on the Katz Group's land. The removal of the height restrictions would also allow developers to address the pent-up demand for these types of amenities in downtown Edmonton—a development that would later bode well for the arena's CRL financing mechanism.

Throughout the spring of 2009, Northlands, the city of Edmonton, and the Katz Group continued to meet in advance of the release of a formal arena development proposal. Publicly, Northlands remained optimistic about its involvement in any future project given its traditional role as the sole operator of the city's NHL facility, as well as its prominent position within the community. As Andy Huntley noted,

> Given our experience and history, we're really confident we'll have a role. Northlands clearly has the core competency. It's just been a get-to-know-you peek at this point. If we had something to say, we would. It's really been very preliminary. The Katz Group has been excellent in just assuring our involvement, but who is going to do what and how it shakes out—that's for another day.[32]

If Northlands initially felt reassured by the Katz Group and supportive of the overall agenda for a new, publicly-financed downtown arena, citizens continued to have doubts. An Ipsos Reid poll dramatically underlined Edmontonians' opposition: of 440 residents polled, 76 percent opposed using taxpayers' money for a new arena development.[33] The popular hockey blog *Battle of Alberta*, having criticized the idea since 2006, started an ongoing Downtown Arena Primer to gather relevant information.

The most significant development of 2009, though, came in September, when Patrick LaForge of the Oilers held a press conference to announce that plans for a new arena and entertainment district were well underway—with no reference to any role for Northlands—and that the Katz Group had purchased two parcels of downtown land from WAM Development, including the Baccarat Casino site at 101 Street and 104 Ave and a parking lot located one block east of the Greyhound bus station at 103 Street, plus options on other sites.[34] In revealing the eventual location of the new, city-owned arena, LaForge also reiterated the findings of the ALC in the *City Shaping* report, including that a new arena had to be publicly financed and built at that location. Although he provided little additional concrete information, he used the press conference to perform more promotional work, including advertising the involvement and expertise of Mark Rosentraub, "the star last February at a well-conceived University of Alberta symposium on The Role of Sports and Entertainment Facilities in Urban Development."[35]

After LaForge's press conference, Mayor Mandel announced his support: "It's a reasonably good location. Putting the [Metro] LRT right there, I think it is reasonably accessible. It's a large enough site to put other things right there."[36] The Katz Group's preferred location was also endorsed by sport management scholar Dr. Dan Mason: "It's a good spot for the development in the sense that there's not much on the land there."[37] In none of the coverage was there any discussion of the HOK site rankings, which hadn't been made public.

Again, we encounter two recurring and related themes in this debate: depoliticization and secrecy. The location of the publicly-financed and city-owned arena would be determined solely by the Katz Group, without significant public input and without community consent. The city's decision to withhold the results of the HOK study ranking the Casino and Greyhound sites below almost every other potential site—including the option of building a new facility on the grounds at Northlands—precluded a fair and balanced public assessment of the merits of this particular location. Not a single council session was dedicated to publicly debating the merits of the site the Katz Group had selected. Few in the media bothered to ask who stood to benefit. The headline of an article by David Staples in the *Journal*, for example, simply stated, "Oilers Confirm Casino Site as Best Place for New Arena," as if it were a fait accompli, and as if it were up to the Oilers to determine where to build a city-owned facility.[38]

It was taken for granted that the city would have to purchase the land from the Katz Group to build a city-owned facility at this location, and many simply turned a blind eye to the fact that the Katz Group—and others in the land development industry—stood to make huge profits from having already assembled significant amounts of land around the eventual arena location. There was, moreover, no analysis of how this particular location supported the city's pre-existing policy commitments or the redevelopment of the Northlands grounds. Finally, while the location was described as a "wasteland,"[39] no attention was paid to the potential displacement of less affluent and homeless citizens as a result of development in the area.

When announcing the Katz Group's development plans, LaForge also took the opportunity to reiterate a now obvious point: the franchise had no interest in remaining at Rexall Place, even if it were extensively redeveloped to fulfill the Oilers' revenue requirements, a point that the Oilers had first made behind closed doors as early as 2004. The Katz Group, of course, was unwavering in its commitment to the new business model of the NHL. LaForge, however, disingenuously asserted that the Oilers maintained a good relationship with Northlands—useful if the team needed to extend its lease at Rexall Place until a new facility was built. While representatives from Northlands weren't at LaForge's news conference, the organization initially offered its "vigorous support" for the Katz Group's plan, projected to be a $1-billion downtown development with a new arena as the centrepiece of a broader entertainment district that would include a practice facility, condos, hotels, a casino, office towers, and student housing.[40]

But the political terrain had already shifted. The Katz Group aggressively pursued the new business model of the NHL with the full support of the city of Edmonton, and Northlands was soon to vanish into the ever-widening cracks in the coalition that had long dominated the professional sports landscape.

7

SHUT OUT

NORTHLANDS WAS NOT YET FULLY CONVINCED that the land the
Katz Group had assembled would be the ultimate location of a new,
city-owned arena, especially given the site's low rankings in the HOK
study and the lack of public input to the process to date:

> JAY SCHERER: *You must have heard the rumours as I did that Katz
> had already bought the land downtown, that the land assembly
> was happening even before the ink was dry on his purchase agree-
> ment with the team?*
>
> ANDY HUNTLEY: *I always felt that could have been a real estate
> play. Anyway, I think there was some tension between Katz and
> WAM at that point because I think his option had lapsed and WAM
> went in and got it tied up. I don't think all was well between the
> two of them at that point, so there were other things playing out.
> We just looked at it and said it's a real estate play anyway, that
> it's not final, that the arena won't be there. We discounted it as a
> location and tried to tell [city] council, "You've got some problems
> associated with it."*[1]

Northlands had, however, underestimated the emerging influence of the Katz Group, especially its increasing interest in land
development opportunities, and its executives assumed that city

administration would perform its own due diligence in comparing all the potential arena sites. Despite initial optimism and public assurances, behind closed doors the relationship between Northlands and the Katz Group was continuing to fracture, while the association between the city of Edmonton and the Katz Group was further solidifying. As the Oilers publicly announced their development plans, they were taking steps to shut Northlands out of any significant role in the operation of a new, city-owned arena.

These developments had been on the horizon for months. Earlier in the year, Northlands had asked the Katz Group to define its role in the development and operation of a new downtown arena. Having received only "vague generalities" in response, Northlands formally asked the Katz Group in August 2009 to draft a "written proposal providing details describing the proposed development and further describing the role that they envisioned Northlands would play in the development and operation of the new arena."[2] At a meeting on September 4, 2009, the Katz Group presented their answer: a two-page draft memorandum with a list of non-negotiable demands. The Katz Group would have full control of a new downtown arena and would receive all its revenues, including non-hockey revenues. Its existing lease agreement with Northlands would be immediately amended to give the Oilers absolute control of Rexall Place and all its revenues. Northlands would still be responsible for covering all operating costs related to the new arena and Rexall Place, using funds from casino revenues and/or the city to do so. According to Northlands, to "further underline the non-negotiability of this 'offer'...[the Katz Group] stated repeatedly that any response to the draft memorandum other than an unequivocal acceptance would constitute a refusal of same."[3] For Northlands executives, this draft memorandum "differed significantly from the substance of...ongoing discussions and was delivered without warning after months of ongoing negotiations."[4]

As Ken Knowles, the former president and CEO of Edmonton Northlands, recalled, this meeting marked a decisive turn and an irreversible erosion of whatever level of trust had previously existed:

Daryl Katz stickhandles new arena deal past Edmonton Northlands, March 4, 2011.

[Malcolm Mayes/Artizans.com]

Unfortunately, that was kind of the way the wind was blowing at the time. You know, we sat down, we put a negotiating team together at Northlands and the Katz Group had a team together. And the first couple of meetings were very amicable and the city was certainly on board, trying to facilitate all parties, the city, Katz Group, and Northlands, because Northlands had been such a huge player, and so Northlands could still stay involved in some way, shape, or form. What that was, you know, we hadn't reached that point yet, but then all of a sudden it went off the rails. The Katz Group issued a proposed contract in one of our joint meetings, and basically said this is the way it is and it's not negotiable. And we just said thank you and got up and left the room. And that wasn't the spirit of negotiations and that's when it really started to go off the rails at that time. But you

know, back then I could see that the Oilers wanted all of the revenue,
and particularly Daryl, and I don't think he had an appreciation or
an understanding of why he's got to be talking to Northlands, who
the hell is Northlands? Here I am, a private entrepreneur, this is what
I'm prepared to do for the city of Edmonton, why do I need them? And
I also think that he couldn't understand why Northlands has such a
strong relationship with the various levels of government. And we did
federally, provincially, and municipally [have] great relationships.[5]

But even with these relationships and its long history, Northlands'
taken-for-granted role as the traditional promoter of sport and
entertainment events in Edmonton was now in trouble. Northlands
increased its own efforts to attract major concerts and shows to
demonstrate its credentials as an organization capable of competing
with any private sector entity in the sport and entertainment
industry. In 2009, Rexall Place ranked tenth in the world for concert
and event ticket sales. Northlands later opened the Expo Centre,
built with money borrowed from the city, to much fanfare, with its
four new exhibition halls, a 13,000-square-foot ballroom, conference
rooms, and the city's biggest commercial centre.

On the other hand, as Knowles suggested, the Katz Group had
established its own priorities: its $100-million investment in the
arena project—and the broader ancillary developments that the city
desperately wanted—would not proceed unless the Oilers controlled
and operated the new facility and received all arena-related monies,
including the lucrative concert revenue that currently went to
Northlands. The Oilers were again claiming to be at a competitive
disadvantage with other NHL teams that controlled all revenues
from their arenas. Patrick LaForge insisted, "The Calgary Flames
and the Edmonton Oilers need to be on the same footing. We need
to compete with them...Our request is, let's equalize. Let's get to
the same place. I don't think that's forbidden fruit."[6] In contrast
to Gary Bettman's earlier statement about the financial health
of the team, LaForge lamented, "We lost money last year. We lost
quite a bit of money."[7] The *Forbes* 2008 "Business of Hockey List"[8]
told a different story. In 2008, *Forbes* reported, the Oilers had an

estimated operating income of US$11.8 million, the seventh highest in the league, behind only the Toronto Maple Leafs, New York Rangers, Montreal Canadiens, Detroit Red Wings, Dallas Stars, and Vancouver Canucks—all teams in much larger markets.

Northlands, as Andy Huntley noted, was well aware that the Oilers wanted the concert revenue that the non-profit organization was getting:

We're running, I think it's well documented, somewhere between the 10th and 12th busiest arena in the world in the 470th largest city and that's documented in Pollstar *[a trade publication for the concert tour industry]. So, we're doing something right, we're very good at Northlands at what we do. We had 44 sold-out concerts. So, of course, they're sitting there being the professional team looking at this and wanting that revenue stream for their own. And I mean, that dynamic is played out in market after market. It's about the business model of pro sports today...From my first meeting—I've only had a couple meetings with Mr. Katz, I actually knew him prior—but it was abundantly clear that where he was headed with his thinking [was] "we need all of these revenues." And he just said, "Andy, it's the new NHL, it's the way things are."[9]*

The financial dynamics noted by Huntley revealed the changing business model of professional sport that was driving these developments. Major league franchises across North America were attempting to secure arrangements to boost their profits and valuations, while securing ancillary land development opportunities that also appealed to municipalities. Katz acknowledged that a new playbook was guiding the actions of NHL owners after the 2004/05 NHL lockout. Still, Northlands was confident that if the Katz Group demanded full control of a public facility and all of its ancillary revenue streams—even with its own investment of $100 million and the promise of additional development—council would simply tell them to build the new arena themselves. They were disastrously wrong.

Northlands was increasingly under attack from both the Oilers and the club's media allies, all suggesting that, without public subsidy, Northlands couldn't compete with big players in the global entertainment industry like AEG, which controlled 93 major venues around the world. Katz had already held meetings with both AEG and Live Nation with the intention of establishing partnerships to run the new arena in Edmonton, providing that Northlands was firmly out of the picture as a potential competitor, especially for the local concert market. Mere days after the press conference at which he had emphasized the good relationship between Northlands and the Oilers, Patrick LaForge undermined Northlands in the local media:

> We're interested in being the best in the world. I'm not trying to poke Northlands in the eye here...Northlands [has] done a good job so far. Nobody would have an issue with that. [But] the new world is big operators like AEG, Live Nation and the like. They are creating a new world of preferred outlets that they bring their best Triple-A entertainment to, and we want our place to be one of those stops and want them probably to be one of our partners.[10]

The Katz Group wanted to emulate AEG's business model, though on a smaller scale and with massive public subsidies, as Rick Daviss, the executive director of the city's Arena Project, noted:

> They were looking at AEG for a while, and they got involved more and more with AEG and seeing how they operate, and they had AEG on contract and consulting, and they said, "you know what, we can do that." And they decided to become the Oilers Entertainment Group (OEG) and I don't know that they're limiting themselves to Edmonton. I think they want to be the AEG of Canada and I think their thoughts are much bigger than even just controlling the entertainment business in Edmonton. I think they're looking across the country...[Northlands] made a big assumption, and their assumption was that they were going to operate the new arena and it was the wrong assumption to make in hindsight. And you can understand why they would have made it given their history and to protect their interests.[11]

LaForge's inflammatory public statements had clearly taken Northlands by surprise, and its representatives made their displeasure clear. As Andy Huntley remembered, "Mr. LaForge was very good at maligning Northlands and did it in that way that only he could."[12] LaForge also had a trusted ally in the media in David Staples, who circulated his arguments against the future involvement of Northlands in a new arena development. "I was not kind to Northlands," Staples acknowledged. "I didn't think they were putting any skin in the game."[13] In response, Northlands tried to defend its operations and its community-based mandate as the most suitable operator of any new, publicly-financed arena. As Andy Huntley remarked:

> [LaForge's announcement] caught us flat-footed. I thought we had agreed together that if there were going to be media releases, that they'd be planned, but that didn't happen. So, we're having a little trouble understanding it. If there's going to be public-sector dollars in this project, our whole point is, how can you put control into the hands of a private developer? You need some steward in there to protect the public good and the community interest. This is why to me, it's best to leave [arena management] in the hands of Northlands.[14]

Northlands also took issue with claims that it was uncompetitive and dependent on public subsidy by trumpeting its return of $196.5 million to federal and provincial governments over the past decade. In retrospect, though, Northlands had overstated its expertise the result of its historical monopoly in arena operations—and minimized the fact that it was not profitable enough to avoid carrying large debt loads. All of these issues, including the secrecy that has historically surrounded Northlands' operations, as well as its long-held power and political influence, fuelled longstanding resentments and the perception of many that the organization protected its own interests rather than the public good. And, by now, the Oilers enjoyed the full support of the mayor and influential bureaucrats.

Despite the shift in the relationship between Northlands and the Katz Group, however, Northlands remained an influential institution within the city and beyond. As a result of its 130-year history, Northlands could count on a long list of allies in both the private and the public sectors, including past presidents and directors, to facilitate direct access to various levels of government. Many, for example, had longstanding ties with the federal Conservative and provincial Progressive Conservative parties. Gary Lamphier, business columnist for the *Edmonton Journal*, wrote:

> *Unlike the Katz Group, where one man, supported by senior execs, makes all the big decisions, Northlands is more like an octopus. Its appendages reach into the backrooms of the legislature, city hall, boardrooms and living rooms all over Alberta. Although the province, the feds and the city are represented on the Northlands' board, and they contribute millions of dollars a year to its operations, Northlands' real power extends far beyond the $140 million in direct revenues or the estimated $1 billion in province-wide economic activity it generated in 2008. Northlands functions more like an extended family of like-minded community power brokers—including Dr. Bob Westbury, Harry Hole and Bob Walker, to name a few—supported by an army of 900 citizen volunteers, 300 full-time staff, and 1,800 part-time employees.* [15]

Some councillors have also traditionally sat on the Northlands board as part of their standing duties, making them aware of the importance of arena operations for Northlands and of Northlands to the city of Edmonton.

Daryl Katz, while undeniably influential, lacked an equivalent network of longstanding local political connections, and he was unfamiliar with, and uninterested in, the democratic process and the workings of municipal and provincial government. The innumerable requirements and complex bureaucratic structures of government differed enormously from his role as chairman and CEO of a privately-owned business empire with a hierarchical corporate model. In the case of a new arena with a proposed financing structure so heavily tilted toward the public sector, the sharp contrast between the corporate model of the Katz Group and the bureaucratic structure of various levels of government was evident from the outset. By the fall of 2009, Katz had yet to set foot in city hall to discuss his vision for a new arena district. Councillors, like the citizens of Edmonton, were still getting updates about the progress of negotiations from the media.

In October 2009, though, they were summoned by email to meet with Daryl Katz in private, away from city hall, and at his convenience—an invitation that a city solicitor later suggested might have violated municipal regulations. Councillors were unaware of the workings of the ALC, had no comparative analysis of other potential arena sites, had not fully discussed the CSL and HOK reports, and lacked basic information about the Katz Group's proposal. As Gary Lamphier noted, serious questions remained about the public–private financing structure and the troubling lack of public support for the development. Moreover, not a single hotel chain, casino operator, condominium builder, or commercial developer had yet endorsed the project.[16]

Lamphier also pointed out the lack of a guarantee from the Katz Group for a certain amount of ancillary development to ensure the success of the proposed CRL financing mechanism in Edmonton. Such commitments had been made by other major league teams, including the San Diego Padres, to secure the use of tax increment financing to build stadium or arena developments. After asking these basic questions, Lamphier received a "cranky response from the folks at the Katz Group," who suggested that the tone of his column was both "snide and insinuating."[17] From this point forward, the Katz Group denied Lamphier information related to the arena development, limiting his ability to approach important sources in his capacity as a business columnist; they kept up a steady flow of information to more cooperative columnists, though.[18]

Playing with Numbers, Smearing the Opposition

By the beginning of November, the organization had adjusted its lobbying strategies at both the municipal and provincial levels to secure public funds. First, Katz began to meet with councillors at city hall to outline his plans for the arena development, while also becoming more familiar with the process of municipal governance and bureaucratic procedures. Then, the Katz Group hired former deputy premier and PC party executive director Peter Elzinga, and Joan Forge, who had run communications for Alberta premier Ed Stelmach's party leadership campaign in 2006, to lobby the provincial government.

The Katz Group's promotional push also intensified near the end of 2009, supported by a broad and seemingly coordinated campaign in the local media, especially in the pages of the *Journal*. An article by David Staples on December 4, 2009 announced that the Katz Group had hired AEG to advise on the proposed arena development downtown. Patrick LaForge touted AEG's experience and its privately-funded LA Live sports and entertainment district that had transformed downtown Los Angeles. Paid sport management consultant Mark Rosentraub confirmed that AEG was the "best and biggest organization when it comes to building these kinds of arena districts. Their project in Los Angeles, the combination of Staples Center and L.A. Live, is simply extraordinary."[19] Staples further wrote about AEG's successful role as part of a four-part, pro-arena series published in November and December. His broader story on Los Angeles, with exuberant quotations from Patrick LaForge, Dr. Mark Rosentraub, Dr. Dan Mason, and AEG vice president Ted Tanner, came out on the 6th of December.[20] Staples was also dispatched to another destination familiar to Edmonton's arena boosters for the promotional series—Columbus, Ohio, with its (at the time) privately-financed Nationwide Arena.

Staples boosted the arguments of the arena's supporters while denigrating those of its critics, including in one article an ad hominem attack by Patrick LaForge against economist Dr. Brad Humphreys. Rather than engaging with Humphreys' critical analysis of the economics of publicly-financed major league sports developments, LaForge simply dismissed him as anti-culture:

> To a large degree, it's people with Humphreys' view that prevents us
> from building the next Eiffel Tower, the next Peace Arch, the next CN

Tower, because people who think like him can't find the economic
rationalization to do it. I think that sports and entertainment is a
unique industry and it adds value to a city...You can't replace it with
a refinery or a pulp mill. They might have similar economic impact,
but it's not a substitute for entertainment for the masses. It's people
like him that are going to prevent the world from being a place of
entertainment, arts and culture.[21]

Although Humphreys was interviewed by Staples, he was not given
an opportunity to rebut LaForge's contemptuous remarks. Such
treatment went well beyond what the economist had experienced in
other cities, and contrasted starkly with the support Staples gave to
pro-arena sport management consultants:

Well, what still stings the most is the hit job that Staples did on me,
when he let Pat LaForge call me an impediment to civic progress and
never solicited a quote from me that might have rebutted that, or
you know, let those people make false statements and never try to
fact check them, like the statement that the Eiffel Tower was publicly
financed when it wasn't. That sticks out in my mind. I was used to
being ignored by the local media, but I've never really experienced this
sort of active attempt to de-emphasize my work as what occurred in
Edmonton, and if you look at the way that Dan Mason was treated, it
was quite different than the way I was treated in the local media.[22]

Besides providing LaForge with a platform to malign Humphreys,
Staples suggested that the economist had reversed his position
in recent years, referring to his new research on the arena district
in Columbus, Ohio, home of the Blue Jackets. Humphreys and
co-author Xia Feng had offered a less "skeptical" conclusion in an
unpublished paper:

A new state-of-the-art facility integrated in a comprehensive urban
redevelopment program and located in the heart of a large city might
be expected to generate increases in residential property values near
hundreds of millions of dollars within a mile of that facility, if the

location, planning, construction, and development is carried out
carefully.[23]

But, as Humphreys explained in our interview, this study was not
representative of his overall research:

> *Well, yeah, he [Staples] tried to place some sort of spin on my work,*
> *which is not reflective of the full body of the research that I've*
> *published on the topic. I have published some papers that show that,*
> *in some cases, property values are higher closer to sports facilities,*
> *but that's highly dependent on idiosyncratic local conditions. And you*
> *know I stand by the research that I've done that shows those effects,*
> *but that's two papers out of 40 that I've published, and that article*
> *comes along and you know Staples and Mark Rosentraub said that I*
> *had "come over to the dark side" or something like that. I just felt like*
> *that they were seizing on a very small part of my research agenda and*
> *blowing it up to make me out to be somebody who has done the same*
> *things that Mark Rosentraub has done, which is be a paid consultant*
> *for property developers. And he's got to be on record saying the right*
> *things, while being on the record as opposing the research that I've*
> *published that reaches different conclusions than what the people who*
> *are hiring him want to hear. I mean, in a lot of other cities, people will*
> *just let sort of dissenting points of view stand, and it seemed like, in*
> *Edmonton, every dissenting view had to be strongly stamped down.*[24]

Such tactics underline the extent to which arena proponents and
their supporters in the Edmonton media worked to neutralize their
challengers through a range of strategies, including publicly misrep-
resenting research and ridiculing legitimate intellectual arguments
and evidence.[25]

Boosters and beneficiaries of the new arena development ramped
up their lobbying efforts, trying to demonstrate its economic impact
through the production of more advocacy reports. Bob Black, an
Edmonton lawyer and long-time friend of Daryl Katz, was hired
as the Katz Group's executive vice president, sports and entertainment, and Janet Riopel, a consultant and former city employee who

would later become president of the Chamber of Commerce, was contracted to engage in a broader community "dialogue." Black was promoted as a fresh face and was "seen less as a man beholden to and speaking for the Oilers than as someone who has signed on with Katz because he was seduced by the billionaire's grand urban vision."[26] Black introduced himself to councillors in a letter dated December 19, 2009, pledging to "begin the process of engaging in a broader community dialogue" and listing the Katz Group's sports and entertainment properties (NHL, WHL, and AHL hockey franchises, the Edmonton Capitals baseball team, and Aquila Productions), suggesting that the holding of such properties was representative of a business model similar to AEG's.[27]

Other influential Edmontonians, land developers, and various quasi-public institutions like the Downtown Business Association also began to increase political pressure. As he had done four years earlier in conversation with David Staples to initiate discussions about a new arena, Cal Nichols, a former co-owner of the Oilers, reiterated the importance of a new facility for the financial well-being of the Oilers: "The future of the Oilers franchise won't be secure in Edmonton unless a new arena is built...[It] has got to work [financially]."[28] The longer the project took to get off the ground, he warned, "the more expensive an arena project will be."[29]

In late 2009, the Edmonton Economic Development Corporation (EEDC), a city agency, released its own economic impact assessment of the proposed development, just as it had done over a decade earlier when it had prepared a glowing, if now discredited, report that the Oilers contributed millions of dollars and jobs to the local economy in order to secure millions of dollars of public funds to renovate Rexall Place. The EEDC produced a "fantasy document"[30] claiming that the construction of a new downtown arena would generate 30,000 person-years of work and $1.5 billion in wages, employing 6,000 people. Patrick LaForge lauded the EEDC's prediction of the project's economic potential: "For me, it frames how do you say 'it's big.' You can say it with language, but the numbers tell a better story."[31] The numbers were, of course, pure speculation, and EEDC President Ron Gilbertson conceded that "the EEDC analysis didn't include a study to determine what demand there might be for office space or other components of the complex."[32] While these types of economic impact analyses often inflate projections to "justify a position that either sports organizations or community elected officials have adopted or are proposing,"[33] the *Journal* published these numbers in a front page story, with no discussion of the methods employed in the report or even an acknowledgement that such reports are produced by lobby groups and organizations with vested interests to sway public opinion.

While boosters celebrated the EEDC's analysis, critics raised concerns, including the fact that it hadn't been made public. The Canadian Taxpayers Federation submitted yet another FOIP request to gain a clearer picture of the economic assumptions underlying the EEDC's claims. As the Federation pointed out, these types of arena developments largely shift existing spending and investment within a city, rather than create new wealth; economic impact assessments, moreover, tend to rely on gross benefit analyses instead of calculating the net economic impact. However, the EEDC refused to release this information, claiming that it was bound by a confidentiality agreement with the Katz Group.

Some city councillors had similar concerns. Councillor Linda Sloan contacted the EEDC to request additional information, including material about the confidentiality agreement the city agency had signed. In response, the EEDC said that it had been approached "a number of months ago" by the Katz Group to provide an estimate of the anticipated, potential economic activity that would accompany the proposed downtown arena development, and had signed the confidentiality agreement as a result of being provided with "some preliminary information regarding the proposed complex."[34] The EEDC conceded that its analysis was not necessarily "an economic impact report on the proposed complex, but more of a high-level estimate," and that once it had delivered its commissioned analysis to the Katz Group, the latter had requested that the EEDC issue a "news release indicating the results and the benefits for Edmonton for the vision of a downtown entertainment district."[35] Finally, in response to Councillor Sloan's request to review written reports and additional documentation, the EEDC admitted that it had not actually provided the Katz Group with a formal report and that it could provide no economic data in support of its claims.[36]

In response to a FOIP request that we submitted in 2017—nearly a decade after the organization was first approached by the Katz Group—the EEDC still refused to release a full, unredacted copy of its impact assessment, insisting that it remained bound by the original confidentiality agreement. We were, however, given access to a portion of the report, and asked economist Dr. Brad Humphreys to review it. He found that the EEDC relied on the usual assumptions and procedures that have historically produced biased and inflated assessments in support of development agendas, including: the use of sales instead of household income multipliers; the misrepresentation of employment multipliers; the inclusion of local spectators; the failure to define the area of interest accurately; and, crucially, the omission of opportunity costs and other costs associated with the development.[37] In sum, he stated, "These estimates are crap for the same reason the Calgary Olympic estimates are crap...as all these things go, no policy should ever be made on estimates like this."[38]

Despite these coordinated promotional efforts, subsidizing a new arena development remained unpopular, especially at a time of economic recession. Considerable skepticism also remained about claims of the Oilers' financial vulnerability in the post-lockout era. Indeed, a month earlier, *Forbes* had released its annual list of estimated NHL team values, in which, for the 2008/09 NHL season, the Oilers ranked 24th of 30 franchises in value, but were considerably more profitable than most NHL franchises, with an estimated operating income of US$9.4 million. By way of comparison, the fourth most valuable franchise, the Philadelphia Flyers, was less profitable than the Oilers, with an estimated operating income of only US$3.1 million.[39]

The *Forbes* numbers were predictably dismissed by the Oilers as inaccurate, although Patrick LaForge later claimed that the franchise had a "break-even" year. In the months ahead, executives from the Oilers categorically asserted, like Peter Pocklington in the

1990s, that the franchise was losing money and had, in fact, been unprofitable for years. And while the Oilers were clearly a profitable franchise even while playing in Rexall Place—at least according to *Forbes* and other sources—Katz was also one of the wealthiest and most influential men in Canada, ranking 17th on *Canadian Business'* annual listing of the 100 richest Canadians, with a net worth of over $2 billion in 2009. It was implausible that he could not afford to build his own arena.

Thin Ice

The coordinated promotional push that marked the end of 2009 continued into 2010—with NHL commissioner Gary Bettman arriving in Edmonton to insist that a new, publicly-financed arena was necessary for the Oilers. Following a meeting with Oilers executives Patrick LaForge and Bob Black, Bettman enthused: "The proposal is very exciting, very compelling and I think it's very important for the franchise." He then spelled out the orchestrated cycle of planned facility obsolescence: "This is the second-oldest building in the league and if this team is going to have success long-term they need a new rink."[40] Of course, long-term success for Bettman meant ensuring that NHL owners garnered as much profit as possible—moving away from revenues based largely on gate receipts to revenues generated by new facilities and land development schemes—thus dramatically increasing the valuation of their franchises.

The next day, Bettman went to Calgary to promote the arena proposal of the Flames' ownership group: "There's an economic reality to what new arenas provide. If the Flames are going to continue to be successful and stable, ultimately, they are going to need a new arena."[41] The Oilers had long argued that they needed to control all revenue from a new, publicly-financed arena to ensure a level playing field with the Flames, and Bettman now claimed that the Flames were not economically sustainable without their own new arena.[42]

In early 2010, Simon Farbrother replaced Al Maurer as city manager. Maurer, a city employee since 1970, when Edmontonians voted down the proposed Omniplex downtown development in a plebiscite, would offer some advice to proponents of a new, publicly-financed downtown arena in anticipation of the emergence of more strident public opposition: "I think the real lesson there is don't underestimate the public, that they support the downtown arena. The Omniplex was a real great idea, but in the end, there wasn't that public support. I could see the same thing happening here."[43] Arena proponents at city hall would heed this advice by rigidly circumscribing public debate, and by sidestepping the prospect of another plebiscite altogether. As Mayor Mandel noted: "I don't believe a plebiscite is in the best interest of the citizens. We were elected to make decisions and those decisions need to be made by city council."[44] Council, though, had never publicly debated the findings of the *City Shaping* report, and some councillors would soon complain about the information gaps that prevented them from making fully informed decisions on behalf of their constituents.

Maurer's departure also meant that Northlands had lost a long-standing contact at city hall, and the organization would quickly discover that the new city manager was not interested in cultivating a similar relationship. Farbrother accepted both the legitimacy of the new business model of the NHL and its ability to sustain the Oilers for the foreseeable future, and the importance of a new, city-owned arena that would revitalize the downtown. Despite the success of Northlands' increasingly lucrative concert business, by 2010, the well-publicized power struggle between Northlands and the Katz Group had reached its nadir; they hadn't met since their acrimonious meeting in September 2009, when executives from Katz Group delivered their "take-it-or-leave-it ultimatum."[45]

Executives from the Katz Group were at the same time aggressively lobbying city councillors to fast-track a rezoning application for the downtown land it had assembled. In anticipation, the Katz Group unveiled in February 2010 its proposal for a $1.4-billion entertainment and sports district with a new arena, a community rink, office towers, a new casino, and an enclosed Winter Garden/public plaza over 104 Avenue—the latter being the costly solution to the main problem associated with this site that had been identified in the HOK report. Instead of showcasing its vision to city council and taxpayers—its supposed partners in the new development—the Katz Group made its first public presentation to an assemblage of local developers from the Building Owners and Managers Association of Edmonton.

The plan, announced by Bob Black, staked out the Katz Group's initial bargaining position for the upcoming negotiations with the city in a manner that was audaciously one-sided. It represented a radical departure from the informal agreement struck behind closed doors years earlier, and from the public–private financing models proposed more recently in the *City Shaping* report. The city would build the arena on land assembled by the Katz Group, to the company's specifications and design, while financing a debt of $450 million. Without any reference to other financing mechanisms— including a ticket tax—the Katz Group further proposed that the city implement a CRL that would capture rising property taxes associated with the surrounding developments in the new arena district to pay off its loan and interest payments. And instead of honouring the organization's original commitment to invest $100 million in the construction of the arena itself, the Katz Group now proposed to direct the equivalent sum of money to ancillary developments— a classic "bait and switch" tactic reminiscent of those deployed by developers in the 1970s and 1980s. Finally, and not surprisingly, the Katz Group proposed that it control and operate the city-owned facility and receive all of its revenues.

To some pundits, the Katz Group's aggressive opening salvo seemed little more than the action of "spoiled, entitled brats"[46] arrogantly dictating to the city of Edmonton, and hence to taxpayers, their expectations for a new facility and an enormous public subsidy. The benefits of this proposal for the Katz Group were nothing short of extraordinary. It would sell re-zoned land, at market value, to the city of Edmonton, which would then finance and build a costly new facility that the Katz Group would operate and control. The Katz Group would benefit from the increase in the value of the land surrounding the facility and would retain a monopoly on ancillary land development, while the city would assume most of the risk associated with repaying the loan and the costs of servicing the debt through a CRL. Still, as the economist Brad Humphreys noted, these types of extravagant claims on public resources were by now common across the continent, and entirely consistent with the professional sports playbook associated with these political debates: "It sounds on the face of it like an outlandish request, but teams all over North America get deals like this done all the time. As a matter of public policy, we let professional sports operate this way."[47]

The Katz Group had, in other words, proposed a number of radical changes to the public–private financing model, and its executives were now attempting to negotiate, at least publicly, an entirely new financing agreement, even before starting formal discussions with the city. There was no mention, for example, of the *City Shaping* report's recommendations, including the crucial one that the full amount of a new arena's annual surplus cash flow be available for arena debt servicing. Nor was there any mention of a user pay model, or the injection of private funds from the Katz Group. Serious concerns remained, too, about the use of a CRL as the main financing mechanism, and whether sufficient property taxes would be raised by it to service the city's arena debt and eventually pay it off.

To illustrate these concerns, consider Edmonton City Centre, a large mall in downtown Edmonton, which in 2010 paid 1.4 percent of its assessed value in property taxes. If, in 2010, it was assumed that the arena would spur $1-billion worth of value in assessed new developments, only $14 million in new taxes would have been generated per year. However, annual payments on a $400-million loan over a 20-year term would have been roughly $31 million.[48] Clearly, in the case of the proposed arena, a CRL would be insufficient to cover the debt and interest payments. The city would also need to consider the potential decline in property values elsewhere if investment and spending shifted to the downtown core. In other cities, most notably San Diego, developers had to guarantee that they would make up the difference in CRL funding if ancillary development did not occur—a commitment that the Katz Group was neither willing, nor required, to make.

Still, the Katz Group's initial proposal aligned with the mayor's promise that the arena would be built "at no net cost to the city and without any increase in taxes or reallocation of civic infra-structure dollars," at least in theory.[49] Bob Black suggested that the city would have to borrow significantly less than the estimated $400 million if it could secure contributions from other levels of government. However, others, including a number of city council-lors, were far from pleased with the details of the Katz Group's proposal, including Don Iveson, who argued that private companies "shouldn't be allowed access to lower-cost government borrowing power earned by the 'fiscal discipline' of the public sector."[50]

Playing the Game

Mayor Mandel expressed his surprise at the proposal's lack of a significant private contribution to the new arena's financing and at the substantive alterations made to the original framework crafted years earlier, but he refused to condemn it. Instead, in the familiar terms of boosterism, he implored citizens not to reject it: "Let's not throw gasoline on it. Let's see what it is and try to be more of a city that wants to be a doing city rather than being a naysayer."[51] Executives from the Katz Group also downplayed threats that the Oilers might leave Edmonton without a new arena. Bob Black commented, "I'd be very disappointed with that kind of character-ization. I can tell you that Daryl Katz is somebody who believes this makes sense in Edmonton and that we will find a way to make sense of this in Edmonton."[52]

Katz rarely commented publicly, but in this instance he did, although his statements were carefully controlled—virtually every statement he made came through his employees or through boost-erish local media. In a pre-recorded interview with Bob Stauffer on 630 CHED, an AM station and the Oilers' official radio broadcaster, Katz "responded to queries lobbed at him by an employee."[53] He conflated public and private interests, emphasizing the importance of a new arena to both the city of Edmonton and the Oilers: "It's crucial as far as we see it. We have a once in a generation oppor-tunity to do something very special for the city. And, at the same time, develop a sustainable model for the long term for NHL hockey and for the Oilers in Edmonton. [It will] put a model in place that solidifies and sustains professional hockey for the long term in our community."[54] Katz also promoted a funding model for a new arena that included absolutely no private investment whatsoever:

> *The funding model that we advanced sees the city owning the arena.*
> *Our contribution in that regard can best be leveraged by facilitating*
> *a tax base that can assist the city in paying for the arena over a long*
> *period of time. The entire funding model would change, of course, if*
> *we, the Katz Group, were to own the arena, but the model that was*
> *advanced contemplated something different...and that's what makes*
> *the most sense in that context.*[55]

Of course, this latter option—with Katz owning and debt financing the arena himself—was never explored, and it was certainly never raised during this or any of the other softball interviews.

Katz's vision for a new downtown arena development was predictably supported by those who had the most to gain from it, namely civic boosters, hotel owners, commercial real estate agents, and downtown developers. There were, however, some concerns. Edmonton was only just emerging from the 2008 economic downturn, and some in the business community noted that new hotels and office buildings could only be filled after a full economic recovery and substantial growth. The downtown office vacancy rate was already at 7.3 percent[56] (before the opening of the city-owned Epcor Tower in 2011, which would increase that rate). Other analysts recognized that a new arena development would shift existing investment and spending within the city and concentrate it downtown around future Katz properties, rather than create or entice new businesses from outside of Edmonton.[57] Hoteliers relished the prospect of attracting new customers, with a downtown hotel vacancy rate that sat at 60 percent in 2009.[58] Developers who had purchased downtown land at reduced prices, meanwhile, knew that they stood to profit handsomely as property values grew around the proposed arena district.

In mid-February, aware that its proposed funding model—with neither a private capital contribution nor a ticket tax—had profoundly irritated both city council and the mayor, the Katz Group implemented a public relations (PR) strategy aimed at swaying public opinion in favour of the arena. On February 13th, the Katz Group's development agenda received a timely and enthusiastic endorsement in a *Journal* editorial:

> *Daryl Katz is absolutely right about seizing the rare and priceless opportunity to boost Edmonton's downtown core with a massive redevelopment centered around a new arena...If we are wise as a community, we will figure out a way to capitalize on these assets, and a way to make our vision of our town a force in the long, hard bargaining that lies ahead.*[59]

On February 14th, a *Journal* op-ed written by Katz promoted his proposal, while defending the reversal of his commitment to invest $100 million in the new arena:

> *That said, I do believe the funding model makes good on my original commitment and that it is a much better way to finance the project than if I were to simply pay construction costs. That's because in the model we have proposed—which was designed for a scenario in which the city would own the arena—you can't separate the private-sector investment from the financing the city would provide to help fund the arena construction costs. The two are tied together. The arena creates the draw for the private-sector investment and the private-sector investment generates the revenues to pay for the arena.*[60]

Of course, neither Katz's op-ed nor the earlier editorial acknowledged that a privately-owned arena that attracted investment and development could also pay for the construction costs. Katz provided a host of arguments similar to those already made by the mayor, including a one-sided explanation of the CRL financing mechanism, while downplaying the extraordinary gains he stood to make:

But the benefits of our proposed model go far beyond that. By lever-
aging my investment in the project to attract more than $1 billion in
additional development, we can expand the city's economic base and
generate sufficient tax revenues to pay back the city's investment. And,
once that's done, the revenue generated by the development will fill
the city's bank account for decades to come. We can do all that with
no increase in property taxes for Edmontonians...Surely this is also a
better investment than putting another $250 million into the modern-
ization of Rexall Place, which would offer no return to the city and do
nothing to revitalize downtown.[61]

The Katz Group also invested in a social media strategy that included a glossy promotional website (www.revitalizedowntown.ca), a Twitter account, an Edmonton arena district fan page on Facebook, and a YouTube promotional video starring Katz. The website featured testimonials from legendary Oilers (and Katz's personal friends) Mark Messier and Kevin Lowe about the importance of a new arena for both the franchise and the city. The YouTube video emphasized Rosentraub's three "successful" case studies of Columbus, San Diego, and Indianapolis. Such carefully controlled digital platforms have become standard elements in the marketing arsenal of professional sport franchises in their attempts to direct the discourse associated with these types of divisive policy debates.[62] In 2010, the debate continued to rage on social media, especially on Twitter, which became a digital battleground in this policy debate as grass-roots opposition groups and other critics contested the claims made by the Katz Group, the city of Edmonton, and their supporters in the media.

Conflicting Interests?

On February 18th, in his first public speech after the Katz Group's initial proposal, the mayor now sternly acknowledged that the Katz Group's withdrawal of its $100-million contribution to the arena represented a "material change" from earlier discussions.[63] However, instead of insisting on a larger commitment of private capital before beginning formal negotiations, the mayor suggested to his audience of developers at the Urban Development Institute a "new" financing mechanism: a ticket tax on all events at a new arena. Of course, this idea was far from new and had been discussed by the mayor and the Oilers behind closed doors for several years as a way to cover 25 percent of the total cost of a new arena. The ALC had also suggested such a tax in the *City Shaping* report, because it would spare the Katz Group the immediate expense of contributing to arena construction and minimize the likelihood that municipal property taxes would have to be raised or existing grants redirected to help pay for it. It was also, as Mayor Mandel noted, a way of capturing some revenue from people who lived outside Edmonton: "And the reason you have to have the ticket tax is as much [for] the people from Sherwood Park, from Lloydminster, from Grand Prairie—all of [the people of] northern Alberta benefit from this arena and they had to pay something, and so the ticket tax is an indirect [way] of them paying their share."[64] The negotiations between the city and the Katz Group were thus well underway, even if they had not been formally sanctioned by city council.

By this point, a pattern was beginning to emerge in the *Journal*'s coverage of the debate. Only a day after the mayor's speech, it published three articles addressing the substance of his talk. The first, by reporter Gordon Kent, described the speech for readers.[65] The other two, an article by city hall columnist (and later city councillor) Scott McKeen[66] and an editorial headlined "Ticket-Tax Idea Will Help Serve Arena,"[67] both lauded the mayor, his plan, and the project itself. They appeared together with no counterpoint. The *Journal* would continue to support the arena project enthusiastically throughout the debate. The tabloid *Edmonton Sun*, in comparison, devoted fewer resources to covering the arena debate, but would also take a more critical editorial stance, although the plan would receive the full endorsement of the *Sun*'s prominent sports columnist, Terry Jones.

More critical coverage of the debate appeared outside of Edmonton, especially in the pages of the national daily newspapers, although these articles were infrequent. An article in *The Globe and Mail* in April 2010, written by Josh Wingrove, a former reporter for the *Edmonton Journal*, offered a sharper assessment of the types of conflicts of interest and political machinations that were already at play:

> the city committee that recommended a new arena included the Oilers' chief executive officer and one of the owners at the time. Also, Mr. Katz is a director of the mortgage company that employs Mr. Huntley, the chairman of the board of Northlands, the team's current landlord. And the husband of popular Edmonton City Councillor Karen Leibovici is an executive at a Katz-owned company [Medicine Shoppe]. (Ms. Leibovici did not respond to an interview request, but the Mayor says it's up to her whether she votes when the issue reaches council.).[68]

According to one of Wingrove's sources, the city of Edmonton and the Katz Group were collaborating on promotional strategies, including the production of a boosterish primer on the CRL that was released by the city but paid for by the Katz Group. Wingrove also quoted a variety of academic sources (beyond the city's hired sport management consultants, such as economist Dr. Brad Humphreys and Dr. Bruce Johnson, a specialist in urban and sports economics), who challenged the economic arguments of pro-arena boosters and were critical of the argument that new arena and entertainment districts genuinely revitalized cities.

To be fair, both the *Edmonton Sun* and the *Edmonton Journal* ran stories that touched on Leibovici's perceived conflict of interest, although they treated it very differently. They acknowledged that Leibovici had secured independent legal counsel (as recommended by the *Municipal Government Act*) to confirm that she was not in a conflict of interest because she did not stand to personally benefit from the arena development. Indeed, as Leibovici reflected in an interview, she had fully considered the issue before the debate:

> That's why I secured a number of legal opinions. The first one that I got was from someone within Edmonton and the city clerk's office has it. But there were rumours that nobody in Edmonton is free from the influence of Daryl [Katz], so with the city's law department we found

somebody in Calgary who had no affiliation, had never done any work
for Daryl, and asked them for a legal opinion as well. But there was
no direct reporting or way that my husband could have been influ-
enced by Daryl [Katz] through his job and, in fact, about a year later
Medicine Shoppe was sold.[69]

While sympathetic to Leibovici and her family, an editorial in the
Sun argued that citizens would perceive her to be in conflict so she
should recuse "herself from decisions involving the Katz Group" to
help maintain the "integrity of democratic systems."[70] The *Journal*'s
city hall columnist, Scott McKeen, on the other hand, reassured
readers that Leibovici was "as impervious to lobbying as they
come," that "she was known for making up her own mind," and that
"she was one of the most thoughtful, hardworking and account-
able people to ever sit on city council."[71] McKeen, who was being
recruited to run for city council in the 2010 municipal election by
the mayor and people in the mayor's office, noted that Leibovici
"and [Stephen] Zepp [Leibovici's husband] have for years kept business affairs out of their private lives" and had "even kept city or
corporate secrets from each other."[72] McKeen provided Leibovici
with the opportunity to "clear the air," and she confirmed that, "At
this point, I imagine I'll be voting on it." Still, he cautioned her
to "keep a close eye on public reaction" in advance of an anticipated mayoral campaign, lest she risk inviting voter cynicism and
mistrust, which could "put a fine political career on ice."[73]

In the end, Leibovici's decision to vote on arena-related
motions was within the scope of the law, but the provincial statute
addressing conflicts of interest for elected officials is vaguely
worded, and this lack of clarity enabled her ongoing participation
in the debate despite what many saw as a violation of the spirit,
if not the letter, of the law. Other councillors were aware of her
predicament and were fielding questions and correspondence from
citizens concerned about it. Her decision to remain involved in the
early stages of the debate was, as Councillor Ed Gibbons recalled,
a source of both controversy and irritation because it undermined
public faith in the political process and in council itself: "I didn't

think she should have stayed while her husband was working for a guy who was blackmailing us basically."[74] In the years to come, Leibovici participated in every council discussion about the arena and consistently voted in favour—a pattern that, in hindsight, may have sowed seeds of mistrust among the electorate for later electoral campaigns and contributed to the failure of her 2013 mayoral campaign, even after the Katz Group sold Medicine Shoppe (and its Drug Trading Company) to the pharmaceutical giant McKesson for $920 million in January 2012.

The early stages of the arena debate, then, had severely eroded public confidence in the political process. There was a lack of transparency with both key reports and significant decisions associated with the arena debate, including the location of the facility, there were perceived conflicts of interest, there was the perception that Daryl Katz was exerting untoward influence on councillors and on the mayor, and there was the willingness of many in the local media to provide only positive coverage. In 2010, as well, the longstanding fiduciary requirement for elected officials to disclose all personal land holdings in the city of Edmonton (as well as those of their spouses) in their annual disclosure statement, submitted to the office of the city clerk, was eliminated just before the start of formal negotiations between the city and the Katz Group. The cumulative impact of all of these factors meant that many Edmontonians were already mistrustful of both their elected officials and of the arena proposal itself. All of these issues would only be exacerbated in the months ahead, as the Katz Group and other boosters intensified their lobbying efforts, and as council avoided public scrutiny by discussing arena-related matters behind closed doors.

8

SHOW ME THE MONEY

BY MARCH 2010, the Katz Group and senior officials from the city
of Edmonton were discussing both the proposed publicly-financed
arena development and the Katz Group's impending application to
rezone the downtown land it had assembled. The Katz Group had
also intensified its lobbying of councillors in advance of its rezoning
application, and various provincial leaders, including Ray Danyluk,
Alberta's minister of infrastructure, were hosted by Bob Black, the
Katz Group's executive vice president, sports and entertainment, in
the company's corporate box at Rexall Place.[1] The lobbying eventually had the desired effect. Councillor Bryan Anderson said: "I
actually looked in his [Katz's] soul in my office and I looked in his
eyes and saw his heart and I really believe that he wanted to transform our downtown in such a way that it would be talked about
forever and I never believed he was going to bail."[2]

Still, despite all of the increasingly intertwined promotional
activities by the Katz Group and the city of Edmonton, another
poll—conducted by TeleResearch for CTV Edmonton—indicated
that most citizens still opposed using public funds for a new downtown arena.[3] Aware of the level of opposition, councillors retreated
behind closed doors in early March to receive a verbal update from
Simon Farbrother, the city manager, on the status of the development. This would mark the first of many in-camera discussions

of this particularly divisive public issue—a pattern that would be amplified and extended once formal negotiations began in January 2011. On March 8th, an 11-page PowerPoint presentation entitled "Strategic Downtown Development," with the subheading "Katz Group Arena Proposal," was sent to all councillors in advance of the next meeting. The slides emphasized the utility of sport-related urban developments in the competition to retain people, featuring familiar images of "successful" developments like Nationwide Arena (Columbus), the Staples Center (Los Angeles), and Petco Park (San Diego), drawn from a March 2010 report written by sport management consultants Mark Rosentraub and Dan Mason called *A New Arena-Anchored Development in Edmonton: A Confluence of Public and Private Needs*.

Mason and Rosentraub had been retained once again on sole-source contracts explicitly to "support the establishment of the City's proposal for a downtown development" and to write a "detailed report that describes some of the arguments for why Edmonton should be considering a comprehensive downtown arena-anchored development project."[4] The consultants strictly adhered to their instructions: one section was simply called "Why Edmonton Should Insist on an Arena District." Administration had also instructed them to outline the "strategies used in Columbus, Los Angeles, and San Diego to highlight for the City's leadership the benefits and drawbacks of different frameworks of public, private, and public-private ownership," and to "look at the issues associated with the attraction and retention of human capital to advance corporate locations and business development of the city."[5] The 28-page report drew heavily on Rosentraub's 2009 book *Major League Winners* that had explored the same cities, although the book itself was not cited.

The in-camera slides, though, included two interesting schematics. The first slide, a broad map of the downtown core, showed the precise location of the Katz Group's proposed arena development to the north and south of 104 Avenue on the land holdings the company had assembled. It also highlighted some parcels of city-owned land between 104 and 105 Avenues, between 102 and 103

Streets—another municipal resource that would be dedicated to the new arena but wouldn't appear as a cost.

The second schematic showed the Katz Group's initial plans for the proposed new arena development adjacent to the Baccarat Casino, which included a community rink and a Winter Garden extending over 104 Avenue, and which would eventually contain restaurants, bars, and concessions, and was the crucial link to the Katz-owned properties to the south. The schematic also showed two towers, including an office building that would eventually become the Edmonton Tower. Remarkably, these two slides showed exactly where the arena would be built (though with some small changes, e.g., the community rink was eventually built on the north-east side of the development), even though city council had not endorsed the plan or even discussed potential locations. The Katz Group had, in other words, decided where the city-owned arena would be built and outlined the location in this "working draft proposal" without any consultation or debate whatsoever. The inclusion of a community rink and the Winter Garden also shows that, even at this early stage, both parties were aware that the arena district would include a range of other amenities that would dramatically increase its final cost beyond the publicly stated $450 million—a fact that proponents didn't want to be made public.

The slides concluded by noting that discussions with the Katz Group and the development of an "integrated communications plan" between the public and private partners were "underway." Foreshadowing its near-complete exclusion from the deliberations between the city and the Katz Group, neither the slides nor the accompanying report made a single reference to Northlands.

Strategic Zoning

In early April, at the mayor's annual speech to the Edmonton Chamber of Commerce (which had already endorsed the publicly-financed arena development), Stephen Mandel reassured his audience that city hall was "starting to see the scope of the plans" and that "the checklist and due diligence on this project will be very big...and transparent."[6] The mayor then met formally with the *Journal*'s editorial board, which repeated his claim that the final price of the arena "may not be as high as the $400-million figure being bandied about...and that money saved on otherwise unavoidable Rexall improvements might make the city's eventual involvement seem less outrageous."[7] Finally, the mayor conceded that, having announced his intention to run for a third term in October's municipal election, he would likely have to sell the arena project to citizens "more, probably, than I want."[8] He wanted to "take some of the emotion out of [the debate]...There's a need for more facts."[9]

By the end of April, the Katz Group had submitted its application to rezone 16 acres of land in the city core to support a sports-entertainment development. Crucial information about the proposed development—design proposals, budget numbers, timelines—was absent from the application, and many councillors thought it was premature given the lack of discussion about either the funding or financing for a new arena or the extent of the city's potential involvement. Moreover, as councillor Bryan Anderson noted, the Katz Group's rezoning application was considerably more extensive than anticipated, and much more public discussion was needed to address the project's potential impacts: "They're asking to get rid of the...park and close a road, then have a discussion about whether the use is a good idea [and] who's going to pay for it."[10] The city would eventually close a portion of 103 Street, which was sold to the Katz Group in 2014 for $465,000.[11]

Even more worrying, the rezoning application was orchestrated to avoid immediate scrutiny from council and to ensure that councillors would be removed from future political deliberations about the broader development. Columnist Paula Simons argued that the rezoning application was designed to limit genuine democratic discussion:

> The zoning application will now be circulated through city administration to garner feedback from all the affected departments, from transportation to parks and recreation to planning. Then, there will

be a public hearing before council. Then council will vote on the total rezoning of the parcel. Now, here's the nifty strategic bit. If and when council votes to accept the proposed rezoning of the parcel, the Katz Group won't have to come back to council for political approval of any of its actual buildings. Council won't get to have any say on the design or site of the arena itself nor on the design, size or precise loca-tion of the casino, the hotels, the condos, the student residences, the office towers or any other part of the hypothetical project. Each time a new piece of the plan comes along, the Katz Group would only need to apply for a development permit. City bureaucrats could still turn them down. Concerned neighbours could still appeal to the Subdivision and Development Appeal Board. But councillors would be out of the discussion. Debate in the "political arena," pardon the pun, would be closed. [12]

Simons' analysis was spot on. The prospect of circumventing city council in this public–private partnership afforded additional polit-ical benefits that could, in turn, be translated into material gain:

By asking council to "pre-approve" the master plan, to give its blessing to the very general proposal in advance, the Katz folks could save themselves a lot of time-consuming and expensive political battles down the road. They'd never again have to go cap in hand to city councillors and the mayor, never again have to lobby and curry political favour. They'd be in a much better position, thus, to recruit investors...to arrange the massive finance package this $1-billion plan would require. [13]

All of these developments, however, only highlighted the extent to which the Katz Group was attempting to manipulate, if not bypass altogether, the democratic process in support of its own interests.

Much of the downtown business community pledged its imme-diate support of both the publicly-financed arena development and the Katz Group's rezoning application. Ignoring all research on the economic impacts of new arena developments, Martin Salloum, CEO of the Chamber of Commerce, a bastion of free enterprise, made the classic booster assertion that a city-financed arena and entertainment district would "significantly benefit Edmonton businesses and all Edmontonians for many years to come."[14] For critics, though, these sentimental retreats to boosterism illustrated the extent to which arena proponents and the business community, especially the Chamber of Commerce, were prepared to lobby for corporate welfare when it suited their economic interests. Nor were these boosters prepared to acknowledge that other buildings (the Epcor Office tower, several high-rise condos, etc.) were already under construction near the proposed arena development "without public largesse," as one letter writer bluntly noted:

> Most importantly, he [Salloum] neglects to tell us why, for the first time ever, Edmonton taxpayers should build something and then hand over all its revenues to a third party—for free!...The foremost principle of free enterprise is that the entity which derives the upside gains also takes the downside risks. If Daryl Katz wants all the revenue from an arena, then by all means let him build it—with private financing.[15]

Certainly, the Katz Group was aware of these types of concerns among both the public and councillors, who were facing a municipal election in October. Councillor Don Iveson summed up these concerns: "There's an irony here, which is that someone else is designing a building, which the last I heard we're being asked to fund and own."[16]

In response to these issues and questions, as well as concerns raised by architects and the Downtown Community League over the proposed pedestrian crossing over 104 Avenue, the Katz Group held an "open house" at the Art Gallery of Alberta on the 6th of May. They exhibited glossy pictures of the proposed development, and representatives from the Katz Group and various consultants were there to give a sales pitch. Details about financing, though, were conspicuously absent. Councillor Iveson thought it was little more than a glib infomercial: "This was about the public and trying to sell them on the concept. The information we need is the banking side of this, who's going to finance the thing...I see that the strategy they're employing is to try to get people onside."[17] Some citizens, though, used the occasion to voice their own opposition and hand out self-produced flyers announcing "Edmonton Taxpayers Say No! To The Mandel/Katz Hockey Arena."

Other councillors, including Linda Sloan, continued to express concern about the political process to date, and the Katz Group's ill-timed rezoning application and the impending public hearing in June: "I think it's very premature...Is their business model reliant on public financing? That's the first question. If we consider and approve the zoning in advance of having the final information, it can be perceived that we have given the first level of approval for the arena district."[18] For many councillors, the effect of the new development on Rexall Place and Northlands also needed to be considered in advance of any rezoning hearing or any commitment of public funds to a new development. And, as Sloan noted, Northlands had now been excluded from the current discussions: "It seems to me it strikes a death-knell for Rexall Place without any consideration for what it means to Northlands, what it means to the historic investment in that facility."[19] City staff stated that the absence of crucial information from the Katz Group's rezoning application meant that administration could not confirm its support.

The Katz Group stressed the distinction between land-use issues and questions of funding—a distinction fully supported by Mayor Mandel. Though technically correct, this distinction provided a convenient and timely loophole, and prevented council from asking questions about financing at a public hearing focussed on land use. Knowing that the Katz Group's proposal was going to require hundreds of millions of public dollars, administration could have convened a briefing session separate from the public rezoning hearing to address such questions, especially in light of concerns already expressed by council and citizens even before formal negotiations began.

Recognizing that they risked derailing the arena development with a rushed rezoning proposal, the Katz Group announced in June that it would defer the public zoning process until after the municipal election. The delay gave the Katz Group more time to work with administration to revise its application and align the rezoning proposal with the city's Downtown Plan, which would be formally approved on July 7th. The plan was structured to help prepare the political terrain for the Katz Group's development by endorsing a sports and entertainment district as a "concurrent catalyst project" on the "station lands"—the precise location of the Katz Group's land holdings.[20]

Still, while municipal bureaucracy was providing assistance to the development, the Katz Group continued to limit political debate by requesting that all future negotiations be held in private, much to the irritation of council. By this point, council's frustration was high: crucial reports were never seen or even discussed; the Katz Group had abandoned its pledge to provide $100 million toward the construction of a new arena; and ties with Northlands had been severed. This last decision angered its influential supporters, especially those on council. Even with a political process designed to support the Katz Group's interests, deliberations were antagonistic as the Katz Group continually tried to strengthen its bargaining position.

With constituents' concerns mounting, and without concrete public information, council met on June 23, 2010 behind closed doors to receive another verbal update from the city manager, and consequently agreed to invite the Katz Group to make a formal public presentation on July 21st, while directing staff to prepare a report on the merits of, and funding options for, a new arena. Council hoped that delaying the rezoning hearing and inviting the Katz Group to make a public presentation would allow more information to be made public and reset the deliberations before the 2010 municipal election. A similar invitation was not, however, extended to Northlands.

The Katz Group, inexperienced in navigating the bureaucratic channels at city hall and frustrated by the lack of clarity over policies and procedures associated with such a divisive political issue, was thus given a chance to regroup. NHL commissioner Gary Bettman and his deputy, Bill Daly, arrived in Edmonton in late June, ready to

help. Bettman and Daly also met with the mayor, who joined Katz
for a private meeting later the same day. Mandel characterized the
meeting with Bettman as little more than a "nice discussion about
the NHL," but said he also provided an "update" on the status of the
arena deliberations "out of respect for the commissioner."[21] Mandel
also explained the importance of the upcoming public meeting with
the Katz Group in mid-July, timed to follow the NHL's entry draft in
Los Angeles (June 25–26), which the mayor planned to attend. These
meetings, plus the mayor's visit to Los Angeles, provided further
opportunities for private discussions. Powerful people in these types
of debates "have far superior 'unofficial access' to decision makers
than do average citizens—access that often occurs in stadium luxury
boxes!"[22] Mayor Mandel also took the opportunity to remind citizens that "Daryl is a great guy and someone who is committed to
Edmonton"[23] in order to quash lingering fears that the Oilers
might leave.

Sucker Punch?

Attempts to advance the political dialogue and restructure the terms
of the arena debate, however, fell apart when news emerged that
Oilers representatives had gone to Hamilton, Ontario, to explore the
possibility of taking over the lease of Copps Coliseum "to control
the potential arrival of a relocated or expansion NHL team."[24] The
Oilers denied that the trip represented a threat to move the franchise, although Patrick LaForge, the Oilers president, conceded that
it was "optically not perfect."[25] Major leagues deliberately restrict
the number of franchises to ensure that aspirant cities—and empty
arenas—can be used as leverage by existing franchise owners in
their negotiations to secure new publicly-funded arenas and other
concessions from municipalities. For example, after the owner
of the Pittsburgh Penguins, Mario Lemieux, had secured a new,
US$321-million, publicly-funded arena, he confessed to having taken
several excursions to other cities simply to apply political pressure
in his negotiations with both the city of Pittsburgh and the state of
Pennsylvania, as per the NHL's playbook:

We had to do a few things to put pressure on the city and the state, but our goal was to remain here in Pittsburgh all the way. Those trips to Kansas City and Vegas and other cities was just to go and have a nice dinner and come back...[Pressure] was felt, and that was the important thing. A lot of things happened throughout the negotiations. Ups and downs. That was just a way for us to put more pressure, and we knew it would work at the end of the day.[26]

Lemieux's threats had been backed up by both Gary Bettman and Bill Daly during negotiations with Pittsburgh. Commissioners routinely make these types of explicit and unpopular threats, more than do owners themselves, and both Bettman and Daly have admirably performed their roles over the years, including most recently in Calgary and Ottawa. In Edmonton, though, Katz soon broke from this pattern by making such threats directly—a bitter reminder to Oilers fans of Peter Pocklington's bargaining tactics, although Katz was asking for far more money than Pocklington ever did.

Despite having been spurned by both the Katz Group and the city, in July 2010, Northlands hired well-known sports executive Richard Andersen to replace Ken Knowles as president and CEO. Andersen had been lured to Edmonton from San Diego, where he had most recently served as executive vice president of the Padres, that city's major league baseball franchise. The Padres play in Petco Park—a facility used by both the Katz Group and the sport management consultants as a successful case study of a publicly-financed sport development. Andersen tried to defend Northlands' interests and its historical role in the sports and entertainment business in Edmonton, and his hiring showed that senior executives at Northlands continued to believe that it would play a major role in the operation of a new, city-owned arena in Edmonton.

Northlands also reminded council that the Katz Group was not the city's only option, announcing a new reduced estimate to renovate Rexall Place for $175–190 million. Outgoing CEO Ken Knowles pointed out that the building was only in the middle of its life cycle and could realistically function for another 30 years.[27]

Applying political pressure. Edmonton Oilers owner Daryl Katz (left) speaks with
NHL commissioner Gary Bettman during the second period in Edmonton at a game
between the Edmonton Oilers and the Atlanta Thrashers on Saturday, February 19,
2011. [Canadian Press/John Ulan]

This assessment was confirmed in a report produced for the city
later that year, which concluded that the building's structural,
mechanical, and electrical components had been effectively maintained and its condition was good. Despite its monopoly in arena
operations, though, Northlands' credibility and status had eroded
since the 1970s, and it just wasn't used to defending itself politically. As Knowles himself conceded, "I'd speak at the functions
and I'd say you know Northlands is well known but it's not known
well and unfortunately the community didn't really understand or
appreciate...the role...Northlands played in the community."[28] For
decades, Northlands had operated behind closed doors through
various political channels and through its connections with the
key players in the local business community and various levels of

government, a pattern that only reinforced the perception of the organization as an old boys' club.

In advance of its public presentation to council, the Katz Group was staking its own claim. In a letter to council from Bob Black dated June 29, 2010 and leaked to *Journal* columnist Scott McKeen for a column published on July 14th, but one which a number of councillors had never actually received, the Katz Group suggested that councillors "should also be aware that our 'ask' of the city will be significantly less than the $400 million that has been so widely reported."[29] According to McKeen, it gave council a "heads-up on Katz's recent foray into Hamilton"[30]—a trip that had ignited a fire-storm of criticism, but was supposedly intended only to facilitate the creation of a national sports and entertainment business.

The letter also confirmed that the Katz Group would honour its original commitment to contribute $100 million to the construction of a city-owned arena. It "goes on to say," McKeen reported, that "Katz and his people have been talking to Mandel and city officials for months. It makes it sound like the $100-million flipflop was merely an idea being batted around, instead of a tactical error."[31] For many councillors, as well as many members of the public, this letter offered a desperately needed demonstration of good faith and some assurance that a crucial piece of the funding plan was in place. It would be pointed to by proponents as further justification for the exclusion of Northlands, which, unlike the Katz Group, was not prepared to invest its own capital in a new arena development. Northlands had, of course, been subsidizing the Oilers for decades with assistance from the city, while also managing its own operations.

The prospect of a new arena development gained further political traction with the publication of a financial report by the city's chief financial officer (CFO), Lorna Rosen.[32] Released on July 21, 2010, shortly after it became public knowledge that the Katz Group had re-committed to contributing $100 million to the construction of the arena, Rosen's well-timed report outlined various funding options to cover the cost of the capital construction of a $450-million arena without raising residential property taxes. These options had, of course, already been determined years earlier behind closed doors.

Rosen identified three well-known potential sources of funding: a ticket surcharge that could generate sufficient revenue to cover debt servicing (raising approximately $110–135 million); a CRL that could cover another $120–140 million; and Katz's $100-million contribution. She noted that the original *City Shaping* report had recommended a "balanced" public–private funding model and a 30 percent equity contribution, but clearly $100 million was as much as Katz was prepared to offer, even though he would receive all revenues from the city-owned facility. Rosen's combined higher-end estimates, though, added up to only $375 million at best, well below the total estimated cost that had been set two years earlier. To cover the gap, other potential revenue sources were needed, including funding from the other two levels of government, the proceeds from personal seat licences, and the transfer to the new arena of the city's existing commitments to the operation of Rexall Place.

While Rosen's report was both "readable and comprehensible,"[33] its conclusions relied on at least two significant assumptions. The first was that property values, and therefore municipal property taxes, would continue to rise in and around the new development, with no consideration of the possibility of an economic downturn during the 20 years of the CRL or a decline in property values, despite the realities of Alberta's oil-based, boom-bust economy. Similarly, her report ignored the possibility of any decline in the value of other downtown properties as a result of an oversupply of commercial office space and condominium developments.

The report's second main assumption was that property taxes from other parts of the city would remain stable. However, increased downtown property tax revenue, which would be dedicated to paying for the new arena, was likely to be offset by tax losses elsewhere in the city, meaning that property taxes would have to go up to cover municipal services and expenses. Other hidden costs that regularly accompany new arena and stadium developments, as well as some that had already been identified—the Winter Garden, a new community rink, an LRT connection, and forgiving Northlands' outstanding debt—were not included in the $450-million estimate.

The CRL, however, would remain the crucial financing mechanism. It would capture "new" tax revenue to pay for the new arena instead of going to the general revenue fund. Moreover, one of the advantages of a CRL—and a considerable attraction for Edmonton's city council—is that it allows a municipality to divert the payment of provincial education taxes to fund infrastructure projects, like Rogers Place, within the CRL boundary. In other words, both parts of the property tax collected by the city would be diverted to pay for the new arena: the city's portion of property tax away from its general revenues, and hundreds of millions of dollars in education property tax collected on behalf of the province.

The risks of such a speculative financing mechanism were obvious. What if there was not sufficient development within the CRL boundary to cover a portion of the cost of the arena? Would a new arena trigger *new development* (i.e., development that would not have occurred otherwise), or would it simply shift existing spending and investment from other areas of the city to within the CRL boundary? What would happen to the city's general tax revenue if increases in property tax revenue within an expansive CRL boundary were, for a long time, unavailable for city-wide services? And, crucially, if other areas of the city declined while increases in downtown property tax revenue remained dedicated to paying for the arena and other downtown infrastructure, would property taxes need to be raised to provide city-wide services? The implications of these questions were never fully addressed; it was simply assumed by city officials that property tax values within the CRL area would continue to grow.

Still, despite these concerns, a substantial amount of coordinated political and promotional work had obviously already happened behind closed doors in advance of the Katz Group's crucial public presentation to council later that month. The Rosen report was, in this respect, intended not only to provide council with specific, if familiar, information, but to guide the political process to a preferred outcome. It also signalled to the Katz Group that the city was prepared to play its part in financing the arena development according to the terms set years earlier, and that the option of renovating Rexall Place had been discarded altogether. In retrospect, however, it's striking that the city's CFO would go on record with a financial report supporting a proposal from the private sector before it had even been discussed at a public hearing.

Meeting Mr. Katz

All of this political momentum was temporarily derailed on the day of Katz's appearance before council, with the publication of an article in the *Journal* entitled "Katz Arena Site Ranked Fourth; City Councillors Never Discussed Consultants' Report."[34] Katz's land had, in fact, been ranked fifth and seventh of eight potential sites evaluated by HOK, and rated poorly in comparison to the preferred site at 106 Street and Jasper Avenue and well behind the option of building at Northlands. Still, the article confirmed that council had not discussed the results of the HOK study (or the *City Shaping* report); some councillors couldn't recall ever seeing the site rankings. As Councillor Brian Anderson asked, "Are we going to confine our discussion to what [land] Katz owns? If he isn't paying for it, how does he get to design it and decide who operates it?"[35] Councillor Don Iveson openly criticized the potential location of the arena, which did not align with the city's pre-existing policies to revitalize Jasper Avenue and The Quarters: "We don't have a revital- ization plan for that parking lot. The point is that we never debated the Leadership Committee report. And now because he [Katz] obtained this land, it's assumed that's the best spot for it."[36]

Nevertheless, executives from the Katz Group, supported by AEG vice president Ted Tanner, appeared before council on July 21, 2010, just a few months shy of the upcoming municipal election. In his address to council—his first public appearance since the arena debate began—Katz led the procession of executives by outlining his commitment to the proposed development and his willingness to sign a long-term location agreement as part of a lease for a new, city- owned downtown arena—a crucial concern for fans and for council. He concluded his conciliatory speech by formally asking city council to provide administration with a mandate to negotiate with the Katz Group to develop a new, publicly-financed downtown arena and entertainment district. While Katz equated the importance of the new arena with the long-term stability of the Oilers and the city of Edmonton's broader growth agenda for the downtown core, he made no mention of the personal gains that he stood to make, especially the increase in franchise value.

Katz was followed by his CFO, Paul Marcaccio, who further outlined the "business realities" of the franchise. The Oilers, he said, played in the second smallest arena in the NHL, with limited opportunities for ticket and premium suite revenue, advertising and sponsorship income, and concession sales. The Oilers' location in Edmonton also limited the value of local broadcast rights and magnified the cost of travel and of the effect of the US dollar on Canadian franchises (revenues are Canadian-dollar based, while expenses, especially salaries, are US-dollar based). These were, of course, the same arguments that small-market Canadian NHL franchises had been using for more than a decade in their regular attempts to secure public subsidies, and money from the NHL.

While Marcaccio claimed that the Oilers' expenses were "in line with other teams," he provided no comparative data to support his contention that the Oilers were financially disadvantaged by playing in Rexall Place or by being located in Edmonton. Both *Forbes* and CSL painted quite a different picture of the profitability of the team that had routinely sold out Rexall Place and whose fans paid among the highest ticket prices in the NHL. In the 2009/10 season, for example, *Forbes* reported that the Edmonton Oilers had an estimated operating income of US$8.2 million and earned more money than franchises in Boston, Pittsburgh, Dallas, New Jersey, Los Angeles, Calgary, Minnesota, Colorado, Washington, Ottawa, San Jose, Anaheim, Buffalo, Florida, St. Louis, Carolina, Columbus, New York (Islanders), Tampa Bay, Atlanta, and Phoenix.[37]

Representatives from Northlands also disputed claims that the Oilers were losing money, even before Katz's 2008 purchase of the team:

> We did have a consultant from the United States who reverse-engineered the numbers; it's kind of interesting...but the NHL has

a transfer system much like the provinces do in Canada and there's
"have teams" and "have not teams" and the Oilers are in the "have
teams." Now, of course, the books are all closed and no one is going
to tell you anything, but the reverse engineering based on the amount
of transfer payment that the Oilers were making suggested about $6
million annually in profit. So, they were claiming being broke [but]
that wasn't exactly the case and we had that evidence. But, there was
a coming together of interests to keep the team in town around the
EIGLP, and everybody put in, including Northlands, to keep the team,
and they obtained $1 a year in rent and when Mr. Katz bought the
team...he just expected the same deal if not more.[38]

In his speech to council, Marcaccio also emphasized the Oilers'
desire to control all non-hockey related revenue from a city-owned
facility, and to exclude Northlands from the deliberations and from
the operation of any new facility. He insisted that the Oilers were
"the ONLY team in the NHL that does not control its arena, and the
ONLY team that does not receive the non-hockey related revenues
from the facility in which they play. For sake of comparison: in
Edmonton, those revenues go to Northlands. In Calgary, they do not
go to the Stampede Board; they go to the Calgary Flames organization."[39] Marcaccio understandably neglected to mention that the
Oilers had previously chosen to abandon the concert business.

Other important information was absent from Marcaccio's
presentation. He made no mention of the generous and unique provisions of the lease agreement between Northlands and the Oilers, for
example, that limited rental payments to only $1 per year; the Flames,
in contrast, paid $1.5 million in rent annually to the Saddledome
Foundation.[40] Nor did Marcaccio explain that other franchises,
including both the Flames and Canucks, had to pay arena operating
expenses that the Oilers were excused from, according to the terms
of their lease agreement with Northlands. Likewise, he ignored the
substantive public investments in Rexall Place made by various
levels of government over the years that had directly subsidized the
Oilers. Summing up, Marcaccio claimed that the Oilers were losing
money and that Katz had been subsidizing them "by several million

dollars in each of the past two years in order for the team to break even."[41] Yet, the Katz Group, like owners of all other professional sports franchises in search of public subsidy, refused to make available their financial records in order to confirm these claims and to acknowledge the tax advantages for franchises that manipulate tax laws by declaring accounting losses.

Marcaccio was followed by John Karvellas, executive vice president and general counsel for the Katz Group, who publicly stated what the Oilers had made clear in private for many years—that the hockey club would refuse to play in a renovated Rexall Place:

> We also know that the financial model to justify any renovation [of Rexall Place] would depend in large part on the willingness of the Edmonton Oilers and Oil Kings to enter into a new lease that runs beyond June 2015. To avoid any uncertainty in this regard, I can tell you that we do not believe a renovation would assist in the sustainability of the Oilers, we will not invest in or otherwise support such a project, and we do not intend to have the Oilers play in a renovated Rexall Place.[42]

He repeated, as well, that the organization had its own "timing concerns" about the "need for a new home for the Oilers by the fall of 2014" when its lease agreement with Northlands ended, and that the Katz Group needed a political endorsement to provide "commercial certainty" as it worked to secure additional investment in the arena and also in entertainment facilities.[43] Karvellas promised that the organization would respect the "City's planning and development process" and fulfill the "City's public consultation requirements." He concluded by underlining Katz's initial request:

> As Daryl indicated, we are asking that you give your administration authority to negotiate with us to develop an agreement dealing with the design, construction and financing of a new arena and related sports and entertainment facilities in downtown Edmonton...It is our desire and I hope that prior to the end of this calendar year, a proposed form

of agreement would be brought back to Edmonton City Council for discussion and, hopefully, approval.[44]

This latter point, in retrospect, was crucial: the Katz Group was increasing the political pressure by introducing deadlines that would, in turn, set limits on the ability of council to engage in prudent and rational analysis and deliberation, especially when the information being provided to elected officials was full of questionable claims and assumptions. The time limit would also constrain any kind of meaningful and genuine consultation with the public.

Despite months of simmering frustration and anger, though, most councillors were, according to one observer, "smitten and content to throw bouquets at Katz and crew," while Mayor Mandel had "nothing but praise for Katz and his offer to invest substantially in our downtown."[45] Some councillors, though, requested clarity on whether the Oilers were threatening to relocate if a new arena was not constructed, to which John Karvellas responded, "I will never say such a thing. I will never imply it either...If that's what's implied with what we have said today, that is not our intention."[46] Others, including Don Iveson, were less than satisfied with Karvellas' response: "We didn't get a straight answer on what will happen after 2014."[47]

Nor was Karvellas willing to respond to other important questions, including whether the Katz Group was prepared to cover any shortfalls if anticipated development around the arena was insufficient to cover future borrowing costs. When reminded that all the other NHL rinks in Canada—in Montreal, Ottawa, and Vancouver—had been privately financed and had cost considerably less than the Katz Group's proposal, Karvellas said that those arenas had failed—a claim presented without evidence or context. Even if those privately-financed arenas had, in fact, "failed," was this failure not simply a reflection of the flawed business model of the pre-salary cap NHL, and of the inherent risks associated with free enterprise? And, even if the former owners of those franchises faced financial challenges—ones that were the result of their broader business interests—the hockey clubs and arenas were purchased by new wealthy owners and, according to *Forbes* estimates, continued to make money, especially the Montreal Canadiens and Vancouver Canucks. Moreover, if those less expensive, privately-financed rinks had been unsuccessful—two in considerably larger markets—as Karvellas claimed, why would Edmonton risk building a substantially more expensive facility in a smaller city?

The implied threat was clear: the Oilers were not willing to play in a renovated Rexall Place or to continue the terms of their lease with Northlands under any circumstances. Nor was the Katz Group willing to finance a new arena or contribute any more than $100 million. The city of Edmonton, then, not the Katz Group, which had set itself up as the main private beneficiary of a new arena, would bear the risk in this public–private partnership.

A host of outstanding issues remained unaddressed, so councillors were invited to submit a list of questions to the Katz Group, Northlands, and administration that would be answered in a written report by the end of the year. This was in itself an unusual development that allowed council to approve a motion despite extensive gaps in information, while signalling to citizens that due diligence would eventually be undertaken before any more significant votes were held. Council could have refused to support any motion without having full and immediate access to information, but doing so would have delayed the process, which both the Katz Group and the mayor were anxious to avoid: an official agreement was needed as soon as possible in order to approach the provincial government for funding.

The decision to present responses to over 140 queries from council by the end of the year in a single report, moreover, offered another advantage to arena proponents. All of council's questions about complex and controversial issues could be bundled together, simplified, or ignored altogether in a written report, instead of being rigorously debated in the public sphere. Crucially, the report was to be received after the municipal election in October, ensuring that the unpopular issue would not be properly debated during the campaign.

However, despite the lack of objective information about a
number of critical issues—the Katz Group's finances and the profitability of the Oilers, the HOK arena site rankings, the potential
financial impacts of a new downtown arena on Northlands and on
other areas of the city, etc.—council approved a multi-part motion
directing administration to enter into discussions with both the
Katz Group and Northlands on a framework for the financing and
operation of a new downtown arena project (not including an
increase in current property taxes), and to begin planning for a
city-wide community consultation process. While Northlands was
identified in the broader motion as a stakeholder in the discussions,
it had not been invited to appear before council along with the Katz
Group. Administration was instructed, though, to develop a report
on the anticipated effects of a new facility on Northlands, which
would be invited to appear before council before the end of the year.

Council also supported two other motions. First, it requested
a report on the CRL financing mechanism and its potential effect
on an existing levy for The Quarters. And, it instructed administration to develop a report that provided a benchmark scenario for
the private development of a new arena and quantified the financial factors precluding the building of a privately-financed arena.
Of course, this option was never seriously contemplated, and the
mayor's Arena Leadership Committee had already concluded in its
City Shaping report, without any evidence, that private financing
of a new facility was impossible. Eight months later, after official
negotiations between the city and the Katz Group to construct a
new, publicly-financed arena development had begun, administration produced a cursory report on the CRL, but it never bothered
to undertake a comprehensive analysis of the feasibility of private
financing.

Game On

The Katz Group's presentation to council put in motion the formal
process launching negotiations for a new, publicly-financed arena
and entertainment district. It was largely a theatrical and promotional

exercise, especially given the presence of senior executive members of the Katz Group, including Katz and his family. It was rather unusual for a private company to be invited to address city council in this way. Council even had to vote to suspend a procedural mechanism to allow the Katz Group to make a presentation and to engage in a subsequent discussion without a motion on the floor.[48] The usual course of action for any potential project that involved the city of Edmonton was to engage in an initial discussion at a standing committee to ensure due process and public scrutiny. In this instance, though, the policy was circumvented to avoid both delays and more public involvement.

Boosters were quick to label Katz's appearance at council as an act of penitence, and they cheered the subsequent discussion of the Oilers' need for a new, publicly-financed arena. An editorial in the *Journal* celebrated the day's events and wondered whether Katz's demand for the non-hockey revenue from a new facility was actually a threat or "just an unpleasant, but unavoidable statement of reality in the modern world of major league sports."[49] Another editorial a week later presented these types of subsidies as common sense: "The way of this world—like it or not—is that hockey clubs collect all the non-hockey revenue from their respective venues. The Calgary Flames possess a $35-million advantage over the Oilers because of such an agreement."[50] These types of boosterish commentaries, though, failed to ask some key questions. Why was it the responsibility of the citizens of Edmonton to resolve the financial problems of an NHL team through public subsidy, while other possible solutions, including greater revenue sharing within the league, remained available? And why, moreover, was it the responsibility of taxpayers to subsidize the business interests of an extraordinarily wealthy man?

Instead of confirming that the Katz Group had the resources to finance a new arena itself—a facility it wanted to operate and from which it would capture all the revenue—the *Journal* continued to toe the party line that had been drawn by Mayor Mandel by suggesting that "the goal should be to finance the project without increasing taxes on existing property owners."[51] But even if taxes weren't raised to pay for the development directly, the dedication of hundreds of millions of dollars of public funds to a new arena would inevitably mean less public money for civic responsibilities like policing and firefighting, for social services, and for public infrastructure, a point the editorial ignored. The *Journal*'s editorial board also took direct aim at Northlands by asserting that the "interests of Northlands must not be the focus of any conversation or even a secondary concern, with all due respect."[52] But Northlands' interests were already aligned with the city in a variety of ways, especially because it had borrowed money. What these types of boosterish editorials ignored, though, was any suggestion that the Katz Group ought to build and finance the arena itself—especially since it wanted to operate it and control all its revenues.

9

END GAME?

DESPITE NORTHLANDS' SUPPORT of a new, publicly-financed downtown arena, dialogue between the organization and the Katz Group remained non-existent. According to Andy Huntley, "a palpable sense of mistrust" had also developed between Northlands and the city because of the association's role in running a money-losing Indy car race in Edmonton, at the city's request, from 2008 to 2010.[1] Tensions associated with the arena debate only made things worse. Executives from Northlands knew that the city was committed to building a new arena downtown, that they were losing their main tenant, and that they were being sidelined in the political process. Northlands now faced the prospect of either forcefully defending its interests or reinventing itself with an entirely new business model for an unknown future. It chose the former.

These issues were outlined in a letter sent by Northlands' solicitor Roger Swainson to the city manager, Simon Farbrother, on July 16, 2010, declaring the organization's opposition to the establishment of bilateral discussions between the city of Edmonton and the Katz Group, and, by extension, to its exclusion "from any meaningful participation in the process in determining issues related to a new arena facility."[2] This latter development, Northlands asserted, was "totally inconsistent with the collaborative process that we have embarked upon for the past few years."[3] Northlands had participated in the early stages of the discussions, contributed to the costs of the ALC and the commissioning of reports, and provided commercially sensitive information and its own expertise on facility operations and development. The letter accused city administration of manipulating information, including in the reports and slides accompanying the in-camera update in March, to justify the exclusion of Northlands from negotiations between the city and the Katz Group.[4]

Northlands also worked behind the scenes to influence the debate. It hired its own academic consultant, economist Dr. Andrew Zimbalist, to prepare a report rebutting the arguments being made by both the Katz Group and the city's sport management consultants. The Zimbalist report,[5] which directly challenged Daryl Katz's claims that the Oilers were losing money, was eventually distributed to council and made public in March 2011, after Northlands had been officially excluded from the negotiations. Northlands had also hired CSL to perform a market analysis to address the potential viability of Rexall Place as a competitor to a new downtown arena in Edmonton. The CSL report noted that, historically, secondary arenas were rarely competitive financially with newer facilities, and that it would be challenging—but not impossible—to sustain a secondary competitive building in Edmonton.[6] It was for this reason that the Katz Group later demanded a non-compete clause with Northlands as it tried to ensure its monopoly in the local sports and entertainment markets.[7] If Rexall Place ceased operations as a sports and entertainment facility, the report continued, it could not operate in a different capacity without significant and costly renovations. These additional costs would be largely ignored throughout the arena debate.

Finally, in autumn 2010, Northlands commissioned Ipsos Canada to conduct public opinion research about the Katz Group's proposal. This poll was designed to defend the interests of Northlands and to discredit the Katz Group's demands to control a new arena. Its results (released in March 2011) mirrored the findings of every previous poll in demonstrating strong opposition to the use of public funds to build a new arena. The following are the key results

of the Ipsos Canada poll,[8] based on 412 interviews that took place
between September 30th and October 5th:

1. *Fewer than 1 in 5 participants identified the arena/entertainment
   district as important to them. Those who did were likely to be male.*
2. *72 percent opposed the use of taxpayers' money for a new downtown arena.*
3. *48 percent thought the city of Edmonton ought to control a new
   arena; 29 percent were in favour of Northlands controlling it; and
   12 percent were in favour of the Oilers controlling it.*
4. *53 percent thought the arena should be funded privately.*
5. *57 percent thought the owner of the Oilers ought to pay for a new
   downtown arena.*

Northlands, though, was increasingly isolated politically. Given its
long history, it had assumed that it would operate any new, city-
owned arena, and that the Katz Group would enter into another
generous lease arrangement that would continue to grant the Oilers
all hockey-related revenue while freeing the club from paying rent
or contributing to operating costs. Northlands had also assumed
that it would retain all non-hockey revenue to cover its expenses
and replace its lost profits. A continuation of its current lease
arrangements with Northlands in a new, city-owned arena would
have dramatically expanded the Oilers' hockey-related revenue and
increased the club's valuation. But this was not enough. Katz wanted
all the revenue from a new arena—and Northlands was in his way.

The mayor and key administrators, including the city manager,
were on Katz's side in this dispute, as they had been from the beginning. Simon Farbrother recalled:

*And very early in the process we actually said the only way this is
going to work is if there's a shared desire to make something happen,
recognizing that we actually have to represent the interests of our
respective constituents. So, we agreed that the concept made sense,
but at the end of the day it had to make financial sense for the Oilers*

and it had to actually make...sense for the city. Philosophically, the city wanted an arena in the core, it wanted it connected to the LRT, it needed to line up with the downtown plan. And within that city-building context...retaining a hockey team is really important in terms of the psyche of the city, in terms of profile, in terms of economic development, but also [in terms of] the physical infrastructure and space and bringing the population to the core, and essentially bringing West Edmonton Mall back into the downtown. And it also needed to do it in a fashion that actually reinforced the fact that successful cities construct cores, and that's true whether you have 20 municipalities or one municipality. The core has to be successful.[9]

Thus, despite polls and reports showing opposition to a new, publicly-financed arena and despite the profitability of the Oilers at Rexall Place, Northlands' once-influential voice was not being heard. The organization simply could not counter the powerful interest groups that had re-aligned the coalition dominating municipal politics in favour of both downtown development and long-term support for the hockey team. As Farbrother noted:

Northlands made that assumption [that they would run the new arena] and they'd also made the assumption that if they didn't there would be an obvious compensation paid to them even if the lease [with the Oilers] was up...We made the commitment to keep them informed and engaged and met with them on a regular basis...and there were some levers that could have been played. All I would say there publicly is that at the end of the day for Northlands, that wasn't their solution, they wanted something else...It was all about Northlands...so you ulti-mately ended up with a situation of Northlands in a sense watching the boat sail and not being on the boat.[10]

Likewise, for Mayor Stephen Mandel, Northlands "played the wrong hand":

I think that's really the demise of Northlands and they had a vision that wasn't as reasonable when they built the Edmonton Expo Centre.

That put them in a financial hole, and then I think they made some
other calculated mistakes [which lost them] their power base and that
made a big difference...But they also started bringing in people who
didn't understand our city. And our city is our city. It has its own
characteristics. You need to understand those and how to make
them work.[11]

Passing the Puck?

The financial model for a new downtown arena, though, remained
incomplete: at least $100 million was unaccounted for. Despite
attempts by the Katz Group and by Mayor Mandel to lobby the
provincial government, Premier Ed Stelmach was not prepared to
invest additional public money in a new facility in Edmonton: "As
I said before, there won't be any public money going to the arenas.
We are trying to catch up with badly needed infrastructure in
health and schools."[12] Stelmach also knew that if his government
provided any direct funding for a new arena in Edmonton, Calgary
would expect the same. He was prepared, though, to provide indirect assistance in the form of an LRT connection and other related
infrastructure.[13]

Political energies in Edmonton now shifted toward the 2010
municipal election in October. Scott McKeen announced that he was
resigning as city hall columnist for the *Edmonton Journal* to run for
council in Ward 7, which includes Rexall Place and its surrounding
communities. He followed the mayor's lead by announcing his
support for a downtown arena, as long as it wasn't paid for by
existing taxes.[14] McKeen was defeated by the incumbent, Tony
Caterina, who opposed the downtown arena. But, after the election,
McKeen was hired by the city on a sole-source contract for $47,250 to
perform "communications services around the arena project."[15] In
2013, after being hired as a "blogger-in-residence" on an additional
$6,000 contract with the city, McKeen was elected to council, this
time having run in Ward 6, which includes the downtown core.

It is, of course, not unusual for former journalists and media
personalities to run for office at all levels of government in Canada.
In the 2010 municipal election, former *Edmonton Sun* columnist

Kerry Diotte was elected to represent Ward 11. Nor is it unusual for journalists to be hired to perform public relations and communications work for government, especially given recent job losses in newsrooms across the country. However, McKeen's explicit remit to perform arena-related communications work for the city of Edmonton underlined, once again, the extent to which the city was trying to control the debate by hiring like-minded consultants. It also underscored the extent to which the city hall columnist was trusted by municipal officials and civic leaders—his former sources—to frame and communicate information about the divisive issue, first as a columnist and later as the city's communications specialist.

While the arena debate had generated heat for several years, it remained on the political margins during an election campaign dominated by the proposal to close City Centre Airport. Mayor Mandel supported the closure and favoured the redevelopment of the airport lands as a "sustainable" mixed-use urban community to entice middle/upper class consumers and families to live just north of downtown, where they would be connected to the city core by the Metro Line LRT. The success of the arena district and its financing through a CRL were also dependent on the closure of the airport, and the related elimination of the existing height restrictions that had hitherto prevented construction of the kind of high-rise condominium and office towers that the Katz Group planned to build on the downtown land that it had assembled, adjoining and across from the proposed arena site. The Katz Group kept conspicuously quiet during the campaign. Unlike the 2007 municipal election, when it had made a substantial donation to Mandel's mayoral campaign, it now made no donations. Though executives from the Katz Group probably did their fair share of lobbying behind the scenes, its public silence was judicious.

Although the arena debate remained in the political background, some candidates and incumbents made their positions clear. The Canadian Taxpayers Federation was also active, distributing questionnaires with a number of questions about the arena. Of the five incumbents who responded, only Don Iveson and Tony Caterina said that they opposed using public funds for a new arena development, including the creation of a CRL. Iveson, in particular, remained a forceful opponent of the project and insisted that he wanted the Oilers to open "their books" to "prove they can't build a new arena on their own."[16] Ward 12 incumbent Amarjeet Sohi said that, while he supported a new arena development, it did "not need any support from taxpayers."[17]

Citizens were also talking about the proposal during the campaign. Gordon Stamp, a local realtor, produced and circulated a pamphlet that took direct aim at the mayor: "Mayor Stephen Mandel...Manipulating the Process From the Very Beginning." Stamp listed facts obtained from published news stories and invited readers to ask: "Can we trust Stephen Mandel to represent our interests? Or do his loyalties lie elsewhere?"[18] After the election, he received a letter from Mandel's solicitors advising him that the re-elected mayor intended to commence legal action for defamation. Stamp was accused of smearing Mandel by insinuating that he and Katz were "operating in collaboration prior to and including May 2007," and that the *City Shaping* report was "prepared for an improper purpose and made improper conclusions and was biased (and known by Mr. Mandel to be so)."[19] Stamp was prepared to apologize in writing if Mandel could prove that any of the questions raised in the circulated pamphlet were factually incorrect, and he reminded the lawyers that both Katz and the mayor could potentially be summoned to the witness stand in any future legal proceedings. A letter from the solicitor dated November 30, 2010 said that Mayor Mandel no longer intended to commence legal proceedings.[20]

Probably the main reason for so little political discussion of the new arena, though, was that both Mandel and his main challenger, David Dorward, were already on the record as supporting it, though Dorward wanted a plebiscite on the issue. He was also firmly opposed to the CRL financing mechanism: "If somebody is going to put a pizza place in Avonmore, and instead they put it in that [downtown arena] area, well, we would have got that property tax increase from the pizza place anyway. The fact that you put it in that area really isn't extra money to the city."[21] But without a strong mayoral candidate willing to oppose the use of public funds—a position that would have alienated Oilers fans as well as developers, construction companies, and others—the arena debate gained very little traction during the campaign.

The main outcome of the election was a third mandate for Stephen Mandel, though his support had eroded from 65 percent three years earlier to a narrower majority of 55 percent in 2010. The influence of developers in the 2010 municipal election was again significant. Their contributions to candidates for council, for example, ranged from 32 percent (Linda Sloan) to 94 percent (Jane Batty) of campaign donations. Other councillors who relied primarily on developer donations included Bryan Anderson (91 percent), Don Iveson (67 percent), Karen Leibovici (63 percent), and Kim Krushell (62 percent). Mayor Mandel, whose campaign raised $628,283, received $366,714 from developers, just under 60 percent of his total. In contrast, he received only $6,000 from unions, just 1.6 percent of his total. All told, 56 percent of contributions for all candidates in the municipal election was tied to the development industry.

Stephen Mandel's victory was greeted with a supportive editorial in the *Journal* entitled "Vindication for Team Mandel." It suggested that citizens had embraced "an aggressive city-building agenda... that could make our town a very different, more modern, more self-assured place as the new century continues to unfold." The editorial also emphasized the significance of the mayor's re-election for Edmonton's central core: "a new downtown arena, as part of a broader entertainment district, is now a lot closer to reality. Mandel has a mandate to drive a tough bargain with Daryl Katz, but he also has received an endorsement for the principle of using a new arena to spark downtown redevelopment."[22] Of course, he had received no such endorsement from citizens, because the issue was barely raised during the election campaign. Nonetheless, proponents now had a three-year window before the next municipal election to solidify an agreement.

Public Consultation?

With the election out of the way, the city announced a public consultation process about the new arena. But first, it sought a legal analysis to "examine the role of the public in relation to various alternatives available to a municipality pertaining to the funding and operation of a new arena."[23] In particular, the analysis explored whether the city was required to hold a plebiscite or a public hearing; whether council, "acting on its own initiative," could put various arena-related questions to a plebiscite or public hearing; and, finally, whether council could be "forced by others" (i.e., citizens) to hold one.[24] All of these issues would be guided by the terms of the *Municipal Government Act*.

Council could, according to the *Municipal Government Act*, voluntarily initiate a plebiscite for a particular issue, although the results would not be legally binding. Council could also be forced to put certain questions to a binding vote of the electorate through a citizens' petition. However, the requirements for a petition are strict, and "in a municipality the size of Edmonton, considerable effort must be invested in order to achieve a petition sufficient to force Council to put an issue to a binding plebiscite."[25] A successful petition would require the signatures of at least 10 percent of eligible voters in Edmonton (over 80,000 people), collected within 60 days of a vote, and the requirements associated with the collection of signatures were equally rigid.[26] Thus, while "a petition to prevent the construction of a major capital project is within the intention of the legislation," the requirements made the prospect of a citizen-triggered plebiscite over the arena virtually impossible.[27] In the end, the analysis concluded that, "in the absence of a sufficient petition, there is no mandatory requirement to hold a public hearing or a plebiscite in relation to the various actions contemplated by the municipality."[28]

The terms of the *Municipal Government Act*, therefore, set powerful limits on the democratic process, allowing council to have the final vote on the fate of any proposal. Thus, even in the face of significant public criticism to date (especially over the findings of the *City Shaping* report and the suppression of the arena site rankings), the rules appeared to favour arena proponents. All they needed now was to secure the support of a majority of council and to guide the issue through administration and the mayor's office.

Still, given the contentiousness of the debate, at least a facade of public consultation and democratic process was needed before any final vote by council. The policies and frameworks for such consultation, as well as the general approach to it, would later be condemned by the city auditor, who "blasted the city's public engagement process," and noted that "meetings on proposed projects have been held to discuss pre-made decisions" and that "barriers have been deliberatively placed between dialogue with the public."[29]

To assist with the process, the city once again hired Margaret Bateman of local advertising agency Calder Bateman, at a cost to taxpayers of $195,300, on a sole-source contract to organize and facilitate a multi-faceted public consultation process.[30] And, while council had formally directed administration to initiate public consultation following Katz's public appearance at city hall in July, city staff and the hired consultants had, in fact, been meeting since March to discuss the process, the accompanying communications strategy, and the need to identify "what communications/consultation [would be] done in conjunction with the Katz Group," as well as what would be done unilaterally by the city.[31]

By May 2010, city staff had already begun discussions with the Katz Group about both the structure and the timing of the consultation process. The Katz Group had asked whether consultation could occur by the end of June, even before Katz's appearance at the council meeting in July, to allow them to finalize an arena deal as quickly as possible with minimal public scrutiny. City staff said no, and that a consultation process for a development of this magnitude would last about six weeks and could be scheduled only "once sufficiently detailed information on key aspects of the project is publicly available to enable informed community discussion."[32] Municipal officials also had "to present more specific information about how the project might impact adjacent communities and the broader community and taxpayers."[33] They also considered running the consultation before the election, but wanted to minimize the prospect of incurring "campaign impacts."[34] Postponing it until after the election would allow administration to present the results just before the next major vote in January 2011, during which council would be invited to initiate formal negotiations with the Katz Group.

Three consultative instruments were ultimately selected: an Internet questionnaire; four public meetings restricted to small group discussions around five generic questions (and the submission of additional feedback on sticky notes); and a telephone survey of 800 residents conducted by the firm Return on Insight, which was hired on another sole-source contract at a cost of over $40,000.[35] Although these mechanisms met minimum requirements, they provided little opportunity for meaningful and informed public debate or active participation in arena-related decision-making. They did little more than create a veneer of democratic involvement. All of the important decisions had been made.

The city and its consultants appear to have structured each of the consultative mechanisms to provide the answers they wanted before the next council meeting in January. In the Internet questionnaire, for example, citizens were asked to respond to the following questions with simple yes or no answers:

1. *Do you think a new downtown arena should be built in Edmonton?*
2. *Do you think a downtown arena is important to the long-term success of our city?*
3. *Do you think a new downtown arena and entertainment district can spur revitalization of the downtown?*
4. *Do opportunities for community use of the arena facilities for hockey and other activities influence how you feel about the funding model options?*
5. *Do you think the City of Edmonton should contribute funds to a new downtown arena as long as it does not raise the property tax rate or reallocate infrastructure funds?*[36]

The framing of the fifth question illustrates how the city sought its desired result, instead of simply asking people if they supported the use of public funds for a new arena. Administration also avoided questions that invited citizens to reflect on who ought to retain the revenue from any new, city-owned facility, or whether a new arena development ought to be privately financed. Nor did it ask, as the Northlands poll did, who should operate and control a new, city-owned facility. The city and the Katz Group had already decided that.

Amazingly, the city did not restrict the number of times one person could respond to the questionnaire or who could complete it. The Katz Group took advantage of both of these deliberate omissions and initiated an automated campaign that called 350,000 phone numbers in the capital region, including people in St. Albert and Sherwood Park (who don't pay city of Edmonton taxes). The telephone recording of Oilers President and CEO Patrick LaForge asked if respondents supported the new arena development; only those who answered yes received a second phone call encouraging them to complete the Internet survey. LaForge defended the expensive telemarketing campaign, which those opposed to the arena could never have afforded, to the *Journal* columnist Paula Simons: "I don't know why you say we have an unfair advantage. Do you think we should just sit back and watch?"[37] A representative from the city of Edmonton, meanwhile, said the Internet survey was never designed to be a statistically valid poll, and that it was only intended to help gauge public opinion.[38]

While the city's telephone poll of 800 Edmontonians raised a wider range of issues than the Internet survey, it also ignored questions about the proposed use of public funds and the inevitable opportunity costs associated with these expenditures, asking instead, "If the project were to proceed, do you think the City of Edmonton should contribute funds to a new downtown arena as long as it does not raise the property tax rate or reallocate infrastructure funds?"

The four public meetings held in November 2010 were also narrowly focused on five pre-determined talking points.[39] Many issues raised in the public meetings were relevant to the arena debate, but, given the limited information available—no business

plan from the Katz Group, no concrete financing proposals or estimates—the discussions at these meetings were often non-specific,
inconclusive, and replete with caveats. The Katz Group also tried to
influence the conversations by ensuring that their community representative was always in attendance. Following the public meetings,
a number of citizens voiced their concern about the "structured
discussions" around pre-determined talking points, which they
considered "undemocratic."[40]

The consultative process, an expensive and time-consuming
undertaking, was thus little more than an exercise in public
relations to solicit favourable responses in support of the city's pre-
determined position. It also inflamed already simmering opposition
to the proposed development, and a grassroots opposition group
called Voices For Democracy (VFD) formed soon after to influence a
debate that had been, thus far, completely dominated by influential
supporters.

Voices for Democracy

The boosterism that had accompanied the early stages of the
debate, as well as the wider level of cheerleading in much of the
media in favour of the proposed new arena development, propelled
three people who had been commenting on arena-related articles
on the *Journal*'s website to contact each other to discuss the issues.
None had met before, and two had remained anonymous while
blogging. However, after an introductory meeting at a coffee shop,
they agreed to form a grassroots organization that would try to influence the political process. VFD was incorporated two months later
as a registered non-profit society. The remaining members of the
board of directors joined the group later in 2011.

From its inception, VFD strove to demonstrate that it was a
credible and responsible citizen-based organization aimed at
offering informed contributions to the arena debate. Its members
hoped it would not be labelled as a collection of special interests,
naysayers, or knockers, especially given the history of boosterism
in Edmonton. VFD sought to provide more objective analyses and
a vehicle through which citizens might influence their elected

representatives. Its campaign was named Speak Up, Edmonton!, and its mission was threefold: 1) to be a critical voice on the arena project; 2) to provide a simple and evidence-based account of the proposed development; and 3) to allow Edmontonians opposed to the arena deal to be heard.

Members of VFD were neither the biggest names in the money game in Edmonton nor experienced activists, but they could draw on a substantial range of personal and professional expertise. Members of the board were all knowledgeable hockey fans, giving them some credibility with like-minded people and undercutting the notion that VFD was anti-hockey or anti-Oilers. As with many grassroots organizations, the political affiliations of board members varied, and VFD courted volunteers from the left-of-centre New Democratic Party (NDP), who focused on the issue of social justice, and from the right-of-centre Wild Rose Party, who denounced the expenditure of public funds as a fiscally irresponsible and unnecessary government intervention in the free market. VFD emphasized reasoned arguments with evidence-based data over more radical tactics that might have garnered greater publicity, but fewer results. The board met regularly to discuss issues, adopting a non-hierarchical, participatory governing structure to facilitate transparent discussions and vigorous debate of political tactics and the establishment of various roles and working groups (e.g., website development, fundraising).

VFD wanted to show councillors and the media that opposition to a publicly-financed facility was widespread, so it commissioned Environics Research Group to conduct a city-wide telephone poll. Unlike Calder Bateman's telephone survey, VFD's poll asked specific questions, such as "Do you agree that the City of Edmonton should provide taxpayers' money to build a new downtown arena?" The poll demonstrated strong opposition to the use of public funds to build a new arena and showed that many citizens wanted reassurances that the city would share in the benefits of any future development.[41]

VFD also purchased billboards across the city with a message taking direct aim at the lack of discussion of the proposed arena during the October 2010 municipal election: "$400 million for a new arena? That wasn't on the ballot! Speak Up, Edmonton!" It produced 70,000 brochures and paid to have copies distributed evenly in wards throughout the city. Board members and volunteers regularly handed out pamphlets on the street, inviting citizens to reflect on the process surrounding the initial arena debate and arguing that it was not the responsibility of the city to subsidize a privately-owned NHL franchise and its billionaire owner. VFD disputed the claim that a new arena would revitalize Edmonton's downtown by highlighting the number of recent developments that were already transforming the downtown core without a publicly-financed facility. It also argued that the city's original cost estimate of $400 million for the new development was far too low; the final cost would probably exceed $600 million (a prediction later proven correct). VFD's website provided detailed information about the arena debate and countered the social media strategies of boosters. The group developed a Facebook page and a Twitter account, and members volunteered hundreds of hours to develop online content, including regular updates on new developments at city hall, links to current media stories, commentary, and press releases.[42]

VFD members and volunteers subsequently explored other political channels to shift the terrain of the debate. They spoke at public consultation sessions and hearings, lobbied councillors, and provided elected officials with research-based evidence from other cities that challenged more optimistic projections and analyses of costs. However, while many councillors were willing to listen to VFD's arguments—with some privately agreeing that the concerns were valid—most had already made up their mind to vote in favour of the arena development. VFD was not alone in its efforts to lobby elected officials; pro-arena groups such as the Edmonton Chamber of Commerce held meetings with public officials to promote their own agenda, and the Katz Group also engaged in lobbying efforts at both the municipal and provincial levels. Thanks to the relationships among the city's power elite, business-driven organizations enjoyed informal access to the corridors of power at city hall that were inaccessible to ordinary citizens.

Q and A with Council, and the Quebec Oilers?

Executives from the Oilers stoked fears of relocation once again by meeting with officials in Quebec City in early December 2010. Patrick LaForge defended the trip as a mere fact-finding mission about the Quebec City arena project: "We are not planning to move the Oilers at this time. We're going to build a building....At this time"[43]—few Edmontonians missed the implication. Meanwhile, on December 10th, city council got the responses to the 140 questions they had posed back in July to Northlands, city administration, and the Katz Group. Representatives from Northlands were invited to appear before council and to respond to specific questions after making a brief presentation. Council again suspended a section of the procedures and committee bylaws (Council Committees Bylaw 18156 and Council Procedures Bylaw 18155) to allow a presentation and discussion without a motion on the floor. The responses were instructive.

First, a number of councillors were, at this point in the debate, unconvinced of the need to replace an arena that was only three decades old. To Councillor Bryan Anderson's question asking if the city really needed a new arena, administration responded:

> *There has been a business decision made by the Katz Group to propose a new sports and entertainment district including an arena to meet the growing demand for a larger and modernized facility, one that will generate additional revenues beyond those created by the arena component. The Katz Group has also indicated that they do not intend to continue to be a tenant at Rexall Place. The committee of community representatives that researched and wrote the 2008 report titled* City Shaping *concluded that a new sports and entertainment district is feasible and desirable, and it presents a unique opportunity to rejuvenate Edmonton's downtown and provide benefits to citizens throughout the city and region.*[44]

Asked by Councillor Sohi if Rexall Place could be upgraded to meet NHL standards, Northlands said that the arena already fully met all NHL standards—an admission it had not publicly made before.[45]

Why then, councillors asked, was a new arena necessary? They requested additional background information from administration about the genesis of the proposed development, to which administration replied:

> The Katz Group has brought forward a proposal for a downtown Sports Entertainment district. The proposal includes the partial City funding of a new arena that the Katz Group would design, build and operate on the City's behalf. Alternatives to this plan have not been considered as the position of the Katz Group is that a downtown Sports and Entertainment District is the only option that they are pursuing at this time.[46]

In response to a question from Councillor Karen Leibovici—Would Northlands be able to attract private capital to renovate Rexall Place and operate Rexall Place without any public subsidy?—Northlands responded, "We are of the opinion that, if we had the same revenue generating opportunities that our current hockey partners [have, i.e., hockey revenue], we would be able to attract private capital without public funds."[47]

Council also asked administration to disclose more information about the HOK report's ranking of potential arena sites. "What is the best site for a new arena?" asked Councillor Bryan Anderson, to which administration responded:

> When factoring in the location criteria as identified in the HOK Study, the proposed location is the best site for a sports and entertainment district including an arena. By attracting more people and investment to the downtown, the proposed sports and entertainment district would act as a catalyst for the redevelopment of the area, including the North Edge, Downtown, McCauley, and The Quarters neighbourhoods.[48]

Councillor Tony Caterina asked administration why the fifth-best location was chosen rather than the first. Administration's response to this was particularly telling:

> *The confidential HOK Study does not prioritize the proposed loca-*
> *tions. Rather, it identifies the essential components required to attract*
> *major sporting and entertainment events and identifies location issues*
> *and the criteria necessary for a successful facility development. The*
> *proposed location for the district is a viable choice when factoring in*
> *the various criteria identified in the HOK Study, particularly related*
> *to the challenges/opportunities of land assembly.*[49]

It is striking that councillors were invited to ask these types of
questions two years after the publication of the HOK and the *City
Shaping* reports. Equally striking were administration's misleading
and evasive answers. HOK had, of course, provided concrete rankings and had prioritized potential arena locations according to
detailed criteria, and the Katz Group's land holdings had ranked
poorly. Despite their attempts to make diligent assessments on
behalf of their constituents, councillors were still not getting
objective, disinterested, or even accurate information from administration. For Councillor Tony Caterina, in retrospect, the entire site
ranking debacle was a less-than-subtle diversion from the obvious
questions about land ownership and private profit:

> *We got the information as rankings to explore what would be the best*
> *site for the arena. And that's the setup, just to get the information.*
> *"Oh, we have five sites. Okay, so what's the rank? Oh, this is the best*
> *site. So, you picked the fifth site? Why?" Well, obviously there are*
> *interests in that fifth site and there are other things at play that they*
> *didn't want put into the mix of making a decision.*[50]

Councillors also invited the Katz Group to provide evidence of the
Oilers' unprofitability and of its ability to finance the types of ancil-
lary developments that would ultimately fund the CRL. The Katz
Group was, however, unwilling to provide answers to these funda-
mental questions. When Councillor Iveson, for example, asked to
see the Oilers' Unified Report of Operations as submitted to the
NHL for the past two years, the Katz Group's answer was blunt:
"We will not do that."[51] Likewise, Councillor Jane Batty tried to get

information about the Katz Group's major creditors and what security it could provide, but the Katz Group insisted that it had "a right to privacy in respect to its financial affairs."[52] Rather than opening their books to demonstrate that the Oilers were unprofitable and that the Katz Group was unable to finance an arena, the organization simply retreated to a standard line: "The Oilers are a private company and do not publicly disclose financial details."[53]

The Katz Group's recalcitrance did little to inspire confidence in the project. If a bank, for example, had been asked to provide a $450-million loan for a new arena development, it would have demanded and received a detailed examination of the Katz Group's finances and credit history. Why would a municipal corporation even contemplate such a significant public–private partnership without having the opportunity to check the private partner's finances? Council and administration could, of course, have demanded that this information be made available before beginning formal negotiations with the Katz Group, but they did not.

Councillors pressed the Katz Group repeatedly for details about its business plan. They were rebuffed. "We are still in the conceptual stage," the Katz Group kept saying.[54] Council also sought clarity regarding the Katz Group's contribution of $100 million to the arena. "These proposed details have yet to be negotiated with the City Administration," the Katz Group replied. The Katz Group also refused to respond to questions about the future involvement of Northlands in the operation of a new arena, or why Northlands should simply turn over to the Katz Group the lucrative concert business that it had successfully developed. Asked to explain why the Oilers were claiming financial duress when *Forbes* had estimated that the club's operating income had been greater than that of the Calgary Flames for the past three years (from US$3 million to US$10 million per year), the Oilers simply claimed, "That is not accurate based on our information."[55]

Only one question was asked (by Councillor Iveson) about the inevitable increase in the value of the Oilers franchise that would result from a new, publicly-financed arena development and from the provision of a "long-term inexpensive lease in hand which

guaranteed all hockey and non-hockey revenue."[56] Relying on *Forbes*
data, the sport management consultants hired by administration
concluded that the eight NHL clubs that had moved into a new
arena since 1999 had seen their franchise values increase on average
by US$37 million from the year before the arena opening to the year
after. According to *Forbes'* estimates, the value of the Oilers franchise would increase by 78 percent—from US$225 million in 2012 to
US$400 million in 2013—with the mere announcement of an agree-
ment between the city and the Katz Group, a figure double the 2008
purchase price. Although he asked both Northlands and administration for information, Mayor Mandel posed not a single question to
the Katz Group.

Making its case for operating a new arena, Northlands pointed
out the generous terms of its lease with the Oilers, its own
successful resurrection of the concert business that it had inherited in 1998 when the club's non-hockey business was losing $2.5–3
million annually, and the fact that its lease with the city would not
expire for decades. Northlands also drew attention to its profit-
sharing agreement with the city, through which it had returned $2.8
million to the city since 2004 to be held in reserve for arena capital
projects. Council therefore instructed the city manager to work
with Northlands to prepare a report to ensure the sustainability of
Northlands if a new arena was constructed, and to prepare an additional report to determine the long-term plans for the city-owned
land on which Rexall Place was located. Neither of these reports was
ever completed.

It was council's last chance to ask such questions. The flames of
boosterism continued to be fanned by influential Edmontonians,
including former mayor Bill Smith, who encouraged citizens to be
cheerleaders: "We need a new facility, not just for the Oilers, but for
Edmonton. Let's show the world that Edmonton is still number 1
and that we know how to get things done and stop all the negative
comments."[57] Northlands came into its share of criticism. Pro-arena
columnist David Staples argued that the organization should
"pull out of the arena deal for the good of all" because it was not
providing grant money or a capital contribution to the new arena,

while he lauded the Katz Group for its willingness to contribute $100 million to the construction of the new arena.[58] He made no mention of Northlands' historical role in subsidizing professional hockey in Edmonton. For Staples, Northlands and its role in arena operations represented an older era—an era in which the organization was politically dominant and could easily access resources—while the Katz Group represented a new vision that would sustain the franchise in the decades to come. Finally, on December 30th, during the holiday season, the city of Edmonton announced that it was prepared to support the Katz Group's rezoning proposal, which had been resubmitted in October and would be discussed by council in January. The stage for formal negotiations was set.

10

THE BEAT GOES ON

COUNCIL HELD ITS FIRST arena-related meeting of 2011 on January 17th, when it received the results of the public consultation process and was asked to agree to start formal negotiations on a framework agreement for a new, publicly-financed arena development with the Katz Group. Mayor Stephen Mandel insisted that council arrive at a final decision on the new arena no later than April. For arena propo- nents, time was of the essence. The Oilers' lease agreement with Northlands expired in 2014, and the team was not going to renew. The Katz Group wanted to begin construction on a new facility as early as 2012. The mayor also needed a firm agreement with the Katz Group before formally approaching senior levels of government, especially the province, for funding.

In advance of this meeting, boosters in the local media continued where they had left off in late 2010, eagerly promoting the results of the public consultation process, which had just been released.[1] Given the problems with the online survey and the open houses, however, they focused on the telephone survey.[2] This survey, which gathered data from 800 randomly selected adults in Edmonton between December 20 and 23, 2010, found the following:

Overall Support

- *59 percent supported building an arena*
- *68 percent believed a new arena could revitalize downtown*
- *82 percent cited perceived economic benefits*

Funding Models

- *56 percent supported a mix of public/private funding*
- *67 percent agreed or strongly agreed that public money could be used as long as it did not raise property taxes or reallocate infrastructure funds*

Sources of Funding

- *76 percent supported a user pay model*
- *53 percent strongly or somewhat disagreed with the CRL concept*
- *88 percent of people were strongly in favour of a public/private agreement on financial risks and benefits*

Assurances

- *60 percent strongly supported a plan for what would happen to Rexall Place*
- *72 percent strongly supported consulting people in the area*
- *68 percent strongly supported a location agreement that would keep the Oilers in town for the life of the agreement*

The *Journal*'s David Staples thought the consultation process confirmed the "simple, undeniable fact...that most Edmontonians want a new downtown arena" and that city council "now has a clear mandate from Edmonton voters to proceed." He acknowledged opposition, but framed it as coming from a "hardcore minority" of naysayers who weren't representative of the broader population.[3] An *Edmonton Journal* editorial also lauded the results of the telephone survey in advance of the January 17th council meeting. Neither mentioned that this was the only poll commissioned to date that had demonstrated any semblance of public support for a new, publicly-financed arena.

A more nuanced analysis of the results came once again from the *Journal*'s Paula Simons, who pointed out that questions in the telephone survey were designed to elicit the precise results that the city wanted to see. Even with such careful management, though, the results were not enthusiastic. Simons identified two other important factors that had been downplayed or ignored altogether by her colleagues: the responses showed a significant gender gap—with male respondents being more supportive of a new arena than females—and, crucially, strong opposition to using a CRL. Simons concluded that respondents were, at best, "cautiously supportive of the idea of a downtown arena but they have a lot of questions and concerns about how it gets built, how it gets funded, and how the city manages the financial risk."[4] These were, of course, the precise questions repeatedly raised by citizens at the public meetings in November 2010. The city, though, promoted the results of its public consultation process—and in particular the claim that 59 percent of Edmontonians supported a new arena—on its website, with a link to the Katz Group's website showcasing the same results.

Simons was also the only writer at the *Journal* to acknowledge that the grassroots group VFD had recently organized to oppose the use of public funds for a new arena development, although she found it difficult to imagine how a small coalition of disparate citizens could possibly summon the resources to cultivate widespread opposition and emerge as a credible political force, especially given the powerful vested interests lined up against them. "Still," Simons reflected, "they're asking the questions we all need to be asking. Is this arena a public good? Does it deserve public monies? And if so, how do we make sure we, the people, protect our stake in the game? Over the roar of the avalanche, getting those questions heard, much less answered, won't be easy."[5] VFD immediately encountered barriers erected by council to prevent genuine political debate. At the January 17th council meeting, for example, representatives from VFD and the Canadian Taxpayers Federation tried to address council about arena-related matters on the agenda and the limitations of the public consultation process. Their requests to speak, however, were summarily denied.

It's remarkable how many councillors endorsed the silencing of their constituents. The meeting was meant as a platform for support, not for skepticism or criticism. After a presentation by the architects of the public consultation process, Margaret Bateman of the consulting company Calder Bateman, and Linda Cochrane, general manager of the city of Edmonton's Community Services Department, council voted to accept their report—a result that might have been different if the public consultation process had allowed for real opposition.

Reports requested in July remained outstanding, including one assessing the feasibility of private financing and another on "potential impacts on City operations, infrastructure and investments of a potential downtown arena and...any commitments of Federal and Provincial funding."[6] A report on the potential risks to CRL revenues from diminished development in The Quarters was unfinished; administration said this information would eventually be provided to councillors, but only after a vote to support an agreement that included a CRL.

Administration recommended a 30-year location agreement with the Oilers and now confirmed that it had been meeting exclusively with the Katz Group, shutting out Northlands completely. A public–private financing framework for a $450-million downtown arena, including a user fee mechanism and a CRL, had been prepared. But, administration acknowledged, it was still $100 million short and the price tag didn't include everything, so the final bill, and the public's share of that bill, would be considerably higher.

Administration wanted to "provide the team with at least the same opportunities for success as the majority of the teams within the NHL if those opportunities are within local control."[7] The threat of relocation had clearly taken hold in city hall. As Mayor Mandel noted, the Oilers' long-term sustainability had been accepted as a legitimate municipal priority: "The NHL's not going to go broke by losing a team in Edmonton. It's a very small market...Our goal in the beginning [was] to ensure the Oilers are successful...[it] doesn't do us any good to have a hockey team that's so under the gun that they're not going to make any money."[8] The key terms of the January 2011 proposed arena framework were:

- *Capital funding: $450-million downtown arena, construction costs only.*
- *Any land acquisitions or swaps to assemble the necessary land "would be based on the fair market value achieved through an independent appraisal at the time of acquisition."*
- *The Oilers would sign a 30-year location agreement.*

The proposed funding breakdown was:

1. *Katz Group contribution: $100 million to the arena construction.*
2. *City's investment: $125-million CRL.*
3. *City's investment: $125-million user fee.*
4. *Unaccounted: $100 million to come from other sources (administration had not yet formally discussed funding contributions with either the federal or the provincial government).*

Administration then requested direction from council to open formal negotiations with the Katz Group. If supported, administration would continue its meetings and return to council in March with a report outlining key components of the financing and operating agreement. However, before voting on a 12-part omnibus motion prepared by Councillor Ben Henderson, Councillor Linda Sloan introduced a two-part motion. The first part requested that administration obtain written confirmation from the Katz Group regarding its willingness to have a third-party firm establish the company's financial ability to "preface any financial negotiations on an arena and arena district."[9] Aware that the Katz Group had already refused to disclose its financial records, council rejected this motion, but it did support the second part of Sloan's motion—that the city manager clarify with the Katz Group the guarantees and collateral that could be provided to minimize the city's risk. Councillor Kerry Diotte, who supported Sloan's motion, was troubled by his colleagues' unwillingness to perform due diligence on behalf of their constituents. As he later explained in our interview:

> *I mean, that was just common sense to me. You couldn't take this deal to a bank. It was incumbent on me as a representative for the people to see the books, and to see where the dollars are. Again, a banker would laugh you out of the bank if you came to the board and said, "I'm not showing my financials, but I want your money." It was ludicrous. It was unlike anything anybody had ever seen, and if it truly was such a great deal, then let's see all the minute details, let's see where the money is, let's have full disclosure. And if that disclosure existed and things added up, I would have supported it, but there never was a full disclosure.*[10]

Council then voted on the broader 12-part omnibus motion, with only Councillor Sloan voting against it.

The pressure being applied to council by the Katz Group, Sloan noted, was reminiscent of the 1990s when the Oilers' former owner, Peter Pocklington, had threatened to move the club in order to secure public concessions: "I hesitate to raise the word 'Pocklington,' but this city has gone down a road before where assurances were made."[11] The mayor rebuked her: "I think that's out of order...I'm sorry, councillor." Undaunted, she persisted: "All I'm offering is a history lesson of what [road] the city has gone down before, and the city ended up assuming the majority of the risk."[12] For Councillor Don Iveson, too, the debate had already been tainted with "emotional blackmail,"[13] and council was under enormous pressure to support the new development or risk being blamed for the possible loss of the Oilers—a tactic routinely deployed by professional sport franchises to undermine cities' bargaining positions.

Despite everything, though, council had agreed to provide administration with the legal and political authority to enter into exclusive negotiations with the Katz Group—without getting the reports that had been commissioned in July 2010 or a fundamental financial background, and without clarity on the precise terms of those negotiations. Proponents tried to downplay all of these democratic limitations, including Mayor Mandel, who assured Edmontonians that "negotiations are just negotiations...We can always say no."[14] Once a city enters into formal negotiations with the owner of a professional sports franchise for a new arena or stadium, though, it becomes all but impossible to walk away.

Going In-Camera

Administration would use the decision to begin formal negotiations to justify holding future council discussions in-camera,[15] away from public scrutiny. The authority for a council to go in-camera can be found in Section 197 of the *Municipal Government Act*, which states that councils and council committees must conduct their meetings in public unless the matter to be discussed falls within one of the exceptions in Division 2 of Part 1 of the *Freedom of Information and Protection of Privacy Act* (FOIP) (Sections 16 to 29). The provincial government provides municipal councils and administrators with the following guidelines:

> It is strongly recommended that an in-camera discussion not be recorded as any notes or minutes taken during the discussion may be requested as part of a FOIP request. The council meeting minutes should reflect that a motion was made to move into an in-camera session and then another to move out of the in-camera session and return to the open meeting. Council members...and any others included in the in-camera discussion are required to keep in confidence what was discussed until the item is discussed at a meeting held in public.[16]

The *Municipal Government Act* emphasizes that councils should avoid holding discussions about contentious issues, budget deliberations, and capital expenditures behind closed doors—and the arena debate met all these criteria. But administration and the mayor's office used in-camera sessions throughout the process, and the project was ultimately approved with minimal public input and scrutiny. The use of in-camera sessions by council was not uncommon. Between 2004 and 2013, for example, council retreated behind closed doors to discuss a variety of actions, such as appointments to civic agencies, the funding of LRT expansion, interviews for the creation of the LRT governance board (an arm's-length body to govern the city's LRT system), and the development of a business case for the Blatchford Redevelopment project. What was different about the arena process, however, was the calling of in-camera sessions over multiple years to construct and continually alter the financial framework for the proposed project, and to gain council's approval for the most significant public–private partnership in the city's history.

Council's in-camera sessions allowed candid, often heated, discussions between councillors and the mayor, and enabled administration and arena supporters to lobby and corral their colleagues to support predetermined motions that would be presented in public only after in-camera meetings. Indeed, as Rick Daviss from the city of Edmonton conceded, it was difficult to balance the need for a series of challenging private negotiations with the Katz Group while also providing information to council, and, to a lesser degree, to citizens:

> We tried to provide as much information as we could to council. I know the public hates it. Council hates it even more when you have an in-private report, but they understood that we're negotiating and that's very confidential, but we didn't hesitate to come back to council every 2 or 4 weeks with an update.[17]

Some councillors, however, disputed this interpretation, and thought the continued reliance on in-camera meetings unnecessary and, to some extent, deceptive, because they placed legal restrictions on what elected officials could reveal in public. As Councillor Kerry Diotte said later on, the in-camera sessions had the effect of undermining the faith of the public and of some councillors in the political process itself, especially given the absence of written reports and minutes:

> Well, there was no debate because there were so many in-camera sessions, and that was frustrating for me personally, because I think

*something this big has to be out there in the public and people should
have a say. I don't like in-camera sessions at all, and when you look at
this situation, there were no competing entities. You can understand
it when you're talking about bids or things like that, but this was one
entity and the city, and if you're in-camera, you can't debate it in
public. I was also frustrated by the lack of paperwork; there were not
a lot of documents that were presented and that's just not right. You'd
come in and have a sense that things had already been set in motion,
and that a decision had already been made, and it should not have
happened this way. It's not good governance and it's not fair to the
public, and that really angered me.*[18]

Councillor Tony Caterina agreed:

*Because of all the in-camera meetings, there were all sorts of details
that you could never say publicly. That was another disadvantage as
well. There are good reasons to go in-camera, if it's going to hamper
negotiations for price or a third party, you know, information on
finances, that sort of thing. On the other hand, you can also go
in-camera because then you limit what you can actually say outside
in public, to prevent the public from understanding exactly what is
going on. And that's something that Stephen [Mayor Mandel] used
very effectively as well, too. So many, many of the verbal reports came
in-camera. We had information, but you couldn't go to the public and
say, "you know what, you don't have the right information. You're
supporting something but you don't know what's going on." And, at
the end of the day, there's nothing in writing, there's nothing you can
actually go back to and say, "well, you said this" or "you did this,
so we're going to cancel this deal." It doesn't exist. We know that
Stephen had a lot of control over this. We know that there were a lot of
directions given by the mayor's office to administration, to push in a
certain direction and come up with the information, facts if you want
to call them that, numbers that would support that position. Well, can
you go back now and say "well, that's what was done" or how it was
done? You can say it, but you can't act on it.*[19]

The in-camera meetings, then, not only kept certain information away from the public, but also ensured that official written reports and accurate historical records were neither produced nor kept.

Northlands Strikes Back

The city's decision to begin exclusive negotiations with the Katz Group was, predictably, endorsed by NHL commissioner Gary Bettman, who reiterated his now-familiar argument about the need for a new arena to *Journal* sports columnist John MacKinnon while visiting Edmonton in February. Bettman applauded Katz's magnanimity and benevolence: "for a market of this size, what [Katz] is doing borders on being generous, as opposed to being an investment."[20] But council was still worried about several aspects of the arena financing proposal, including its reliance on a speculative CRL and the $100-million shortfall.

In advance of another council vote scheduled for three weeks later, these worries were magnified when Northlands released the report that it had commissioned earlier in 2010, by Dr. Andrew Zimbalist, Robert A. Woods Professor of Economics at Smith College in Northampton, Massachusetts. The timing of the release was deliberate. Northlands had been officially excluded from the arena negotiations, and the organization knew that another important vote was on the horizon. In retrospect, though, Northlands may have erred by not releasing the Zimbalist report sooner. Delaying its publication until after council had voted to start exclusive negotiations with the Katz Group caused the impact of Zimbalist's arguments to be minimal, and the report was largely ignored by boosters and the general population. Arena proponents could now point out that executives from Northlands (who had supported a new arena when serving on the Arena Leadership Committee) were only speaking out because they had been excluded from the deliberations—a claim not entirely without foundation.

Nonetheless, unlike with the reports commissioned by the city from its sport management consultants, observers like the *Journal*'s business columnist Gary Lamphier found Zimbalist's analysis "measured and balanced," "neither categorically for nor against the basic concept of downtown arenas as economic engines."[21] While Zimbalist agreed that "under certain financial and economic conditions, a sports facility can anchor a broader, more integrated development in the downtown core," he added several caveats and sharply disputed the Katz Group's claim that the Oilers were losing money. He also took issue with the work of pro-arena sport management consultant Mark Rosentraub, who had supplied pro-arena reports to the city.

Zimbalist further noted that the Oilers were the beneficiaries of one of the most favourable lease agreements in the NHL, thanks to ongoing support from both Northlands and the city of Edmonton. He disputed claims that the Oilers were disadvantaged because they did not collect non-hockey revenue at Northlands, and pointed out that, since the 2004/05 NHL lockout, the Oilers had ranked as one of the league's most consistently profitable franchises, despite failing to make the playoffs every season since 2005/06. Even though the Oilers had not accumulated a nickel of playoff revenue for over five years, the 2010 *Forbes* analysis estimated that the Oilers had generated US$8.2 million in operating profit, eighth-highest in the 30-team league.[22] Zimbalist also highlighted the strength of the local market, which had allowed the Oilers to continually sell out home games, despite having among the highest ticket prices in the league and despite a succession of teams that were, to be charitable, among the worst in the NHL. Zimbalist acknowledged that Rexall Place was not without limitations and lacked the revenue-generating amenities of more modern facilities. Still, he cautioned the city to resist the temptation to arrive at a hasty decision on constructing a new facility in the absence of full information and due diligence, especially given the profitability of the Oilers and the overall functionality of Rexall Place.

Zimbalist provided the kind of balanced review of the scholarly literature on the economic impact of sports facilities and professional sporting teams that had, thus far, been absent from the information that administration had provided to council:

*The virtually unanimous conclusion that has come out of the academic
literature on this subject is that a city, county or state should not
anticipate a positive economic development or fiscal impact from
a new sports facility. That is, a new sports facility by itself should
not be expected to raise employment or per capita income levels in a
community.*[23]

He then challenged Rosentraub's self-selected case studies of
"successful" integrated development projects in Columbus, Ohio;
Indianapolis, Indiana; Los Angeles, California; and San Diego,
California. He offered a more cautionary analysis, noting that the
main result in each of these cities was simply a relocation of existing
economic activity within the metropolitan region. There was no
significant increase, for example, in the levels of employment or
income per capita in any of these case studies, while a host of other
developments in St. Louis, Brooklyn, and Dallas, among other cities
with sports and entertainment districts that were never acknowledged by the sport management consultants in Edmonton, had
encountered significant financial difficulties.

Zimbalist provided salutary advice about the risks of a Tax
Increment Financing mechanism (a TIF is essentially a CRL), none
of which had been acknowledged by Rosentraub or the city's chief
financial officer:

*First, there is a strong possibility that incentives to develop one area
will result in the relocation of economic activity from other areas of
the city, and not in the creation of new activity. Hence, any increase in
tax revenue from redeveloped area A may be offset by a decrease in tax
revenue from area B, leaving the city with no additional funds to pay
the debt service on the public's new investment. If the new integrated
development is launched at a time when the economy is weak and
commercial and residential vacancy rates are appreciable, then the
likelihood of this cannibalization effect is greater.*

*Second, the TIF/CRL district may yield tax revenue increases from
the normal inflationary process. This process usually engenders gener-
alized increases in property values as inflation proceeds over time.*

Such tax revenue increases would have occurred with or without the new development. Indeed, in some cases, the district may have developed on its own without any special public intervention.

Third, as an area develops, the need for new public services grows as well. The city must provide additional public safety, sanitation, infrastructure, and perhaps education, inter alia. *Thus, even if the total tax revenue grows in the city as a result of the new development, the net tax revenue (after incremental costs) will be smaller.*[24]

Zimbalist encouraged the city of Edmonton to secure a legally binding commitment from the Katz Group to proceed with ancillary developments and to guarantee funding for public debt service in the event of any financial shortfalls in projected tax revenue. A similar commitment had been made by developers in San Diego before being granted public funding for Petco Park, the home of the San Diego Padres. As per the terms of their public–private partnership, the Padres agreed to share evenly all ballpark revenues with the city, and the Padres also agreed to cover any construction cost overruns. "The private developers [in Edmonton]," Zimbalist concluded, "stand to profit from the partnership, and they should bear a good part of the risk. A letter of credit to meet any potential shortfall could be considered."[25]

Zimbalist's arguments prompted the city to invite Professor Rosentraub to offer a rebuttal. Rosentraub defended his position by suggesting that *Forbes'* estimates were unreliable, and that the city's alternative subsidizing of Rexall Place operations was likely to increase. As for his selected case studies, he offered a brief rejoinder that, in the case of Los Angeles, was buttressed by a copy of a promotional travel story on the success of the LA Live entertainment district that had been featured in the *New York Times*.[26]

Rosentraub's position had, of course, already been endorsed by a familiar ally, David Staples, who claimed that "all citizens" would enjoy the benefits of downtown revitalization and a new arena.[27] Staples tried to discredit Zimbalist in an online piece by suggesting that the economist was contradicting an earlier feasibility study that he had been hired to produce by Bruce Ratner, the developer of the Atlantic Yards arena in Brooklyn. Notably, his only source for this claim was a commentary on a blog post.[28] Despite having interviewed both Rosentraub and Dr. Dan Mason repeatedly to promote the pro-arena agenda, Staples did not interview Zimbalist for a piece clearly intended to undermine the findings of his report and impugn his professional reputation.[29]

Council instructed administration to invite Zimbalist, Rosentraub, and Mason to a special meeting on March 24th to respond to questions and engage in a public debate. Scheduling conflicts derailed the meeting (and a later phone conference), and administration never contacted Zimbalist again to make alternate arrangements. Zimbalist's arguments were swiftly relegated to the sidelines of the debate. He was not surprised by these developments, including the cancellation of the debate and subsequent media criticism: "You know how it works, there are powerful people who want these things to happen, and usually politicians bend to that pressure, not always but usually."[30] Nor was he surprised by the boosterish arguments that Rosentraub had promoted in the debate and in his commissioned reports: "Mark is not an economist, even though he allows himself to be called an economist. He was involved in Columbus and in Los Angeles, so he's basically just saying that he did a good job in those places when he writes his case studies and reports. All that had to happen [in Edmonton] was for them [administration] to contact Mark and indicate what they wanted done."[31]

To Council in March

Less than two months after officially voting to start exclusive negotiations with the Katz Group, council met again on March 2, 2011, for further deliberations over the proposed arena development and an update from administration. The CRL report that council had requested in July would not be available until April 6th, but CFO Lorna Rosen did make a brief presentation suggesting that enough tax revenue could be generated over 20 years to pay the costs for borrowing $160 million in initial infrastructure investment. None of Zimbalist's cautionary advice was acknowledged in this speculative update, though administration did say that it had met with representatives from the Stadium Capital Financing Group to discuss the information required for a proposal for a private development. An update was promised in a month.

Knowing that ongoing delays were damaging its credibility, administration emphasized its continuing engagement with various experts to provide the requested information. It had spent roughly $450,000 in 2010 alone on external consultants and would soon spend even more. It had also hired accounting firm KPMG, as an independent financial advisor, to assist with negotiations and to verify the Katz Group's financial ability to meet its commitments; this analysis was never provided to council. And, administration re-hired architectural design company HOK (now Populous) to report on the sustainability of Northlands and to assist in developing options for city-owned land. But much of the information that council requested remained incomplete. Nor would other information like a cost-benefit analysis be provided.[32]

The most revealing information pertained to the incorporation of a community benefits agreement (CBA) into the deal. CBAS are now part of the lexicon of sport-related urban developments, and are pro-actively negotiated by developers and community groups to secure genuine redistributive and legally binding provisions before developments start. They include such things as arrangements for affordable housing, commitments to living wage ordinances, and the inclusion of local job creation strategies. These types of agreements ensure that sport and entertainment districts—especially in vulnerable communities—are as equitable as possible, and that they minimize and mitigate any potential harmful effects, including the displacement of pre-existing businesses and community members as a result of gentrification and, crucially, the loss of housing. While gentrification adds value to property, it changes the character of communities and leads to competition for space and public resources. But less affluent residents often face personal, social, and cultural dislocations as a consequence.

The new arena and entertainment district was to be built in one of the poorest parts of downtown Edmonton, an area that has, historically, been home to the city's most vulnerable residents and the organizations that serve them. For several decades, as mobile working-class and immigrant families and businesses relocated to the suburbs and more Indigenous people moved from reserves to Edmonton's inner city (the only urban space available to them), the concentration of racialized poverty in the downtown core had intensified. These developments were exacerbated by the demise in the 1990s of the federal government's national housing strategy, and by the cumulative impact of the conservative agenda of the Ralph Klein-led provincial government, which brought dramatic cuts to social services, the deinstitutionalization of mental health services, and diminished transfer payments to cities. In 2008, the year that the ALC concluded that a new, publicly-financed arena was feasible and that it "had to be downtown," Edmonton had over 3,000 home-less community members, most of whom were Indigenous and lived in the downtown core.[33] Many social service providers—like Boyle Street Community Services, located a block away from the new arena development—are concentrated in the inner city, along with affordable and subsidized housing, like the MacDonald Lofts building, just across from Rogers Place on the corner of 102 Street and 105 Avenue.

However, instead of providing the types of commitments contained in many well-documented CBAs in North America and Europe—including the LA Live CBA negotiated in 2001 as part of the privately-financed arena and entertainment district development in Los Angeles, and offered up as a key "success story" by Edmonton's arena boosters—administration concluded that the community benefits of a new arena development would derive from "enhancing the city's image," "enhancing the stability of the Oilers' franchise," "attracting and retaining human capital," and "contributing to a more desirable/livable downtown."[34] Although the arena and enter-tainment district was to be built near a pre-existing community of vulnerable and marginalized residents, and adjacent to other less affluent and ethnically diverse neighbourhoods like Central McDougall, McCauley, Boyle Street, and Chinatown, administra-tion argued that a traditional CBA, one that included substantial commitments by developers to provide affordable housing, was simply unnecessary:

A community benefits agreement is a contract between two or more parties which establishes the benefits that one or more parties will receive from a development. Circumstances which typically lead to an agreement of this type are driven by expropriations and displacement which affect a distinct community. A community benefits agreement is typically used as a legal instrument to help mitigate these impacts. The proposed downtown arena site in Edmonton is approximately six acres and is currently unoccupied. The conditions and benefits related to the development of the downtown arena district in Edmonton are different than the conditions and benefits typically addressed in community benefits agreements. For this reason, Administration proposes incorporating a community benefits component into the negotiated agreement with the Katz Group instead of developing a separate community benefits agreement.[35]

While technically correct, as the proposed site was a parking lot, administration ignored the pre-existing, community-use values of the land, as a longstanding and familiar space for homeless community members to socialize, to camp, to feel safe, and to recreate community relations. Indigenous communities have striven to remake livable spaces for themselves in the inner city—a space repeatedly described by arena proponents as simply a "wasteland," even though there were businesses around the final location of the arena and significant amounts of redevelopment (including the Art Gallery of Alberta, which opened in 2010) were already occurring. Both administration and the Katz Group regarded this land and community space as a "new urban frontier" that needed to be reclaimed and resettled with young, affluent members of the professional and largely white creative class.[36] No consideration was given to the inevitable broader impact of gentrification on the surrounding neighbourhoods, leading to the displacement of community members and challenges for affordable housing, social service agencies, and longstanding businesses in the area.

Despite repeated pleas from various social service agencies and community members, and from some councillors, a legally binding

CBA was never negotiated. What passed for a CBA for administration—a three-paragraph attachment to the broader master agreement between the city of Edmonton and the Katz Group—was drafted without community involvement, and without the input of council. As Councillor Tony Caterina reflected,

> For the Community Benefits Agreement, we said to administration, "okay, so you're going to do this?" Again, the consistent theme from administration was, "don't worry about the details now, just approve the arena and we'll get you the community benefits, and we'll look after the displaced people." It never happened.[37]

In retrospect, former city manager Simon Farbrother conceded that the CBA "could have been a bit stronger,"[38] when, in fact, it had been overlooked in the complex negotiations with the Katz Group. The Edmonton arena CBA is an unenforceable agreement with no provisions for affordable housing; no contributions to social service agencies; no commitment to a living wage or binding job-creation strategy for community members; no contributions to parks and recreational facilities; no provision of daycare facilities; and no revenue sharing with the community (let alone the broader city). Nor would the city, which spent hundreds of thousands of dollars on other arena-related research and reports, commission a social impact study or any type of diligent assessment about the potential effects of gentrification and displacement, despite the anticipated increase in property values in the area—the very foundation of the CRL that both the Katz Group and the city were literally banking on.

In Private

Council may have been given a broad and encouraging update in public, but a very different set of discussions took place afterwards in secret. During the 4.5-hour in-camera update, from 11:38 AM to nearly 4 PM, the city manager explained to councillors that, over the past four weeks, the Katz Group and the city had agreed in principle to a number of terms set out in the pre-negotiated financial framework revealed to council in January. But major issues remained, and the initial financing framework had already been considerably altered. In retrospect, it's clear that the Katz Group was trying to minimize any risk associated with the arena and various ancillary developments, while also trying to maximize its profits from the new facility and from the surrounding developments that it expected the city to subsidize.

By this stage in the negotiations, many of the salutary recommendations of the *City Shaping* report had already been abandoned by administration, including the recommendation that surplus cash flow from the facility be made available for debt servicing. The Katz Group also steadfastly refused to agree to a cap of $450 million on the arena's cost. This fictitious estimate had been made years earlier, and they correctly anticipated far higher costs. The Katz Group additionally insisted that the terms of its $100-million contribution to the construction of the arena be altered; while the city expected the full amount to be paid over the course of construction, the Katz Group now wanted to extend its payments over the terms of its lease agreement—a crucial change from its earlier position.

The Katz Group also rejected a $125-million facility ticket tax/user fee as a financing mechanism. While the city had hoped to increase this revenue source as a means of addressing shortfalls associated with the CRL, the Katz Group considered it income for the Oilers. The city also wanted to pursue the use of personal seat licences to minimize the public sector's contribution, but the Katz Group also refused to support this proposal, arguing that it too would diminish its revenue streams. And, while the city wanted to limit funding requests from other levels of government to $100 million, the Katz Group insisted that there should be no ceiling on these types of subsidy demands. Its concerns about fiscal responsibility were not, of course, to be extended to the public sector.

The Katz Group aggressively sought both cost certainty and subsidies for its proposed ancillary developments as well. It refused to commit the promised $100 million that had been a key component of the city's CRL calculations, insisting instead that its private investment be contingent on the development's viability. The Katz Group also demanded that the city commit to leasing office space in a new Katz Group-developed office tower that, it suggested, would fulfill its $100-million contribution to the development. The Katz Group was minimizing its risk while staking its claim to financial advantage in all elements of both the arena and the surrounding property development. In this instance, it demanded another subsidy in the form of an untendered lease agreement with the city of Edmonton. As Rick Daviss from the city of Edmonton pointed out,

> one of the arguments that the Katz Group had was that, in order for them to make the real estate development around the arena work, they needed to have a hotel. For a hotel to work, they needed surrounding retail. For retail to work, they needed an office tower. They all work together, and they said, "We can't commit to all that retail if there's no office space, because if we have retail and restaurants coming in that are depending on 200 nights a year at the arena, they'll go broke, and you're not going to get a hotel that's interested in coming in if the area's only active 200 nights a year, so we need that office density and activity to sustain the hotel, people coming in for conferences and meetings, and to sustain the retail to make it all work. So, you have to commit...The city will be an anchor tenant in our building." And, at the time, we [the city] were looking at consolidating all of our offices, and so we said, "Well, that sounds good, but we can't deal with you directly. We're a public organization, [and so] we do this very transparent and public." They said, "Yeah, but you're investing in an arena, and to make that arena work, you need this to work, so you should invest in this." "It's really part of your arena investment," they said. Yeah, that makes a lot of sense, but we're not going to do it.[39]

In response to the Katz Group's insistence that the city lease space in a new, Katz-owned office tower, a demand that would be made repeatedly during the negotiations, the city's negotiators stated the obvious: formal tender processes would need to be respected for any leased office space.[40] The city was already contemplating the consolidation of its employees in a centralized office tower in the downtown core and would announce its request for proposals in

Daryl Katz brings arena demands to Santa, December 17, 2012.

[Malcolm Mayes/Artizans.com]

2012, but in a way that, arguably, favoured the Katz Group's downtown land holdings. Finally, the Katz Group also sought additional revenue from other properties, including taking over the contract for the city hall parkade, then held by Oxford Properties (yet another subsidy).

A consensus had, however, been reached on other crucial elements. First and foremost, the Katz Group and the city of Edmonton had agreed that the Katz Group would exclusively operate the arena and would receive all operating revenue from the city-owned facility, including non-hockey revenue. The Katz Group would, in turn, pay all operating expenses (excluding, for now, capital maintenance). The city would levy a fee on all tickets sold at Rexall Place from the time of the agreement, with the proceeds dedicated to paying the capital cost of the new arena, further restricting the ability of Northlands to compete with a new, Katz-operated arena. This fee, it was agreed, would continue even after the capital costs were paid to fund capital repairs. The city would continue to finance *up to $250 million* of the total cost of the arena: $125 million to be funded by the ticket tax, and the city's contribution of $125 million, which would be funded by the CRL.

The Katz Group agreed in principle to commit to a location agreement for the Oilers over the duration of its lease with the city of Edmonton—a commitment that shows just how lucrative the new arrangements would be for the franchise. The arena would be made available for use by the city for community events for a certain amount of time per year, and a CBA would be implemented, although the details remained unspecified. Finally, as an indication of just how intertwined the city and the Katz Group had become in this corporate–civic project of building Edmonton, both agreed that the sustainability of the Oilers was a "prime consideration."[41]

To secure a monopoly on all sport and entertainment events in Edmonton (and an additional subsidy), moreover, the Katz Group secretly demanded the inclusion of a non-compete clause with Northlands, as well as the transfer of the city's $2.4 million per year funding arrangement with Northlands, to offset its operating expenses for the new arena. The city refused to commit to any further operational subsidy for the Katz Group, and, while it agreed to explore ways to achieve a non-compete clause with Northlands, administration had no legal recourse to force the non-profit organization to sign any type of non-compete agreement, let alone to alter the terms of its longstanding lease, at least without significant compensation. Strategies to restrict the ability of Northlands to compete with the Katz Group would be hammered out behind closed doors in the months to come, which would prove costly for both Northlands and the city.

11

HEAD GAMES

AFTER THE COUNCIL MEETING on March 2, 2011, pro-arena pundits in the media encouraged councillors to push forward with the arena development, even without crucial information and with considerable gaps in the financing agreement. In a column called "Clarity from Council Proves New Arena is a Must," David Staples attempted to ease concerns about the expenditure of public funds, falsely suggesting that "70 per cent of the arena funding is private—coming either from Oilers owner Daryl Katz or from a user fee in the form of a ticket tax—and just 30 per cent is public, paid for by the Community Revitalization Levy."[1] He also said there were "half-truths coming from folks who don't care at all about revitalizing our downtown, or actively dislike professional sports, or have an interest in the team staying at Rexall Place."[2] As a columnist who was strongly supportive of a publicly-financed arena development, Staples was well connected to sources, both in city hall and in the Katz Group, and was the recipient of a steady flow of partisan information throughout the duration of the debate: "I was observing Mandel for years, talking with Patty Mitsuka [Mayor Mandel's chief of staff] constantly, observing the other side, talking to them constantly."[3]

Council, on the other hand, was worried about the Katz Group's ever-increasing demands, as well as both the lack of information about key issues and the negotiations happening behind closed doors. Had proposals, for example, been exchanged between the city of Edmonton and the Katz Group over the past week? When and where did the meetings occur? Had any records of the negotiations been kept? Who had determined the bargaining priorities and non-negotiable items on behalf of the city and taxpayers? Why was the Katz Group unwilling to provide firm collateral guarantees? How did the city's negotiating team respond to the Katz Group's bargaining positions? Some, including Councillor Linda Sloan, took issue with the pro-arena bias in many of the reports prepared for council: "I feel as though council is being corralled...I don't know why a report from Administration would not be more neutral."[4] Councillor Tony Caterina later concurred, suggesting that the reports were targeted at councillors already in support of the development:

> They were not balanced at all. That was the frustration: administration
> came with their reports and they were steered towards where they
> wanted this to go, and that was obvious from the beginning. But, at
> the end of the debate, they knew there were 3 councillors that opposed
> the arena funding formula and 10 that were on board, so
> administration played to that 10 and so did the mayor's office.[5]

But even Mayor Stephen Mandel, after having imposed his own deadline for a decision, was frustrated with administration's lack of progress. As a result, he continued to pressure both council and administration, stating publicly that he expected a final decision to be made by April 6th, only a few weeks away. He lambasted councillors who questioned the political process, and retreated to classic boosterish arguments: "Either we build a new arena or we become a second class city."[6] He wanted an immediate vote even if it undermined both the city's bargaining position and the ability of councillors to make an informed decision.

Aware of the pressure that council was under, and having been shut out of the negotiations, Northlands tried to reassert its interests. First, it released the results of its Ipsos Reid poll demonstrating the widespread opposition to the use of public funds to build a new arena; the public's expectation that a new, city-owned facility would be operated by either the city of Edmonton or Northlands; and the public's belief that revenue from any new, publicly-financed arena development ought to belong to the city. Perhaps aware that Katz was trying behind closed doors to secure a non-compete clause, Northlands also instructed its solicitor, Roger Swainson, to draft a letter to city manager Simon Farbrother to be shared with members of city council.

Dated April 1, 2011, the letter reminded council that Northlands was entitled to exclusive possession and control of Rexall Place (and the Northlands site) until at least 2034, and that any discussions about the future of Rexall Place therefore had to involve Northlands. Second, Swainson made it clear to council that, whatever the intentions of the Katz Group, Northlands intended to operate Rexall Place as a competitor, "regardless of whether a new license agreement was signed with the Oilers following the expiration of their current agreement in 2014."[7] Finally, the letter from Northlands noted that council was being asked to make urgent and important decisions about the new downtown arena without due diligence on a host of issues:

> *Much of this time-constraint pressure appears to be based upon the fact that the Oilers current lease arrangement with Northlands expires in 2014. Please be advised that Edmonton Northlands is fully prepared to enter into a new license agreement with the Edmonton Oilers Hockey Club for a period after 2014 in order to allow sufficient time for the negotiation and due diligence required for the proposed new arena to be properly completed without unnecessary time constraints.*[8]

Farbrother responded to all of these concerns in a letter dated April 7, 2011, confirming that Northlands' communication had been distributed to council, and that administration would continue to work with both Northlands and HOK to ascertain the effect on Northlands of a new arena.

As a result of all of these concerns, at least 9 out of 13 councillors were not prepared to vote on any impending agreement, while others publicly expressed their concerns about continuing closed-door discussions. For Councillor Caterina, after two months of "supposed negotiations" the deal had only gotten "worse for the city and better for the Katz Group."[9] Councillor Ed Gibbons publicly questioned whether he could trust Simon Farbrother, the new city manager, to be "strong enough to negotiate tough" with the Katz Group.[10]

In advance of the next council meeting on April 6, 2011, Mayor Mandel not only intensified his lobbying for a revitalized downtown as a centre of arts and culture, but also began to promote a new arena financing plan to assuage council's concerns. He used his annual state-of-the-city speech to the Edmonton Chamber of Commerce to laud the arena development, while announcing that the government of Alberta had approved up to $492 million for the completion of the NAIT LRT line that included a stop at the proposed arena site—a timely announcement, as city officials had become increasingly concerned that the money wouldn't arrive in time for the scheduled 2014 opening of the new arena. The funds, requested in the fall of 2010, represented the first substantive investment of Alberta's GreenTRIP transit program. Thus, while the province remained unwilling to support the arena directly, it was prepared to support it in other ways, including ensuring that the NAIT LRT line was prioritized for funding and would be built in time to meet Katz's original deadline for the opening of the new facility. The mayor also continued to insist that, without a new building, "we won't have a hockey team."[11]

That same day, he met with the *Edmonton Journal*'s editorial board to defend the publicly-financed arena development as part of a broader downtown growth agenda, and not "as an act of generosity to a private business."[12]

I say this time and again to my council colleagues: "This is about Edmonton. About what kind of city we can build." And I know he [Katz] is a part of it...But we sat as a city for 50 years and watched our young people leave. We sat as a city that did nothing to create opportunity for people. The time has come for us to be competitive,

*to build the kind of city that will have my children come back here
because they see this as a place of the future.*[13]

Similar anxieties—especially the fear that young people would leave
Edmonton if world-class cultural amenities were not provided—
were regularly recycled by arena proponents even though Edmonton
was in the midst of a sustained period of growth.

Mayor Mandel also told the editorial board that he planned to
put forward a revised financing plan minimizing the use of the
unpopular CRL financing mechanism and raising $95 million from
revenues related to the arena business, including $2.4 million that
the city currently gave Northlands in support of Oilers hockey. This
new plan, he said, would minimize the city's risk. If nothing was
built around the new arena to fund the CRL, the city would have to
make up only $2.4 million per year:

> *My God, I cannot believe that this city cannot support something that
> is going to be in that area [$2.4 million per year]. My God, it would
> just be beyond my imagination. If you boil this down to a couple of
> million dollars, is Edmonton not worth it, with or without Katz?*[14]

Despite the councillors' doubts, and despite not even knowing the
arena's full cost, the *Journal*'s editorial board endorsed the new plan,
and David Staples' subsequent column was simply called, "Time
Has Come for Council to Green-Light Arena Proposal."[15]

April Arm Twisting

All of these promotional efforts were, however, undermined by the
Katz Group, which continued to aggressively defend its interests.
Indeed, before the April 6, 2011 meeting, news emerged that Daryl
Katz had written a letter to Mayor Mandel outlining his refusal to
support a $125-million ticket tax/user fee. Mandel had originally
proposed it to minimize the need for additional public funds and
prevent a tax increase, just as he had promised taxpayers. In a province without a provincial sales tax, a ticket tax/user fee was regarded
by administration as a legitimate way to collect money directly

from hockey fans and concertgoers without a significant additional financial burden on the city. The Katz Group, on the other hand, considered a $125-million ticket tax/user fee to be revenue for itself.

Owners of professional sports teams regularly take such stands in their negotiations with municipalities in order to claim a higher contribution to a public–private financing package, and to accumulate political capital that can be deployed later on. When they eventually concede to the inclusion of a ticket tax in a financing package, as Katz did, they can then claim to have made a substantive concession in the negotiations, even though the money was never theirs in the first place. As Mayor Mandel explained, "For the longest time, it was about the ticket tax. You know, I said, 'We have to have a ticket tax,' and they said, 'Well, that's our money.' But it's like the GST—is that your money? No. Well then, this isn't your money either. It's a tax."[16]

The Katz Group also wanted to keep the ticket tax subsidy that the Oilers currently received at Rexall Place, even if they were now owned by a billionaire who, unlike Northlands, would receive all hockey and non-hockey revenue. Katz invited Mandel to attend a private meeting with NHL commissioner Gary Bettman to discuss the ticket tax issue, but the mayor insisted that the ticket tax was a non-negotiable part of the proposed financing model and "quite properly, refused to be drawn into private, back-channel negotiations with Katz or Bettman."[17] Bettman was in regular contact with Mandel throughout the arena debate, though, and the mayor soon accepted another invitation to engage in private negotiations with Bettman and Katz in New York.

On April 6, 2011, council met to discuss a wide range of reports about the CRL, community benefits, arena governance, and alternative funding methods, including the long-requested report on a private financing option. Council also received a report, *Is a New Arena a Good Fit for Downtown Edmonton?*,[18] by Tom Sutherland, the consultant who had helped the city prepare the pro-arena Capital City Downtown Plan; perhaps unsurprisingly, it was full of supportive quotations from both the plan and from the original pro-arena report produced, at the city's request, by Dr. Dan Mason.

In its report on the CRL, administration provided additional property data about the collection of municipal and business taxes in Edmonton between 2000 and 2010.[19] In contrast to the rhetoric of arena boosters, it confirmed that Edmonton's downtown had experienced substantial growth in recent years—without a new arena and entertainment district. In 2000, the entire downtown had produced only $23.2 million in property tax revenue; by 2010, it produced $86 million, an increase of 271 percent. City-wide growth, in comparison, had been only 152 percent. While downtown municipal taxes had accounted for 6.86 percent of total municipal taxes in 2000, by 2010, this number had grown to 10.11 percent. Downtown business taxes had also steadily increased, from 4.31 percent of total city-wide business taxes in 2000 to 16.45 percent in 2010. Still, even though the report undermined the argument that a new arena district was required to "revitalize" downtown, the expansion of property and business tax values in the downtown core, as well as the growth of the downtown population, assured administration that these values would continue to grow—the crucial gamble associated with the CRL financing mechanism.

Council also received a preliminary CRL boundary map that covered a massive, 29-block radius. Administration argued that a new arena would spur development in this area, and that over the next two decades, the CRL would provide between $125 million and $160 million toward the $450-million cost of the facility. Administration conceded, though, that there would be CRL shortfalls *for the next decade* until enough new development occurred, and that these shortages would have to be covered through an interim financing source, probably a temporary increase in the ticket tax to 9 or 10 percent.

For critics, like the *Journal*'s Paula Simons, the redirection of all future property tax revenue within such an extensive CRL boundary—an area already experiencing significant growth—exclusively to pay for the new arena over the next two decades would

rob municipal and provincial coffers of millions of dollars that could
be spent on things other than subsidizing a hockey rink for the benefit

of a private company. Last year, the residential and commercial prop-
erty within the proposed CRL zone generated almost $16 million in
municipal and provincial tax revenues. Does it really make sense to
freeze or cap that revenue pool for the next 20 years—just as another
property and development boom begins—and divert the entire
increase to one project?[20]

The CRL was a gamble for the public sector—not for the Katz Group. Would there be enough of a lift in tax assessments to cover most of the arena debt and other infrastructure expenses over two decades?

Administration had also been directed to engage the Chicago-based Stadium Capital Financing Group, which had argued that it was possible to finance the cost of a new arena through a seat condominium/mortgage model. In this model, a number of seats (2,000–3,000) within a facility are made available for fans to purchase upfront, and subsequently own, for a period of decades, at a cost of hundreds of thousands of dollars; this money can then be applied to the capital cost of construction. However, this model had yet to be applied in a professional sport setting (although it has been used to finance NCAA stadiums in the United States), precisely because it would decrease revenue from annual ticket sales. Thus, it runs against the dominant business model of major league sport franchises. Even though it could limit fiscal participation from the city of Edmonton and taxpayers, it was vigorously opposed by both the Katz Group and the NHL. On the issue, Gary Bettman wrote to the city manager:

> *The NHL does not believe seat mortgages work as a general matter, or*
> *that seat mortgages could work in Edmonton. In our view, the concept*
> *of seat mortgages has a number of weaknesses which renders it an*
> *inappropriate model for financing NHL clubs and construction of NHL*
> *arenas. Perhaps most important, we believe that the model serves to*
> *severely limit the NHL club's ability to receive in future years a steady*
> *stream of fundamentally important revenues that is [sic] necessary*
> *for the club's long-term viability—essentially, in this instance, seat*

mortgages would mortgage the club's future financial viability in order to fund construction of the arena. [21]

While cities are invited by the NHL to embrace risky financing ventures in building costly arenas, the league's wealthy owners, on the other hand, demand a "steady stream" of guaranteed revenues for decades to come.

In response to council's request for a detailed report on the private financing option, administration simply provided a brief update: "Given the costs of operating such a facility and the costs of operating an NHL franchise," it said, "the business case to proceed with 100 per cent private funding may not be positive." And, it added:

> *Funding a $450-million arena in downtown Edmonton from totally private sources would be difficult. Assuming an owner equity contribution of $100 million, the mortgage on $350 million would amount to approximately $23 million annually for 30 years at a 5 per cent interest rate. The mortgage payments would need to come from the operational revenue of the facility.* [22]

However, administration did not provide revenue and operating income projections to demonstrate conclusively that the Katz Group could not afford to make payments on a $350-million mortgage, including CSL's earlier conservative projections that the Oilers would benefit from an average annual increase in profitability of $16.6 million over the first five years in the new arena. Nor did administration identify other potential sources of funding such as the ticket surcharge/user fee ($125 million or more) that would have reduced the mortgage amount to $225 million, or the potential redirection of the city's annual contribution to Rexall Place ($2.4 million per year). Administration had also anchored the cost of a new arena at $450 million, and a less expensive facility—one that may well have been within reach of private financing—was never considered. To our knowledge, this short note, lacking any detailed analysis, including an analysis of other revenue streams available to the Katz Group, was the only civic document that discussed any type of private financing option.

Council also received another lengthy verbal, in-camera update from administration on the status of the ongoing negotiations with the Katz Group, beginning at 4:33 PM and ending at 8:23 PM. Councillors are discouraged from leaving in-camera meetings, and all support staff who could have provided important resources and information had gone home for the night. Council was now pushed to support a motion authorizing administration to negotiate a firm deal with the Katz Group, having given them only three options:

1. *Do nothing: Oilers' lease expires.*
2. *Renovate Rexall Place: requires $200 million and Oilers will not stay.*
3. *Build a new arena: requires $450 million, provides downtown development opportunities, Oilers will commit to staying in Edmonton for 30 years and will provide $100 million in private investment.*[23]

Clearly, administration had simply accepted the Oilers' threats to leave Edmonton without any evidence whatsoever (e.g., a market analysis) to support these claims, not even acknowledging the routine nature of such threats. Administration had also accepted a host of other assumptions about the status of the NHL in Edmonton: that the Oilers needed a sustainable income stream (as if one hadn't been provided already); that they required a larger arena with greater capacity; and that they needed access to both hockey and non-hockey revenue from a publicly-financed facility to provide them with a "competitive advantage." Some councillors, like Karen Leibovici, also accepted these assumptions as fact. As she recalled in our interview:

KAREN LEIBOVICI (KL): *The Oilers leaving Edmonton, I think, would have left a huge hole for us, and, you know, there's some who say, "No, they wouldn't have left." They would have left. There's a*

lot of other cities that are more than willing to build a new arena to
bring the team there.

JAY SCHERER (JS): *So, I'm one of the people who said they would*
never have left.

KL: *Okay. I can tell you that they would have left.*

JS: *And what was the basis for that?*

KL: *Because Daryl said so.*

JS: *But owners say that all the time.*

KL: *Well, my understanding was that at a certain point, teams don't*
stay and they move.

JS: *This was a profitable...*

KL: *Actually, they don't make money. They actually don't make money*
until they're in the playoffs. No team makes money—maybe New
York does or Chicago or Boston, but they don't make money unless
they're in the playoffs. So Edmonton has been less than profitable.
Even the concessions and all the rest don't cover what the costs are.
I know that.[24]

Behind closed doors, too, council saw an updated financing framework that had been negotiated in response to the reluctance of senior levels of government to contribute $100 million. The new proposal shifted the city's subsidy of Rexall Place to the new arena and dedicated new downtown parking revenue to the cost of the facility. In other words, the new proposed framework transferred a greater portion of the cost (and the risk) to the public sector, while keeping the Katz Group's contribution anchored at $100 million.

Over the course of the four-hour meeting, council ultimately supported various aspects of the new financing framework, with a wide range of concessions and commitments, many of which would never be fulfilled. Upon the conclusion of the in-camera session, Mayor Mandel moved a pre-prepared, 17-part omnibus motion that outlined the specific terms and conditions that administration would be instructed to secure as part of their negotiations with the Katz Group, in order to finalize the financial framework for a new arena development. The logic was simple: by approving this motion, council signalled its willingness to endorse a deal with the Katz Group, if these precise terms were met.

The public motion confirmed a maximum cost of $450 million (excluding infrastructure costs); a user fee contribution of $125 million, which Katz continued to contest; the Katz Group's $100-million contribution to the capital cost of the arena; the city's contribution of $125 million; and a 30-year location agreement. The $100-million contribution to ancillary development had disappeared. Given the considerable funding gap that remained, council requested that administration negotiate a revenue-sharing agreement for arena-related revenue (including naming rights and parking), which both administration and Mayor Mandel knew the Katz Group would never agree to. Council also asked for a firm CBA to ensure tangible benefits to the inner-city community, and for information on the possibility of a lottery with proceeds directed toward community benefits. Council directed administration to continue to work with Northlands to address the city's financial challenges, and to refuse to proceed with the arena development until the full balance of funds had been confirmed—another commitment that would never be fulfilled.

The most substantive concession that arose from this meeting, though, was a new model associated with the CRL financing mechanism, one that many councillors and the broader electorate continued to identify as a wager whose stakes were simply too high for the city to bet on. Now, only $20 million of the estimated $160-million tax uplift would be dedicated toward the arena, and the remaining funds would pay for improvements in other parts of the downtown core. The balance of the city's contribution of $125 million would, in turn, come from other sources, including the city's existing financial support of Northlands, new downtown parking revenue that would have otherwise gone to Northlands, and other unspecified municipal revenue streams. As Karen Leibovici recalled,

Stephen is great at making deals and people's taxes weren't being increased. The arena was being paid for through this combination of the CRL, the parking revenue, the ticket tax which is a user tax, and

some upfront dollars, and then we took the money that we were giving
annually to Northlands to the new arena.[25]

Not all councillors, including Tony Caterina, were convinced of
the merits of the deal, especially with the radically fluctuating CRL
figures and estimates:

It was all speculative. We actually had two projects that were based
on CRLs that had gone nowhere, and we spent millions on supportive
infrastructure to spur them. So, when someone else comes by and says,
"No, CRLs are good, this is going to happen," well, it's hard to believe
or justify, especially with that type of investment. Looking at it now,
in 2016/2017, I go, okay, it worked to a certain degree. But, a number
of the projects were already slated to go regardless of the arena or not.
They were already announced and prepared to go. But the numbers
were always changing, and even some of Katz's commitments were
changing, and that made it awfully difficult to support. You know, is
this guy serious? Is it true? Are we just getting sucked into funding this
and not realizing any of the development benefits? So even the process
of going through—the CRL was changed so many times, and it was
like the 11th hour on everything, everything's pressing, you've gotta
support it now. Then you change the CRL, you've gotta support it now.
Then you change the CRL again and you gotta support it. Until it actu-
ally fit the end result of what they needed to justify. Yeah, it was last
minute. You know, pressure's on, make the decision.[26]

However, on this day, the concessions were enough to sway many
councillors to vote in favour of the motion.[27] Many on council
thought that the entire city centre now stood to benefit from the
uplift of municipal property tax revenue, and all but three councillors (Don Iveson, Linda Sloan, and Tony Caterina) voted in favour
of the omnibus motion. The mayor was prepared to introduce a
motion with commitments that could not possibly be fulfilled—
including revenue sharing and a radically reduced reliance on the
CRL—to secure the council votes necessary to ratify the financial
framework and keep the political process moving forward. In May,

though, council would be asked to approve an altogether different deal. Administration would claim that it had fulfilled the 17 commitments that council had ratified, even though CRL numbers would continue to fluctuate.

While many lauded the mayor's negotiating skills and his ability to establish a consensus on council, others were unconvinced, including the *Journal*'s business columnist, Gary Lamphier, who took direct aim at issues ignored by administration in its negotiations with the Katz Group:

> *I'm not willing to adopt the mayor's perspective just because he tells me to. When he says the Oilers will move if they don't get a new home, I want to know where one of the league's most profitable teams (according to* Forbes*) would go. Winnipeg? Quebec City? Kansas City? That seems unlikely. Especially when so many existing NHL clubs are struggling. Threats of a move in 2014 sound like little more than blackmail to me. And if a project is attractive, it shouldn't require such threats to proceed.*

He continued,

> *I'd like to see Katz or Bob Black—Katz's designated arena czar—at least try to answer some basic questions. Questions like the ones I sent to Black's media relations guy, Steve Hogle, back in early March...* Forbes *magazine's latest annual survey shows the Oilers are among the top 10 teams in the NHL on an annual operating-profit basis. Yet Katz Group's representatives told council last summer the team has lost money for 10 years. Why not put this issue to rest by opening the Oilers' books? Katz has committed $100 million to the new arena and $100 million to adjacent private development (although the latter conspicuously went missing from last week's council motion). Since the arena funding model remains short of the $450-million target, why doesn't Katz simply commit $200 million to the arena itself? San Diego's Petco Park development—which has been held up as a success by many—calls for a revenue split between the city and the Padres, which shared the financing costs for the stadium. If taxes are used to*

help fund a new Edmonton arena, why shouldn't taxpayers here also
share in some of the upside?[28]

As outsiders to the negotiations, executives from Northlands
continued to insist that they intended to remain in the sports and
entertainment business even without the Oilers, and even if the
city of Edmonton reallocated its operational funding to pay for
the downtown development. As Richard Andersen noted, the $2.4-
million subsidy that Northlands received from the city fell well short
of the $6-million operating costs that the organization incurred
from Oilers' games, and the organization fully intended to compete
with a new, Katz-run facility: "I know I haven't made a career out of
playing bluffs and Northlands hasn't. When we say something, we
mean it."[29]

Success for the Katz Group

Just weeks later, another decision loomed as council was invited
to approve—without any notice and without any documentation—
the "final" framework negotiated between the city and the Katz
Group. The city council agenda for May 18th noted that council
would receive a verbal update from the city manager, but there was
no mention of a formal agreement on the agenda. Nor had any
background documents been provided in advance of the meeting,
although normal protocol required that councillors have two business days to review public documents before a vote. Council had
just concluded three long days, including two days of 12-hour
public hearings, on an unrelated matter, and councillors were not
prepared to engage in an extensive discussion about the arena, let
alone vote on a financial agreement. However, the impetus for all
of these tactics was clear: administration felt that, over the course
of four weeks of negotiations, it had fully secured the requisite
commitments from the Katz Group, as stipulated by council earlier
in April. However, other political pressures added to the urgency of
this controversial vote. Both the Katz Group and the city needed an
official agreement to formally approach the provincial government
and Ed Stelmach, the Edmonton-area premier who was soon to

leave office, to secure the missing $100-million contribution, plus, they hoped, another $125-million loan to cover the ticket tax. (Prime Minister Stephen Harper had already refused to contribute federal funds.)

Before the vote, the Katz Group informed council of its rejection of the equity seats rights financing model proposed by the Stadium Capital Financing Group. Having just spent the past four weeks negotiating a public financing framework with administration, and with key proponents including the mayor already on board, council knew that a private sector option was never really a genuine consideration. At best, discussion of it, however cursory, offered a veneer of diligence; at worst, it distracted a council now overloaded with arena-related information and documentation.

Just as in April, council met behind closed doors, beginning late, at 4:20 PM, and ending over four hours later at 8:46 PM, after a day that had begun at 9:30 AM. Administration claimed that it had fully addressed the 17-part omnibus motion that council had passed in April. Many of the 17 points had been addressed, but others had been altered, and an entirely new amendment had been inserted—a non-compete clause with Northlands.

Administration was, predictably, unable to secure a revenue-sharing agreement with the Katz Group, which would be the sole operator of the city-owned facility. However, the organization had now agreed to pay for all maintenance and upgrades, as well as operating and capital expense costs. In turn, the Katz Group would be the sole recipient of all revenue from the new arena, including the lucrative naming rights and parking revenue from the facility, along with non-hockey revenue. The Katz Group stood by its earlier commitment to invest $100 million in ancillary developments "subject to commercial viability," but continued to attempt to defer paying the full amount of its $100-million contribution to the capital cost of the arena during construction. Importantly, the Katz Group agreed to reintroduce the $125-million user fee financing mechanism under the guise of a "facility improvement fee"—wording that would allow the organization to claim that this source of income was not part of its NHL revenue stream—but with several new strings attached. The city would now be required to request an interest-free loan from the province to cover the $125 million of borrowing that would fund the facility improvement fee. (The city is able to borrow money at lower rates than companies like the Katz Group, and would, in effect, be subsidizing the organization by holding the debt for this loan.) Furthermore, the ticket tax/facility improvement fee would be managed and collected by the Katz Group, even though the city would be responsible for the $125-million loan needed to finance construction costs—a concession of concern for some councillors because it increased the public sector's liability to the benefit of the Katz Group.

The Katz Group was now prepared to extend the length of the location agreement from 30 to 35 years, while granting the city access to the arena for four weeks per year. According to administration, the Katz Group had, in fact, been prepared to sign a 40-year agreement with an option to extend—an indication that the Katz Group knew the value of the proposed agreement and the profit that it stood to gain in Edmonton in the decades to come, especially if it secured a non-compete clause from Northlands and established a monopoly on the sports and entertainment industry.

In contrast to the April agreement, administration agreed to increase its CRL commitment from $20 million to $45 million, and to purchase land from the Katz Group at current fair market value. Finally, the city continued to commit to financing a maximum of $250 million (including the facility improvement fee), and agreed again that the project would not proceed until the balance of funds was confirmed, and that the provincial government ought to be approached to make up the $100 million still unaccounted for. The biggest difference between the May agreement and the earlier one in April, though, was the introduction of the non-compete clause with Northlands.

The in-camera meeting was a tense affair, with administration claiming that it had "dealt with" the 17 conditions in April's motion and that there was "no additional liability for the city." Several councillors disagreed, especially in light of the Katz Group's new non-compete demand. Indeed, as Councillor Sloan's notes outlined, "This is not a response to council's April 6 motion. This is a new proposal, one in Katz's favour, that increases the public commitment and front-end investment in subsidies. In no way, shape or form is this the final deal—administration is seeking council's endorsement to be used as a platform for seeking provincial funds."[30]

Council also challenged the Katz Group's ongoing refusal to share revenues and administration's capitulation to this refusal. Administration's response contradicted the public narrative crafted by boosters, including both Katz and Mayor Mandel, about the importance of a new arena for the city, especially for its downtown core. City manager Simon Farbrother asserted: "It's about significantly increasing their revenue streams to increase their sustainability over the next 35 years. This isn't about building a building. This is about building a viable NHL franchise."[31] Administration had always known Katz's non-negotiable position on revenue sharing, despite including it as an option in the April motion. Behind closed doors, in contrast to his public pronouncements, Mayor Mandel now also conceded that the project's real cost could be $525 million, while emphasizing the benefits of a new downtown facility: the city would have no operating costs and maintenance expenses, and there would be increased downtown parking revenue and additional investment in the downtown core.

Administration was equally frank about the Katz Group's demand for a non-compete clause with Northlands: "If they don't get it we won't be building an arena downtown. From the point of view of the Katz Group, it is their position that they are building an arena, and they won't unless they have a non-compete clause."[32] Some councillors refused to accept this new demand, including Kerry Diotte: "That's huge. That's new and was not a part of the April motion."[33] Administration was convinced that this demand was non-negotiable. The stakes were enormous, especially because no notification had been given to Northlands of what was being considered by council behind closed doors—arrangements that would inevitably damage the viability of its business.

A new partnership. Arena deal sees Edmonton bypass Northlands for Katz Group, May 23, 2011. [Malcolm Mayes/Artizans.com]

Nevertheless, administration, the mayor, and various pro-arena councillors pressured remaining councillors not only to support the new deal, but also to keep its precise terms private—especially the non-compete clause with Northlands—even though council had made public the 17-part motion endorsed in April. "Considering that all other 17 points were made public," asked Kerry Diotte, "why wouldn't we make the non-compete clause public? Shouldn't this all be in public?"[34] The city manager, Simon Farbrother, though, said that fully disclosing the deal—a deal that had been altered in significant ways from the April framework—would "compromise your ability to get the $100 million [from the province]."[35] Farbrother had earlier conceded that, "A large amount could be discussed in public, a majority of this piece could be discussed in public. But the Katz Group said if council agrees to this package that they wouldn't agree to parts of the deal being debated in public."[36] For administration, not only would an official agreement apply pressure on the provincial government to secure additional funds, but it would also position Edmonton as a city that was prepared to keep an NHL franchise, thereby responding to two problems, namely, "the Oilers say they are going to leave and the NHL says the city is difficult."[37]

Councillor Tony Caterina was concerned about the changes made since April, but administration was adamant that the agreement had to be approved by council immediately, without any further negotiation or oversight:

> *TONY CATERINA (TC): So we don't have the opportunity to hit the ball back to the other court?*
>
> *SIMON FARBROTHER: It is our position that it would be counter-productive.*
>
> *TC: Given the magnitude of this decision, regardless of the hours spent negotiating, I don't think that's valid.*[38]

Administration was willingly ceding opportunities to push back harder in the negotiations and had accepted the Katz Group's demands despite the opposition of some councillors, all without public input. As Caterina reflected,

> *My point was that I didn't feel that administration was pushing them at all. I felt more that Simon was working for them. Like it just felt that way, that if we're sitting here having negotiations, if he's [Katz] threatening to go to Quebec, I don't know, threaten to pack for him. You know, say, "Here, we'll hire the truck if you want to go." Because he played hardball. And again, I can't blame him for that. Katz did what he needed to do to advance his position. We could have done a much better job in negotiating that from the people we sent there to do it and that. And Simon, it was obvious right from the beginning…but it didn't feel like he was actually acting on our behalf. It felt like he was acting on their behalf.*[39]

Certainly, administration had wholly accepted the position of the NHL team. Caterina raised other important questions during the in-camera discussion, including how much property tax would be foregone in light of the city owning the land upon which the arena would be built—a question that was never answered. He also asked for a guarantee that administration would not come back to council to "cover the missing $100 million from the province," to which the city manager responded, "We've never suggested we'd backstop the provincial funds."[40]

Despite all of these concerns, late in the evening, council met publicly to vote on a motion by Councillor Jane Batty to approve the financial framework to build a new downtown arena. As requested in-camera by administration, all of the specific terms of the agreement—especially the controversial non-compete clause with Northlands—remained secret.

The vote was far from unanimous, with five councillors voting no (Don Iveson, Linda Sloan, Ed Gibbons, Kerry Diotte, and Tony Caterina). But most councillors and the mayor voted yes—demonstrating that there was enough support on council to push the deal through, despite glaring gaps in financing and a lack of revenue sharing. For critics, like business columnist Gary Lamphier, however, the "staged late-night theatrics" at city hall had simply been designed to "ram through...a half-baked deal in the hope that it can be used to extract funds from a lame-duck premier before he makes his official exit."[41] As Councillor Sloan reflected to Lamphier,

I don't think manipulation is too strong a word. I have to say I feel to a degree that councillors were puppets, with Mr. Katz and Mr. Bettman and the mayor pulling the strings. We had just come through three long days, including two 12-hour public hearing days discussing the Kanata gravel pit application. And we had a published city council agenda that made no mention of this draft agreement being an item on the agenda. Even in the presentation in the [closed-door] session there was no report. It was just a series of Power-Point [sic] slides. So councillors were left to ask questions, and again there was really nothing [in terms of] written commitments or even draft written commitments. The justification for bringing this [motion] with no

advance notification and no written report was hinged completely on
the imminent departure of the premier. It was made clear to council in
the [private] session.[42]

Without revealing the full extent of the discussions, Councillor
Sloan noted some worrying statements made behind closed doors
about Northlands, including suggestions that the city would attempt
to prevent the organization from competing against any Katz-run
facility: "There were things said in that [closed-door] session
that would have a direct impact on Northlands, and there was no
clear indication that Northlands had been advised in advance."[43]
Councillor Ed Gibbons was equally perplexed by the closed-door
meeting: "What was the rush? Was it that the Katz Group had to
rush in and glad hand? I just felt like I was corralled and pushed
to the chute. I don't mind losing votes, but I do dislike if I can't
digest what everybody has voted 'Yes' on."[44] Despite these concerns,
though, arena proponents were understandably elated, if unsur-
prised; unbeknownst to councillors, a press conference had already
been organized by the Katz Group in anticipation of a favourable
vote. Mayor Mandel, meanwhile, personally called Daryl Katz in
Vancouver to pass on the good news. Katz took the call in his suite
in Rogers Arena, while watching a Canucks playoff game with Gary
Bettman.[45]

12

LOBBYING THE PROVINCE, SLAMMING NORTHLANDS

STEPHEN MANDEL, Daryl Katz, and Gary Bettman were not the only people overjoyed with the terms of the agreement crafted in May 2011. So were several media boosters, who were also quite untroubled by the democratic deficit accompanying the in-camera deliberations and council's late-night vote. Terry Jones, the sports columnist for the *Edmonton Sun*, crowed that it was a "great day in the history of the City of Champions," writing somewhat more ominously the next day that "somebody ought to make sure to record the names of the five councillors who voted against [the agreement]."[1] Jones had been personally invited by Bettman to join Katz in his suite in Vancouver for an exclusive interview after the deal was approved. An editorial in the *Edmonton Journal*, meanwhile, boasted that the arena development "took a major and wonderful jump forward Wednesday,"[2] while acknowledging the $100-million shortfall and the likelihood that Northlands would not agree to a non-compete clause.[3]

On June 6, 2011, Mayor Mandel wrote to Premier Ed Stelmach to say that "general terms of an agreement framework between the City of Edmonton and the Katz Group to build a new arena in the North Central Alberta region" had been reached after "two years of due diligence, extensive community consultation and negotiations." Moreover, he wrote,

> *Based on a maximum of [sic] $450 million budget, we must raise an*
> *additional $100 million in order to move forward. Given the impor-*
> *tance of the project, not solely to the City of Edmonton, but across the*
> *Capital Region and central and northern Alberta, City Council has*
> *authorized me to ask your Government to begin a process to determine*
> *a role for the Province of Alberta as a funding partner to the City on*
> *this project, helping to bridge the remaining gap of $100 million.*[4]

He believed that a firm agreement between the city and the Katz
Group would force the premier's hand to support the arena development financially, but Stelmach repeated the government of Alberta's
refusal to grant directly public funds for a new arena. This time,
though, his statement appeared to leave the door open for other
more creative and indirect solutions to addressing the $100-million
funding gap.[5] Boosters therefore intensified their lobbying of the
province, including David Staples, who repeated the old threat that
the Oilers would leave if they didn't get what they wanted:

> *a new arena is needed to keep the NHL in Edmonton; a massive public*
> *investment in Rexall Place makes little sense; the proposed downtown*
> *project enjoys massive public support; it will provide a huge benefit*
> *to Edmonton's neglected downtown; it is normal for the government*
> *to help build this kind of infrastructure; it's a fair deal by NHL stan-*
> *dards; and, finally, a $100-million investment is much less than other*
> *provincial governments in Quebec and Manitoba are now set to pay*
> *for NHL arenas.*[6]

Staples was exaggerating public support, as boosters tend to do,
and he ignored the obvious facts that the premier recognized the
existence of significant opposition, and, as a political conservative,
believed that the private sector should be responsible for a new
arena. Staples, who had supported all previous iterations of the
agreement between the city and the Katz Group, was equally selective with his other claims: a fair agreement by the standards of the
NHL and its billionaire owners, for instance, could by no means be
equated to a fiscally responsible deal for the citizens of Edmonton.

And, to suggest that the Alberta government had no choice but to provide $100 million for a new arena simply because other provincial governments in Manitoba and Quebec had contributed to new facilities was another weak argument, one that ignored the lower cost of the MTS Centre in Winnipeg—$133.5 million—and the use there of money from casinos and other gambling revenue, not from taxpayers. Staples also greatly exaggerated the Katz Group's contribution: "He's investing $225 million through a direct $100-million investment and a $125-million ticket tax on Oilers fans and concert goers. That amounts to half of the $450 million project."[7]

The premier did suggest that money from the Municipal Sustainability Initiative (MSI) might be used to finance the new arena development. The MSI was a 10-year program implemented in 2006 by the province to help municipalities address a profound provincial infrastructure deficit inherited from the Ralph Klein era (an era of debt and deficit elimination), to be used for such things as transit systems, bridges, roadways, libraries, and recreational and sports facilities. Under the program, municipalities could determine their own priorities for the use of the funds, and Edmonton's share was estimated to be $2.1 billion over the duration of the MSI. Moreover, the provincial government had already invested in Edmonton's downtown by providing funds for the new Royal Alberta Museum and the NAIT LRT line, despite, as Stelmach pointed out, "the worst economic recession in half a century."[8]

The premier's MSI proposal had the effect of diffusing the pressure he was facing to provide $100 million in arena funding and deflecting the political spotlight back onto Mayor Mandel and council. But it was also, as it turned out, a complete non-starter. Having met with the mayor in late July, Stelmach knew that the city of Edmonton had already dedicated the full amount of its existing MSI funding to other projects, as Mandel reminded him in a follow-up letter on August 8, 2011:

> Edmonton's current MSI projections have been fully allocated for the
> duration of the program on key priorities including roads, transit and
> community facilities. Thus, as was discussed in our meeting, only by

adding new money to the program would Edmonton be in a position to consider funding any new projects.[9]

Mandel was optimistic, but the province now faced challenging economic circumstances and Stelmach was under pressure from his own party to retire as soon as possible. A new leader was unlikely to view any new financial commitments more favourably.

Both the Katz Group and the mayor recognized the increasingly urgent need to secure more MSI funding to cover the $100-million gap, and so the Katz Group intensified its lobbying of the provincial government, asking MLAs to redirect phone calls from constituents with questions about the arena deal and the potential use of MSI funding to the Katz Group's own communication team. This offer to perform communications work, which had been at least partially accepted in other forms by the city of Edmonton, was viewed by MLAs, according to Liberal Hugh MacDonald, as "political interference."[10]

Arena boosters also continued to sharpen their criticism of Northlands, whose executives had refused to comply with the wishes of both the city and the Katz Group that they sign a non-compete clause. Following the submission of its 2011 Capital Budget to council, which contained a line amount of $770,000 to replace seats in the lower bowl of Rexall Place, executives from Northlands emphasized that they were prepared to compete with the Katz Group for concerts and other events, even if the Oilers relocated to a new arena, and even if the city withdrew the funding that it provided to the organization. Council approved Northlands' budget, which also included $4.7 million in other upgrades across the site.

While Mayor Mandel had publicly stated that he hoped "Northlands would be a co-operative partner,"[11] he knew that the city had concluded bilateral agreements with the Oilers behind closed doors. In response to Northlands' recalcitrance in these matters, Mayor Mandel embraced an altogether different tactic in an attempt to sideline the organization further; he demanded that Northlands make public its complete financial records to demonstrate its projected continued viability after the new arena opened, especially in light of the organization's remaining $56-million debt for the Expo Centre. This was a demand that had never been made of the Katz Group, even though the city was prepared to make a considerably greater investment in a new facility than it had made in its loan to Northlands. Northlands responded by simply noting that, unlike the Katz Group, it annually filed its independently audited financial statements online, and that it was not bound to disclose any additional information to council, especially if that sensitive information could benefit its direct competitors. As Richard Andersen explained in a letter to city manager Simon Farbrother, Northlands was prepared to defend its interests in a new era in which the "City and the Katz Group will be our competitors."[12]

A New CRL

News came in August that the Katz Group had met with representatives from Enoch Cree Nation about building a new arena on the reserve just west of Edmonton. The motive for this meeting was transparent. It was yet another a clumsy attempt to pressure the city into making additional concessions. Councillor Don Iveson was prepared to call the bluff: "I think there's just another round of collective eye-rolling online and, I'm sure, out there in public. A veiled threat to put it in the region is better than a veiled threat to move it somewhere else in Canada, so I guess we're making progress."[13]

With no provincial funding, the Katz Group's unwillingness to contribute more money, and the mayor's commitment that no existing municipal grant money would be used to finance the new arena, the city was left with one remaining option: relying even more heavily on the CRL and property tax revenue. Despite public opposition, and the mayor's promise to minimize the use of the CRL to pay for the arena, the city announced in August a new proposed CRL boundary that would cover 60 blocks of Edmonton's downtown, more than double its initial proposal. Existing office buildings and major hotels and amenities would therefore be subject to the CRL, and any growth in their tax revenues would no longer be going to support general revenues, but would be dedicated to supporting the arena district. This expansive CRL, administration suggested, would be used to finance not only the arena development, but also some of its ancillary costs, including land purchases, the LRT connection, and roughly half the cost of the 104 Avenue pedway. It would also now fund other infrastructure projects in the downtown core like wider sidewalks, parks, streetlights, and decorative paving.[14]

The inclusion of other downtown development projects was designed, in part, to secure provincial approval for such an expansive plan. The new CRL would generate an estimated $1.2 billion in funding over 20 years that would be redirected to pay for all of these amenities, including $242 million that would otherwise have gone to the province for school taxes. The inclusion of these projects, though, created a problem for those councillors who supported the broader development of Edmonton's downtown, but not the arena deal, like Councillor Iveson: "I would feel really conflicted about voting on a CRL which funds a lot of projects I support, and the arena project."[15]

The new proposed CRL boundary was enthusiastically endorsed by Edmonton's boosters, including the Downtown Business Association, whose membership stood to benefit from infrastructure investments and the prospect of increases in property values and business activity from the arena development. As the association's executive director, Jim Taylor, remarked, using a well-rehearsed narrative that had long been deployed to justify public financing of the new facility, "It's not just the arena. Downtown is about to substantially change. The beauty of it is you're not going to be paying your house taxes toward these things."[16] This argument suggested, though, that the CRL was new money rather than just a redirection of existing property taxes. In other words, any increases in property tax revenue from the revitalization zone would be dedicated solely to paying for those amenities, rather than other public services and needs that would then have to be paid for by the city at large. And, if other areas of the city declined in value as investment and spending shifted to the downtown, there would be an even smaller municipal base of property tax to draw from, resulting in the need to either raise taxes or cut the budget.

The government of Alberta was, of course, aware of all of these issues. And, as the Minister of Alberta Municipal Affairs, Doug Griffiths, noted, the province had never intended that a CRL be used to pay for an arena development for a professional sports franchise. Beyond this, as Griffiths explained, he had a number of other philosophical issues with the size of the boundary that the city of Edmonton was proposing, as well as with the fact that the city had simply assumed that a CRL would be automatically approved by the province:

> The challenge we had was that the downtown redevelopment zone...I mean, it didn't capture just parts that were supposed to be redeveloped. It captured parts that were already redeveloped...and some very expensive new buildings had gone up and the property taxes had gone through the roof for those buildings. And the city was essentially saying, "We want to keep that revenue too, from the province, so that we can put it into the new development."...I would use the Epcor building as an example. It had just gone up and you include it [in] the redevelopment zone, but it was there before you were introducing the CRL, it's not really part of the new [one]. It's already happened, right? But the challenge is, if they didn't put new buildings in for a project of that size for redevelopment of an area that needed investment, and all that infrastructure and the area didn't generate any property taxes, you wouldn't have any money to put back in. It was sort of a catch-22, so in order to raise the funds to have money to put into the redevelopment, you needed to put some new buildings in there, which wasn't the intent of the CRL...We did discuss this with the city and we narrowed down the land that was included in the CRL, so that it was more reasonable and realistic. Otherwise, I thought, the way this is escalating...the entire downtown core will be the CRL...We negotiated it down with the city to get it a lot more reasonable, knowing they still needed revenue from somewhere to put back in to pay for the sidewalks and lot of the sewer and the LRT and that redevelopment stuff.[17]

Still, as Griffiths explained, the provincial government had already approved a CRL for Calgary, and there was pressure to provide

Edmonton with an equivalent financing mechanism to support the arena: "The legislation was there, [so] it was really hard to deny them one. It was more about what area they were going to include in the CRL, but they hadn't actually got official approval from the province when they began the process."[18]

The city came clean about some other expenses that fall. It had, for example, already spent $1.15 million on lawyers and external consultants, and expected to spend another $600,000 before the end of the year on other arena-related matters, pushing the total to over $1.75 million. Some councillors, like Tony Caterina, thought engaging in these considerable expenses in advance of having secured a definitive funding model for the new arena premature: "The city is moving too fast. We shouldn't have actually started [negotiations]. We've known for a long time that this [$100 million] isn't coming."[19] Likewise, for other councillors, including Ed Gibbons, these costs indicated an increasingly one-sided public–private partnership: "If Mr. Katz wants the deal, why isn't he paying for some of the costs?"[20] These types of expenses, often fully disclosed only after the fact, contribute substantially to the overall cost for the public sector of such projects.

The Katz Group's negotiating tactics continued to be both divisive and irritating for some members of council and many citizens, and public resentment rose even higher with the revelation that Katz himself had moved to Vancouver and had been living in the penthouse suite at the Fairmont Pacific Rim Hotel, purchased for over $15 million.[21] The discrepancy between the PR accompanying Katz's purchase of the Oilers franchise and his vision of a new downtown arena for his "hometown" and his own lack of commitment to making Edmonton his permanent home was glaring. Unsurprising as it may be that a plutocrat would have multiple homes across North America, the revelation highlighted Katz's wealth and privilege at a time when he was demanding hundreds of millions of dollars in public subsidy and continuing his threats to relocate the Oilers.

New York, New York

Katz ignored the criticism, and in mid-September he announced another deadline for the completion of a final financing framework with the city: October 31, 2011. Council had received a private update from city manager Simon Farbrother on September 14, 2011 that the latest deadline was related to the impending expiration of the Katz Group's options on land holdings for the arena development; in other words, the cost of the land was about to go up for the Katz Group, and, by extension, for the city.

In particular, the Katz Group had offers to purchase two sizeable parcels of land in the downtown core whose options were set to expire: a 4-acre site just south of 104 Avenue and to the east of the Greyhound bus station (a parking lot owned by Edmonton businessman Cam Allard), and a 12-acre site north of 104 Avenue that included the Baccarat Casino and the attached parking lot (owned by WAM, a local property developer). The plan was for the Katz Group to purchase both the north and south sections, with the intention of immediately selling most of the northern section—the proposed location of the arena—to the city of Edmonton at cost (i.e., the Katz Group would not profit from this land sale). The Katz Group would, however, benefit from the arrangement in other ways, including being spared property tax (until subdivision) and any expenses or debt associated with the purchase of this particular piece of land. The Katz Group wanted a final financing agreement in place before exercising its option to purchase the land by the end of October. Still, the need to enter into an agreement to purchase the land and the need to finalize an agreement on the arena's financial framework were not mutually exclusive. The two issues had been bundled together to apply additional political pressure on council to approve a financing agreement as soon as possible, without public input or further due diligence.[22]

Meanwhile, behind the scenes, the city was putting together the package that would become arena land. It had purchased the land at 10205-105 Avenue for $2.5 million in 1995 and designated it a municipal reserve. The title to 10157-105 Avenue was owned by WAM Development Group (since renamed ONE Properties and currently located in the Edmonton Tower), which had purchased it for $4.5 million in 2009. Although the land was assessed at $14.5 million in 2011, the city bought it from WAM for $30 million that same year. A second WAM-owned property at 10128-104 Avenue, worth $7.5 million in 2009, was assessed at $11.7 million in 2011; the city purchased the title for $25.25 million also that year. The land was packaged into a single property to be developed for the new arena and a casino.[23]

All of the risk associated with the purchase agreement now fell on the city. If the financing agreement with the Katz Group fell through, the city would be on the hook for a significant amount of land in the downtown core. Still, many on council thought the risk minimal; the land was an increasingly valuable commodity as a result of the broader redevelopment of the area, even if buying it meant that the city was becoming a downtown property speculator. All of these matters prompted a request for a special city council meeting on September 23, 2011, during which councillors received another in-camera update about the status of the negotiations.

Behind closed doors, administration emphasized the latest time pressures, while acknowledging that several conditions of the May framework remained unmet, including the non-compete clause with Northlands and the missing $100 million. Neither of these issues would be resolved by the Katz Group's October 31st deadline, even though council had stated that it would not sign any agreement until the full balance of funds had been secured. The city manager also revealed that he had been in regular discussions with Northlands in an attempt to determine how to monetize a non-compete agreement with the intention of reimbursing Northlands if it agreed to abandon the concert industry. One important question remained, though: Who would reimburse Northlands for this concession? The city or the Katz Group? The Katz Group, of course, believed that the responsibility fell to the city.[24] The city was prepared to underwrite the arena development until all of the financing was securely in place, even though the Katz Group had not provided its own financial statements to verify its ability to meet the $100-million commitment.

In public, the mayor was adamant that a deal had to be made by the end of October, while some councillors, including Dave Loken, were unconcerned about the missing $100 million: "The $100 million isn't the crux of the conversation. We hear from the province that's going to happen."[25] The odds of the province providing the $100 million for the project were, however, low, and they would get even lower when Alison Redford won the Progressive Conservative leadership race in early October to succeed Ed Stelmach. Redford, who didn't share Mandel and Stelmach's close friendship, would quickly confirm the province's unwillingness to contribute any funding to the new arena.

As a result of Redford's decision, the Katz Group took direct aim at council, emailing its supporters to make their "voices heard" by demanding that councillors negotiate a final arena agreement by the end of the month.[26] The email, written by Patrick LaForge, contained a host of questionable pieces of information, including the disingenuous claim that the inclusion of the ticket tax had more than doubled the contribution of the Katz Group to the new arena— an argument that Councillor Tony Caterina labelled "idiotic."[27] On October 5th, meanwhile, a letter from Richard Andersen to city manager Simon Farbrother dated May 18, 2011 was anonymously leaked to the media in Edmonton, revealing that Northlands had put a price on its withdrawal from the concert business: $250 million in compensation.[28] The leak, as Councillor Caterina noted, was little more than a "ploy to paint Northlands in a bad light."[29]

Many of these issues were taken up in a point-form editorial in the *Edmonton Sun*. Unlike the boosterism of the *Journal*'s editorial board, the *Sun* took aim at a host of outstanding issues and worrying trends in light of the new October deadline:

1. *There had been no explanation of why a new arena could not be privately financed.*

2. *There had been no public discussion of the enormous borrowing costs that the city would incur.*

3. *There had been no capitalization on the amount of money that the city would forego in ceding all revenue to the Katz Group.*

4. *Surveys showed that the majority of Edmontonians remained opposed to paying for the new arena.*

5. *The study supporting the arena looked at just three examples, and was partly written by "an author who has advocated in his own book for similar developments across North America, a clear conflict."[30]*

In light of the Katz Group's imposed deadline, the lack of provincial funding, and the refusal of Northlands to abandon the concert business, the NHL commissioner once again inserted himself into the debate. In early October, the mayor, his chief of staff and strategic advisor Patricia Mitsuka, and city manager Simon Farbrother were summoned to the NHL's head office in New York to hammer out the financial framework behind closed doors with Gary Bettman and Daryl Katz. The trip to New York, for meetings on October 11th and 12th was, of course, on the public's dime—a cost of just under $15,000—not paid by the NHL or the Oilers.[31] Beyond representing an additional public expense, the trip to New York concerned some councillors, with Tony Caterina noting that "those meetings were used to their [the Katz Group's] advantage to gain something from us,"[32] while Kerry Diotte indicated his surprise that other elected officials had not attended the meeting and that no records of the discussions were provided to council:

Something like that, it's highly unusual. Let's face it, a trip like that, if you're going down, there should have been a delegation that included a couple of councillors. That would have been a more reasonable and transparent way to do something like that, if indeed it was necessary at all.[33]

Former city manager Al Maurer agreed:

I kind of knew Katz was going to get his way when Mandel and Simon went to New York. If I was there, I would have certainly opposed that. If the NHL commissioner wants to meet, he can come to our playground. We won't go to his. Of course, the mayor, I guess he can go where he wants, but I certainly wouldn't have wanted that. But,

I guess it's an easy thing to say. The pressure does become kind of intense, and when you're on the pot getting mixed reviews from all over the place, it's a little different than sitting on the outside saying well, "Why the hell did they do that?"[34]

The private meeting in New York was significant, as Mayor Mandel recalled, because it provided the time and the space to broker a deal with Katz, with the NHL commissioner acting as mediator:

I'll be very clear. There were two times in the negotiations that anything ever happened. One when I went to New York, and Daryl and I and Gary and Daryl's team and our team sat across the table, [and] we came up with a deal, and [the second] when Gary came to the city before the last meeting we had, to close the deal [in 2013]. Other than between those two periods...very little happened...So, it wasn't until...I was in one room and Daryl was in another and Gary went back and forth between us to finalize the deal. He's [Bettman] able to quietly gain control of the meeting...of what needs to be done, what's reasonable, what's fair.[35]

The key terms of the deal, then, were not negotiated by council or by administration, as was suggested in public, but by the mayor and Katz, along with Bettman, behind closed doors. This raises worrying questions about democratic transparency and due process, as Mayor Mandel later conceded:

I wish I would have been more diligent in taking notes [during] these meetings, but most of the time it was myself and Gary and Daryl talking about, you know, the last meeting. Especially, "Can you do this?" "No, I can't get it through council," and he'd go back to Daryl and say, "We can't do this, how about this?" And then they'd come back, "How about this?" Back and forth, and we finally finalized the deal.[36]

In response to our FOIP request, the office of the city clerk confirmed that there are no available records or communications from the discussions in New York.

Upon returning from New York, the mayor and the city manager gave council a private update during a hastily called meeting on October 14th, from which four councillors were absent. It was a critical meeting in that, in addition to receiving an update on a new financial framework, council was also asked to endorse the land purchase arrangements for the arena development. In other words, council was being asked to consider a broad range of complex issues that had been quickly bundled together by administration during another closed-door meeting.

As Councillor Linda Sloan recorded in her notes from the private update in New York on October 14, "Mr. Bettman was used as a mechanism by the Katz Group to introduce new costs/commitments by the City."[37] Council was now told that Katz had made a substantial "concession" in New York, dropping his longstanding demand for a non-compete clause with Northlands—a version of this demand would, however, be re-inserted into the final agreement in 2013. In exchange, though, the city agreed to a number of amendments to provide additional support for the Katz Group, based on a similar financing agreement between the city of Pittsburgh and the NHL's Penguins. In a crucial decision, the city's negotiating team agreed to absolve the Katz Group from its original commitment to provide $100 million to the cost of the arena. The Katz Group had, of course, long desired to minimize its upfront costs in a variety of ways throughout the negotiations, and its $100-million contribution now became annual lease payments of $5.5 million (with interest) over the course of the arena agreement.[38] This substantive concession erased the longstanding commitment of the Katz Group to invest private capital in the arena, showing again that each agreement between a municipality and a major league franchise sets powerful precedents that subsequent cities are "invited" not just to meet, but to exceed, in the continuous cycle of league-wide facility renewal. It also meant that the city would now debt-finance nearly the total cost of the new arena—especially in the ongoing absence of provincial funding—and would assume far greater borrowing costs, despite its earlier stated commitment to finance no more than $250 million. Put another way, by agreeing to transform the Katz Group's original commitment to invest $100 million of private capital into the construction of the arena into annual lease payments, the city facilitated the deal without the Katz Group paying the money up front.

The city of Edmonton's generosity, though, went well beyond that offered by other cities. At the meetings in New York, the city agreed to enter into a marketing and branding partnership to provide the Oilers with $2 million per year for the next decade—a subsidy that reduced the Katz Group's annual lease payments to $3.5 million per year. The city also endorsed the imposition of a new municipal surcharge on tickets sold at Rexall Place (to be collected by the city) to further restrict the ability of Northlands to compete with the Katz Group. Finally, the city confirmed that it would discontinue its current subsidy for Rexall Place once the new arena opened— another key demand by the Katz Group. For many on council, including Councillor Ed Gibbons, these actions were simply unprincipled: "I just think it's unfair the city can come up with this kind of decision without even going and talking to Northlands. Is this their way of shutting the [Rexall] operation down for sure?"[39]

The city and the Katz Group also agreed that the latter would pay 50 percent of the Winter Garden pedway, with the city's contribution capped at $25 million, and confirmed a guaranteed maximum price for the arena at $450 million to ensure no cost overruns. Both parties confirmed that any required land assembly would be undertaken by October 31st, and that design work on the arena would commence immediately, even without a resolution for the outstanding $100 million. In other words, over the course of the meetings with Bettman and Katz, the city had abandoned another of its stated commitments: not to proceed with the arena development until the full balance of funds had been confirmed. Council, though, voted in favour of holding a non-statutory and non-binding public hearing on the new financial framework on October 25th. Before voting on purchasing the land from the Katz Group, Councillor Linda Sloan requested additional information:

1. *A list of the parcels of land the City is required to purchase with both the legal description and municipal addresses for the subject properties.*

2. *The names of the current owners of the subject lands and if the owner is a Corporation, the names of the directors and shareholders.*

3. *When the current owners purchased the subject lands and the purchase price they paid for the said lands at the time of purchase.*

4. *Has the City of Edmonton performed any appraisals on the subject lands as part of its due diligence? If yes, provide a summary of the appraisals; if no, why not?*

5. *If the arena project does not proceed and the City has acquired the subject lands, what will the City do with the subject lands? For example, will the City become the owner/landlord of a casino.*[40]

Sloan's motion was supported by just one other councillor, Kerry Diotte, while the rest of her colleagues endorsed the land purchase agreement, the details of which would remain hidden from the public until the land transactions had been concluded at the end of the month. Only Councillors Sloan, Diotte, and Caterina voted against the original motion. Councillors were invited, once again, to submit any outstanding questions in writing to administration by October 17th.[41]

The radically revised financial agreement that had been negotiated by the city and the Katz Group under the supervision of NHL commissioner Gary Bettman was defended by the mayor as "a reasonably fair deal."[42] Chief media booster David Staples suggested that the most recent version represented a "massive step forward."[43] Terry Jones, the *Edmonton Sun* sports writer who had travelled to New York to report on the negotiations, meanwhile, heralded the mayor as "Edmonton's MVP" and "Daryl Katz...as the first star."[44] On the other side, *Journal* columnist Paula Simons reminded readers of how many of the terms from the May 2011 agreement—a substantially amended version of the April 2011 iteration—had been altered during the closed-door negotiations in New York, and asked who stood to benefit from these developments:

I am honestly awestruck at Katz's audacity—and his brilliance. The city takes two large parcels straight off his hands, at cost, allowing

him to assemble and flip the land, with no expense or debt. The city
pays all the upfront costs of the arena but still agrees to let the Katz
Group choose and hire the architect, come up with the best design, and
keep all the revenues. We actually pay the team to promote the city.
And, at Katz's behest, we slap a tax on his business rival. It's the most
stunning power play in Oilers history.[45]

Moreover, as Simons noted, the land-sale agreement that had been
outlined to council in private, including information about land
costs and whether the city had purchased the Katz-optioned properties on both the north and south side of 104 Avenue, was restricted
as a result of third-party confidentiality, and would only be made
public after the sale closed on October 31st. The city was also
required to file official legal notice of its intent to purchase the land
by October 21st, just four days in advance of the scheduled public
hearing on October 25th.

Administration's response to written questions by councillors
was, as always, revealing. For example, in reply to a question about
the risks of not proceeding with a downtown arena and maintaining the status quo, administration simply stated: "The most
significant risk of maintaining the status quo would be the loss of
the Edmonton Oilers franchise. The Oilers ownership has publicly
stated that they are not willing to continue with the status quo. The
risk of not building an arena downtown would be the continued
underdevelopment of significant property in the downtown core."[46]
Of course, administration had already acknowledged that significant development in the downtown had happened over the past
decade. When it was suggested that the city of Edmonton was using
its borrowing powers and access to financing at lower interest rates
from the Alberta Capital Finance Authority for the benefit of the
Katz Group, administration only noted that, technically, the city was
"not making a loan to the Katz Group."[47] Another councillor asked
to see a financial breakdown of the city's costs and revenues if the
city paid for the arena and collected all of the revenue from it. "This
scenario would not be feasible," administration insisted, "as the
most significant amount of revenue generated would be from the

Edmonton Oilers, which would belong to the Edmonton Oilers."[48]
Administration also refused to explain the value of the proposed
$2-million sponsorship agreement.

Finally, administration was asked to provide annual cost estimates
for a new arena, including interest payments and other infrastructure expenses. Administration claimed that the city's contribution to
the arena was only $125 million and that other infrastructure costs
would be a maximum of $82 million. In other words, its analysis was
based on a total cost estimate of $207 million. Using these numbers,
administration provided estimated expenses for annual payments
based on a 20-year loan at then-current interest rates for the construction of the arena ($125 million) and related infrastructure ($82 million),
as well as total interest costs over 20 years. The breakdown was as
follows:

> *Annual Payments for Arena ($125 million): $8,705,521*
> *Annual Payments for Infrastructure ($82 million): $5,710,822*
> TOTAL: *$14,416,343*
>
> *Interest for Arena Over 20 Years: $49,110,419*
> *Interest for Infrastructure Over 20 Years: $32,216,435*
> TOTAL: *$81,326,854*[49]

Debt and infrastructure payments would be fully covered by the
CRL, new parking revenue, and the redirection of current expenditures related to Rexall Place. However, administration conceded that
interim funding would be needed until the CRL was sufficient to
cover debt repayment.

Administration acknowledged that the city might eventually have
to pay the missing $100 million. However, it provided no estimates
of the cost of covering a $100-million loan over 20 years. (Based on
the city's figures, our calculations suggested that the city would
incur another $6,964,416 in annual costs as a result of this additional
loan.) Administration also failed to include the annual $2-million
expense of the 10-year marketing and sponsorship agreement with
the Katz Group. In other words, the city of Edmonton's true annual

principal cost for a new arena—including the missing $100 million and the $2-million sponsorship agreement—would be $23,380,759, not $14,416,343. This figure paints a remarkably different picture from the one presented to council. By way of comparison, administration provided a similar cost estimate for renovating Rexall Place: the total cost would be approximately $200 million; annual payments over 20 years on $200 million would be $13,928,833, and total interest payments over two decades would come to almost $80 million. However, rather than suggesting alternative methods of financing these costs (e.g., user fees, etc.), administration simply noted that a potential renovation of Rexall Place would result in a 1.4 percent property tax increase for 2012.

A competing analysis was put forward by a former mayor of Edmonton (1977–1983), Cec Purves, who questioned the city's calculations and creative financing claims. He argued that the city was about to provide the Katz Group with what amounted to a subsidy of over $1 billion. The Katz Group, Purves explained, would operate the new arena for 35 years without any equity investment whatsoever. It would receive all revenue from the city-owned building (conservatively estimated at $581 million over 35 years based on the earlier CSL report), and $2 million per year for the next decade, thanks to the marketing and sponsorship agreement. The city would incur hundreds of millions in interest costs, while the Katz Group would benefit from an increase in the value of the Oilers franchise, and from other ancillary development opportunities and increases in land value. Purves' report[50] to council contained the following estimated figures:

Arena and Infrastructure Estimated Cost in 2011: $532 million
Interest on Borrowing Costs: $364 million
Estimated Operating Surplus Over 35 years: $581 million
Advertising and Sponsorship Over 10 years: $20 million

TOTAL: $1.497 billion over 35 years
LESS $198 million for Katz Group lease payments

TOTAL: $1.299 billion over 35 years

PLUS $150–$250 million increase in Oilers franchise value

TOTAL: $1.5 billion + ancillary land development

The Katz Group Contribution:

- *$5.7 million in annual lease payments for 35 years (Total: $198 million; $98 million interest)*
- *$25 million for half of estimated cost of overpass*
- *Responsible for all capital costs and maintenance throughout lease (no reports showing projected costs)*

It's hard to judge the accuracy of Purves' analysis because the city refused to release its full revenue and cost projections, despite a FOIP request, claiming once again that this information was commercially sensitive and that to release it would harm the Katz Group's business interests. Later news reports claimed that the Katz Group's estimated operating expenses would amount to approximately $10 million per year, or $350 million over 35 years, thus reducing the city of Edmonton's total "gift" to the Katz Group to roughly $1.15 billion, using Purves' figures.[51] It is still an alarming figure, and notably did not include the Katz Group's potential profits from real estate transactions (e.g., the sale of the Edmonton Tower in 2018).

In advance of the public hearing on October 25th, the drums of boosterism continued to beat. Paul Douglas, the head of the influential construction company PCL, which was eventually awarded the contract to build the arena, called on council to support the deal because the Oilers would leave without a new arena and "some other city will capitalize."[52] Other business leaders launched a pro-arena website (buildthearena.com) that included a "who's-who of Edmonton business people and companies."[53] Nearly all of them claimed to be fiscal conservatives believing in limited government intervention in business; but, in this case, they were prepared to abandon their political beliefs—as boosters in Edmonton always have—in support of the publicly-subsidized growth agenda. When challenged, they side-stepped questions about the use of public funds to subsidize private interests: "We don't think it's our job to negotiate or define that. We think it's our job to let our elected leaders know that this is a project that we support and we want them to find a way to make it happen."[54] Many of these boosters, of course, would benefit from the publicly-financed development, just as they always had through organizations like the Chamber of Commerce. Moreover, the day before the public hearing, the *Journal* published a lengthy op-ed piece written by Dr. Dan Mason, who defended both the arena development and the city's "highly qualified and ethical project team" that had negotiated the financing agreement.[55] On the same day, a *Journal* editorial was equally boosterish, headlined simply "Say 'Yes' to a New Arena."[56]

Not everyone was convinced of the merits of the arena development, though. The *Journal*'s business columnist, Gary Lamphier, continued to ask challenging questions about the new framework that had been negotiated behind closed doors in New York, and, unlike the boosters in the media, included in his column a lengthy commentary from economist Dr. Brad Humphreys:

> It's a terrible deal. They're still short $100 million and I don't see it going very far until they come up with the remainder of the funding. I notice in the reporting to date, people are saying that Katz is paying $165 million, which is $5.5 million over 30 years. But that's not right. That calculation ignores the time value of money, which, believe me, is coming out of the taxpayers' pockets...I've been saying this to anyone who will listen for a year now. This $450-million estimate is several years old, and it's not based on any actual architectural plans, either. It's just a number that's been thrown out there. This arena is going to cost more than $450 million when all is said and done.[57]

Humphreys would be prophetic, but boosters of the arena were united in their promotional aspirations and were less than concerned with these types of questions and perspectives.

The public hearing was a divisive affair. About 85 people used the occasion to address council, and, according to one observer, "a slim majority...most from companies or business groups...called for the project to go ahead."[58] A number of citizens from across the political spectrum took the time to voice their concerns about the financing agreement, including representatives from Voices For Democracy and former mayor Cec Purves, who continued to cast doubts on the deal. The process was temporarily disrupted by Occupy Edmonton, which protested subsidizing a billionaire and limiting the democratic process. Mayor Mandel, for his part, suggested that critics simply did not understand the financing agreement: "They tried to make it more complicated than it is—we said $450 million for the cost, not $480 [million], not $490 [million]. No, it's $450 million. If it's higher, we won't go ahead."[59] Of course, he had already acknowledged behind closed doors that the cost of the total development would be substantially higher, making nonsense of this public assertion.

Supporters included influential members of the business community and the broader local growth coalition: businessmen Irv Kipnes and Bruce Saville, Jim Taylor (Downtown Business Association), Simon O'Byrne (Stantec), Bob Walker (Ledcor Construction), representatives from the Edmonton Economic Development Corporation and the Edmonton Chamber of Commerce, and many from the restaurant and hospitality sector and the land development industry. These boosters employed now-familiar rhetoric in their attempts to sway council to vote in favour of the arena development. Bruce Saville, the founder of an international telecom software/services company, a well-respected philanthropist, and himself one of the former owners of the Oilers, made an emotional pitch:

> *Edmonton is on the verge, with the correct decision here, of becoming a world-class, urban and cosmopolitan city that simply no longer needs an agricultural society playing a major role. But this is not about Northlands. It is also not about the Edmonton Oilers, Daryl Katz, the Katz Group, Rexall Sports or concerts or ice hockey. It's about an iconic downtown arena and entertainment district that will make a new, revitalized city core, just as Toronto, Montreal and Vancouver have experienced with new downtown arenas. Do we want*

to be a world-class city? Do we want to be grouped with Montreal,
Toronto and Vancouver? Or do we want to be grouped with Regina and
Hamilton and Windsor and Moncton? Any of you who do not see the
wisdom of this project, any of you who vote against this development,
shame on you, shame on you.[60]

Proponents trotted out familiar narratives associated with boosterism, at times resorting to shaming and intimidating opponents
instead of engaging in rational and reasoned dialogue. Earlier in
2011, for example, Saville had written Councillor Sloan an email:
"Linda...So which are you: you don't care about revitalizing downtown; you actively dislike professional sports; you have an interest in
the team staying at Rexall Place?"[61]

Inundated by these emotional and boosterish appeals, and
unmoved by the arguments of critics, council voted in favour (10
to 3) of the agreement re-negotiated in New York. Only Councillors
Sloan, Diotte, and Iveson voted no, with Iveson saying after the
vote, "I have not yet seen a compelling argument specifically justifying the funding formula before us—most of the arguments boil
down to a leap of faith."[62] He remained unconvinced that the team
needed a subsidy, and continued to demand concrete evidence of
the Oilers' unprofitability: "We're simply told over and over again
that the Oilers won't be sustainable without this specific deal."[63] In
an attempt to secure an upfront commitment for private ancillary
development, Councillor Tony Caterina moved that the Katz Group
invest $30 million before construction on the arena began; that the
$2 million per year marketing agreement be capped at 10 years with
a review every two years; and that the new ticket tax on Northlands
not be used to fund the downtown arena. The deal negotiated in
Gary Bettman's office, though, remained basically unchanged, and
firmly in favour of the Katz Group.

Only days later, the cost of the city's land purchases dramatically
increased to $75 million, over three times higher than the original
estimate of $20 million put forward by both parties throughout the
negotiations. The city had purchased not only the land upon which
the arena and the community rink would be built (for roughly $25

million), but also the adjacent land (for $15.4 million) and another separate parcel south of 104 Avenue (for $33.6 million). The Katz Group had already agreed to (re)purchase this latter piece of land, paying the city $16.8 million toward that total purchase amount. There was yet another twist in these arrangements. In light of Councillor Caterina's last-minute amendment to propose that Katz make commitments up front, and after consulting with Katz, administration agreed that the Katz Group's purchase of the south parcel of land would fulfill the commitment to invest $30 million in development before construction began. In response, Paula Simons noted,

> once again, I can't help feeling that the goalposts just got moved. Katz is a tough negotiator—and with this land swap he's just reduced his capital commitment in the ancillary developments to $70 million. In effect, Caterina's amendment didn't make this a better deal for the city—it made it a better deal for Katz. The money for the land purchase is not included in the $450-million cost for the arena, and will not be covered by any future ticket tax or the proposed community revitalization levy. It's coming, instead, out of general revenues. But no matter how you add the numbers, it's a lot more money than Edmontonians were led to believe.[64]

The better question, though, was: Why were administration and council willing to continually cede terrain in these important matters?

As the year ended, design work on the new arena began, but other enduring issues still remained unresolved, including the ongoing $100-million funding gap. A number of hard questions were also being asked about the state of the city's finances; it was close to $2 billion in debt, and citizens faced another property tax increase. The Oilers, on the other hand, continued to do well despite playing in Rexall Place and despite missing the playoffs—and the opportunity to accumulate lucrative playoff revenue—yet again. According to the most recent figures in *Forbes*, the value of the Oilers had increased to an estimated US$212 million in the 2010/2011 NHL season, a 16 percent increase over the previous season. The Oilers remained one of the most profitable teams in the NHL, with an operating income of an estimated US$17.3 million—behind only the Toronto Maple Leafs, the Montreal Canadiens, the New York Rangers, and the Vancouver Canucks in terms of profitability. As *Forbes* noted, Edmonton's franchise valuation and operating income would dramatically increase with a new arena.[65] Executives from the Oilers had, of course, only a year earlier claimed that the club was losing money, while arena proponents, including those at city hall, had consistently argued that full private financing of a new arena was simply impossible. *Forbes* also offered a cautionary note to the boosters who feared that the franchise would relocate to another city if negotiations over a new arena collapsed: "But if the city does not pony up for the new arena it would appear Katz has few options, given the strong Canadian dollar is a strong incentive to remain in Canada and there is already at least one other U.S. NHL team looking to move north of the border."[66] In other words, despite the arguments that the city was a weak Canadian market and that the Oilers were losing money, Edmonton remained a coveted location, and the franchise continued to be, as it had been for years, one of the most profitable in the NHL.

13

THE ART OF THE DEAL?

AFTER ASSEMBLING THE LAND for the arena development, and after the Katz Group had dropped its non-compete demand with Northlands in exchange for additional concessions, the arena financing agreement was still $100 million short. But the shortfall didn't stop the city from announcing, in January 2012, deals worth CA$30 million with US-based ICON Venue Group and 360 Architecture of Kansas City (later acquired by HOK in 2015). The companies were to serve, respectively, as project manager and architect. Like so many of the city's arena-related contracts, there was no public tender process, as required by provincial legislation. Both companies were handpicked by the Katz Group and approved by administration behind closed doors. Calder Bateman, once again, got a sole-sourced contract for design-related public consultation worth $246,750. Public input on these matters was minimal and after the fact—a "hollow replacement for an open design competition."[1] The contract to build the arena with a guaranteed maximum price of $450 million—a price that had not changed since the *City Shaping* report four years earlier—had yet to be awarded, and a further controversy over the final cost of the arena was on the horizon.

All of these developments and closed-door decisions were questioned by concerned citizens who wondered why the Katz Group should receive all of the revenues from a city-owned facility, including its naming rights, plus a $2 million per year marketing subsidy, even if the organization was paying operating and capital expenses. Former mayor Cec Purves found it unfathomable that the Katz Group was allowed to plan and develop the arena without paying for the cost of the design, let alone for a substantive portion of the upfront construction costs. As Purves noted in a letter to the editor published in the *Edmonton Journal*, council had also allowed Daryl Katz to renege on his original contribution of $100 million, and many of the 2008 *City Shaping* report's constructive recommendations had been ignored in the negotiations. Purves rebuked Edmonton's elected officials, who appeared determined to push through the deal:

> Council has a motion on the books saying that the arena will not go ahead unless the government puts in $100 million. Premier Alison Redford has made it very clear that the province will not. Why, then, have the mayor and council approved a $30-million expenditure for design and planning? Income to support the servicing of the debt is not in place. The $125-million ticket tax does not have any detailed financial study to show the seven-per-cent surtax is reasonable...
>
> There will be $125 million from the city and $45 million from community revitalization levies with no detailed financial report showing timelines on how this cash is going to flow, starting with all the vacancies downtown. Where do the payments come from when the cash flow isn't there? There will be a balance of $80 million with no detailed financial report on how this is going to be raised, except for the $2.6-million subsidy to Northlands...All the boosterism in the world won't make these facts go away...In the 45 years I have been involved in city politics and watching I have never seen a more irrational, irresponsible or reckless move by council.[2]

But boosterism prevailed, as it always has in Edmonton.[3] When the city ignored his concerns, Purves held a press conference in early February 2012 to publicize the benefits to the Katz Group from the deal, and called on the city to halt design work until all of the funding was in place. For his troubles, Purves was labelled a naysayer and "a nervous Nellie" who was stuck in the past. He was also tarred with the decline of Edmonton's downtown core because he had supported the construction of the West Edmonton Mall.[4] That his concerns were so quickly rejected, and that such a prominent and influential Edmontonian was derided as a "knocker," shows the ongoing power of boosterism to divide even as it unites.

All of these issues—especially the lack of an upfront commitment by the private sector and the failure to make up the $100-million shortfall—were further inflamed in January when the Katz Group announced that it had sold a portion of its assets to US pharmaceutical giant McKesson Corporation for just under $1 billion. Despite being flush with cash from this sale, the Katz Group was still unwilling to contribute more to the arena development, even though it was becoming clear that it was getting out of the pharmacy business in order to be restructured as a sports/entertainment and land development empire.

The Katz Group announced in February that it had partnered with the local company WAM Development Group to develop the land around the new arena. The city, for its part, initiated negotiations with another influential local company, PCL Construction, to build the arena for a guaranteed maximum price of $450 million. The total cost of the arena—including land, the Winter Garden, the community rink, and pedestrian connections—already exceeded $550 million, and additional expenses like debt servicing and interest payments would increase it further by hundreds of millions of dollars. Where was this money to come from?

Cost estimates for such projects routinely exclude all sorts of expenses. Supporters of these developments across North America have sometimes justified their exclusion by using a home mortgage analogy: lenders often inform borrowers of just the principle, not the total cost of the principle and interest over the duration of the loan.[5] Still, by law, financial institutions must disclose the estimated total costs of a loan to potential borrowers upon request.[6] *Journal* columnist David Staples attempted to deflect growing calls for full disclosure by Cec Purves and Councillor Kerry Diotte in a column entitled "Very Bad Day for 'Grumpy Grandpas' in Edmonton Arena

Debate," by calling these concerns "unusual" and not "how the city talks about funding the LRT or a recreation centre or a bridge."[7] "The city," he continued, "says how much these things will cost now, not what the total cost, plus interest, will be over time. Why talk about the arena project in different terms?"[8]

The problem with this argument, though, is that citizens have the right—regardless of the project—to an accurate and objective accounting of all public expenditures, in order to understand the overall state of municipal finances, including the city's debt, which was soon to exceed $2 billion (over half of its provincially mandated limit of $3.8 billion). The arena, moreover, was an entirely different proposition from other pieces of public infrastructure because the city would be incurring substantial long-term debt to support the interests of the Katz Group, which would control the facility and receive all of the revenue from it as part of the agreement. And, unlike other capital projects, such as the LRT or a bridge, the arena would not be equally accessible to all Edmontonians because not everyone could afford the high ticket prices. If the full costs of borrowing—tens of millions of dollars—had been fully disclosed as part of the total price tag for the arena, though, public opposition would have been harder to ignore.

Free Falling?

Behind the scenes, concerns about the financing gap and the overall state of the negotiations over the arena project continued to grow. The head of WAM, Darren Durstling, for example, expressed his trepidation about how "the arena project is playing out" in a conversation with the city's executive director for the arena, Rick Daviss, and requested a meeting with Daviss and the city manager, Simon Farbrother, to discuss moving the project forward. The developer also planned to meet with Mayor Mandel and acknowledged that the two met on a "regular basis."[9]

Meanwhile, the price of oil continued to fall, and the government of Alberta, facing its own multi-billion-dollar deficit for the 2012 fiscal year, refused to cover the $100-million shortfall. The construction budget for the arena alone was now projected to exceed $450

million. The city prepared to massage this bad news in advance
of an upcoming council meeting: "[The] key message is we are
continuing to build the arena in partnership with the Katz Group,
and that we are meeting councils [sic] target of $450 million."[10] Cuts
to the arena budget had to be made before the meeting on July 17,
2012, which had been delayed to allow administration more time to
revise the design, prepare an update, and draft a report on the CRL.
The problem for administration was clear: given continued opposition and the mayor's stated commitment to the $450-million total
price for the arena, senior public officials were reluctant to appear
before council with a proposal for a significant cost increase.

The price tag now was between $475 and $485 million. While
some savings had been found, by using a less expensive exterior
finish, for example, other expenses had gone up, largely the result
of a design change associated with shifting the arena slightly to
the west and building parking underground to improve its appearance—and, of course, to provide the Katz Group with another
guaranteed revenue stream. The cost of the Winter Garden, it was
reported, had ballooned—from $50 million to $80 million. Yet, only
months earlier, the city had limited its contribution to $25 million.
When administration suggested that underground parking could be
decreased by 50 percent to save $10 million, the Katz Group balked
at reducing its revenues. Rick Daviss then conceded, "Whether the
revenue streams are still sufficient to allow the hockey club to keep
its operations sustainable, that will be the subject of negotiations
between the Katz Group and the city."[11]

The arena's latest price tag further stretched the patience of many
councillors, including those who had consistently supported the
development. But a revised CRL revenue forecast was both encouraging and politically reassuring. Administration was now projecting
$1.6 billion in property taxes over 20 years—including $173 million
that would otherwise be redirected to the province for education—
based on the Katz Group's and WAM's joint construction plans,
though these were still qualified by the insistence that they would
proceed only when an anchor tenant (i.e., the city of Edmonton) had
been secured for their office tower.[12] The city was soon to announce

its own request for proposals to consolidate staff in a new, central-ized, downtown office tower[13] as a cost-saving measure and "catalyst for a vibrant downtown that boosts economic activity, density, land values and taxes, as well as providing a showcase for Edmonton."[14] The competition for such a lucrative long-term lease with the city was, arguably, structured to favour the Katz Group because its land holdings were well-positioned to fulfill the city's criteria: "within downtown Edmonton in close proximity to City Hall, located on or near major public transit and strong pedestrian connectivity."[15] The company was further advantaged in this competition because it had already designed an office tower as part of the arena and entertain-ment district; unlike other developers, the Katz Group could meet the city's stringent occupancy deadlines that coincided with the opening of the new arena, and, in turn, contributed to the CRL.[16] Still, as Rick Daviss explained, given the interests at play, the city brought in an "independent fairness advisor [who was] involved in the preparation of the tender, the evaluation of criteria, the judging of submissions, and the awarding of the bid."[17]

In 2014, after another private debate and vote, the city of Edmonton would announce that the Katz Group had emerged victorious in this competition, over 13 other bids. The Edmonton Tower, which opened in 2016 and is located just across from Rogers Place on 104 Avenue, would fulfill Katz's $100-million commitment to ancillary develop-ment. The city of Edmonton would sign a 20-year lease to be the principal tenant, *at increasing rates* in a commercial office space market that was vastly oversupplied. The Katz Group, whose annual arena lease and property tax payments were *fixed* for 35 years, was again the beneficiary.

Beyond the city's request for proposals for a new office tower—a development that would have occurred with or without a new arena—a number of other significant construction plans had been announced for the downtown core as the area continued its decade-long trend of growth and redevelopment. For example, the development company Westrich Pacific had just broken ground on construction of the Ultima condominium building (10238–103 Street). The sales manager explained that much broader economic forces were at play in the company's decision to invest in the down-town core, beyond the prospect of a new arena development: "I wouldn't say [the proposed arena] was the main driver of sales, but it definitely helped. We saw a great opportunity downtown. The arena was something we thought was a huge bonus."[18] Westrich had also committed to building another residential tower (Encore) the following year, and Langham Developments was set to announce its own plans for two new high-rise condominium towers on 104 Street.

Was the arena responsible for these developments? Or were these investments now largely being made thanks to unrelated changes, like the removal of height restrictions after City Centre Airport was closed or increasing wealth in Edmonton that spurred demand for upmarket accommodation in the downtown core? Jim Taylor, the executive director of the Downtown Business Association, said that over the previous decade (long before the arena had been announced) the downtown had been growing steadily; between 1998 and 2010, the number of people living there had increased from 5,000 to almost 13,000. "Now," he said, "we'll just keep building... because people want to live downtown, not just because there's an arena."[19] Taylor also emphasized the potential for $4.8 billion in downtown development projects over the next five years, with "the largest ones...not tied to the arena."[20]

In other words, the 10-year trend of downtown growth would intensify in the years to come, thanks to a number of develop-ments that would have occurred without a new arena—a point with profound implications for the implementation of a CRL that would capture and dedicate future increases in municipal property tax revenue to paying off the city's arena-related debt. The arena would largely concentrate *already existing investment and spending* in the downtown core, and the construction of new hotels, condo-miniums, and the Stantec Tower would accelerate the wave of development begun years earlier, including public investments like the expansion of MacEwan University and the construction of the Royal Alberta Museum and the Art Gallery of Alberta. Stantec, as an example of this trend, committed to leasing office space in the arena district to centralize and relocate staff from five other offices in Edmonton. Stantec had been preparing to move to a new building anyway and had explored other downtown sites, but committed to Ice District once the arena deal was finalized. The 66-storey Stantec Tower was developed by the Katz Group/WAM. Stantec, in turn, provided architectural and engineering services for the new tower, and also worked on designing the new arena and the planning for the broader entertainment district.

In light of rising costs, some boosters returned to familiar rhetoric in advance of the council meeting on July 17th, when councillors would be asked to approve additional arena design work. The *Journal*'s editorial board reminded readers (and councillors) that the "extra money pales next to the long-term promise of a downtown arena...a once-in-a-generation chance to revitalize the downtown core of Edmonton."[21] This narrative of generational change had been associated with many other past revitalization projects, like the Omniplex, Edmonton Centre, and Eaton Centre. The *Journal* also attempted to be clever by suggesting that "when the project is a success—think the Montreal and Vancouver Olympics—controversies about the preparation phase are wiped from public memory like purged Bolshevik leaders."[22] Mayor Stephen Mandel, meanwhile, had retreated from his promise that the new arena would cost no more than $450 million, and he urged council not to fret; Edmontonians would not tolerate the construction of a "crap" arena, whatever the cost.[23] The boosters' campaign worked. Council voted in favour (10–3) of proceeding.

Spending even more public money on an arena received the blessing, once again, of the boosterish Edmonton Chamber of Commerce. In an op-ed in the *Journal* in August, the Chamber suggested that, in light of rising construction costs, anything less than $516 million was a "good financial deal," and that other levels of government ought to fund the shortfall of $100 million.[24] Its own members, however, remained conspicuously silent when it came to investing their own money in the development, a stance lambasted by Paula Simons as hypocritical and reflective of "crony capitalism."[25]

John Karvellas, executive vice president and general counsel for the Katz Group, wrote to the city manager, Simon Farbrother, in September to reinforce the point that a new arena meeting the revenue-generating demands of the Oilers could not be built for $450 million. Further delays, moreover, would only invite additional cost increases. New economic circumstances in the hockey world had to be addressed, he said, and the Katz Group now wanted even greater subsidies from the city to reflect "Edmonton's standing as the second smallest market in the NHL and commensurate with the public support given to the NHL franchises in Winnipeg and Pittsburgh." He further reminded the city manager, and the mayor, of the Katz Group's interests in the negotiations:

> It has proved impossible to achieve these budget goals without violating a key condition of the [October 2011] New York framework, which is that the Katz Group's revenue streams from the arena will be sufficient to ensure the Oilers' long-term sustainability and provide a return on the hundreds of millions of dollars of capital we are putting at risk (including through a 35-year lease and location agreement).
>
> As we have feared, these cost pressures have been exacerbated by the time it has taken since we met in New York to get to this point... We have made tremendous progress, together, on arena design. In addition to earning strong public support, this work has enabled us to develop reliable models, based on the arena's actual design, of the arena's anticipated revenues and expenses. These estimates, plus the fact of a competitive facility (Rexall Place), have implications for the management of capital and operating expenses that must be given fresh consideration if we are to arrive at a deal that makes economic sense for the Katz Group and the City.[26]

Without opening the books to show revenue and expense projections, or offering any additional private capital whatsoever, Karvellas suggested that it made economic sense for the city to dedicate an even greater amount of funding from the CRL to cover both the new cost increases and the missing $100 million. He concluded by emphasizing Katz's unwillingness even to meet with council to discuss his latest demands.[27]

Council Pushes Back

In response to Karvellas' bellicose letter, administration outlined to council, in another in-camera session on September 12th, the Katz Group's new demands. The most significant was for a $6-million annual subsidy to minimize the company's operating and main-tenance costs—totalling $210 million over 35 years. This proposed grant, an addition to the $2-million annual marketing subsidy that the city had already provided, would offset the full amount of the Katz Group's annual lease payments of $5.5 million.[28] The company also returned to one of its earliest demands, a long-term commit-ment from the city to be the anchor tenant in the new Katz/WAM office tower, a commitment that would largely offset the cost of this ancillary development. The Katz Group demanded a host of other concessions: relief from paying municipal property taxes; a casino license (which fell under provincial, not municipal, jurisdiction); the naming rights for the city-owned community rink; assistance with other additional costs associated with team facilities; and consid-eration of a lease extension at nominal cost beyond 35 years.[29] The Katz Group also wanted a provision that the entire arena agreement would be reviewed if the Canadian dollar fell below US$.90.

Given the generosity of the framework negotiated in New York only a year earlier, councillors were flabbergasted by the new demands. For Councillor Tony Caterina, they were mind-boggling: "They don't want to pay taxes. They want help in operating the arena. They want a guaranteed subsidy. They want the city to be their tenant in a major office building. They want the casino license."[30] The company's demand to avoid taxes was especially ridiculous, he said: "Mr. Katz is a private company and for him to ask for no taxes, for example, really is a non-starter, because part of the taxes coming out of that building were going toward the [CRL] to actually pay for it. That was always the discussion when we were negotiating."[31] Council supported a motion outlining its commit-ment to the framework that had been negotiated in October 2011, with a proviso to cover increased costs. Having spent an enormous amount of his own political capital to secure that framework, an increasingly frustrated Mayor Mandel set a "drop-dead date" of

October 17th for the Katz Group to appear before council to justify its demands.

In light of mounting public outrage and having refused to meet with council to explain his position, Katz chose to give his rebuttal in an interview with the *Journal*'s David Staples and John MacKinnon and the *Sun*'s Terry Jones, all fervent supporters of the arena project. Katz expressed his disappointment that a version of his latest demands had been leaked and claimed that the operational subsidy he wanted was similar to what other NHL franchises received. The Winnipeg Jets, for example, got approximately $12 million per year of operational assistance from multiple sources, including gaming revenues: "We don't care if it's a casino and gaming initiative, or something else. We need a mechanism to offset operating and maintenance costs, just like Pittsburgh and Winnipeg."[32] Yet the Katz Group had been granted all revenue from the brand-new facility, as well as a $2-million annual subsidy for the next decade, to cover these expenses. Katz also emphasized the benefits of his proposal to "centralize city employees in an office tower to be built adjacent to the arena, along with a hotel and other parts of the surrounding development."[33] Despite his unwillingness to open his books, which went unchallenged in the interview, Katz insisted that he had incurred operating losses since he purchased the team in 2008, and that, outside of Toronto, all of the other NHL owners who had privately financed their arenas had "lost their shirts."[34] To justify the additional concessions, he once again donned his booster's hat, suggesting that "Edmonton is a great hockey town, not necessarily a great market," despite having had continuous sellouts since 2006/07 and among the highest ticket prices in the league.[35] Finally, he offered a unique interpretation of the role of professional sports franchises in fostering arena developments.[36] Without the Oilers, Edmonton

> would have to pay all the capital and operating costs [of any new arena], just like Quebec City will, just like Kansas City, just like Phoenix, just like Seattle, just like Hamilton, and just like other cities that would all like an NHL or an NBA team to subsidize their arenas.

So, you see, in our view, it is the team that acts as a subsidy for a city's arena, which is effectively infrastructure, not the other way around.[37]

Only days later came news that senior executives from the Oilers, including Katz himself, plus Wayne Gretzky, had gone to Seattle after that city had approved a new $490-million arena development in the hope of attracting both an NBA and an NHL franchise. Although Katz had repeatedly made similar threats, some on council were still concerned that the team might leave Edmonton, including Mayor Mandel: "Unlike many other people, I felt they would move the team, and I didn't think it was an idle threat...There was a point in time that we were told...by other owners that they would not say no if Daryl wanted to move the team."[38] Still, in the midst of another NHL lockout, with no Oilers' hockey in Edmonton, the visit was a publicity nightmare for Katz, prompting unprecedented outrage on social media and talk radio—not just from long-time fans, but also from the boosters who had long supported the arena development. Such vituperation forced the Oilers' owner to write a public apology, published in both the *Edmonton Journal* and the *Edmonton Sun*, promising to continue negotiations with the city to forge a mutually beneficial deal.

Despite Katz's apology, many critics of the negotiations felt he hadn't made a legitimate case for additional public funding, and his recent actions had only amplified the longstanding calls for financial disclosure to demonstrate the need for more subsidies. In this respect, as Gary Lamphier, business columnist for the *Journal*, noted, the arena development was different from other business negotiations because it had been coloured by issues of cultural identity, fan loyalties, and boosterism:

Most successful business deals only happen after both sides have had a hard look at one another's books and come to a mutual agreement on terms that make sense for both parties. That's not the case here. The Oilers' books have remained closed from the start, even though team owner Daryl Katz has been playing hardball with the city, and Oilers fans, in order to swing the best deal he can get. After years of

*closed-door discussions between the city and Katz Group, even the
most basic facts are still in dispute, leaving taxpayers—who will be on
the hook for a big chunk of the project's costs, no matter how you slice
it—in the dark. Since Katz has never opened the team's books to scrutiny and cherry picks the journalists he's willing to talk to, how can
city council possibly know whether the Oilers actually lose money, as
Katz insists, or generate a profit, as* Forbes *magazine suggests?...Now
is the time for him to take the next step and provide the kind of financial disclosure to city council that should have been made available
long ago. If Katz has a case to make, it's time for him to make it.*[39]

According to *Forbes*, the Oilers had another profitable season in
2011/12, generating an estimated operating income of US$16.2
million—more than that of 22 other teams, including Boston, Los
Angeles, St. Louis, and, especially, Calgary. The Oilers had benefitted
from a lucrative new local television deal with Rogers Sportsnet
for an undisclosed amount.[40] Moreover, even with annual lease
payments of $5.5 million (minus the $2-million annual marketing
subsidy) and operating costs of roughly $10 million per year (largely
paid in US funds), a new arena would raise revenues by 30–40
percent because of concerts and other non-hockey events.[41]

Katz may have offered a public apology, but he refused to back
down. Nor was he willing to appear before council on October 17th.
That same day, in response to what many councillors considered
an insulting two-page letter from Katz to Mayor Mandel—a letter
in which a bitter-sounding Katz recommended yet another intervention by NHL commissioner Gary Bettman to help facilitate a
resolution—council unanimously voted to suspend negotiations
with the Katz Group. Even the most ardent supporters of the new
arena on city council—including Jane Batty, Dave Loken, Kim
Krushell, and Karen Leibovici—were now at the end of their collective tethers. Mayor Mandel was astonished by the Katz Group's
intransigence: "The deal we offered to Mr. Katz was incredibly profitable. I know the numbers and I can tell you he wasn't going to lose
money."[42] As the mayor pointed out, Katz was low-balling revenue
projections to strengthen his case for additional subsidies: "That

was a big point of contention...We kept saying that, 'You're going to generate far more money than you're saying,' and then we said 'That's why you can afford to pay this,' and the numbers we gave were less than what he's now charging!"[43] None of these figures had ever been released to the public. The city had always been prepared to fund the arena project, while Katz was simply making a final push, as part of a multi-year negotiating strategy, to secure additional concessions. Former city manager Simon Farbrother recalled:

> I think Daryl Katz went to a board of governors meeting and the other owners told him he could get a better deal. And he came back and he didn't accept the deal, and then a year later he signed the deal, because over that year he realized that what was on the table actually made sense.[44]

Katz's petulance reminded many of Peter Pocklington's. Even some ardent supporters now suggested that the city build the arena on its own and have it managed by Northlands, with the Oilers as the principal tenant. This was, of course, the business model that Northlands had proposed years earlier for an arena that would have been considerably cheaper, and without add-ons like the Winter Garden, the purpose of which seemed largely to be guiding people to other Katz properties.[45] As the associate dean of the University of Alberta's Faculty of Engineering noted in a letter to the *Journal*, the cost of the proposed arena vastly exceeded the price of other comparable single-use facilities in North America, and the capital cost per seat of the new facility was estimated at $26,000, while the average capital cost per seat of arenas in Pittsburgh, Columbus, Ottawa, Phoenix, and Winnipeg ranged "from about $10,000 to $18,000."[46]

Another Katz Group Controversy: *Resuming Negotiations*
While the Katz Group continued to alienate some of its allies on council, news emerged that Daryl Katz, his family, and various senior executives, including Bob Black, John Karvellas, and Paul Marcaccio (a resident of Ontario), had together contributed $300,000 to the Progressive Conservative Party during the provincial

Daryl Katz floats lead trial balloon with trip to Seattle, September 29, 2012.

[Malcolm Mayes/Artizans.com]

election campaign in April 2012, 20 percent of the total $1.5 million raised by the party. *The Globe and Mail* later reported that Katz had actually donated $430,000—fully one-third of the total amount—broken up into smaller amounts.[47] Katz, who had given money to Mayor Mandel's 2007 election campaign as well, wanted provincial funding for the new arena development and a casino licence. In making this donation, far exceeding the individual limit of $30,000, the Katz Group was widely perceived as trying to buy influence.[48] By accepting it, the Progressive Conservative Party seemed willing to be bought. As one political commentator joked, the party ought to be renamed the "Progressive Katzervatives."[49] In her criticism of the donations, Danielle Smith, leader of the Opposition Wildrose Party, attempted to draw other connections, and noted that Katz was on the board of AIMCO, the Crown Corporation that manages $70 billion of Alberta's financial assets: "Daryl Katz's partner in the arena project, WAM Development Corp, also receives hundreds of millions for joint land development projects with AIMCO. Katz, AIMCO, WAM, arenas, donations—doesn't anyone in this government have a problem with that?"[50] The scandal killed any lingering chance of provincial funding.

The Katz Group now had no other option than to return meekly to council to plead its case. Once again, it was allowed to speak to council directly, rather than at a committee meeting, the usual venue for addressing councillors. A municipal election loomed in the fall of 2013. Everyone involved was anxious to avoid debating the project before an increasingly irritated electorate, and the Katz Group wanted the matter resolved with the current incumbents, rather than face the possibility of a new mayor and a new council that might not be so supportive. Some councillors were facing significant pressure from their constituents over the unpopular deal. Councillor Amarjeet Sohi, for example, acknowledged that there was little support for the development in his ward, and that he would not consider moving beyond the financing framework that had been struck in New York.[51]

And so, in yet another act of theatrical penitence, the Katz Group appeared before council on December 12, 2012—the final council meeting of the year—to request that the city re-open the negotiations. The Katz Group agreed to drop its demands for an additional annual subsidy of $6 million and a guarantee that the city be its tenant in a new downtown office tower. It consented to the appointment of an independent mediator who would facilitate future negotiations, and appoint an independent financial analyst to examine the Oilers' revenue and expense projections.

But the Katz Group didn't want to leave council empty-handed, so it put forward an entirely new proposal: that a portion of the property tax revenues in the arena and entertainment district be directed to pay for the operating and maintenance costs of the new arena through a dedicated "arena reserve fund." The Oilers suggested that this money, which would diminish the CRL financing mechanism, was necessary to offset shortcomings in arena revenue "because Oilers fans from outside the city might be too nervous to come to downtown Edmonton to see a game, or because outside bars and restaurants might compete too effectively with arena concessions."[52] They had even prepared a draft motion for councillors' approval.[53]

Council ultimately voted to re-open the negotiations, with only Councillors Sloan and Diotte opposing.

The *Journal* appeared to have forgiven Katz for everything, publishing a lengthy, multi-page promotional piece on him at the end of the year.[54] With negotiations now back on track (despite the glaring gap in the financing), arena proponents were optimistic that a final agreement would be completed in early 2013, at which point political energies could focus on the upcoming election.

The Deal Finally Gets Done

The new year began with the NHL chiming in again. In advance of the scheduled council meeting on January 23rd, news emerged that NHL commissioner Gary Bettman had been in Edmonton for secret meetings on Friday, January 18th. The agreed-upon independent mediator would not be appointed, nor would the independent financial examination ever be performed. Council had not even been informed that the meeting with Bettman was planned. Relevant material was only made available to councillors just before the meeting on January 23rd, prompting speculation that administration was making last-minute revisions as a result of Bettman's intervention.[55] Still, many councillors were optimistic that a new deal had been reached, though some were frustrated by the current state of the negotiations. Ed Gibbons doubted that the city's negotiating team had done enough to defend the public interest: "You play tough at the start. You don't play tough at the end after you lose things."[56]

On January 23, 2013, with five Edmonton Oilers sitting in the front row of the council chambers, Councillors voted 10–3 in favour of a new agreement similar to what had been decided in New York in October 2011. Councillor Don Iveson, who with Councillors Sloan and Diotte had voted against the previous proposal, was reluctant to support an agreement he had already voted against in principle: "I know the politically astute thing to do is for me to vote yes...However, I'm confronted with the reality that this is essentially the same funding formula that council voted on in 2011."[57] The Katz Group had dropped all of its latest demands, and both parties agreed to a maximum price of $480 million for the arena,

Alberta Tories and Katz Group use loopholes in campaign finance laws, May 3, 2013.
[Malcolm Mayes/Artizans.com]

an increase of $30 million over the projection of $450 million, and to split the difference. The city agreed to build a $21-million community rink, "originally slated to proceed only if the province and Ottawa provided two-thirds of the budget," and the Katz Group would pay the city a maximum of $250,000 annually—a fixed amount over the entire term of the deal—for business undertaken during events, in addition to paying provincial education taxes.[58] The total price tag for the development, including related infrastructure, was now revealed to be $601 million. But the financing agreement was still short $100 million. Proponents remained optimistic that the provincial government would make this money available in its upcoming budget in March, despite the donation scandal. Both Mayor Mandel and city manager Simon Farbrother noted in our interviews that the highest levels of the provincial government had promised this funding behind closed doors, despite what was being said publicly.

But just as the government of Alberta had publicly and repeatedly stated, the $100 million was not included in the provincial budget, though Edmonton did get a $3-million boost to its share of the MSI. On April 10, 2013, councillors voted in favour of a motion put forward by Councillor Dave Loken to use these funds to cover annual payments on a $45-million loan over a 20-year borrowing period to help pay for the new arena. Five councillors (Ben Henderson, Linda Sloan, Don Iveson, Tony Caterina, and Kerry Diotte) voted against it. For Ben Henderson, who had supported the arena agreement in January, the use of MSI funding went against the commitment he had made to his constituents because it would affect the city's ability to undertake other projects. The additional MSI funding was intended to support all forms of municipal infrastructure (e.g., libraries, roads, transit, recreation centres, etc.) and to help alleviate growth pressures. To divert it to pay for a new arena, in other words, represented a "disingenuous violation of the spirit of the framework agreement."[59] Nor had the government of Alberta confirmed that the increase in MSI funding would remain in place for the foreseeable future. While the city had discarded its commitment not to proceed without having fully secured the $100 million in provincial money, the new motion insisted that council would not endorse a final deal with the Katz Group until the government of Alberta provided the remaining $55 million—which was never going to happen.

For Councillor Tony Caterina, all of these developments, especially the abandonment of so many public commitments, violated democratic procedures:

> Everything just kept changing, and it seemed like it was changing in
> order to justify the end result, which was a new arena. So that was
> frustrating and what I learned probably more than anything else
> during that process was that when we make motions—you would
> think that a motion is a motion. If it's "subject to X," provincial
> funding, for example, that that would be the norm, and if the provin-
> cial money wasn't available, then the project was off the table. But
> that "subject to" just kept being dismissed and dismissed, no matter
> what subject we added to the motions to try to mitigate risk and those
> sorts of things. There always seemed a way out of it for administra-
> tion and those in favour of moving this project forward. And that

*happened a number of times over the course of this, where, I'm joking
now, every time there's a "subject to" any motion, I'm not interested.
I don't believe in "subject to's" anymore because they can be removed
and bypassed.*[60]

As former city manager Simon Farbrother conceded, administration
had indeed framed certain issues in ways that were designed to keep
the political process moving forward in the hope that solutions to
problems would eventually be found:

*what was interesting is, if we'd have said in our first presentation we
made to council, "We're 25 percent short" [progress on the arena negotiations might have stopped]. But instead of shutting it down and then
making that the headline, it was, "Don't worry, let's keep building."
So, you go down a path where the obstacles become the news, or you
keep building on the good stuff and then you find a way to figure it out.
And at the end of the day, we filled the gap.*[61]

Worried, Edmonton's boosters and some of the city's biggest
downtown corporate players, including the Edmonton Chamber
of Commerce and Stantec, held a press conference to "demand"
that an arena deal between the Katz Group, the city of Edmonton,
and the government of Alberta be concluded. The newly formed
"Downtown Vibrancy Coalition," chaired by Simon O'Byrne, a vice
president with Stantec, began a pro-arena email campaign to pressure councillors. Councillor Tony Caterina dismissed the coalition
as nothing more than a group of businesses that stood to benefit
from the new arena: "I don't see any of them coming up with cash
to help. They look out for their own interests. Their rationale is old,
old, old, news. Maybe they don't hear that most people do want a
new arena, but they're not happy with the framework and
the funding."[62]

Still short $55 million, council voted to postpone its next arena-
related meeting with the intention of approaching the Capital
Region Board to support a grant application to be made by the city
of Edmonton for a $25-million regional collaboration grant from

the provincial government. The board voted to support the application, despite concerns that the vote was recorded incorrectly—but this source of funding was never pursued. The council meeting was disrupted by citizens demanding that any agreement be subjected to a plebiscite in the municipal election only four months away. And, it appeared that most Edmontonians remained opposed to the financing agreement, although council ignored their concerns. Using $5,000 of her own money, Nita Jalkanen (a volunteer for Voices For Democracy) commissioned one last poll in May 2013 that demonstrated continued opposition to the use of public funds for a new facility: 62 percent of Edmontonians disagreed with putting taxpayers' money into the project, and 82 percent of residents opposed the city incurring over $500 million in debt to support it. But on May 14th, the same day that Jalkanen's survey results were released, a special council meeting was hastily called for the next day to push through the final version of the financing agreement.

After voting to deny a request to address council by members of Voices for Democracy, councillors overwhelmingly supported the final iteration of the arena-financing agreement (10–3), with only Councillors Caterina, Diotte, and Sloan voting against it. The final deal included a number of changes, including an additional cash contribution of $15 million from the Katz Group. While Katz would contribute $27.7 million in cash to the overall development, he would receive $26.5 million from the city of Edmonton as per the terms of the arena land purchase; in other words, his upfront cash contribution was just over $1 million, a far cry from the $100 million that had been initially agreed upon. Council also agreed to alter the source of the $45 million in arena funding that it had supported earlier in April; no longer would MSI funding be used for the arena. Instead, an additional amount of money would be drawn from the CRL. Council also anticipated dedicating funds from its regional collaboration grant to make up the difference (but this would never happen). The price tag for the overall development had now risen to $604.5 million and would eventually grow to $613.7 million. Despite all of its previous stated commitments, the city of Edmonton would now debt-finance nearly all of this amount. Still, the final changes were enough to sway some councillors to support the new deal, including Ben Henderson, who had voted against the agreement in April.

Finally, while the Katz Group had dropped its demand for a non-compete clause with Northlands from back in October 2011—in exchange for numerous concessions including the $2 million per year marketing subsidy and the restructuring of its $100-million upfront contribution to the arena as annual lease payments— administration now added a new condition to the master agreement, giving the Katz Group a veto over the redevelopment of Northlands, whose executives vowed to compete against the new arena. Thus, not only had the city provided the Katz Group with a new, $613.7-million arena, but it had also granted the organization control over the old one to secure a monopoly in sport and entertainment, all without public knowledge. Councillor Caterina said,

> I was happy that the non-compete clause with Northlands was origi-
> nally removed, because it was bad for Northlands, bad for the city,
> and just bad in general—that we would support entering into any
> agreement that would put someone else out of business. But then it
> was reintroduced at the back-end with the master agreement. The
> master agreement was delegated to the city manager; we do the high-
> level stuff and then delegate the city manager to negotiate the final
> details. And, they re-entered that with the clause in there, the master
> agreement that says that Katz has a veto power over anything that's
> related to sports and entertainment. It was signed by the city manager,
> and so legally it's in place. But that's the process, the city manager
> is delegated the responsibility to sign and work out the final details
> along with law and everybody else. Is that a great system? Under
> these circumstances, absolutely not a great system. And they purposely
> left it so vague, it could be anything. You want to play marbles in
> that building, Katz can say, "No, that's entertainment." Somebody's
> having fun watching or you're playing a sport, he can say no. That's
> probably the biggest hurdle right now in repurposing or doing some-
> thing with that building. So, with that clause in there and his [Katz's]
> unwillingness to move on it, we can't sell it, we can't program it, we

Edmonton Mayor Don Iveson chants with the crowd at the Edmonton Oilers' Orange Crush community rally in Sir Winston Churchill Square in Edmonton on Thursday, April 20, 2017, during the team's first-round playoff series against the San Jose Sharks.
[Canadian Press/Codie McLachlan]

can't do anything with it because it would enter into the master agreement where we can't have those activities in there. The building has another 50 years of life, and we've had dozens of non-sports related entities come forward and express interest in purchasing or leasing the building. But, again, with that clause in there, he deems everything to be sports or entertainment. And our legal department has basically said it's hard to argue that it's not sports because it's so vague, and it makes you wonder why they didn't think of that at the time to protect the city's interests.[63]

The biggest surprise of the day, though, was the decision by Councillor Don Iveson to vote in favour of the arena-financing agreement. Despite having regularly voted against the agreement since January 2011, and despite his emergence as a forceful and eloquent critic of public subsidies for professional sport franchises, Iveson justified his reversal in two ways. First, even though the arena deal had gotten progressively worse for the city, in his opinion, a better arrangement with the Katz Group was never going to happen. As he candidly noted, council had been "outmanoeuvred at a number of points...and pushed back far too late."[64] His second reason was "his gut" feeling that the new arena would be beneficial for the city's downtown core. The more credible motive for Iveson's reversal, however, was that he had decided to run for mayor, and to have voted against the final arena deal would have damaged his ability to secure the support of influential developers and business interests and to appear as an Edmonton booster. Iveson would win the mayoralty in October 2013, and, on the opening night of the new downtown arena in 2016, would stand on the red carpet with Daryl Katz. Iveson's change of heart about the arena, and his subsequent victory, were astutely summed up by Mayor Mandel: "Smart politician."[65]

14

CONCLUSION

FOR MANY EDMONTONIANS, Rogers Place has achieved exactly what
city policymakers and Oilers executives set out to do over a decade
ago: it triggered a visible transformation of a depressed area of
Edmonton's downtown core, while securing the future of the hockey
club for years to come. And, for the main boosters and beneficiaries
of the heavily-subsidized arena development, this end has justified
the political means. Still, this transformation has come at an enormous public cost, and has brought with it a host of intended and
unintended consequences. That said, the final chapters on the
success and the impacts of the whole development will take years
to play out.

The arena agreement has, however, raised important questions
about the use of municipal resources to support the financial interests of the Edmonton Oilers and the club's billionaire owner, as well
as the associated opportunity costs. Is it the best use of limited
municipal funds to spend taxpayers' dollars on a new arena development at the expense of essential city-wide services such as police,
fire, transportation, transit, LRT, drainage, waste collection, libraries,
local recreation centres and arenas, culture, and so on? Should the
city of Edmonton spend hundreds of millions of dollars on a new
arena when community services and programming for women and
families remain woefully under-resourced? Across North America,

billions have been spent on new facilities—what Bruce Kidd calls "men's cultural centres"[1]—to support the male owners of sports franchises; the players and their agents; the mostly male business community, which rents luxury suites to entertain largely male clients; the male-dominated sports media who cover the games; the media corporations that provide mostly male audiences for advertisers; and the predominantly male sports fans who attend the games.[2]

Most important, was a new arena even needed when another publicly-funded facility, the Northlands Coliseum, which opened in 1974, was still profitable, functional, and safe? From the 1990s until the conclusion of the deal in 2051, Edmontonians will have added well over a billion dollars to the coffers of the Oilers franchise. Meanwhile, at the time of this book's writing, the city of Edmonton has over $3 billion in debt and a funding gap of $3.8 billion in potential infrastructure needs over the next decade.[3] Municipal tax levels have continued to increase since 2013. Predictably, this latter development has been greeted with vitriol by many citizens and business leaders, including those who were among the most influential boosters of the publicly-financed arena, including the Edmonton Chamber of Commerce—now headed by former Katz Group employee Janet Riopel—as well as *Edmonton Journal* columnist David Staples.

Despite billions of dollars of investment in the downtown core, the city's Capital City Downtown CRL projections have been negatively revised.[4] The assessment baseline for the Capital City Downtown CRL was struck on December 31, 2014; all increases in municipal property tax revenue from this point forward will be dedicated to paying for a host of downtown projects, including Rogers Place, until 2034. Both the size of the CRL boundary and the date of the baseline assessment are of crucial importance. Indeed, the Capital City Downtown CRL will capture increases in property tax revenue across much of downtown, including from a number of new office towers and condominium developments *built before the arena development began.*

There is inevitably a timing issue in terms of the recovery of these types of speculative financing mechanisms. Specifically, the city of Edmonton's expenditures on catalyst projects like Rogers Place—including debt servicing—occurred previous to the tax uplift in the CRL area actually being generated; thus, the CRL will incur losses to the reserve position for a number of years before revenues exceed annual expenditures. The city hopes that CRL revenues will improve sooner rather than later, finally pushing the reserve into a positive position. At that point, council will be able to fund new projects from the reserve for the remainder of the 20-year duration of the levy, instead of having to borrow funds.

Recent documents presented to city council show that the Capital City Downtown CRL tax levy will not be available to the general pool until 2031, just three years before the expiration of its 20-year term. In January 2018, for example, the city of Edmonton projected that the CRL would generate between $675 and $864 million over the next two decades, and that this amount would be "sufficient to fund most or all of the downtown catalyst projects," including part of the total cost of Rogers Place and its related borrowing charges. However, as the result of a significant recession beginning in 2014, after the collapse of the price of oil, as well as an oversupply of commercial office space downtown, the assessed value of existing properties within the CRL boundary has decreased, resulting in diminished revenue forecasts.

This can be illustrated with three financing milestones: positive annual cash flow (when the CRL revenues no longer need to be supplemented by other city revenues); positive reserves; and loan repaid. In 2015,[5] council was told that the Capital City Downtown CRL would have an annual positive net position by 2019; three years later,[6] the city had revised this estimate to 2020. In 2015, council was also told that the CRL reserve would reach a positive position by 2022.[7] In 2018, this estimate was revised to 2024.[8] Finally, in 2015, council was told that by 2027, the CRL tax levy would be available to the general tax pool (i.e., all remaining debt services and administrative costs would be covered).[9] In 2018, this was revised to 2031.[10]

The city of Edmonton, moreover, has yet to provide a full economic assessment, i.e., of how the city's net tax revenue has been, and will continue to be, affected as investment and spending shift to Ice District, and as other parts of the city decline. Thus, in light of the devaluation of other areas of the city, especially around Northlands, as well as the CRL's deficit reserve position, the city's overall tax base has been negatively affected. In other words, taxes continue to increase each year.

The Capital City Downtown CRL may eventually turn out to be a tremendous success story for the city, and may fully cover the costs of a significant portion of Rogers Place and a host of new downtown amenities by 2034. However, at this point, it is too early to come to any definitive conclusions about the success of this public financing mechanism, and the gamble that city council made in 2013 when it voted in favour of the arena agreement without a full economic analysis. Still, as a creative public financing mechanism, the CRL has only further aligned the city's interests with those of the Katz Group and various downtown land developers to cover a substantial portion of the costly arena development. It also spared the Katz Group from having to contribute to the upfront cost of the arena itself.

And, at the expiration of its 35-year deal with the Katz Group (an organization that may no longer even exist by then), the city of Edmonton will own what will probably be called an antiquated facility—at least by the ever-increasing standards of the business model of professional sport—and the land on which it sits. Of course, by that time the city may already have paid for a costly renovation of Rogers Place or been pressured into building yet another arena.

Power and Democratic Practice

Throughout this book, we have tried to foreground all of these questions in our analysis of the development of urban policy, the limitations of the democratic process, and the mobilization of political and economic power in Edmonton. Since the city's beginnings, council has been influenced by boosters in the local business community, especially those in the property development sector, and it has vigorously pursued a growth agenda, often at the expense of addressing social issues. This experience is not unique to Edmonton, though. It is consistent with that of other cities, not just in Canada but throughout North America.

The city's historical development has also been uniquely shaped by the Edmonton Exhibition Association, later Northlands, originally run by a small group of wealthy local families with strong ties to other levels of government, who worked behind the scenes to promote the interests of Edmonton, as well as their own. These groups have consistently sought to generate economic development and promote the image of Edmonton in the region, in the country, and, increasingly, on the world stage. One of the central ways that these influential boosters sought to achieve their goals was through the promotion of sports, especially men's professional hockey, as we saw in the challenges for the Stanley Cup before World War I and in the 1920s, and during the 1960s and 1970s when civic leaders wanted to attract an NHL franchise to Edmonton. These same interest groups were prepared to have the city spend significant amounts of public money on sporting facilities to support that quest, and their goal was achieved when the WHA's Edmonton Oilers franchise, owned by businessman Peter Pocklington, was absorbed into the NHL in the 1979 expansion.

The most recent arena debate in Edmonton, like its historical antecedents, raises important questions about power in municipal governance and about democracy itself. While plebiscites were held for the city to borrow money for the Omniplex in 1970 and for facilities for the 1978 Commonwealth Games—excluding the Coliseum, which had already been funded, largely with provincial and federal money—a referendum was never triggered to allow citizens to vote on the arena-financing agreement between the city of Edmonton and the Katz Group. Whether taxpayers supported the deal or not, council decided to fund a billion-dollar project in a deal negotiated mostly in secret and with minimal public input.

The disproportionate power of dominant business interests and certain businessmen in municipal affairs was evident throughout the debate on the new arena. From our interviews, it would appear that the broad structure of the financing agreement was arranged by newly elected Mayor Stephen Mandel and the Oilers' owners (then the Edmonton Investors Group Limited Partnership, or EIGLP) as early as 2004, around the same time as discussions about closing City Centre Airport were occurring. Influential members of the EIGLP and key developers had supported Mandel's mayoral campaign, and a new arena was soon linked to a municipal growth agenda to revitalize the downtown core. This goal was fully endorsed by the mayor's handpicked Arena Leadership Committee.

Once the hockey club was sold by the EIGLP in 2008, the influence of the Katz Group, which had contributed to Mayor Mandel's campaign in 2007, was obvious during the multi-year negotiations with the city. We also now know that vital information was withheld from council throughout the debate, including objective analyses of the Katz Group's finances. Claims that the Oilers were unprofitable went largely unchallenged. Crucially, despite an exceedingly wealthy owner, and despite council's requests for reports, a detailed assessment of whether a new arena could be privately financed was never made. And, in faithful service to the "owners' playbook," the citizens of Edmonton and their elected representatives were regularly subjected to the threat that the franchise would be relocated if the demands of the owners—first the EIGLP and then the Katz Group—weren't met. Few civic politicians wanted to be held responsible by Oilers fans for "losing" the team, even though polls consistently showed that most Edmontonians opposed using public funds to build a new arena. Tremendous pressure was brought to bear on council from within city hall and from influential boosters and lobbyists in the private sector.

The city's administration, committed to the idea of a public–private partnership with the Katz Group from the beginning of the debate, both manipulated and limited information, and largely abandoned its traditional remit of providing unbiased analyses of issues to council, instead acting as one of the biggest boosters of the arena project. The use of like-minded external consultants allowed administration to control the political narrative in support of the arena, rather than provide council with a full and balanced summary of the risks and benefits associated with the proposed development. One-sided analyses were also commissioned by the Arena Leadership Committee, which subsequently refused to make public the recommendations offered in crucial documents, including the HOK report that had ranked the Katz Group's land holdings well down the list of preferred arena sites and included the option of building at Northlands.

Administration treated the Katz Group as its partner, routinely granting the company favourable treatment throughout the challenging and lengthy negotiations. The city purchased and held land for the Katz Group until the land was subdivided so that the organization did not have to pay property taxes. It agreed to restructure the original terms of Katz's promised $100-million investment in the arena as capped annual lease payments, allowing him to avoid spending his own money. It limited the Katz Group's annual property tax payments for the arena to $250,000 for the next 35 years. It sold the Katz Group a portion of a city street (103 Street between 103 Avenue and 104 Avenue) for $465,000 to allow the organization to build additional amenities for Ice District. It provided massive amounts of tax dollars to a private venture without predetermined repayment terms for the principal and interest for the total duration of the agreement (terms were only provided for five years), and without demanding security for the loans. It allowed the Katz Group to determine the location of the city-owned arena and to design the facility according to its terms and specifications, including the costly Winter Garden overpass.

Despite including Northlands at the beginning of the process, the city engaged in exclusive negotiations with the Katz Group and granted a private company full control over a city-owned facility. It also gave the Katz Group a monopoly on the Edmonton sports and entertainment market, and control over another city-owned facility by inserting veto clauses into the master agreement, resulting in the closure of the Coliseum and the demise of Northlands. Thus, a radically different political economy of major league sport has emerged in Edmonton, and elsewhere—one that features billionaire owners and a more integrated business model at the expense of a more traditional elite, or stratificationist, model of community power. And despite significant public opposition, Edmonton's City Centre Airport was closed in 2013—in part, to remove the height restrictions that had prevented the construction of high-rise towers in the downtown core and to support the new integrated business model of major league sport. The intended redevelopment of the airport lands as a mixed-use urban community has, however, been a slow process for the city. As of 2019, only a small portion of the land has been prepared for development, with construction on the first phase slated to begin later in the year.

The city also agreed to lease office space in the Katz-owned Edmonton Tower for 20 years at increasing rates—a demand that the Katz Group had made from the outset of the discussions as a crucial element in its integrated development plan for the arena district. After the negotiations were halted in 2012, the Katz Group claimed to have dropped this demand, but administration knew that the Katz Group's plans for a new office tower were integral to the development, and that if the office contract was awarded to another developer, the arena project would likely fall through. This was never, at least according to Councillor Linda Sloan's memory and notes, made explicit to council.[11]

While the subsequent public tender process, overseen by a fairness commissioner, appears to have been a genuine competition, some observers believed that the playing field was tilted in favour of the Katz Group. Administration was also aware of the effect of a new office tower on an already oversupplied market, which will continue to depress the value of various properties downtown (and the Capital City Downtown CRL), much to the chagrin of many commercial land developers and business owners. This, despite the claims of arena proponents, including the Downtown Business Association, that all of downtown—indeed, all of the city—would benefit from the new arena and entertainment district. While the construction of the Edmonton Tower further fulfilled the Katz Group's $100-million commitment to ancillary development, in July 2018, the organization sold the Edmonton Tower for an estimated $400 million to the

Alberta Investment Management Corporation[12]—a reminder that the arena deal was always, at its heart, a heavily publicly-subsidized real estate play.[13]

Funding for the new arena from other orders of government was harder to come by. Facing its own multi-billion-dollar debt and knowing the lack of support in constituencies across the country for the use of public funds to subsidize NHL hockey, the government of Canada declined to make a significant investment in the arena, but did provide $7 million through the Federal Gas Tax[14] to help build the community rink. The government of Alberta, which had covered some of the construction costs for both the Northlands Coliseum and Commonwealth Stadium in the 1970s, rejected the city's pleas and the Katz Group's less-than-subtle lobbying attempts. The premiers, first Ed Stelmach and then Alison Redford, would not provide direct funding for such an unpopular project, partly because an equivalent level of funding would, in turn, be expected by Calgary, where the owners of the Flames were also seeking a new, publicly-financed facility (see Epilogue). The provincial government did, however, support the arena project and the development of downtown Edmonton in other ways, including approval for the Capital City Downtown CRL and the funding of infrastructure like the Metro Line LRT that connects to Rogers Place.

Crucially, the government of Alberta, which is constitutionally responsible for municipal governance, remained silent during the arena debate, despite obvious problems. Should it have intervened to discourage the frequent use of in-camera sessions that, it has been argued, contravened the terms of the *Municipal Government Act*? Should the government of Alberta have initiated revisions to the *Conflicts of Interest Act* and regulations requiring signed disclosures from all elected officials and municipal administrators involved in the negotiation of the arena deal and land purchases? Should the province have approved a CRL that was designed from the outset to finance an arena development and support the interests of the Edmonton Oilers, while diverting hundreds of millions of tax dollars away from provincial education coffers? Should the province have allowed the city of Edmonton to use its municipal borrowing power and the resources of the Alberta Capital Finance Authority to debt-finance the arena development in support of a privately-owned hockey franchise? Finally, should it have placed limits on how much the city could borrow to finance a private development project like Ice District, including specific limits on the amount of public debt and the length of borrowing?[15]

All of these issues raise important questions about the democratic process in Edmonton, transparency in council deliberations, and the lack of genuine citizen participation in the arena debate. While it might be argued that Edmontonians were able to voice their opinions on arena-related issues at promotional open houses and at rigidly controlled and carefully scripted public consultation sessions, citizens never had a real opportunity to directly influence the structure of the deal itself, or have a say on the key terms of the final agreement. In fact, the arena issue was barely raised over the course of two civic elections.

Most of the real political action occurred behind closed doors, away from public scrutiny, and sometimes far away from Edmonton. This was especially true of the secret meeting held in the NHL's head office in New York, where Mayor Mandel and the Katz Group convened in 2011, with NHL commissioner Gary Bettman serving as "mediator." Yet, even as many of the Katz Group's commitments fell by the wayside, and even as administration abandoned a number of its own pledges to citizens and to council, most councillors continued to support the project and its financing mechanisms. Despite never having the genuine opportunity to debate the findings of the pro-arena *City Shaping* report in 2008, for example, council accepted its conclusions at face value, without full consideration of the far-reaching implications of these decisions for all of Edmonton, not just for the downtown core, and especially with respect to the Capital City Downtown CRL. The few councillors prepared to ask hard questions and vote against the arena financing agreement were, thus, easily contained and consistently outvoted.

All of these efforts were supported by prominent members of the business community (many of whom directly benefitted from the arena development), the Downtown Business Association, the

Edmonton Chamber of Commerce, various legal firms, and trusted private consultants, and by the young professional representatives of the Downtown Edmonton Community League, who had endorsed the project and were often called upon by arena boosters to speak on behalf of "the community." And yet, many businessmen who demanded that significant amounts of public money be used to build the new arena were unwilling to invest their own money in the development, resorting to populist appeals to justify their position, including the argument that the arena would benefit "all of downtown," the "city as a whole," and even "all of northern Alberta." All this in a historically conservative province known for its advocacy of free markets, minimal government intervention, and fiscal conservatism.

It is important to remember, though, that there is a difference "between public spending intended to provide public services, such as subsidized housing and recreational facilities, and public spending intended to attract private investment and stimulate economic growth through offering tax incentives or providing infrastructure—in short, by subsidizing the normal costs of development."[16] And, while governments across North America continue to subsidize the latter, and promote various image-making and public relations strategies to attract development and "people of the right sort," they are unwilling to spend money to address important social issues and less glamourous infrastructure projects. In their pursuit of "world-class" status and funding of "fantasy city"[17] developments like Ice District, municipal priorities in cities like Edmonton are laid bare.

These decisions will always produce winners and losers, especially as the inner city further gentrifies and property values increase. In Edmonton's case, the turnover of population and of retail that has followed from these developments has been entirely predictable. Indeed, it is the main objective of a growth agenda designed to bring young, upper- and middle-class professionals—members of Richard Florida's so-called "creative class"—back downtown to live, work, and spend, thus increasing prosperity and the tax base that, in turn, contributes to the CRL intended to fund development in the city core.

The absence of any sort of legally binding CBA has also been keenly felt. In November 2016, only two months after the new arena opened, the Katz Group announced that it had purchased the MacDonald Lofts building, whose units had been allowed to deteriorate to unsanitary and unsafe conditions by its previous owners (Mac Lofts Capital Corp. and Paragon Properties, a Calgary-based capital corporation) and by its private management company, Martyshuk Housing, which had assumed responsibility for the provision of social housing. In April 2017, the Katz Group issued eviction notices to all 66 residents, mostly Indigenous people on fixed incomes and income assistance, to leave the building within a year. The Katz Group did provide residents with a "relocation package"—furniture, cleaning of personal items, and a subsidy for the move to new premises—but non-profit organizations had to help find new accommodation for these citizens in a city with a drastic shortage of social housing. Many of them have been forced to relocate, pushed further away from friends, from familiar spaces, and from trusted networks of support and social services. Facing criticism from community members and other concerned citizens about these developments, Glen Scott, senior vice president of real estate for the Katz Group, simply remarked, with no sense of irony about a company that had received hundreds of millions of dollars of public subsidy and a new "home" for the Oilers, "We're obviously not a social agency and, historically, we haven't been in the business to provide social housing."[18]

Manufacturing Consent?

The mainstream media, especially the *Edmonton Journal*, always a key booster of the city and of professional sports, played a prominent role in promoting the arena agreement and accepting at face value the arguments in its support. Some pundits fuelled a moral panic about the state of Edmonton's downtown core to promote the dominant growth agenda. After Rogers Place opened in 2016, for example, *Edmonton Sun* columnist Graham Hicks expressed relief that there were now more "normal people" downtown as opposed to "the panhandlers, the intoxicated and generally tough-looking characters."[19]

There were, of course, exceptions to this media boosterism, including *Journal* columnists Gary Lamphier and Paula Simons, but their voices were consistently drowned out by the cheerleading of various pro-arena sports writers, columnists, and the editorial board itself. Stories supporting the arena were more likely to appear on the front page than were critical ones. Dissenting opinions were noted and critical letters to the editor printed, including op-ed pieces by the Canadian Taxpayers Federation and Voices For Democracy, although these critics' voices were also overwhelmed by the chorus of pro-arena commentary. While the *Edmonton Sun* published a number of critical editorials during the debate, these declined in frequency as the negotiations continued. The *Sun*'s sports columnist, Terry Jones, though, remained an exuberant promoter of the new arena throughout the debate and he received access to key sources, including Katz himself on occasion. More critical coverage was found in smaller alternative publications like *VUE Weekly* and *SEE Magazine*, both now defunct, but they lacked the reach and influence of the larger daily newspapers. As *Journal* columnist Fish Griwkowsky noted, "I think some of the media lost credibility by not standing up to the process loudly enough."[20]

To be fair, covering the arena debate over the course of many years was extraordinarily complex and challenging. The unavailability of critical reports and financial information certainly hampered reporters and columnists in their assessments of the deal. In addition, as sports journalist John MacKinnon reflected, the vortex of promotion and boosterism was difficult to avoid:

> I think a lot of my coverage was basically just fair coverage, but my financial knowledge is null and void, so...I should've been more careful and I should have sought out more expertise...In that sense I guess, to some degree, I became part of the cards they [the city and the Katz Group] were playing in a certain way...Some of my...work...was

insufficiently critical...[I should have said] "Okay, guys...we're calling
bullshit. You're not going anywhere."[21]

The media was also at a disadvantage because council met behind closed doors so often. Information was often not provided publicly by administration, and the Katz Group was not obligated to release its own documentation. Lacking concrete information, some journalists were asked by administration to "take us at our word" when covering certain aspects of the debate, although, as *Journal* reporter Gordon Kent noted, this request was not unusual in confidential deliberations, especially those involving land transactions.[22] The cultivation of key sources within both administration and the Katz Group throughout the debate was crucial for reporters and columnists, and those who were prepared to "call bullshit," like the *Journal*'s business columnist Gary Lamphier, were subsequently squeezed out of the debate. Substantive cuts to Postmedia newsrooms across the country in recent years also help to explain the absence of sustained local investigative journalism.

All of these pressures made it difficult to provide in-depth, critical coverage of the debate. Later, some writers, including the pro-arena columnist David Staples, conceded that they had simply ignored the principle of transparency, and that the lack of financial disclosure by the Katz Group was not a "deal breaker...especially because the city was open to a great degree."[23] A routine dependence on the same sources within administration and the Katz Group, and on the pro-arena consultants deemed to be "authoritative," undoubtedly influenced the coverage of the debate. These problems were exacerbated by the tendency of some people in the media, like Staples, to denigrate opponents without offering an opportunity for them to respond.

That much of the local media promoted the arena development and the interests of the city's corporate elite shouldn't be surprising. Their main source of revenue is advertising, and the key media interests in Edmonton are owned and operated by large corporate empires. The *Edmonton Journal* and the *Edmonton Sun*, for example, are both part of the Postmedia Network, and "it would be naïve to

Critical media coverage in Edmonton, October 20, 2011. [*Mike Winters/coppernblue.com*]

expect that such media corporations would be anything other than sympathetic to the corporate community of which they are a part."[24] Both papers, and the media in general, are also heavily reliant on sports coverage to secure an audience of largely male viewers and readers, and so remain dependent on local professional sports teams for access to games and players. The Oilers media rights holders (e.g., CHED Radio, Rogers Sportsnet, etc.) were also loath to jeopardize their symbiotic relationship with the team.

Beyond this, as the business writer Max Fawcett (then writing for *Alberta Venture*) noted, it was hard to ignore the impact of power and boosterism in the coverage of the arena debate in Edmonton:

> *Edmonton is a small town at the best of times where politics, and journalism, and power interact. Journalists are not dumb, and they are aware of the fact that they may need a life after journalism. And in Edmonton it doesn't really behoove you if you want to stay in Edmonton to take a steaming dump on the shoes of Daryl Katz, because he's a very powerful man. And the other thing is, I think a lot of people wanted to see this succeed, they wanted it to work, they wanted it to be a good news story, they wanted it to go well for everyone.*[25]

In light of these political and economic pressures, there was a need for national papers like *The Globe and Mail* and *National Post* to provide more critical coverage of the debate. Both the *Globe* and the *Post* did run stories critiquing a publicly-financed arena, but these were largely ignored in Edmonton. There was, though, little economic incentive for either of the national newspapers to pursue a rigorous and time-consuming investigation of land transactions in a small Western Canadian city that may not have resonated in the country's larger markets.[26]

In the end, then, few reporters at the local and national levels asked the hard and necessary questions. What was the city-wide impact of the CRL? Why was there no legally binding community benefits agreement? Where was the comparative assessment of all potential arena sites? Where was the detailed assessment of a fully privately-financed option? Where was the investigation of land sales and transactions associated with the development and its surrounding area? What impact would the financing of the arena have on the city's future spending and borrowing limits? And what were the consequences of the development for the inner-city community, especially for people experiencing homelessness and at risk of displacement to other parts of the city that lack shelters and social services?

The Futility of Resistance?

Throughout the arena debate, those who opposed the financing agreement were largely ignored or framed by promoters and beneficiaries of the development as knockers and naysayers, as anti-Oilers, and sometimes even as anti-hockey. This is precisely the type of invective that has for over a century been leveled at those who have challenged the dominant growth agenda and boosterism in Edmonton. In thinking about the larger lessons of this story, though, it is worth considering why various critics of the deal—including Voices For Democracy, the Canadian Taxpayers Federation, and a number of hockey bloggers—failed to cultivate a wider political base and why citizens did not fight the arena deal in more significant numbers. The popularity of the Oilers and of hockey offers an important explanation. Yet, polls regularly demonstrated significant opposition to the project.

The lack of sustained public dissent was perplexing precisely because of the well-known precedents in Edmonton, especially during the Pocklington era of the 1990s. Fast forward to 2010, though, and the rising value of the franchise, a booming local economy, a collective bargaining agreement between the NHL and the NHLPA that included a salary cap, and an extraordinarily wealthy team owner (much wealthier than Peter Pocklington) rendered implausible any claims that the Oilers were struggling financially or that the local private sector lacked the capital to build the arena district without public assistance. If history repeats, "the first time as tragedy, the second as farce,"[27] why did citizens not fight the arena deal more forcefully?

First, all of the opposition groups faced fiscal challenges in competing against an influential and deep-pocketed growth coalition. Without the financial backing of wealthy supporters, well-paid public relations people, and marketers, such as those employed by the Katz Group and the city to work collaboratively on the arena development and its promotion *on a full-time basis*, and lacking allies in the local media and the endorsement of well-known people in the community, these pockets of opposition were too under-financed, politically inexperienced, and isolated to mount a sustained political campaign that could capture the attention and imagination of citizens or effectively cultivate public anger.

Second, the debate spanned many years, and ordinary citizens with jobs and family responsibilities were not always able to oppose the arena deal over such an extended period of time. As columnist Fish Griwkowsky, who had written a number of critical stories on the arena in *SEE Magazine*, reflected,

> *I came up with the idea of a book called "Oiled," that was going to be 99 reasons the rink was a sham, including little icons like a key in cases we handed Katz—who wouldn't even open his fucking books— the keys to the city. Some artists I know were going to contribute, but unfortunately Trevor Anderson and I started having a lot of success with our films on the international festival circuit, and I had to throw my energy into that...But basically, like anything else, it came down to the fact people don't have time to get out there and protest something that was repeatedly advertised as "a done deal," digging holes in the ground before it was even approved and properly financed. Is it properly financed yet? I lost track.*[28]

Andy Grabia, a prolific hockey blogger (*Battle of Alberta*), made a similar point:

> *It burned me out. There were only a few of us really fighting this thing and it was exhausting. I mean, you're battling an established organization and brand in this city who has their tether hooks in all sorts of places, who frankly bully people in either the public sector or*

the private sector to get what they want. The Edmonton Oilers are a firmly entrenched organization and they are so integral to our self-identity. So, I would hear things like, "Why do you hate Edmonton? Why do you hate the Oilers?" I don't. I grew up an Oilers fan. I love my city. So, I'm not sure if we made a huge difference, but we made people look and pay attention to stuff that they weren't paying attention to. We made journalists talk to us and to other people like Brad Humphreys. I think we also opened a few eyes for the next debate coming down the road in Calgary, and hopefully what we did will make a difference there. But there was no way that the mayor of this city was going to let citizens actually decide and vote on this issue. I learned to become very cynical about municipal governance.[29]

Indeed, while social media and rigorously researched blogs and websites played a role in fostering debate and critical assessments of the claims being made by the growth coalition, at the end of the day, these conversations had virtually no impact on decisions made at city hall.

Third, over the course of the debate, opponents of the arena financing agreement were continually reacting to a wide range of reports, media coverage, and selective financial projections. They had to familiarize themselves with the intricacies of various municipal governance policies, zoning bylaws, and the terms of the arena financing agreement, in order to offer a credible and understandable commentary that might sway not only public opinion, but the voting patterns of individual councillors. Even people with professional and educational expertise and experience in public communication had a hard time responding. As Scott Hennig of the Canadian Taxpayers Federation explained,

I feel like we lost the public relations battle on the Community Revitalization Levy. I didn't feel like I explained it well enough for people to grasp, and the city explained it better. They had a better video, it was simpler, and everyone wanted to believe there was free money. Because when you think of it, as I said to a lot of people, if you think about it for 10 seconds, it makes sense. If you think about it for

a minute, it makes no sense. And more people think about it for 10
seconds, so if you can't win the 10-second battle, they're never going
to think about it for the minute. So, I think if that would've been done
better, maybe [it would have worked], because I think a lot of the coun-
cillors were swayed by it [the city's campaign].[30]

In the end, the sheer complexity and secrecy of the deliberations removed ordinary citizens from fully participating in a political debate over the distribution of scarce public resources and the future of their city. All of these aspects of public life, plus the sheer volume of information withheld from citizens, are now driven by "experts" from both the public and private sectors, and effectively critiquing the conclusions of those technocrats requires significant resources and cultural capital. Perhaps most important, though, the withholding of vast amounts of public information in the name of "commercial sensitivity," a tactic that could be drawn from a Franz Kafka novel, underlines the democratic consequences that flow from the intermingling of the Katz Group and the city of Edmonton. As we discovered in writing this book, the former has been able to harness the resources and the protection of the city, while the latter is now able to hide behind its corporate partner in the face of any request for information—placing both beyond the reach of demo-cratic transparency and citizen accountability. New policies have now been enacted by administration, for example, to ensure that past election donor and contribution lists for the mayoralty and council candidates are permanently destroyed.

Finally, it is important to emphasize how power and intimi-dation, as well as boosterism, worked in this particular debate. Opponents of the agreement had to make serious personal calcula-tions in deciding whether to challenge the powerful supporters of the arena project in the real estate, land development, hospitality, and construction sectors, as well as the Edmonton Oilers orga-nization, the Katz Group, and city hall. Members of the board of directors of Voices For Democracy, for example, were repeatedly told by people, including high-profile businessmen, that while they privately supported the group's objectives, they were fearful of the financial and professional ramifications if they publicly opposed the arena deal. As well-known activist Mimi Williams, who also opposed the use of public funds to finance the arena throughout the debate, recalled, "The business community is just so connected that I think people were fearful for their livelihoods and future prospects. It's a small, small town. As big as we think we are or want to be, not much happens in this town that doesn't get around very, very quickly, and people just didn't want to stick their heads up."[31] The ability to push opponents to the sidelines and marginalize alternative perspectives underscored the power of the growth coalition and boosterism in Edmonton, and often led to self-censorship, in that many stayed silent or publicly endorsed the arena development while privately opposing it.

Critics of the arena agreement also understood the consequences of engaging in public opposition in Edmonton. After one of the authors presented at a public hearing at city hall in October 2011—an appearance that afforded this author some media coverage for denouncing the arena deal as an "egregious use of public funds"—a wealthy booster and donor to the University of Alberta (and a former member of the EIGLP) called the Dean of the Faculty of Kinesiology, Sport, and Recreation, Dr. Kerry Mummery, to demand that the lead author be made to "shut up."[32] Other opposition groups were also attacked, as Scott Hennig of the Canadian Taxpayers Federation attested: "I also had a mildly threatening letter from the Katz Group claiming that I had been publishing false information and then cc'ing other lawyers of theirs on the letter, which we've seen before and we know is intended to be a mild threat."[33]

Fish Griwkowsky summed up perhaps the biggest problem facing critics:

There was precious little resistance because, sadly, this place has such an inferiority complex—the little sibling issues I think we inherited from Canada in general comparing itself to the US—that you can pretty much slap "world class" on anything and all the boosters start salivating about finally having an excuse to live here. I've always loved the city, especially when the economy was slow and we had to

make our own fun—it was a golden age. This whole young entrepre-
neur idea that "we love Edmonton more than anywhere—now here is
a list of needed changes!" thing has always stunk of hypocrisy to me—
not that there's anything wrong with building things. Just quit saying
we live in Asgard [home of the Norse gods] if you want to reshape the
whole place. It's the dumbness, the dishonesty, of the pitch that always
kills me.[34]

At the end of the day, many citizens concluded that there was simply
nothing to be gained from opposing the arena development more
forcefully, especially in the absence of a plebiscite. And, despite
the many polls demonstrating city-wide opposition, local political
organizations, community groups, churches, and other constituencies inevitably retreated from a political process that was rightly
perceived to have been stacked in favour of proponents. One of the
most salient lessons from the arena debate in Edmonton is simply
that when opposition groups are confronted with significant obstacles—including a lack of external resources, nominal alliances with
other interest groups and civic elites, a largely boosterish media,
and a restrictive municipal system dominated by proponents—there
is little chance to alter the "world-class" growth agendas of a devel-
opment-oriented government and its influential corporate partners.

Coda

The arena debate in Edmonton skewed municipal priorities and
dominated political energies for almost a decade—just as similar
debates had during the Pocklington era in the 1990s. And, beyond
the significant financial costs, these matters will continue to affect
municipal governance for the next 30 years. Indeed, since Rogers
Place opened in 2016, council has had to address a number of
additional arena-related matters at the request of the Katz Group.
In 2016, for example, despite having endorsed an arena financing
agreement that was dependent on tens of millions of dollars in
downtown parking revenue only three years earlier, council granted
the Katz Group approval for a temporary parking lot on underdeveloped land north of Rogers Place (a request that the city granted

in exchange for a $150,000 donation to the Central McDougall Community League, although the community itself was not consulted about this decision). Council and administration were, of course, well aware that the Katz Group was also building amenities that featured significant numbers of additional parking spaces. Predictably, in December 2018, it was revealed that the city was not capturing enough downtown parking revenue to meet its repayment obligations for just under $50 million of arena-related debt. This amount was subsequently added to the Capital City Downtown CRL. While administration has estimated that this additional debt will not impact the year in which the CRL reaches an annual surplus position (2020), other key milestones have been pushed back yet again. The CRL reserve will now become positive in 2027, and the reserve will only cover remaining debt servicing costs by 2033—the year before the CRL itself expires. What this also means, though, is that there is now substantially less money to fund a variety of catalyst projects in Edmonton's downtown core through the CRL, as was originally envisioned.[35]

The Katz Group, also sought a bylaw exemption to open a liquor store in Ice District. Council approved this exemption in December 2018. Finally, earlier in 2018, in yet another private meeting with city council, the Katz Group reportedly asked for an additional $10 million in public funds to assist with the construction of a plaza within Ice District.[36]

There are also significant issues associated with arena-related infrastructure, including the crucial LRT stop outside Rogers Place (MacEwan Station), which cannot handle more than 100 riders at a time.[37] The much-touted community rink, meanwhile, is woefully under-utilized, thanks, in large part, to high parking fees (which mostly go to the Katz Group). Moreover, the city has only used a handful of its total "free use" days at Rogers Place since 2016.[38] Finally, the city of Edmonton controversially voted to close the Coliseum, despite interest from the private sector in repurposing the building, and despite minimal consultation with the surrounding neighbourhoods. In exchange for the preservation of its monopoly in sports and entertainment and the permanent closure of a valuable civic asset worth tens of millions of dollars, the Katz Group offered to terminate the "marketing agreement" that was included in the broader arena master agreement, potentially saving the city $17 million. In 2018, the city initiated a call for proposals to redevelop Northlands; however, submissions that included repurposing the Coliseum were simply not considered. The vast grounds at Northlands now sit empty and unused. In April 2019, a new city redevelopment plan proposed the creation of an "urban village" on the Northlands site, with two LRT stations and a mix of housing and commercial spaces. The Coliseum and the racetrack would, of course, have to be demolished.[39]

As for the arena itself, Rogers Place was built to an entirely predictable template, which is hardly surprising given the involvement of HOK in its development. In fact, while many in Edmonton consider Rogers Place a spectacular building, only the exterior shell is at all novel. Following now standard facility design patterns, Rogers Place was built as a "corporate-entertainment complex"[40] to allow the Katz Group to extract as much money from affluent consumers as possible—with high ticket prices and opulent luxury suites/corporate boxes that cost thousands of dollars, overpriced concessions and merchandise stores throughout the facility, and parking in Rogers Place and in the Edmonton Tower.[41] Every aspect of seating in Rogers Place has been monetized. If you want a seat close to the ice or at centre ice, it will be expensive. If you want a bigger seat, that will cost you more. A cup holder, more still. A seat on the aisle can cost an additional several hundred dollars more per season than a seat just two over. "Loge" seating, even more. Likewise, everything in the city-owned facility is for sale: naming rights were sold to Rogers and Ford for tens of millions of dollars, and continuous advertising (including advertising for the city of Edmonton) is central to the Katz Group's revenue streams.

There are hundreds of television screens around the concourse so that fans can watch the game, and consume, without having to return to their seats to see the game live. Fans are invited to engage in various interactive experiences throughout the game on their mobile devices, preferably on the Rogers wireless network, as part of the new mediated experience of being a hockey fan. Likewise, the structure of live hockey games now follows league-wide, carefully choreographed patterns, with loud special effects and music, and replays on oversized jumbotrons. Watching an Oilers game is now about the experience of being in the rink and about "entertainment value," with the game itself secondary to the consumption of costly beer, food, and team "merch"—the exact experience you can have in any modern NHL arena anywhere in North America.

"Corporate-entertainment complexes," writes Howard Shubert, "are private enterprises (even though publicly funded) but clients prefer that they are designed to appear public." Rogers Place has also followed this template to a T by incorporating expanses of exterior glass and a large plaza (the Winter Garden/Ford Hall) that allows fans who miss out on tickets, or cannot afford them, to feel like they are part of the game, and, of course, consume beer and concessions. As Shubert underlines,

Transparency conveys openness. Even the non-paying fans get a look inside. Patrons on the inside feel connected to the surrounding city. Entrance plazas and clock towers act as civic signifiers. They define these buildings as public landmarks even though they are decidedly private, commercial enterprises. [42]

The comforts of nostalgia are also called upon to obscure all of these dynamics, and to ensure a smooth transition into a new arena that is often not as accessible as the old one. In Edmonton, images of players and teams from the club's golden era in the 1980s, as well as of star players from the modern era like Connor McDavid, are featured on the exterior and interior walls of Rogers Place, and a statue of Wayne Gretzky was transplanted from Northlands Coliseum.

Just like every other spectacular sports and entertainment district in North America, everything about Ice District has been designed to capture ever-greater amounts of consumer spending, discretionary income, and investment money from amenities unrelated to the sport of hockey. There are restaurants, bars, casinos, hotels, an office tower, and, for those with even deeper pockets, condominium units that have been developed by the Katz Group and WAM (now ONE Properties). All of this takes existing money and investment from other parts of the city and from other parts of the downtown and concentrates them in Ice District. Moreover, while hockey games and concerts have shifted 5.8 kilometers down the road from the Coliseum to Rogers Place, other popular events like the Canadian Finals Rodeo, which was held in the Coliseum for 44 years and had a significant economic impact on the city, have left town.

Thus, despite the celebration of the arena and the various high-profile construction projects in Ice District as landmark events in the city's history, Edmonton has simply followed in the footsteps of countless other urban places that have already built similar developments. These types of highly speculative investments are often vulnerable to devaluation, especially in boom-bust markets like Edmonton, which perhaps explains why, in 2018, the Katz Group initiated the sale of some of its commercial properties. And, in the pursuit of yet another leisure and consumption district downtown, any claim to unique urban design and distinct local character has largely been ceded, despite the presence of a piece of art as remarkable as Alex Janvier's *Tsa tsa ke k'e* (Iron Foot Place), a 45-foot diameter circular mosaic set in the floor of Ford Hall. Thus, a big question remains: Could Edmonton's downtown core, which had undergone steady growth and development since the late 1990s, have been further "revitalized" in a truly unique and inclusive manner other than through the construction of a sports and entertainment district? Alternatively, rather than investing $100 million in "world-class" amenities that exclude a great many people, or building the new Edmonton Tower, what if the Katz Group had been required to invest the same amount of money in affordable and/or social housing, or in creating truly public spaces?

We have entered the new Gilded Age, and the billionaire owners of major league sports teams are the new robber barons, primarily interested in accumulating as much money as possible through ever-increasing and ever-expansive demands for public subsidy. In Edmonton, the city capitulated to numerous demands from the

Katz Group, and secured the company's interests for decades to come through the provision of a new, heavily publicly-subsidized arena (which has dramatically increased the franchise's value and revenue streams); a 20-year lease for office space in the Edmonton Tower; and a monopoly in the sports and entertainment market and valuable downtown land development around the new arena. In thinking about these issues, then, what might other municipalities consider when they are "invited" by the owner of a professional sports franchise to build a new, world-class facility and entertainment district?

We must understand, first and foremost, that any benefit to the community is secondary to the desire of owners to make as much money as possible out of the deal. Therefore, here is our list for consideration by citizens and their elected representatives:

1. *Be well-versed in the steps of the owners' playbook that will be deployed over multi-year negotiations, including the inevitable threat to relocate a franchise. Councils should gather the evidence necessary to call such a bluff.*

2. *Demand independent analyses of any claims of facility obsolescence and unprofitability. In other words, insist on full financial transparency from the franchise and the provision of verified evidence that a facility cannot be privately financed.*

3. *Set the terms of the negotiations from the outset. City councils are stewards of not only the public interest, but taxpayers' money. They should not simply capitulate to the demands of a team owner for an iconic arena or stadium.*

4. *Ensure that final decisions about any prospective deal are debated publicly, and that complete minutes and relevant documents are made available to the public for all meetings.*

5. *Be prepared for both the owners of the professional franchise and the larger league to intervene in municipal elections. City councils should be prepared to counter this type of political pressure.*

6. *Make no public investment whatsoever in a new facility without getting security for investments or loans.*

7. *Insist that if a new arena/stadium is built using public funds,*

the value of the franchise must be reviewed annually, and any increases tied into the repayment plan. If the franchise increases in value, the loan component should decrease or be repaid.

8. *Provide for a revenue-sharing agreement and an extensive and legally binding community benefits agreement (created collaboratively with surrounding communities).*

9. *Ensure that local interests have the first right of refusal on any sale of the franchise.*

10. *Agree upon the total investment of public funds, which should also be ratified by a plebiscite or city-wide referendum. The city must also ensure due diligence and disclose any concessions associated with ancillary property developments.*

In addition to these suggestions, more substantial structural changes will be required to alter the broader political terrain associated with these boosterish debates in North America and to check the power of the major league sports cartels, including the formation of a North American-wide grouping of cities to collectively bargain over terms of public subsidy. Equally important, federal legislation should be considered to end the monopolies that major league franchises continue to enjoy, and which allow wealthy owners to benefit from franchise scarcity. These same tactics, incidentally, are now used by companies like Amazon to secure extravagant public enticement packages, as cities and governments compete against each other to attract jobs and investment in a continuous cycle of "lotteryism" in the global and continental economy.[43] As economist Brad Humphreys has concluded,

Owners can threaten to leave because there are open markets [like Quebec City] that would support an NHL team. Those markets exist because North American public policy decisions [exemptions to anti-trust legislation] have allowed sports leagues to have complete control over where franchises are located. You could change that law [and end monopoly conditions], so that owners would not have a viable open market to threaten to move to, and it would substantially reduce their power in the bargaining. I think that's one thing that could be done and really should be done to allow more entry into the NHL or the NBA. So that, you know, if Hamilton, Ontario, can support an NHL team, the Maple Leafs shouldn't get to block a team from springing up there. And that's a public policy we could change, altering the implicit anti-trust protection that leagues enjoy.[44]

Still, there does not appear to be enough political will or public pressure to pursue these types of initiatives, at least for the time being. Until these changes occur, though, the political decisions over spending scarce tax money to build facilities for professional sports franchises must be scrutinized carefully and critically. Most important, these decisions must be made by an informed electorate that is genuinely involved in shaping the urban landscape in which they live, work, and play.

EPILOGUE
The Oilers Get a New Arena, So the Flames Want One, Too

SHORTLY AFTER THE ARENA DEBATE ENDED in Edmonton, the
Calgary Flames ownership stepped up its campaign to get a new
arena of its own. The Scotiabank Saddledome was just over 30 years
old and the organization's management contract with the city of
Calgary was expiring.[1] In June 2014, Brian Burke, former president of
hockey operations for the Flames, played the facility obsolescence
card, telling the local Chamber of Commerce that: "There's absolutely
no reason why we should watch a new building going up in Edmonton
and we've got to play in a 1988 building here." The Saddledome, built
in 1983, was "embarrassing," he said, and it didn't "generate NHL
economics," putting the Flames at a competitive disadvantage.[2]
Although it had 19,289 seats, more than in Rogers Place for hockey
games, and the Flames played to sold-out crowds (attendance was
actually 100.1 percent of capacity for the 2013/14 season),[3] it wasn't
making enough money because there weren't enough lower bowl
seats, suites, or fan amenities.

Moreover, according to Burke, preaching directly from the gospel
of the owners' playbook, a new arena had "the potential to revitalize
Calgary's downtown," just like in Edmonton, and without more revenue
the Flames would fall "into second-class status." Local boosters were
quick to jump on board; one Calgary councillor welcomed the idea

of a new rink, and the president of the Chamber of Commerce
added, "It's another meeting and convention facility that Calgary's
really in desperate need of."[4] The narrative that the Calgary franchise
required a new arena because it was not making enough money was
entirely consistent with the needs of the corporate NHL, and resonated
with the corporate growth ideology that shaped the dynamic of
Calgary's economy, politics, and culture.[5] But it marked a significant

shift in emphasis from the goals of the first ownership group of the
Flames, boosters who said they didn't want to exploit their team for
personal profits, but instead wanted to raise the profile of Calgary.[6]

The original ownership group directed much of the team's profits
into local amateur sports groups, hockey scholarships, research into
hockey, and the national men's and women's hockey teams. These
were seen as the best way to promote Calgary. One of the owners,
Norman Kwong, later Lieutenant Governor of Alberta, said of the
Flames in the 1980s, "It's certainly no money-making scheme but
there are advantages to be gained. I have no quarrel at all with the
way it is set up and...I'm glad to be able to share in a significant
contribution to the betterment of the game and to the city of Calgary."[7]
The owners received a tremendous amount of goodwill because of
how they ran their operation, but their success was also due to the
support of various levels of government and contributions from
taxpayers. The bill for the Saddledome, built for the 1988 Olympics
at a cost of $97 million, was paid by city, provincial, and federal
governments, not by the team.

In the 1990s, the Calgary ownership group became less boosterish and more in line with the corporate orientation of the NHL. It
argued that the team was a small-market franchise, players' salaries
were rapidly increasing and paid in US funds at a time when the
Canadian dollar was low, and its net income was shrinking. But, at
the same time, it was able to buy out the Saddledome Foundation's
stake for $20 million rather than extend the lease, and it received the
facility's revenues, including concessions, parking, and advertising.
It wanted renovations to the Saddledome, to which the city agreed
when the owners threatened to relocate the team. "We don't want
to move," said Bill Hay, the club president. "But we need to increase

our revenue so we can remain competitive. It's a business deal."[8] Harley Hotchkiss, a member of the ownership group, would later say of this period, "We went through a really bad time. It was doubtful if we could stay in Calgary. We missed the playoffs seven straight seasons. We lost a lot of our fan base...It got to the point we were losing $6 million a year. The money had to come out of our pockets... That wears thin pretty fast. Two things let us survive: our determination not to give up and our relationship with the community."[9] Boosterism remained alive and well in Calgary.

In June 2013, Calgary experienced a major flood that left much of downtown, including the Saddledome, under water. The facility wasn't upgraded, though, because the Flames were pushing for a new arena, supported by NHL commissioner Gary Bettman, who came to Calgary in January 2015 (as he had done repeatedly in Edmonton) promising a bright future for the city with a new, publicly-funded arena: "[The Saddledome] needs to be replaced. And, hopefully, it can be worked out in a way that not only provides a great facility for the city for family shows and concerts and cultural events as well as the team...it can be used to create something special in the city as it's done in other places, like Columbus, like downtown Los Angeles...A new facility can be a catalyst for a whole host of things that positively impact the city."[10]

Just a few months later, the Calgary Sports and Entertainment Corporation (CSEC; the Flames' parent organization) announced a plan for a downtown sports complex, including an 18,000-seat arena for hockey and concerts and a 30,000-seat field house for CFL football and other sports. The city would own the facility and the company would operate it, covering the operating expenses and receiving all the revenues. The project was called CalgaryNEXT and would cost an estimated $890 million, to be paid for by a CRL (assuming the provincial government approved it), a ticket tax, and a $200-million contribution from the Flames—a financing model similar to the one developed in Edmonton. The city was expected to contribute $200 million. Calgary's mayor, Naheed Nenshi, called the proposal "intriguing," but said, "There are very significant requirements for public funding beyond the field house funding, and there is currently no money. I have said for a long time, and continue to strongly believe, that public money must be for public benefit and not private profit."[11] Perhaps the biggest challenge facing the CalgaryNEXT proposal was its location on the site of an old creosote plant in the West Village section of downtown on the Bow River. The cost of the cleanup, which it was assumed would be picked up by the city and other levels of government, was estimated at upwards of $300 million.

Undaunted, Calgary's boosters quickly gave their support to CalgaryNEXT, including deputy mayor Diane Colley-Urquhart:

We don't build great cities by saying "we have no funding."…At this particular time, with the economy the way it is, and the downward turn that we are seeing, we want to come out of this much sooner if possible in any way that we can. Having people, like these philanthropists, stepping forward at a time like this, provides a lot of confidence in the city and the economy and where we are going, and even in diversifying our economy.[12]

As in Edmonton, the project would include condo and office towers and hotels, attracting investments totalling $2 billion. Calgary, proponents argued, was now the only major city without a field house, and the CEO of Tourism Calgary, Cindy Ady, argued that the complex would "give the city an opportunity to host major amateur and professional sporting events." Ken King, president and CEO of CSEC, said it "would create jobs and is exactly what Calgary's economy needs right now."[13]

Others were quick to jump on board, making the same arguments as had been made in Edmonton. "People can live anywhere. They don't have to be here, which is why it's important to have amenities that will attract and keep people in your city," said Michael Brown, president and CEO of Calgary Municipal Land Corporation. The local media boosted the plan, with the *Calgary Herald* editorializing that the city must attract "the creative class," who are the basis of the new knowledge-based economy and will solve the "complex problems in everything from business and finance to health care....It's incumbent on our leaders—in business and government—to make sure the city continues to grow with the younger population. [Mayor Nenshi has said,] 'When we make investments in arts and culture and sports and recreation, in vibrant public spaces, and even great public transit, those are hard-nosed economic development decisions.'" The greatest tragedy would be that, without CalgaryNEXT, "Calgary risks becoming a city like Buffalo, N.Y." Calgary, in other words, had to become a more vibrant and economically viable city: "World-class venues attract world-class events that generate tourism dollars and enhance the overall tax base...In tough economic times it's easy to focus on the short-term challenges—like creosote contamination—rather than the long-term benefits. Calgary has long been seen as a 'can do' city, known for an entrepreneurial spirit that includes a high tolerance of risk if the endgame is compelling."[14]

Not all reactions to CalgaryNEXT were so boosterish. The national press was more critical, as it had been about Edmonton's arena plans. *The Globe and Mail* quoted the chief economist of the Conference Board of Canada: "It's not a great financial use of taxpayer money, but it can be a good addition to the chemistry of making a city a good place to live."[15] The *National Post* was harsher in its assessment. CalgaryNEXT, it said, was a "rotten idea"; if Calgary, "a business-minded city" in an economic slump, "has this kind of money sloshing around, we can think of any number of uses for it that would more nearly meet the public benefit test than subsidizing the profits of the Flames owners."[16] Columnist Scott Stinson wrote in the same edition about arguments that private businesses and boosters would make about the project. It would lead to, he wrote, "a massive redevelopment of a blighted part of the city, one that will include housing, shopping and restaurants and bars. It will be transformative... It points to the jobs that will be created; the rejuvenation; civic pride." The problem with this argument, he continued, is that arenas do attract money, "but only money that would have been spent locally anyway...The case for an actual public benefit to the public funds spent on them, other than good feelings, is non-existent...Why should the public be expected to provide the bulk of the funding for a project that, at its root, is about expanding the profits of a private business?"[17]

There was also strong local criticism. Kent Wilson, then a blogger and now a writer for *The Athletic* and a passionate Flames fan, argued that owning an arena offered no benefit for Calgary. He deserves to be quoted at length because he represents the perspective of many opponents:

> *Stadiums and arenas are huge, illiquid, depreciating assets. Like a car, they lose value each and every year of their lifespan. On top of that, you can't simply sell an arena if it has become obsolete or you need the cash. They take up massive parcels of land...only have a handful of uses and are almost as expensive to demolish as they are to build. As a rule, arenas are terrible investments (which is why team owners don't like to pay for them). The only real reason to build them is their ability to generate revenue during their life cycle. But that benefit often doesn't accrue to the city in whole or in part in many of these deals...If Calgary is to own the arena(s) and the Flames are to keep all (or a vast majority) of the revenue, then they will have passed the obligations of ownership to the public while keeping all of its attendant benefits. Assuming a 30-year lifecycle, the Flames will have sucked the asset dry of all value by the time it's time to ask for another (taxpayer-funded) arena. And because the public will "own" the structure, the Flames will be able to walk away from the obsolete, dried-up husk of a building without blinking.*[18]

The Flames would be the major beneficiary of the deal, he pointed out, because they would operate the facility and get the revenues from hockey and non-hockey events, including ticket sales, concessions, merchandise, advertising, and naming rights. They would design the facility, thus establishing the seating capacity, retail and concessions space, numbers of luxury boxes and premium seats, and they would pay no property tax. Moreover, he wrote,

> *Billionaires often don't get involved with sports teams simply for the yearly profit and loss statement...but for what the teams can garner as*

overall assets. Forbes *estimates that the Flames alone are worth more than [US]$400 million (they were bought for $16M in 1980), though the valuation is an educated guess at best. We can't really be sure what the Flames would actually be valued at since they don't tend to voluntarily share their books but given that the* NHL *is now charging a [US]$500-million expansion fee, it might actually be a lowball. A lopsided deal with the city for brand-new buildings would no doubt add value to the Flames group's various sports assets.*

On top of all that, team owners also tend to get involved with the development efforts around the arena sites. By taking advantage of sweetheart deals with the city (such as new infrastructure and beneficial CRLs*), team owners can strike up fresh real estate investments outside of the sports franchise—a profitable way to "double dip" on the city's subsidy.*

*This is especially beneficial because it's bonus money beyond the reach of Hockey Related Revenue (*HRR*)—that is, the stuff that gets split 50/50 with the players. If an owner can leverage arena development to create real estate holdings, then he or she doesn't have to share that new source of profit with the players' unions.*[19]

The CSEC also wanted a new facility to generate more concert revenue because, it argued, the Saddledome's iconic roof wouldn't support the equipment used for performances. Plus, as it was responsible for the costs of renovations after the 2013 flood, it wanted to avoid future hits to its bottom line.

Journalist Taylor Lambert provided an equally thoughtful critique. CalgaryNEXT was "brazen" rather than bold because it required so much public spending, while the CSEC would contribute less than 25 percent. The proposal was corporate welfare. He especially singled out the CRL component for criticism:

The idea of a CRL *is that all these new buildings and businesses that sprout up around this new development will pay additional tax, so let's just put that revenue towards the development (often in the form of debt repayments)...[This mechanism is] controversial. Regardless of how you package it, in the end it's a form of public money that could*

go elsewhere...Except that studies have shown that these types of
projects often only revitalize urban areas in the sense that they draw
planned investment away from other parts of the city. And in this
case the people profiting from the public money aren't even funding a
quarter of the project.

He also pointed out that the money would benefit the wealthy
businessmen who owned the Flames rather than the people of
Calgary:

Two of the men, billionaires Murray Edwards and Clayton Riddell,
have a combined fortune of [US]$4.8 billion according to Forbes. The
Flames are the 13th-most-valuable team in the NHL, worth [US]$451
million, and they are just one of the teams that will benefit from this
project. Meanwhile, Calgary lacks a dedicated cancer centre, adequate
drug rehab facilities, social services and sufficient affordable housing,
to say nothing of funding for truly and broadly beneficial infrastruc-
ture such as the Green Line LRT...Given how jealously we guard our
tax dollars in Alberta, I'm amazed at how brazenly this proposal
demands we subsidize a wonderfully profitable corporation.[20]

Calgary City Councillor Druh Farrell was equally blunt: "This isn't
a great deal for the citizens of Calgary."[21] When council met later in
the fall to discuss the project, Mayor Nenshi called it "half-baked"
because the CSEC had not done its homework. Councillor Farrell
estimated that the overall cost to the city would be closer to $1.5
billion, making it, in Nenshi's words, "the most expensive public
works project in Calgary's history. As such, Calgarians deserve to
be able to really know that their council has gone through this in a
very methodical, very transparent and very open way."[22] Nenshi was
proving to be a far more demanding negotiator than Mayor Stephen
Mandel had been in Edmonton, at least for now.

The NHL, as it always has, stepped in to redirect the narrative in
Calgary. In January 2016, Commissioner Gary Bettman gave a speech
to the receptive boosters in the Calgary Chamber of Commerce,

giving his full support to the CalgaryNEXT proposal. "If Edmonton," he said, "could get a 'visionary' new arena project approved via a private-public partnership, then Calgary should be able to manage it as well." He also dredged up familiar tropes—it was not corporate welfare because "that is a view not based on a realistic assessment of the important infrastructure and economic benefits that facilities bring to a community." But, he concluded, "If your attitude is this has to be all [privately financed], it's not going to get done—because *it's not an investment that's cost-justified*. What you need is an understanding of how these projects can generate revenue that not only pay for themselves but spur other economic activity that can make a city stronger."[23]

The next day, Mayor Nenshi offered a sarcastic response that indirectly alluded to Edmonton: "Perhaps in other cities that he has come to, the city councils have just written cheques based on back-of-the-napkin proposals, without any consultation from the public, or without any analysis. That's not how we operate here. I know Calgarians require very wealthy people from New York to come and tell us what we need to do in our community—because they understand vibrancy better than we do." His conclusion, though, was serious: "In other cities, these sorts of deals are presented to the public as a *fait accompli*, with a gift-wrapped ribbon on them. That is not how we have chosen to operate. That's not how council, in public, unanimously decided to move forward. The idea here is, we're going to let the public in."[24] His stand impressed many Calgarians. Even *The Hockey News* praised him: "for the leader of a major North American metropolis to tell any professional sports league to shut its pie hole takes an enormous amount of guts."[25]

Chris Selley, in a *National Post* column called "When Bettman Comes to Town," wrote that the NHL commissioner suggested that the "long-term stability" of the Flames was under siege, raising the prospect that Calgary would not get the draft or an all-star game, all the while reassuring his audience that he was not threatening the city. When asked if the franchise was profitable, Bettman demurred: "I don't comment on clubs' economics. And frankly the question is irrelevant to the discussion we are having." The proposal was, apparently, "about quality of life."[26]

The debate on the plan was deferred until April, when city administration reported to council that CalgaryNEXT was now estimated to cost $1.8 billion, more than double the CSEC's original estimate. Ken King challenged the figure much later, asserting that the bill "would be $1.3 billion before financing, if land remediation is included."[27] The city's current economic state made such a project unfeasible, and so when council met in June, it voted to table the proposal and have administration report back with a Plan B. Brian Burke, who had initiated the conversation in June 2014, said later, "Frankly, when we put out CalgaryNext, I was personally amazed the city didn't say, 'Thank you, let's do it.'"[28]

In December 2016, the CSEC admitted that it was still meeting with the city to discuss Plan B, which would see an arena and events centre built in Victoria Park on the grounds of the Calgary Stampede and north of the Saddledome; a field house built near the University of Calgary; and renovations made to the McMahon Stadium football field.[29] Ken King had earlier revealed in a letter to Flames season-ticket holders: "While we question the logic of building separate structures and a temporary solution for McMahon, we are encouraged that the city is taking the need for new sports infrastructure seriously. We enter this process with an open mind but also a strong belief that CalgaryNEXT is the most logical solution that will benefit all Calgarians."[30] But Mayor Nenshi announced on March 27, 2017 that the proposal was "dead,"[31] and in April, council voted to support Plan B.[32]

Brian Burke responded in June with an announcement that the Flames might leave Calgary if the team didn't get a new, publicly-funded arena. CBC Calgary wrote, "He said the reluctance of Canadian cities to spend on professional sports puts them at a significant disadvantage: 'In the U.S., it has long been acceptable to use public money to construct arenas and stadiums. It's long been acceptable to give a pro team a favourable lease based on the benefits pro teams bring to the marketplace.'" Unlike Mayor Mandel, Nenshi was not fooled by Burke's tactics: "This is page 26 of the script. It's always page 26 of the script in every city, and...I'm supposed to go to page 27 and 28 in the script when I point out that Rogers has given billions of dollars [for the broadcasting contract] and they're not going to let them remove a team from a western Canadian market; that in order for them to go to Quebec, they'll have to sell the team to Pierre Karl Peladeau, and he's not going to give them a deal the way they're going to get in Calgary; blah, blah, blah. I'm not interested in doing that."[33]

Funding the $500-million arena became the focus of the municipal election in October 2017, when negotiations between the city and the CSEC broke down and both sides went public with their positions. The CSEC walked away because, Ken King said, the talks were "spectacularly unproductive." King rejected the city's proposal that Calgary pay for a third of the total and be repaid; the Flames pay a third; and the remainder be generated through a ticket surcharge. Instead, he insisted that the ticket tax was part of team revenues, not a separate component; the Flames should not have to pay property taxes or rent; and the city should pay for policing at the facility and allow fans to ride public transit to games for free. Otherwise, he said, the CSEC would be paying "120 per cent" of the project. Not revealed at the time was the CSEC's simultaneous negotiation of a real estate deal to develop (and gentrify) the Victoria Park properties around a prospective arena with new housing, hotels, and restaurants. It also wanted some of the Stampede Casino's revenue, all parking revenue, and the city to pay for flood insurance. King insisted in his letter to the city that, "Our proposals...outline the minimum requirements for a robust competitive sports environment and the infrastructure needed to compete on the world stage from an entertainment perspective."[34]

Gary Bettman, after a meeting with the ownership group, directly injected himself into the mayoralty campaign to remind Calgary voters that there was a new arena in Quebec City, so, "You need to make your voice heard if you think the city is moving in the wrong direction." Nenshi responded: "The city has negotiated in good faith and we remain at the table...Council understands the importance of the Flames to the city. Council understands the importance of having the Flames downtown. We have worked very hard to come up with a deal that makes sense in this economy without impacting people's taxes."[35]

As expected, many members of the Calgary sports media came down on the side of the Flames. The most vocal booster was Eric Francis, writing in the *Calgary Sun*, who insisted that if the Flames didn't get the deal they wanted, the owners would sell and the team would relocate: "The question is whether city hall will ask taxpayers to pay for a reasonable part of it now or pay much more for it once the Calgary Flames leave." He accepted uncritically the CSEC's argument that revenues from the ticket surcharge belonged to the team and should not be included in the ask. He also believed that the project qualified for a CRL: "The ownership wanted a [CRL], like Edmonton's, which would generate $225 million as a result of developments generated by the new facility. Should the mayor's vision for an entertainment district around a new arena come to fruition, the transformation of empty Stampede-area parking lots into businesses and developments of all kinds would help pay for the driving force of it all—the rink."[36] And, of course, the issue was not just about dollars and cents; although the Flames generated "gobs of money for the local economy and charities," its relocation would also damage Calgary's "psyche." The city "would lose one of the main drivers in putting Calgary on the map." Nenshi had "lost sight of the fact this deal shouldn't be all about dollars."[37]

King, while insisting that he was not trying to influence the election, told a press conference (with Gary Bettman back in town and in the audience) that the Flames were no longer interested in a new arena. The Flames, he said, were now beneficiaries of the NHL's revenue-sharing system, as they were no longer a top-10, revenue-generating franchise.[38] Later, Bettman said, in an exclusive interview with the sympathetic Eric Francis, that he didn't want to "weigh into politics...[but there was] no prospect of [the Flames] getting a new building" in Calgary with Naheed Nenshi leading the city. He again raised the threat of relocation: "They're not moving this season, but I don't know how long they can hang on."[39]

According to Bettman, Calgary's mayor had told him that he didn't believe sports franchises and arenas were central to a city's economic well-being and outlined "the terms of a deal that I knew were just not from the real world."[40] Nenshi struck back, saying that Bettman had misrepresented him. He outlined what he considered to be the real intentions of the Flames' owners: "The goal of building a new arena is not to win a Stanley Cup. The goal of building a new arena is to make more money."[41] New arenas are built to attract a wide variety of events, not just hockey, and "simply watching" an event "is no longer sufficient to attract adequate numbers of spectators." The facility must be "a pleasure palace"[42] and part of a larger real estate development. Nenshi didn't believe that it would be the main engine for economic growth and the revitalization of Calgary's depressed downtown core. Numerous studies show that he's right.

Bettman's intervention may have backfired. On a political panel held before the election, Jen Gerson, a columnist for the *National Post*, said:

> One of the reasons Calgary is in this situation right now is because so many other cities have so weakly capitulated when Bettman and their [sic] billionaire buddies have made the exact same threats. Edmonton is the clear example of this. I mean...so much of Edmonton's flagging, sad, little ego is tied up in their hockey success that they needed to sign a scam of a deal to give a sweetheart arena over to Daryl Katz. And now all of a sudden, the expectation is that Calgary is going to fall in line? We're just not that pathetic as a city.[43]

The Globe and Mail also weighed in with an editorial accusing Bettman of "inexcusably insinuat[ing] himself into the campaign. Doing so represents an appalling lack of judgment from someone who absolutely knows better."[44]

In the end, the scare tactics didn't work. On October 16, 2017, Naheed Nenshi secured a third term as mayor of Calgary with 51.4 percent of the vote.[45] After the election, *The Globe and Mail* editorialized,

The result stands as a rebuke to Mr. Bettman and his disgraceful attempts at meddling in the election campaign, which he did by essentially calling on voters to boot out the incumbent for being insufficiently generous in offering taxpayer funds to the Flames' proposed new arena. Sadly, the defeat of the plutocrats is not how these games usually end. Bully tactics and relocation threats have been a boon to sports leagues for decades. And this game isn't over yet; it's safe to assume the Flames, who are owned by some of Canada's richest people and who are angling for a new $500-million barn, will not go meekly into the night...We encourage him [the mayor] to stand firm. Calgary faces deep financial challenges due to stagnant revenues and flagging downtown commercial occupancy rates. It should focus its energy, and its taxpayers' money, on projects benefiting all citizens, such as a long-planned public-transit expansion.[46]

Mayor Nenshi did say right after the election that "the city remains at the table...and we will stay at the table, and whenever Calgary Sports and Entertainment Corporation [CSEC] is ready to come back to the table we will be there."[47]

Gary Bettman continued to pressure Calgary to build a new arena, though without mentioning the city directly. In an interview in November 2017, he said: "We're not looking to threaten markets, but there is a certain inevitability if a club needs a new arena to stay competitive, to stay viable and have stability, that if it can't for whatever reason get a new facility then at some point ownership has to look at what options it may have."[48] Nenshi's victory also did little to silence his most vocal critics. Eric Francis continued to insist that if they didn't get what they wanted, the Flames would be sold and would leave the city for the greener pastures of Houston. The problem was Mayor Nenshi, Francis said:

the political and business climate is such that the reality may just be that the Calgary Flames have outgrown this town. While profitable, the Flames lose ground on all 30 NHL rivals every day they stay in the 34-year-old Saddledome where the team has maxed out the revenue it

can generate. The team can't possibly continue to play there long-term.
Mayor Naheed Nenshi, whose attitude has proven to be the biggest
impediment to having meaningful negotiations on the possibility of
a much-needed new venue, is here for at least another four years...
In sport, winners and losers are essentially decided by who wants it
more. At this point it's clear Calgary doesn't.

The people of Calgary and their mayor would only be short-term winners if the arena discussion was dropped.[49]

The arena plan refused to die, though; it became intertwined with Calgary's bid for the 2026 Winter Olympics. Olympic boosters, who in this instance included Mayor Nenshi, only promoted the benefits to the city. Emma May, a volunteer who supported the Games bid, advanced the same old arguments: "I was here in the depression of the 80s. People were losing their homes and businesses were going bankrupt. But in 1988, the town gathered around and lit itself on fire and we had the 1988 Olympics. We underestimate what that did to the city's consciousness. It shifted us onto a new path and gave us a global outlook that has helped us thrive."[50] Opponents focused on how much the Games would cost; the total was pegged at $5.2 billion and was dependent on $3 billion in funding from external sources. The Alberta government would only provide $700 million, and the federal government only promised funding up to $1.4 billion.[51] Moreover, the supposed benefits were downplayed. Councillor Druh Farrell cautioned: "We have a tendency to pursue the unicorn, the one big thing that is going to solve our problems. We know that with this particular recession it's very different, very complicated and we're not just going to rebound because of hosting an event eight years into the future."[52]

And then, just months after the municipal election and during the debate about the Olympic bid, in April 2018, developers presented another plan for the land east of Victoria Park (which is north of Stampede Park and the BMO Centre). It promised "a vibrant, high-density, mixed-use community that draws on the spirit of entertainment that resides in its DNA, as well as its natural surroundings." It also included a new arena.[53] This prompted Calgary's city council, which had a number of new faces, to establish a committee to "move forward" on the arena issue and offer a "fresh perspective."[54] Mayor Nenshi would not be part of the committee because, according to one councillor, "A deal won't get done if the mayor is involved."[55] The committee met on June 19th and contacted the CSEC. The reply from Ken King revealed how any new negotiations with the city would go: "While we would never decline your formal request for a meeting, we do have some concerns based on past practice...If we are to proceed, a simple and preemptive imperative is media silence. Public and/or media involvement must only be rendered in the event of an agreement."[56] The Flames clearly saw themselves back in the saddle once again.

In October 2018, during the lead-up to a municipal plebiscite on the Olympic bid, the city council invited the CSEC to discuss the larger property development project. Council commissioned an impact study and one councillor said: "We're actually talking about how do we actually build this into a district that adds value for every single Calgarians [sic]. This isn't just a hockey deal. This is a land deal." Mayor Nenshi was more circumspect: "I'm happy we're doing an economic study, but I think it has to go further than that because we know many, many academics and economists in the world have studied this and they've all come to the same conclusion: there's no direct economic benefit from this. That said, we have to see if in fact we're the exception to the rule or in fact there's other social or public benefit that outweighs the lack of economic benefit."[57]

Economics, once again, came to the fore during the plebiscite on Calgary's Olympic bid. The uncertainty surrounding the support from these other levels of government, and the unwillingness of the city to be on the hook for more than the provincial contribution, hung over the plebiscite, and, the larger property deal, including a new arena, remained in the background. In the end, Calgarians rejected the Olympic bid by a decisive margin of 56 to 44 percent.[58]

The boosters, of course, were disheartened and predicted Calgary's doom. Sports writer Eric Francis clutched his pearls and banged the same old drum, writing that he had fallen "in love with this town...because of its youthful energy, entrepreneurial spirit, sense of community and can-do attitude. Those days are gone." Hosting the 1988 Olympics, he said, had "put us on the map. Made us world class." Another Olympic event "could have been a catalyst for change," but the no vote "killed the best chance Calgary had at turning its economic fortunes around...This city's outlook could have changed, things could have been better...[T]his bid needed to be taken out of the hands of the government and fostered by smart, progressive business-leaders—the real people who shape and spearhead our community."[59] Nothing from Francis, though, on whether these "real people" should use their own money rather than public funds to support the Olympics and build new facilities, including an arena.

The property development project for the Rivers District east of downtown Calgary, though, remained on the table. In January 2019, the city council once again raised the possibility of building a new arena, now re-branded as an "event centre" because it would host more than just Flames' games; the price—between $550 and $600 million.[60] At a council meeting on March 4th, council approved $1.5 billion in capital projects which included the new event centre. Mayor Nenshi stated that, "It does not leave the city overextended" because Calgary has a "rainy-day fund" and will seek grants from other levels of government, including a CRL.[61]

Finally, after months of closed-door negotiations, it was announced on July 22, 2019 that the city of Calgary and the Flames had reached an agreement on a proposed arena deal, the cost of which was estimated at $550 million. The city's tab would be 50 percent of construction costs. As expected, Mayor Nenshi argued that there were public benefits: "This is a good deal for Calgary... [It] makes sense on its own merits."[62] Just like with the Edmonton agreement, the city of Calgary would own the new 19,000-seat facility; the CSEC would keep all the operating revenues, and would cover the operating, maintenance, and repair costs over the 35-year life of the deal.[63] The city also agreed to pay $12.4 million toward the demolition of the Scotiabank Saddledome, in addition to covering the $3 million in transaction costs.

Boosters argued that the project would generate an estimated $400.3 million over the course of the deal for the city from property taxes and facility fees (a ticket surcharge retained by the city), as well as a portion of the facility's naming rights for ten years, all while ensuring that property taxes would not be raised to pay for the building. Support would also be provided to local community sports groups, although a broader, legally-binding, community benefits agreement was not included. Moreover, according to Michael Brown of the Calgary Municipal Land Corporation, the project would be built on time and on budget. Ken King, of course, assured Flames fans that with this deal in place, the team would remain in Calgary thanks to a location agreement.[64]

While Mayor Nenshi argued that the process was very transparent, negotiations were entirely private. And as far as public consultation went, Calgarians were told by pro-arena Councillor Jeff Davison on the day that the proposed deal was announced that citizens had one week to contact their representatives with their feedback: "people have access to councillors' emails and phone and social media channels...So there's many, many ways that the public can let us know how they feel about this."[65] There was, of course, no plebiscite, especially after Calgary's failed bid for the 2026 Winter Olympic Games; boosters were anxious to prevent sustained opposition from coalescing as had happened earlier with the proposed Olympic bid.

Despite being supportive of the deal, Mayor Nenshi conceded that, "The optics of this stink," in part because the city was simultaneously preparing to pare some $60 million from its operating budget and the cuts would affect the fire department, policing, public transit, and other social services.[66] For Davison, a staunch proponent of the arena deal, though, the cuts amounted to just a small amount of the total budget: "The sky is not going to fall for two to three percent."[67] Notably, earlier on the same day that the arena deal and its public consultation process were announced, Davison, along with other councillors, had voted to disallow a coalition of citizens from speaking to council to voice their concerns about the proposed cuts.

Just eight days later, Calgary City Council voted 11–4 to approve the deal, with Mayor Nenshi among the majority. The now boosterish mayor proclaimed: "I'd rather live here than anywhere else in the world precisely because we dream big and we get things done."[68] Ken King, whose Flames got what they wanted, said: "I've been asked if I'm happy. Of course, we're happy—for Calgary. But I think the most fun will be proving to the city of Calgary that we can exceed their expectations...and we'll over-achieve."[69] For Davison, the most vocal proponent of the deal who also chaired the negotiations committee, "This signifies that this council has a vision. We've got a plan to move this city forward."[70] In an op-ed written the day before, he had trotted out now-familiar arguments about a new arena, now termed an event centre, and how it would transform Calgary: "It will create a facility for significant community events, allow us to attract major performing artists, enhance the Stampede experience, and be the new home for our great sports teams...It will spur the development of the culture and entertainment district, help attract and retain young talent in our re-energized city, and solidify Calgary's place as a vibrant destination for visitors from around the world."[71] All boosters, it appears, make use of the same rhetoric.

The economic costs of the deal were, of course, downplayed in light of the cuts to social services noted above. And, while the city projected revenues of over $400 million over the life of the deal, University of Calgary economist Trevor Tombe questioned these projections, which he argued were flawed and misleading; he also calculated that the project might actually have a net cost of $47 million for the city in the end.[72] Councillor Jeromy Farkus lamented: "I love the Flames, but not this deal...The timing is not right, especially considering the economics of our city. I cannot support a new arena deal at the same time as council cuts essential services, inflicts crushing taxes on small business and continues to nickel and dime residential homeowners....We [have] a fiduciary duty to Calgarians."[73] For Nenshi, though, civic benefits outweighed this concern: "the city invests in things all the time for social return... We spend money on swimming pools and hockey rinks and libraries that have no direct economic impact—they have social return." He continued: "These things actually do have a value. It's just not a value you can quantify. Economists agree that is a value that means something to the city."[74] Councillor Davison, too, emphasized the "intangibles" as Nenshi put it: "public money is being used for public good...[W]hat this all comes down to is, are we willing to build community?"[75] Boosters in the media were ecstatic. Don Braid, a columnist in the *Calgary Herald*, wrote: "There's the sense that Calgary is rolling again...By a whopping majority, councillors sent a clear message that Calgary is still a big-league city, both in hockey and urban development."[76]

Lost in all the hoopla about the arena deal has been the fact that central to this agreement is a private real estate development for a sports and entertainment district. CSEC has also been granted options to acquire two city-owned properties valued at $100 million in the Victoria Park area.[77] Once the arena is built, land prices will likely rise significantly. Just like Edmonton, then, Calgary is buttressing a profitable NHL franchise owned by an extraordinarily wealthy group of individuals who could have financed the development themselves, and who stand to benefit in significant ways, including from the inevitable increase in the valuation of the Flames franchise.[78] In the end, though, it will be worth it for boosters, even in the face of significant lost opportunity costs and cuts to important social services. Like the Saddledome, which in 1983 boosted "morale in the city as it was experiencing a significant economic downturn," the new arena will "likewise raise spirits in Calgary, which is in the midst of another oil-related downturn."[79] At the very least, Calgary, unlike Edmonton, is only planning to pay half of the upfront construction costs of the arena. But, yet another costly precedent has been set for other cities in North America that aspire to retain NHL teams.

Post Script: *The Song Remains the Same*

On November 10, 2017, a story appeared in the *Ottawa Sun* entitled, "NHL Commissioner Gary Bettman Says Ottawa Senators Need a New Home." In words familiar to hockey fans in Edmonton and Calgary, Bettman asserted: "A new downtown arena is vitally important to the long-term future, stability and competitiveness of the Senators."[80] There had been meetings that summer between the federal government's National Capital Commission (NCC; which controlled the land in LeBreton Flats, just west of Ottawa's downtown core on the Ottawa River), the owner of the Ottawa franchise, Eugene Melnyk, and the NHL brass, Bettman and his deputy, Bill Daly, about a new facility to replace the Canadian Tire Centre that had been built in the suburb of Kanata and had opened its doors in 1996. Attendance at games had been declining, and the answer, it appeared, was a new downtown arena, rather than improving the team. To emphasize his point, Melnyk made the now-familiar threat to relocate the franchise.[81]

In January 2018, an agreement in principle was announced between the NCC and the development group RendezVous LeBreton (in which Melnyk is a partner) to redevelop the LeBreton Flats. The $4-billion project would be a dense, mixed-use community with an 18,000-seat arena, community rink, and athletic facility, plus hotels, shops, restaurants, condominiums, and affordable housing, all serviced by Ottawa's new LRT, scheduled to open in 2018. Melnyk enthused: "I am thrilled to be moving a step closer to bringing the fans a more enjoyable experience."[82] John Ruddy of the Trinity Development Group, the other major player in RendezVous LeBreton, called it "a transformative project for the city." The NCC boasted: "A community is reborn and it shines like never before." The mayor of Ottawa, Jim Watson, declared: "It's a great day for the city...[After] 50 or 60 years of seeing that land sit vacant, I'm very optimistic in the next couple of years we'll see shovels in the ground and eventually [be] cheering on the Senators downtown."[83] The mayor provided no details on what this "franchise-saving" real estate deal was going to cost the citizens of Ottawa, but he assured taxpayers that the Senators "wanted the city to build the arena, and I said that we're not in the business of building arenas. We're not going to use tax dollars to pay for it."[84]

Just a year later, though, the project fell apart, as partners Melnyk and Ruddy could not come to an agreement and each served a lawsuit on the other. Melnyk stated that his organization "didn't have the confidence and the comfort that we would actually be building a viable project for the city at LeBreton." Ruddy, meanwhile, presented himself as a booster: "I will always find ways to build Ottawa up and continue to make a contribution to our great City."[85]

Although mediation had been offered before a late January 2019 deadline for the partnership to be confirmed, the situation remains unclear. Melnyk has since said that the Senators are prepared to just be tenants in the arena (although the team would pay no rent for 30 years and collect the revenues from the facility and its naming rights), while giving up their share of the profits in the property development, in exchange for Trinity guaranteeing $500 million in financing for the facility, with the city of Ottawa paying half the costs of construction.[86] Another group has stepped up to take over the project, and the NHL commissioner, while "disappointed" with the situation, has offered to get involved in the process: "There are some places where we have been involved in [sic] and I think been very constructive. Edmonton, Pittsburgh, among others come to mind."[87] A member of the NCC board, though, was not optimistic, and said the negotiations were "long on process...and...kind of short on reality."[88] In late December 2018, the organization moved to terminate its agreement with Melnyk's RendezVous LeBreton group, and by March 2019, the deal was dead.[89]

Yet, one reality remains. The owner of the Ottawa Senators, with a case of "Edmonton envy," still wants a new arena built with other people's money.[90]

NOTES

FOREWORD

1. Northrop Frye, "The Cultural Development of Canada," *Australian-Canadian Studies* 10, no. 1 (1992): 16.

PREFACE

1. This argument is taken up more fully in Kevin Taft's *Democracy Derailed: A Breakdown of Government Accountability in Alberta and How to Get It Back on Track* (Red Deer: Red Deer Press, 2007).

IMPORTANT TERMS

1. Details of the financing agreement can be found on the City of Edmonton website, at https://www.edmonton.ca/attractions_events/rogers_place/the-agreement.aspx.

1 INTRODUCTION

1. Unless otherwise noted, all figures are in Canadian dollars.

2. The downtown has been undergoing constant development over the past two decades, thanks to enormous public and private investments, including, most recently, the new provincially-funded Royal Alberta Museum, a new city-funded art gallery (Art Gallery of Alberta), a new office building (Edmonton Tower) for city staff, the expansion of the downtown MacEwan University campus, and an expanded public transit system, plus a host of condominium developments announced before the arena agreement.

3. Elise Stolte, "Residents say Rogers Place Falls Short on Community Benefits," *Edmonton Journal*, August 23, 2016, http://edmontonjournal.com/business/local-business/residents-say-rogers-place-falls-short-on-community-benefits.

4. Bill Mah, "Rogers Place Divides Opinions Even on Opening Day," *Edmonton Journal*, September 9, 2016, http://edmontonjournal.com/business/commercial-real-estate/rogers-place-divides-opinions-even-on-opening-day.

5.   In Winnipeg, for example, taxpayers contributed just $40.5 million toward the construction of the $133.5-million MTS Centre, which opened in 2004. The Jets' ownership group, True North Sports and Entertainment, contributed $93 million and owns the arena, now named the Bell MTS Centre. The facility underwent significant renovations totalling $14 million between 2014 and 2017, and these were paid by True North Sports and Entertainment, not the government of Manitoba or the city of Winnipeg. That said, True North Sports and Entertainment is also the recipient of a significant amount of annual operating subsidies and public funding: $14.1 million in 2018 alone, including $5.5 million from gaming revenues. Likewise, over $45 million in public funding has been provided for True North Square—a luxury condominium and apartment development in downtown Winnipeg—in the form of a Tax Increment Financing mechanism (or TIF) (similar to Edmonton's Capital City Downtown Community Revitalization Levy, or CRL), which rebates taxes for the residential buildings over a 20-year term and provides money for the surrounding infrastructure. So, whether it is Winnipeg or Edmonton, the business model of professional sport—and the story of arena funding—remains much the same. See Bartley Kives, "Winnipeg Pro Sports Clubs to Collect $16.3M in Public Assistance in 2018," *CBC News*, November 29, 2017, https://www.cbc.ca/news/canada/manitoba/budget-pro-sports-contributions-1.4423605; and Dan Lett, "Public Funding for True North Square Rises to $45 Million," *Winnipeg Free Press*, September 14, 2018, https://www.winnipegfreepress.com/local/public-funding-for-true-north-square-rises-to-45-million-493339051.html.

6.   Moving staff to the new building cost $16.4 million, though the Katz Group did pick up half of that bill.

7.   See Scott Johnston and Phil Heidenreich, "Edmonton Tower Sold to AIMCO, City to Receive $5M by Giving Up Right to Buy Building," *Global News*, July 5, 2018, https://globalnews.ca/news/4316121/edmonton-tower-aimco-katz-group-city-edmonton-ice-district/; and *Edmonton Commercial*, "Edmonton Office Tower Sells for $400 Million," July 20, 2018, https://www.edmontoncommercial.com/edmonton-office-tower-sells-for-400-million/.

8.   Howard Schubert, *Architecture on Ice: A History of the Hockey Arena* (Montreal: McGill-Queen's University Press, 2016), 236–42.

9.   Known as Tax Increment Financing (TIF) in the United States.

10. Judith Grant Long suggests that the value of foregone property tax exemptions is significant for municipalities. According to her calculations, where the total cost of a new sports facility is US$350 million, the annual property tax payments are estimated at $67 million over 30 years. See Judith Grant Long, *Public/Private Partnerships for Major League Sports Facilities* (New York: Routledge, 2013).

11. Gordon Kent, "City Looking at Ways to Reduce Edmonton's High Downtown Office Vacancy Rates," *Edmonton Journal*, July 3, 2017, https://edmontonjournal.com/business/commercial-real-estate/city-looking-at-ways-to-reduce-edmontons-high-downtown-office-vacancy-rates.

     Information about office vacancy rates in downtown Edmonton varies. For the first quarter of 2019, estimates range from 13 percent to 18.4 percent. See Elise Stolte, "Calgary's Tax Fiasco Underlines How Fragile Edmonton's Budget Is, Too," Edmonton Journal, June 12, 2019, https://edmontonjournal.com/opinion/columnists/elise-stolte-calgarys-tax-fiasco-underlines-how-fragile-edmontons-budget-is-too; and CBRE Research, *CBRE Edmonton Office MarketView, Q1 2019,* 1.

12.   Cec Purves, "Report on the Downtown Arena," January 31, 2012.

13.   Certainly, other men's sports like baseball and professional football have played important roles in boosting Edmonton. Of course, the most successful sports team in Edmonton's history—a team that was also used to promote the city—was the legendary women's basketball team, the Edmonton Grads. For a discussion of the history of baseball in Edmonton, see Brant E. Ducey, *The Rajah of Renfrew* (Edmonton: University of Alberta Press, 1998). For a history of the Edmonton Grads, see M. Ann Hall, *The Grads Are Playing Tonight!* (Edmonton: University of Alberta Press, 2011).

14.   Chris Heller, "The Impossible Fight against America's Stadiums: The Shady Money and Politics Behind the Country's Biggest, Most Expensive Sports Arenas," *Pacific Standard*, September 2, 2015, https://psmag.com/economics/ the-shady-money-behind-americas-sports-stadiums.

15.   Judith Grant Long, *Public/Private Partnerships*, 18. See also Judith Grant Long, "Full Count: The Real Cost of Public Funding for Major League Sports Facilities," *Journal of Sports Economics*, 6 (May 2005): 119–43; Brad Humphries and Li Zhou, "Sports Facilities, Agglomeration, and Public Subsidies," *Regional Science and Urban Economics*, 54 (2015): 60–73; Kaitlyn Harger, Brad R. Humphries, and Amanda Ross, "Do New Sports Facilities Attract New Businesses?" *Journal of Sports Economics*, 17 (2016): 483–500.

16.   Neil deMause and Joanna Cagan, *Field of Schemes: How the Great Stadium Swindle Turns Public Money into Private Profit,* revised and expanded (Lincoln: University of Nebraska Press, 2008), 62–82.

17.   Interview with Neil deMause, November 17, 2017.

18.   Interview with Brad Humphreys, October 12, 2017.

19.   Richard Gruneau and David Whitson, *Hockey Night in Canada: Sport, Identities and Cultural Politics* (Toronto: Garamond Press, 1993), 224.

20.   In 2017, the Commissioner of the NHL, Gary Bettman, argued that economists' scholarly work was simply wrong: "There are academicians who...disagree with this in theory, but I disagree with them. Having a professional sports team as your anchor tenant, if you do it the right way, can literally transform a city. Look at Chinatown in Washington, D.C., after the Verizon Center was built. Look at L.A. Live, built around Staples Center. Look at what's happened in Edmonton, where they're revitalized downtown. Look at what's going on in Detroit. All of these around new arenas, where an entire area of a city has been vitalized, or revitalized, created a new tax base, brought businesses, residences, people downtown to live" (see a partial transcript of Bettman's interview with *Yahoo Finance* on October 25, 2017, at http://www. fieldofschemes.com/2017/10/26/13076/bettman-says-feh-on-economists-cant-you-see-publicly-funded-arenas-are-the-bees-knees/). Correlation becomes causation.

2 BOOSTING EDMONTON

1.   See, for example, Ray Turchansky, *Edmonton Oilers Hockey Club: Celebrating 25 Years in the Heartland of Hockey* (Edmonton: Edmonton Journal Group, 2003).

2.   Shannon Proudfoot, "Long-Time Listener, First-Time Caller," in *Best Canadian Sports Writing*, eds. Stacey May Fowles and Pasha Malla (Toronto: ECW Press, 2017), 30.

3.   Alan F.J. Artibise, "Boosterism and the Development of Prairie Cities, 1871–1913," in *Town and City: Aspects of Western Canadian Urban Development*, ed. Alan F.J. Artibise (Regina: Canadian Plains Research Centre, 1981), 214–16. See also Paul Voisey, "Unsolved Mysteries of Edmonton's Growth," in *Edmonton: The Life of a City*, eds. Bob Hesketh and Frances Swyripa (Edmonton: NeWest Publishers, 1995), 320–24.

4.   *Edmonton Bulletin*, February 13, 1892.

5.   Artibise, "Boosterism," 214–16.

6.   Carl Betke, "Sports Promotion in the Western Canadian City: The Example of Early Edmonton," *Urban History Review* XII (1983): 47–56. See also James Lightbody, "Edmonton," in *City Politics in Canada*, eds. Warren Magnuson and Andrew Sancton (Toronto: University of Toronto Press, 1983), 255–90.

7.   Artibise, "Boosterism," 227. See also Voisey, "Unsolved Mysteries," 320–22.

8.   Artibise, "Boosterism," 211–14.

9.   Carl Betke, "The Original City of Edmonton: A Derivative Prairie Urban Community," in *Town and City*, ed. Artibise, 329–36.

10. David Whitson and Donald Macintosh, "Becoming a World-Class City: Hallmark Events and Sport Franchises in the Growth Strategies of Western Canadian Cities," *Sociology of Sport Journal* 10 (1993): 223. For excellent discussions of the connection between the commercialization of hockey and boosterism, see Richard Gruneau and David Whitson, *Hockey Night in Canada: Sport, Identities and Cultural Politics* (Toronto: Garamond Press, 1993), 199–221; and Bruce Kidd, *The Struggle for Canadian Sport* (Toronto: University of Toronto Press, 1996), 184–231.

11. Morris Mott, "The British Protestant Pioneers and the Establishment of Manly Sports in Manitoba, 1870–1886," *Journal of Sport History* 7 (1980): 25. Mott is both a historian and a former professional hockey player.

12. For an outline of Alberta's sporting history, see David Mills, "100 Years of Sports," in *Alberta: A State of Mind*, eds. Sydney Sharpe et al. (Toronto: Key Porter Books, 2005), 197–231.

13. See Betke, "Sports Promotion," 48.

14. There is a significant body of literature on the cultural value of hockey in Canada. In addition to Gruneau and Whitson's *Hockey Night in Canada*, see Bruce Kidd and John Macfarlane, *The Death of Hockey* (Toronto: New Press, 1972); Bruce Kidd, *The Struggle for Canadian Sport* (Toronto: University of Toronto Press, 1996); Colin Howell, *Blood, Sweat, and Cheers: Sport and the Making of Modern Canada* (Toronto: University of Toronto Press, 2001), esp. 128–46; and Don Morrow and Kevin B. Wamsley, *Sport in Canada: A History* (Don Mills: Oxford University Press, 2013), especially chapters 1–4, 10, and 11. See also Michael McKinley, *Hockey: A People's History* (Toronto: McClelland & Stewart, 2006); and Michael McKinley, *Putting a Roof on Winter: Hockey's Rise from Sport to Spectacle* (Vancouver: Greystone Books, 2000).

15. Gruneau and Whitson, *Hockey Night in Canada*, 67–71.

16. Men paid 25 cents and women 15 cents to see the game. For an excellent analysis of the influence of hockey on the two communities, see Terence O'Riordan, "The 'Puck-Eaters': Hockey as a Unifying Community Experience in Edmonton and Strathcona, 1894–1905," *Alberta History* 49, no. 2 (2001): 2–11. Karen L. Wall also talks about the

enthusiasm for the games and the need for crowd control in *Game Plan: A Social History of Sport in Alberta* (Edmonton: University of Alberta Press, 2012), 109.

17. Gruneau and Whitson, *Hockey Night in Canada*, 39.

18. Gruneau and Whitson, *Hockey Night in Canada*, 70–71; David Whitson, "Hockey and Canadian Popular Culture: The Making and Remaking of Identities," in *Method and Methodology in Sport and Cultural History*, ed. K.B. Wamsley (Dubuque: Brown & Benchmark Publishers, 1995), 191–92.

19. Karen Wall accepted local historian Tony Cashman's claim that the arena could seat 2,000 people, suggesting that the bigger the better; see Wall's *Game Plan*, 109.

20. *Edmonton Bulletin*, December 19, 1902. The *Edmonton Journal,* on November 1, 1913, called it "nothing more than a big barn" after it burned down. See also David Leonard, John E. McIsaac, and Sheilagh Jameson, *A Builder of the Northwest: The Life and Times of Richard Secord, 1860–1935* (Edmonton: Richard Y. Secord, 1981), 90–91. Secord was a big supporter of Edmonton sports. He helped organize a cricket team in 1884 and supported amateur baseball and curling. As a patron of the Thistle Club, he bought uniforms, hockey nets, and other equipment; he also donated the Secord Shield for the hockey champions of the region.

21. Stephen Hardy, "Two-Way Hockey: Selling Canada's Game in North America, 1875–1935," in *Playing for Change: The Continuing Struggle for Sport and Recreation*, ed. Russell Field (Toronto: University of Toronto Press, 2015), 203.

22. Bruce Kidd and John Macfarlane, *The Death of Hockey* (Toronto: New Press, 1972), 106.

23. *Edmonton Bulletin*, January 5, 1904, quoted in Leonard, McIsaac, and Jameson, *A Builder of the Northwest*, 92 and 120.

24. In this period, competition for the Stanley Cup came from challenges by one team to the team that currently held the trophy. Stanley Cup trustees decided which challenges would go forward. See John Wong, "From Rat Portage to Kenora: The Death of a (Big-Time) Hockey Dream," *Journal of Sport History* 33 (2006): 175–91.

25. *Edmonton Bulletin*, September 10, 1908, quoted in Wall, *Game Plan*, 295.

26. The *Edmonton Journal* was established in 1903 as a Conservative newspaper by local Tories, like Richard Secord, to balance Liberal Frank Oliver's *Edmonton Bulletin*.

27. Whitson and Macintosh, "Becoming a World-Class City," 224–25. See also Stacy Lorenz, "A Lively Interest on the Prairies: Western Canada, the Mass Media, and a 'World of Sport', 1870–1939," *Journal of Sport History* 27 (2000): 195–227, and Gruneau and Whitson, *Hockey Night in Canada*, 83.

28. *Edmonton Bulletin*, March 26, 1907, quoted in Wall, *Game Plan*, 295. See also Gruneau and Whitson, *Hockey Night in Canada*, 236.

29. Quoted in A.W. Cashman, *The Edmonton Story: The Life and Times of Edmonton, Alberta* (Edmonton: Institute of Applied Art, 1956), 180. It should be pointed out that Lester Patrick was paid $100 for expenses but mailed back a cheque for $38, which is how much money he had left when he returned to Nelson, BC.

30. Quoted in D'Arcy Jenish, *The Stanley Cup: A Hundred Years of Hockey at its Best* (Toronto: McClelland & Stewart, 1992), 75.

31. Cashman, *The Edmonton Story*, 180.

32. Cashman, *The Edmonton Story*, 180; Jenish, *The Stanley Cup*, 78.

33. Quoted in Wall, *Game Plan*, 119.

34. Charles L. Coleman, *The Trail of the Stanley Cup*, Vol. 1: 1826–1926 (Dubuque: National Hockey League, 1966), 401–39.

35. Quoted in Henry Roxborough, *The Stanley Cup Story* (Toronto: The Ryerson Press, 1964), 36. The National Hockey League was created in 1917, with teams in Toronto and Ottawa and two in Montreal, the Canadiens and the Wanderers; the Wanderers folded in 1918 and teams in Quebec and Hamilton were added by 1920. In 1924, the Montreal Maroons joined the NHL, as did the first team in the United States, the Boston Bruins. By 1926, there were five more US teams, in Pittsburgh, Chicago, and Detroit, and two in New York, the Americans and the Rangers.

36. Whitson and Macintosh, "Becoming a World-Class City," 224.

37. Kidd, *The Struggle for Canadian Sport*, 207.

38. Both quotations in James Andrew Ross, "Hockey Capital: Commerce, Culture, and the National Hockey League, 1917–1967" (PhD diss., University of Western Ontario, 2008), 133.

39. John Herd Thompson and Allen Seager, *Canada, 1922–1939: Decades of Discord* (Toronto: McClelland & Stewart, 1985), 188. See also Stephen Hardy's "Two-Way Hockey," where he argues that hockey in the United States had different and distinct hockey roots; it was not "stolen" from Canada.

40. Carl Betke, "Winter Sports in the Early Urban Environment of Prairie Canada," in *Winter Sports in the West*, eds, E. Corbet and A. Rasporich (Calgary: University of Calgary, 1990), 52–68; see also Whitson and Macintosh, "Becoming a World-Class City," 224.

41. Voisey, "Unsolved Mysteries," 325.

42. Tony Cashman, *The Best Edmonton Stories* (Edmonton: Hurtig Publishers, 1976), 17–18.

43. Cashman 1976, 17–18. The secretary-treasurer of the council refused to make the minutes public, with the support of his colleagues. Because secret meetings violated the city charter, "the council appealed to the [provincial] legislature and sought an amendment...making it legal to hold meetings in secret. This, of course, the government very wisely turned down." See J.G. MacGregor, *Edmonton: A History* (Edmonton: Hurtig Publishers, 1975), 156.

44. Quoted in Tony Cashman, *Edmonton Exhibition: The First Hundred Years* (Edmonton: Edmonton Exhibition Association, 1979), 68–69. See also the *Edmonton Bulletin*, February 11, 1913, and the *Edmonton Journal*, January 2, 1914.

45. *Edmonton Journal*, January 22, 1934.

46. Quoted in Wall, *Game Plan*, 119.

47. *Edmonton Journal*, April 15, 1966.

48. Lawrence Herzog, "The Edmonton Gardens," *Real Estate Weekly*, November 19, 2009.

49. Christopher Leo, "Global Change and Local Politics: Economic Decline and the Local Regime in Edmonton," *Journal of Urban Affairs* 17 (1995): 281.

50. Lightbody, "Edmonton," 262–67. See also James Lightbody, *City Politics, Canada* (Peterborough: Broadview Press, 2006), 211–12, 216–17.

51. City of Edmonton Planning Department, *General Plan for the City of Edmonton: Part I: The Problem* (Edmonton: City of Edmonton, 1963); quoted in Russell Cobb, "Retrofutures: Edmonton's Omniplex—Part 1," http://citymuseumedmonton.ca/2015/01/26/retrofuture-edmontons-omniplex-part-1/.

52. City of Edmonton Planning Department, *General Plan for the City of Edmonton: Part X: Downtown Edmonton* (Edmonton: City of Edmonton, 1963); quoted in Russell Cobb, "Retrofutures: Edmonton's Omniplex—Part 1," http://citymuseumedmonton.ca/2015/01/26/retrofuture-edmontons-omniplex-part-1/.

53. City of Edmonton, *General Plan for the City of Edmonton: Part X*, i.

54. *Edmonton Journal*, July 11, 2015. Similar claims would be made for Ice District when it opened almost 50 years later.

55. See Russell Cobb, "Retrofutures: Edmonton's Omniplex—Part 1," http://citymuseumedmonton.ca/2015/01/26/retrofuture-edmontons-omniplex-part-1/.

56. Voisey, "Unsolved Mysteries," 332. See also Gruneau and Whitson, *Hockey Night in Canada*, 199–246.

57. Whitson and Macintosh, "Becoming a World-Class City," 226–27.

58. Whitson and Macintosh, "Becoming a World-Class City," 226–27.

59. Voisey, "Unsolved Mysteries," 334; Whitson and Macintosh, "Becoming a World-Class City," 235. Whitson and Macintosh briefly discuss Edmonton's quest for "world-class" status because of "the benefits—both real and imaginary—that...major league sports franchises are presumed to bring to cities." Franchise owners can "extract major subsidies and financial concessions from civic governments that are anxious both for the immediate business and for the longer term benefits. They are supported not just by the sports fans but also by businessmen seeking to promote the economic benefits from which they will profit and by the local media which often emphasizes the issue of civic pride" (222). In short, the process is shaped by neo-boosterism.

60. Gruneau and Whitson, *Hockey Night in Canada*, 235.

61. Interview with Cecil Purves, April 5, 2016.

62. City of Edmonton, *Alternative Locations of Proposed Sports Arena to Replace the Edmonton Gardens: A Report Prepared for the Special Projects Committee of City Council and the Board of Directors, Edmonton Exhibition Association* (Edmonton: Urban Renewal Section, City Planning Department, 1964), 17.

63. City of Edmonton, *Alternative Locations of Proposed Sports Arena*, 4.

64. City of Edmonton, *A Coliseum, Trade Centre or Domed Stadium for Edmonton* (Edmonton: Planning Department, 1968), 3.

65. Tony Cashman, *Edmonton Exhibition*, 149.

66. See Russell Cobb, *Recap: Retrofutures—Edmonton's Omniplex Debate*, December 17, 2014, at http://thewandereronline.com/omniplex-to-the-rescue-by-russell-cobb-and-katherine-krohn/. See also *Edmonton Journal*, October 17, 2010; a column by David Staples on plebiscites in Edmonton asserted that Edmontonians had supported arena projects in the past, notably in 1968. Similar proposals in 1947 and 1963 were rejected, however.

67. Russell Cobb, "Retrofutures: Edmonton's Omniplex; Part 1," at http://citymuseumedmonton.ca/2015/01/26/retrofuture-edmontons-omniplex-part-1/.

68. *Information Concerning a Proposal for Edmonton's Omniplex: A Trade, Convention, and Sports Complex* (City of Edmonton, 1968), quoted in Russell Cobb, "Retrofutures: Edmonton's Omniplex; Part 2," at http://citymuseumedmonton.ca/2015/01/26/retrofuture-edmontons-omniplex-part-2/.

69. Interview with Cecil Purves, April 5, 2016.

70. Whitson and Macintosh, "Becoming a World-Class City," 228.

71. Allard had two careers; he was chief of surgery at the Edmonton General Hospital until 1973, and he was a successful businessman. For more on Allard's business dealings, see Hans J. Dys, *Gut Instinct: The Life and Times of Dr. Charles Allard* (Edmonton: Camary Holdings, 2010); Paul Grescoe and David Cruise, *The Money Rustlers: Millionaires of the New West* (Markham: Penguin Books Canada, 1985), 71–91; and Peter C. Newman, *The Acquisitors: The Canadian Establishment*, vol. 2 (Toronto: McClelland & Stewart, 1981), 287.

72. Bill Hunter (with Bob Weber), *Wild Bill: Bill Hunter's Legendary 65 Years in Canadian Sport* (Calgary: Johnson Gorman Publishers, 2000), 179–80.

73. Dys, *Gut Instinct*, 230. Allard, Dys argued, was "enticed by the potential advantages a professional hockey team could bring to the local economy, as well as the positive effects it might have on the psyche of a sports-hungry city." The third member of the ownership group was Zane Feldman, president of Crosstown Motor City and the long-time business partner of Dr. Allard. They owned restaurants, hotels, real estate, and radio and television stations. He was one of the owners of the Edmonton Oil Kings, and later, the WHA's Edmonton Oilers; Feldman was the team governor.

74. See Ed Willes, *The Rebel League: The Short and Unruly Life of the World Hockey Association* (Toronto: McClelland & Stewart, 2004).

75. Edmonton's mayor and council wanted to boost the city; the federal government supported cities seeking international spectacles; and the provincial government wanted to make Alberta "a national power centre, with its own head offices, banks, and nationally respected institutions." See Whitson and Macintosh, "Becoming a World-Class City," 228–29.

76. David Staples, "The Rise and Fall of the Edmonton Coliseum" in the *Edmonton Journal*, April 6, 2016, https://edmontonjournal.com/sports/hockey/nhl/cult-of-hockey/david-staples-the-rise-and-fall-of-the-edmonton-coliseum.

77. Whitson and Macintosh, "Becoming a World-Class City," 229; emphasis original.

78. *Edmonton Journal*, March 21, 1974.

79. Interview with Cecil Purves, April 5, 2016.

80. Tony Cashman, *Edmonton Exhibition*, 141.

81. David Staples, "The Rise and Fall of the Edmonton Coliseum" in the *Edmonton Journal*, April 6, 2016, https://edmontonjournal.com/sports/hockey/nhl/cult-of-hockey/david-staples-the-rise-and-fall-of-the-edmonton-coliseum.

82. See David Staples, "The Rise and Fall of the Edmonton Coliseum" in the *Edmonton Journal*, April 6, 2016, https://edmontonjournal.com/sports/hockey/nhl/cult-of-hockey/david-staples-the-rise-and-fall-of-the-edmonton-coliseum.

83. Brian Conacher, *As the Puck Turns: A Personal Journey through the World of Hockey* (Mississauga: John Wiley & Sons Canada, 2007), 161.

84. Tony Cashman, *Edmonton Exhibition*, 151. By 2005, the facility was being continually criticized for having too few luxury boxes, narrow concourses crammed with people, and long lines to the washrooms. It was "antiquated," according to the NHL. The last Oilers game in the arena was played on April 6, 2016; Peter Pocklington had earlier described it as "just an old barn. It was nice 35 years ago" (*The Globe and Mail*, March 26, 2016). And the area around the arena on 118 Avenue, far from being revitalized,

had experienced a steady economic decline since the 1970s. See Marty Klinkenberg, *The McDavid Effect: Connor McDavid and the New Hope for Hockey* (Toronto: Simon & Schuster, 2016), 30.

85. Brian Nelson, "Baseball," in *The Theater of Sport*, ed. Karl B. Raitz (Baltimore: Johns Hopkins University Press, 1995), 61, quoted in Howard Shubert, *Architecture on Ice: A History of the Hockey Arena* (Montreal: McGill-Queens University Press, 2016), 148.

86. Andrew Zimbalist, *The Bottom Line: Observations and Arguments in the Sports Business* (Philadelphia: Temple University Press, 2006). See also Gruneau and Whitson, *Hockey Night in Canada*, 211.

87. Schubert, *Architecture on Ice*, 148.

88. Voisey, "Unsolved Mysteries," 334.

89. Gruneau and Whitson, *Hockey Night in Canada*, 211. Interestingly, it is a player and not an arena that has been memorialized as "world class." The plaque on the statue of Wayne Gretzky, originally created for Northlands and now outside of Rogers Place, describes him as "A true champion and gentleman of dedication and character whose talents brought world recognition to the City of Edmonton."

3 THE BLUE LINE AND THE BOTTOM LINE

1. James Quirk and Rodney D. Fort, *Pay Dirt: The Business of Professional Team Sports* (Princeton: Princeton University Press, 1992), 19. See also Paul Staudohar, *The Sports Industry and Collective Bargaining* (Ithaca: Cornell University Press, 1986).

2. This interpretation of the general motivations of businessmen is outlined in Michael Bliss, *A Living Profit: Studies in the Social History of Canadian Business, 1883–1911* (Toronto: McClelland & Stewart, 1974).

3. It has been suggested that, by 1976, the club's financial losses approached $3 million, even though average attendance was 10,722, the highest in the WHA. See John Short, "The Edmonton Oilers: A History," in *Positive Power: The Story of the Edmonton Oilers*, ed. William F. Dowbiggin (Edmonton: Executive Sport Publications, 1982), 83. The whole question of team profitability is problematic, and readers should be warned that reports of profits and losses can be unreliable given the absence of hard data. The Oilers, for example, are privately owned and therefore do not have to release audited financial reports. We are often left with unsubstantiated claims, gossip, or lies. Owners generally control information about how much a franchise makes.

4. Hans J. Dys, *Gut Instinct: The Life and Times of Dr. Charles Allard* (Edmonton: Camary Holdings, 2010), 283–84. Bill Hunter (with Bob Weber), *Wild Bill: Bill Hunter's Legendary 65 Years in Canadian Sport* (Calgary: Johnson Gorman Publishers, 2000), 237–38. Hunter did not want to sell, but could not raise enough capital himself to buy the team. The other partner, Zane Feldman, said that they actually paid Skalbania $400,000 to keep the team in Edmonton.

5. The price was reported to be a 1928 Rolls Royce, two oil paintings, a diamond ring, and a mortgage note for $500,000 worth of real estate (*Edmonton Journal*, August 10, 1988).

6. For details on Pocklington's business career, see David Mills' articles, "The Blue Line and the Bottom Line: Entrepreneurs and the Business of Hockey, 1927–90," in *The Business of Professional Sports*, eds. Paul D. Staudohar and James A. Mangan (Urbana: University of Illinois Press, 1991), 175–202; "The Battle of Alberta: Entrepreneurs and

the Business of Hockey in Edmonton and Calgary," in *Alberta*, vol. 2 (1990), 1–25; "Peter Pocklington and the Business of Hockey," in *Edmonton: The Life of a City*, eds. Bob Hesketh and Frances Swyripa (Edmonton: NeWest Publishers, 1995), 306–15; and "The Visible Hand and the Management of Hockey," in *Method and Methodology in Sport and Cultural History*, ed. K.B. Wamsley (Dubuque: A Times Mirror Higher Education Group, 1995), 244–80. For Pocklington's own take on his business dealings, see Terry McConnell and J'Lyn Nye with Peter Pocklington, *I'd Trade Him Again: On Gretzky, Politics and the Pursuit of the Perfect Deal* (Bolton: Fenn Publishing, 2009).

7.   *Edmonton Sun*, September 10, 1978.

8.   Peter C. Newman, *The Acquisitors: The Canadian Establishment*, vol. 2 (Toronto: McClelland & Stewart, 1981), 293.

9.   *Edmonton Sun*, April 1, 1979.

10.   *Edmonton Sun*, April 4, 1979 and November 28, 1979. The television contract paid the team $2 million upfront and $75,000 annually for five years. The Oilers would have generated higher revenues but for a dispute between Pocklington and Northlands over the sale of concourse seats. The following year, an additional 1,500 seats were installed in the Coliseum. Expenses during the 1979/80 season were estimated as follows: salaries, $2.5 million; travel, $500,000; training, $100,000; supplies, $75,000; hospital and medical, $525,000; and rent, $920,000. Oilers' profits can be compared with losses of $2 million in Colorado, Washington, and Pittsburgh, and of $1 million in Chicago, St. Louis, Los Angeles, and Atlanta. Pocklington pointed to high operating costs, league dues, and winding up the WHA as the causes of his losses. His own company administered the team, and he paid himself first. The losses were really just on paper.

11.   *Edmonton Journal*, August 18, 1988.

12.   Christopher Leo, "Global Change and Local Politics: Economic Decline and the Local Regime in Edmonton," *Journal of Urban Affairs* 17 (1995): 287.

13.   Mordecai Richler, "King of the New Canada," *New York Times Magazine*, September 29, 1985, https://www.nytimes.com/1985/09/29/magazine/king-of-the-new-canada.html.

14.   Decore and Hurtig were quoted in a story in the *Edmonton Journal* on December 22, 2015.

15.   Leo, "Global Change and Local Politics," 289–90. See also James Lightbody, *City Politics, Canada* (Peterborough: Broadview Press, 2006), 214.

16.   Leo, "Global Change and Local Politics," 290.

17.   Leo, "Global Change and Local Politics," 282.

18.   Leo, "Global Change and Local Politics," 288–89.

19.   See Leo, "Global Change and Local Politics," 284.

20.   Brian Conacher, *As the Puck Turns: A Personal Journey through the World of Hockey* (Mississauga: John Wiley & Sons Canada, 2007), 161–64.

21.   Conacher, *As the Puck Turns*, 158.

22.   *Edmonton Sun*, July 28 and 31, 1983.

23.   *Edmonton Journal*, December 7, 1988. He also dumped failing companies before they collapsed, and left the taxpayers holding the bag, and he was a union buster who wanted to crush his striking workers at Gainers in 1986. All this in addition to trading "The Great One" in 1988.

24. Ticket prices were once again among the highest in the NHL; they ranged from $15 to $23 (*Edmonton Sun*, June 6, 1984). Player costs had increased significantly since the Oilers joined the league. In 1979, the average salary was $101,00; by 1983, it was $125,000. (Staudohar, *The Sports Industry and Collective Bargaining*, 123)

25. Conacher, *As the Puck Turns*, 164–65.

26. *Edmonton Sun*, October 8, 1987. Sports economist Paul Staudohar wrote that in 1984/85, "about a third of the teams in the NHL were profitable, a third were breaking even, and a third losing money." See Stauolohaur, *The Sports Industry and Collective Bargaining*, 120.

27. The figures are from unaudited pro forma financial statements presented to the NHL Board of Governors, on March 11, 1987. These were sent to one of the authors anonymously. Although the source of the material may be questioned, the accuracy of these figures was not challenged by either Mr. Pocklington in an interview in 1988 or by officials with the Calgary Flames at the time. See Mills, "The Blue Line and the Bottom Line," 175–202.

28. Tony Cashman, *Edmonton Exhibition: The First Hundred Years* (Edmonton: Edmonton Exhibition Association, 1979), 153.

29. John F. Gilpin, *Edmonton: Gateway to the North: An Illustrated History* (Edmonton: Windsor Publications, 1984), 267–68.

30. *Edmonton Journal*, May 20, 1984.

31. *Edmonton Sun*, May 20, 1984.

32. *Edmonton Journal*, October 31, 2003.

33. Ticket prices for the 1988/89 season were the eighth highest in the NHL (*The Hockey News*, October 28, 1988). His business empire, though, was in trouble and his handling of striking workers at the Gainers plant in 1986 brought bad publicity. The Alberta government finally pressured Pocklington to settle after six months with the promise of a $55,000,000 interest-free loan through ATB, although Gainers was put up as collateral and could be seized if the company defaulted. One of his friends said, "Sometimes Peter is his own worst enemy. He wants to grab every nickel." See Douglas Hunter, *The Glory Barons: The Saga of the Edmonton Oilers* (Toronto: Viking, 1999), 196–216.

34. Peter Pocklington interview, October 11, 1988. Gretzky was 27 in 1988. Players are generally at their peak at this age, although Gretzky had been playing at the highest level for a decade. He had scored 215 points in the 1985/86 season, and followed it up with totals of 183 and 149 points in the 1986/87 and 1987/88 seasons, respectively. He would go on to score 168 points for the Kings in the 1988/89 season.

35. Hard feelings toward the owner took a long time to dissipate. But 30 years after the trade, Pocklington was given a standing ovation when Rogers Place opened in 2016.

36. *Edmonton Sun*, February 28, 1989.

37. *The Globe and Mail*, March 3, 1989.

38. According to the *Edmonton Journal*, July 17, 1989, he donated $12,200 in 1988.

39. *Edmonton Sun*, October 5, 1989; *The Globe and Mail*, October 7, 1989.

40. *Edmonton Journal*, June 9, 1990.

41. *Financial World*, July 9, 1991. It has been argued that ticket prices are set to maximize revenues, and that demand for those tickets depends on the team's success and the popularity of individual players, plus the state of the local economy and the strength

of the city's sports culture. See Andrew Zimbalist, *The Bottom Line: Observations and Arguments in the Sports Business* (Philadelphia: Temple University Press, 2006), 34.

42. *Edmonton Journal*, April 6, 2016.

43. David Staples, "The Rise and Fall of the Edmonton Coliseum," *Edmonton Journal*, April 6, 2016, https://edmontonjournal.com/sports/hockey/nhl/cult-of-hockey/david-staples-the-rise-and-fall-of-the-edmonton-coliseum. The failure of the Coliseum to transform the neighbourhoods around the Northlands property continued to cause discontent. In 1990, the city drafted another redevelopment plan for the Northlands area, but didn't act on it. See *Northlands Area Redevelopment Plan (1990)* (Edmonton: City of Edmonton Planning & Development, 2003).

44. *Financial World Magazine*, May 10, 1994.

45. Expansion fees were US$50 million per team, to be divided among the other owners. Pocklington wanted more expansion and pressed for higher fees.

46. Without a salary cap, the average NHL player salary of US$560,000 in the 1993/94 season would jump to US$630,000 just two years later.

47. McConnell and Nye, *I'd Trade Him Again*, 231–32. Pocklington's figures cannot be confirmed.

48. *The Globe and Mail*, July 1, 1995.

49. Interview on CFRN-TV on March 21, 1995; see also, *Edmonton Journal*, March 22, 1995.

50. *Edmonton Sun*, April 21, 1995. The Oilers would change their uniforms for the 1996/97 season in order to exploit the lucrative merchandising market as the culture of hockey in Edmonton continued to change: the familiar blue and orange were replaced by copper and blue.

51. Staples, "Rise and Fall of the Edmonton Coliseum." See also *Edmonton Journal*, April 6, 2016. Dana Warg was, at the time, CEO of the Target Center in Minneapolis and Vice President of Ogden Entertainment; Pocklington tried to hire him to run the Coliseum, so he was hardly an unbiased analyst. See *Sports Illustrated*, December 20, 1993.

52. Interview, February 20, 2018.

53. Hole was quoted in the *Edmonton Journal*, April 6, 2016; see also Staples, "Rise and Fall of the Edmonton Coliseum."

54. Westbury was quoted in the *Edmonton Journal*, March 21, 2010; see also Staples, "Rise and Fall of the Edmonton Coliseum."

55. *Financial World Magazine*, May 10, 1994. The franchise was still worth considerably more than the approximately $6.5 million that Pocklington had paid for it in 1977.

56. *Edmonton Journal*, April 6, 2016; see also Staples, "Rise and Fall of the Edmonton Coliseum."

57. McConnell and Nye, *I'd Trade Him Again*, 234–35.

58. *Edmonton Journal*, April 6, 2016; Westbury was also quoted in Staples, "Rise and Fall of the Edmonton Coliseum."

59. Interview, February 20, 2018.

60. *Edmonton Journal*, April 28, 1993.

61. Interview, February 20, 2018.

62. McConnell and Nye, *I'd Trade Him Again*, 233–34. The EDE leased the facility from Northlands and then rented it to the Oilers. Northlands continued to administer it.

63. *Edmonton Journal*, April 6, 2016; see also Staples, "Rise and Fall of the Edmonton Coliseum."

64. Tickets costing $7–28 would have $2 added, and 7 percent would be charged on tickets over $28 (City of Edmonton, S. 3, Bylaw 11336, revised September 24, 1996). Pocklington received about $2 million from the ticket tax.

65. Interview, February 20, 2018. Reimer was also critical of the influence of boosters, especially property developers, in local politics: "You would go to places, any event, and there would be the same people, and so that's what council would get exposed to. So, you don't have the exposure to other people in the same way. And so, you get your information from one source and that's what you're hearing and you're hearing it from a number of people, and they are nice people. So, that's kind of often what drives it. And some are very adept. Some would in fact write out exactly what motion they wanted and members of council would read the motion. That took me aback. They're being prepared. At the same time, it does speak to the fact that there's a certain group of people that can exert a lot of influence if you let them."

66. *Edmonton Journal*, July 27, 1994.

67. *Edmonton Journal*, April 12, 1994

68. *Edmonton Journal*, May 8, 1995. Even NHL commissioner Gary Bettman could be a booster, if required. He recalled much later, regarding the Oilers' situation in the 1990s, that "Edmonton is not only a great sports town with great people, it's a great hockey town and the history, the tradition, the fans, the players who played here. I was always committed to making it work" (*Edmonton Journal*, March 15, 2017).

69. Charles Euchner, who has written on the economics of sports, was quoted in *Alberta Report*, November 22, 1993, 33–35. Oilers fans, not just boosters, generally support subsidizing the team. Their identities are aligned with its success or failure. See also, Charles C. Euchner, *Playing the Field: Why Sports Teams Move and Cities Fight to Keep Them* (Baltimore and London: Johns Hopkins University Press, 1994).

70. Nichols was quoted in the *Edmonton Journal*, May 31, 1996.

71. See Richard Gruneau and David Whitson, *Hockey Night in Canada: Sport, Identities and Cultural Politics* (Toronto: Garamond Press, 1993), 238.

72. Interview, February 20, 2018.

73. Brian Bergman, "Tale of Two Cities," *Macleans.ca*, February 12, 2001, https://archive.macleans.ca/issue/20010212#!&pid=20.

74. Scott Messenger, "Back From the Brink," *Avenue Edmonton*, September 2016, 61.

75. *Capital City Downtown Plan*, adopted by the City of Edmonton, April 30, 1997, ii. See https://issuu.com/aesdl/docs/edmonton__alta.__-_1997_-_capital_c.

76. *Capital City Downtown Plan*, i–iv.

77. Revenues were paid in Canadian dollars, while expenses, including players' salaries, were paid in US dollars. The Canadian dollar was worth US72 cents in 1997.

78. David Staples, "How Citizen Cal Nichols Saved NHL Hockey in Edmonton," *Edmonton Journal*, December 14, 2007, https://edmontonjournal.com/sports/hockey/nhl/cult-of-hockey/how-citizen-cal-nichols-saved-nhl-hockey-in-edmonton.

79. Nichols was quoted in *The National Post*, November 19, 2002.

80. EDE, *Economic Impact of the Edmonton Oilers in the Edmonton, Alberta Capital Region, 1996–1997* (Edmonton: Economic Development Edmonton, 1998), 4–5. Commissioned

reports like this one generally "prove" that a professional sports franchise generates huge economic benefits for the community.

81. *Edmonton Journal*, March 15, 1998.

82. *Edmonton Journal*, October 31, 2003.

83. McConnell and Nye, *I'd Trade Him Again*, 243–45. He believed the motive was personal because he had criticized the provincial government.

84. The process took on all the elements of a farce when a conman named Michael Largue, a convicted fraudster who lied about his background and his ties to a prospective buyer from Switzerland, claimed he had CA$100 million to buy the Oilers. He had previously tried to buy the NHL's Tampa Bay Lightning and the CFL's Calgary Stampeders. When *Edmonton Journal* reporters investigated, they uncovered the scam, and Largue disappeared from Edmonton as quickly as he had appeared. See Hunter, *The Glory Barons*, 326–29.

85. *Edmonton Journal*, December 14, 2007; see also Staples, "How Citizen Cal Nichols Saved NHL Hockey."

86. Now living in the United States, Pocklington continues his questionable business practices. He had a criminal conviction for perjury in 2010. In 2013, he had to pay US$5 million to settle fraud charges. In October 2017, he tried to cut a deal with the Alberta government over his debt of $21.5 million, but it was blocked by an Edmonton judge. In April 2018, he was accused of securities fraud, misappropriating funds from investors for personal use, and unethical practices (*Edmonton Journal*, April 5, 2018).

87. *Edmonton Journal*, December 14, 2007; italics original. See also Staples, "How Citizen Cal Nichols Saved NHL Hockey."

88. See Paul Voisey, "Boosting the Small Prairie Town, 1904–1931: An Example from Southern Alberta," in *Town and City: Aspects of Western Canadian Urban Development*, ed. Alan F.J. Artibise (Regina: Canadian Plains Research Centre and University of Regina, 1981), 171.

89. Interview with Patrick LaForge, March 7, 2018.

90. LaForge pointed out that the EIGLP was concerned with managing only the team, not the non-hockey events: "The group was so focused on caring for the Oilers that we didn't run the whole building, although it was given to us. Before I came in 2000 [Northlands said] here's the whole thing, concerts and everything, just take it and [the EIGLP] looked at it and said we don't know anything about that stuff" (Interview, March 7, 2018).

91. *Edmonton Journal*, April 6, 2016; see also Staples, "Rise and Fall of the Edmonton Coliseum." The name of the facility was changed to the Edmonton Coliseum in 1995. Then, in 1998, the rights were sold to Skyreach Equipment Ltd. for $3.3 million for 5 years, whereupon it was called Skyreach Centre.

92. Hunter, *The Glory Barons*, 332–33.

93. *The Globe and Mail*, January 19, 2000.

94. David Whitson and Richard Gruneau, "Introduction," in *Artificial Ice: Hockey, Culture, and Commerce*, eds. David Whitson and Richard Gruneau, 1–25 (Toronto: Garamond Press, 2006), 13; emphasis original. See also, Jay Scherer and Steven J. Jackson, "From Corporate Welfare to National Interest: Newspaper Analysis of the Public Subsidization of NHL Hockey Debate in Canada," *Sociology of Sport Journal* 21 (2004): 36–60.

95. *Edmonton Journal*, December 14, 2007.

96. Quoted in *Edmonton Journal*, November 22, 2009.

97. *Edmonton Journal*, November 26, 2003.

98. According to *Forbes* in 2004, the Oilers averaged about US$2 million in operating income annually, although any profits had to be divided among several owners, if they weren't ploughed back into the team. But improvements like a new $3.1 million scoreboard were paid for by the city (Bylaw 12611); see Michael Ozanian, "The Business of Hockey," *Forbes*, November 10, 2004.

99. Nichols, who had "saved" the Oilers for Edmonton, dropped the boosterism and became an ardent defender of cost certainty for the team. He had said earlier, "if there isn't some correction on cost controls—and player salaries are a big part of that—it's going to get more difficult to operate" (*The Globe and Mail*, January 19, 2000).

100. Staples, "How Citizen Cal Nichols Saved NHL Hockey."

101. *Edmonton Journal*, December 14, 2007. The attachment of the Oilers' fans to the team made it easy for the owners to get popular support for concessions that benefitted their own economic interests.

102. Pocklington made this comment shortly after he traded Wayne Gretzky to Los Angeles. See *Edmonton Journal*, August 10, 1988.

4 PREPARING THE POLITICAL TERRAIN

1. Jason Markusoff, "Door Not Quite Shut on Provincial Aid; Despite Stelmach's Stand, City MLAs Say They'd Consider a Funding Request," *Edmonton Journal*, March 25, 2008, A2.

2. Neil deMause and Joanna Cagan, *Field of Schemes: How the Great Stadium Swindle Turns Public Money Into Private Profit* (Lincoln and London: University of Nebraska Press, 2008).

3. David Goldblatt, *The Game of Our Lives: The English Premier League and the Making of Modern Britain* (New York: Nation Books, 2014), 4.

4. deMause and Cagan, *Field of Schemes*, 49.

5. Arena Leadership Committee, *City Shaping: The Summary Report of the Leadership Committee for a New Sports/Entertainment Facility for Edmonton* (Edmonton, 2008), 13.

6. deMause and Cagan, *Field of Schemes*, 49.

7. Income Tax Act (Canada), R.S.C., 1985, c. 1 (5th Supp.), Expenses for food, etc. [or entertainment], 67.1 (1).

8. Dan Mason, *Sports Development Projects: Current and Proposed in North America*, report prepared for the city of Edmonton, 2007, 4.

9. deMause and Cagan, *Field of Schemes*, 142.

10. David Staples, "The Man who Saved the Oilers (Part 2)," *Edmonton Journal*, October 2, 2005, E6.

11. Interview, January 26, 2018.

12. David Staples, "Edmonton at a Crossroad; Once Again the City Faces a Decision on a Hockey Arena That Will Shape its Future for Years to Come," *Edmonton Journal*, December 13, 2009, E1.

13. Interview, March 7, 2018.

14. There was no public discussion of a new arena in the 2004 municipal campaign. The city of Edmonton was struggling to balance growth with modest tax increases, while still enduring the residual constraints produced by then-Premier Ralph Klein's debt elimination strategy and the corresponding reductions to municipal grants. Voters, meanwhile, were primarily concerned with unfinished or poorly maintained aspects of their communities and associated municipal infrastructure, as well as with keeping property taxes down.

15. Staples, "Edmonton at a Crossroad."

16. Staples, "Edmonton at a Crossroad."

17. Shawn Ohler, "Skyboxes a Big Draw as Firms Seek That Deal-Closing Edge," *Edmonton Journal*, December 5, 2005, A1.

18. Interview, December 20, 2017.

19. Interview, March 7, 2018.

20. Interview, March 7, 2018.

21. The team was, however, required to pay an annual fee of approximately $900,000 as a contribution toward a reserve for capital repairs of Rexall Place, although the actual operating costs for Northlands exceeded this amount by upwards of $800,000.

22. As discussed, Rexall Place had originally been named Northlands Coliseum (and has, at the time of this writing, reverted to its original name), was called the Edmonton Coliseum from 1995 to 1998, and was renamed Skyreach Centre (from 1998 to 2003) in a 5-year deal worth $3.3 million. In 2003, the Oilers signed a 10-year marketing and sponsorship agreement with the Katz Group that included the naming rights to the arena (Rexall), the value of which was rumoured to be worth $1,000,000 per year.

23. Interview, October 25, 2016.

24. Conventions, Sports & Leisure International, *Report on the Potential New Arena in Edmonton*, 2009, vi.

25. Interview, December 15, 2015.

26. Executives from the Flames, in turn, complained once plans for the construction of Rogers Place had been finalized that the Saddledome was itself antiquated and obsolete, in order to try to secure their own new, publicly-funded arena; see Epilogue for further details.

27. Interview, March 7, 2018.

28. Hockey-related revenue includes revenue from seat sales, gate receipts, television contracts, etc.

29. For a discussion of the new CBA and the division of revenue, see Andy Grabia, "The CBA," *Why Downtown?*, September 29, 2010, at https://whydowntown.wordpress.com/?s=CBA&submit=Search.

30. In 2007, the Canadian Broadcasting Corporation and the NHL agreed to a new, six-year broadcasting deal, estimated at $100 million per year. Those funds would be divided amongst the Canadian franchises. In 2010, the Oilers signed a lucrative, ten-year regional television deal with Rogers Sportsnet. Regional television revenue is retained solely by the franchise.

31. Conventions, Sports & Leisure International, *Report on the Potential New Arena in Edmonton*, 2009, iv.

32. Kevin Taft, *Follow the Money: Where is Alberta's Wealth Going?* (Calgary: Detselig Enterprises, 2012), 8.

33. Jay Scherer and Judy Davidson, "Promoting The 'Arriviste' City: Producing Neoliberal Urban Identity and Communities of Consumption During the Edmonton Oilers' 2006 Playoff Campaign," *International Review for the Sociology of Sport* 46, no. 2 (2011): 157–80.

34. Ohler, "Skyboxes."

35. Over a decade later, Florida would recant many of his earlier proclamations following his belated assessment of the economic and social impacts of gentrification associated with such a revanchist development agenda, including the displacement of less-affluent African Americans and other ethnic minority residents from US inner cities. See Richard Florida, *The New Urban Crisis: How Our Cities Are Increasing Inequality, Deepening Segregation, And Failing the Middle Class—And What We Can do About It* (New York: Basic Books, 2017), 57–78.

36. Richard Florida, "The Never-Ending Stadium Boondoggle," *CityLab*, September 10, 2015, https://www.citylab.com/equity/2015/09/the-never-ending-stadium-boondoggle/403666/.

37. Interview, December 20, 2017.

38. Interview, July 31, 2017.

39. Sarah O'Donnell and Stephanie Classen, "Taxpayers Unlikely to Pick up The Tab Even in This Hockey Town," *Edmonton Journal*, October 3, 2005, A12.

40. Interview, July 31, 2017.

41. John MacKinnon, "Downtown Rink Could Trump Backyard," *Edmonton Journal*, January 7, 2006, C1.

42. Gary Lamphier, "Misunderstood and Ignored, Edmonton Has to Rebrand Itself," *Edmonton Journal*, January 7, 2006, F1.

43. Gary Lamphier, "Corporate Sector Has Role to Play in Downtown Revitalization," *Edmonton Journal*, March 28, 2006, E1.

44. City of Edmonton, "Agreement Form: New Edmonton Arena," September 21, 2006; emphasis added.

45. See, for example, Dennis Coates and Brad Humphreys, "The Effect of Professional Sports on Earnings and Employment in the Services and Retail Sectors in U.S. Cities," *Regional Science and Urban Economics* 33 (2003): 175–90; Dennis Coates and Brad Humphreys, "Do Economists Reach a Conclusion on Subsidies for Sports Franchises, Stadiums, and Mega-Events?," *Econ Journal Watch* 5, no. 3 (2008): 294–315.

46. Dan Mason's scholarship has not emphasized the economic impacts of arena construction on city development, but has focused instead on the public good of such projects to justify the use of taxpayer money. He has discussed how an arena project increases a city's profile and status, affects tourism, and improves the quality of urban life. See Gregory H. Duquette and Daniel S. Mason, "Urban Regimes and Sport in North American Cities: Seeking Status Through Franchises, Events, and Facilities," *International Journal of Sport Management and Marketing* 3, no. 3 (2008): 221–41; Daniel S. Mason, Ernest Buist, Jonathon Edwards, and Gregory Duquette, "The Stadium Game in Canadian Communities," *International Journal of Sport Finance*, 2, no. 2 (2007): 94–107; Michael T. Friedman and Daniel S. Mason, "A Stakeholder Approach to Analyzing Economic Development Decision Making: Public Subsidies for Professional Sport Facilities," *Economic Development Quarterly*, 18 (2004): 236–54.

47. Paula Simons, "It's Time to Begin Debate on a New Downtown Arena," *Edmonton Journal*, November 14, 2006, A14.

48. Gordon Kent, "Oilers Have Mayor Onside for $1B Downtown Complex," *Edmonton Journal*, December 22, 2006, A1.

49. Kent, "Oilers Have Mayor Onside."

50. Kent, "Oilers Have Mayor Onside."

5 MAKING THE TEAM

1. HOK, *Rexall Renovation Study*, 2007, 2.

2. Interview, December 15, 2015.

3. Interview, December 15, 2015.

4. HOK, *Rexall Renovation*, 4.

5. The cost of the other four Canadian NHL arenas built after 1993—entirely privately financed in Ottawa, Vancouver, Montreal, and Toronto—averaged only US$192.2 million. In Winnipeg, a smaller but comparable Canadian market to Edmonton, a new facility (the MTS Centre) had been built only three years earlier in 2004 for a total cost of only CA$133.5 million, with contributions from all levels of government. In 2011, the Atlanta Thrashers relocated to Winnipeg, where the Jets would play at a facility with less seating capacity (15,294), fewer corporate suites (55), and less total building area (440,000 square feet) than Rexall Place.

6. Conventions, Sports & Leisure, *Proposed Edmonton Arena Feasibility Study—Preliminary Draft*, 2007, 29.

7. Rexall Place provided fewer spectator facilities (163,537 square feet) than the Prudential Center, (210,200), and less total building area (Rexall: 497,700; Prudential: 718,714). The City of Newark contributed $210 million to the Prudential Center's construction.

8. *Forbes* annual valuations lists can be found by year at forbes.com.

9. Neil deMause and Joanna Cagan, *Field of Schemes: How the Great Stadium Swindle Turns Public Money Into Private Profit* (Lincoln and London: University of Nebraska Press, 2008).

10. deMause and Cagan, *Field of Schemes*, 145.

11. The total public development cost of Comerica Park was US$156 million out of the total cost of US$310 million. See Judith Long, *Public/Private Partnerships for Major League Sports Facilities* (New York: Routledge, 2013).

12. deMause and Cagan, *Field of Schemes*, 145.

13. deMause and Cagan, *Field of Schemes*, 145.

14. Bill Mah, "Plan for an Aging Rexall Place," *Edmonton Journal*, February 22, 2007, A3.

15. David Staples, "Public Cool to New Arena; U of A Survey Finds 50 Per Cent Opposes Use of Civic Funds," *Edmonton Journal*, July 20, 2008, A1.

16. The HOK report suggested that a renovated Rexall Place could be a catalyst for additional development given the city of Edmonton's existing revitalization policy for Alberta Avenue, yet neither a CRL nor any of the other funding mechanisms, including a ticket tax—both essential to funding the new downtown arena—were contemplated.

17. Mayor Mandel would later use these arguments to justify the use of public funds for the construction of a new downtown arena; see Chapter 6.

18. Ron Chalmers, "Rexall Place Reno Report Due Next Month," *Edmonton Journal*, January 13, 2007, B4.

19. Dan Mason, *Sports Development Projects: Current and Proposed in North America*, 2007, 3.

20. Mason, *Sports Development*, 4.

21. Mason, *Sports Development*, 3.

22. Such a study would include the evaluation of: potential sites; costs of site acquisition; costs of site infrastructure improvements; availability of parking and public transportation accommodations; construction costs and identification of other project costs; and an overall project schedule.

23. Arena Leadership Committee, *City Shaping: The Summary Report of the Leadership Committee for a New Sports/Entertainment Facility for Edmonton* (Edmonton, 2008), 1.

24. Mah, "Plan for an Aging Rexall Place," A3.

25. Gary Lamphier, "Will Katz Win Crusade for Oilers?; Mayor Says Whoever Owns Team Will Have to Chip in for Arena," *Edmonton Journal*, August 2, 2007, E1.

26. Gordon Kent, "Candidates Pitch Boycott, Tax Breaks; Snow Clearing, Downtown Arena among Topics Raised," *Edmonton Journal*, September 21, 2007, B1.

27. Interview, October 25, 2016.

28. Notably, not a single elected official was appointed to provide public oversight of the ALC, and the committee itself was far from demographically balanced, with only one woman, Patricia Mackenzie. It thus provides an instructive example of the gendered nature of the political debates over the construction of sports facilities for men's professional sport, or what historian Bruce Kidd has referred to as men's cultural centres. The ALC also lacked racial and ethnic diversity, and any meaningful community representation. Indigenous leadership was excluded—a significant oversight given that the arena was proposed for downtown Edmonton, an area with a substantial Indigenous population at risk of displacement. See Bruce Kidd, "The Men's Cultural Center," in *Sport, Men, and the Gender Order: Critical Feminist Perspectives*, eds. Michael A. Messner and Donald F. Sabo (Champaign, Ill: Human Kinetics Books, 1990), 32.

29. Scott McKeen, "New Hockey Arena Must Be Big, Bold and Iconic—Just Like Our City," *Edmonton Journal*, April 25, 2007, B1.

30. Paula Simons, "Downtown Was Not an Ideal Site for New Arena; Hard Questions— Rather Than Cheerleading Will Get Us the Answers We Need Before Proceeding," *Edmonton Journal*, April 26, 2007, B1.

31. Paula Simons, "Questioning Touted Arena Black Heresy; Hockey Crowd Furious With My Suggestions," *Edmonton Journal*, May 1, 2007, B1.

32. Interview, January 11, 2018.

33. See *The Battle of Alberta* (http://battleofalberta.blogspot.com) or *Why Downtown?* (https://whydowntown.wordpress.com) for examples.

34. Interview, March 7, 2018.

35. Interview with Patrick LaForge, March 7, 2018.

36. Rick McConnell, John MacKinnon, and Gary Lamphier, "Daryl Katz," *Edmonton Journal*, December 15, 2012, E1.

37. Marty Klinkenberg, "The McDavid Effect: The $6-Billion Business of Rebuilding a City Around its Hockey Team," October 30, 2015, https://www.theglobeandmail.com/sports/hockey/connor-mcdavid-and-the-remaking-of-downtown-edmonton/article27045484/.

38. Interview, March 7, 2018.

39. Interview, March 7, 2018.

40. Interview, October 25, 2016.

41. Interview, July 31, 2017.

42. Staples, "Edmonton at a Crossroad," *Edmonton Journal*, December 13, 2009, E1.

43. Interview, March 7, 2018.

44. David Staples, "Group of Five Fight to Keep Oilers; Minority EIG Owners Try Organizing Counter-bid, But Realize in the End It Won't Work," *Edmonton Journal*, July 1, 2008, B1.

45. Interview, December 20, 2017.

46. Interview, December 20, 2017.

47. Interview, March 7, 2018.

48. Scott McKeen, "A Victory for Big Ideas; Mandel's Sweeping Re-election Relegates Era of Penny Pinching to the Past," *Edmonton Journal*, October 16, 2007, A1.

49. Josh Wingrove, "The Puck Stops Here," *The Globe and Mail*, April 11, 2010, https://www.theglobeandmail.com/news/national/the-puck-stops-here/article4315510/?page=all.

50. When the authors attempted to review the campaign disclosure statements from municipal elections in 2001, 2004, and 2007 as part of our research for this book, we were informed by city staff via email that all of the records from these elections had been destroyed. Personal communication, Kristan Cook, Acting Director Corporate Information Elections and Corporate Information, August 24, 2017.

51. John MacKinnon, "'Location Agreement' Bogus; New EIG Chair Butler Merely Stalling to Work Backroom Deal," *Edmonton Journal*, January 4, 2008, C1.

52. Only two years earlier, after a long court case between two groups of former partners, Francesco Aquilini had purchased both the Vancouver Canucks and Rogers Arena for $207 million. The Canucks were valued at US$192 million the year after the 2004/05 NHL lockout, but this total had increased to an estimated US$236 million by 2008; see *Forbes* annual valuation list at forbes.com.

53. Interview, December 12, 2017.

54. Interview, December 12, 2017.

55. Interview, December 12, 2017.

56. David Staples, "Hottest Thing on Ice," *Edmonton Journal*, January 20, 2008, E1.

57. In anticipation of the release of the ALC's report and recommendations, the boosters were given further traction in early February 2008 by a high-profile conference on "The Role of Sports and Entertainment Facilities in Urban Development." The conference was organized by Dr. Dan Mason and jointly sponsored by the University of Alberta's Faculty of Physical Education & Recreation and the Edmonton Chamber of Commerce (whose president at the time was Patrick LaForge, also the president and CEO of the Edmonton Oilers and a prominent member of the ALC). While the conference boasted a relatively balanced lineup and included sports economist Dr. Brad Humphreys, who had consistently opposed public subsidies for professional sport, this was undeniably a growth-coalition sponsored event. The local media spotlight firmly shone on the conference's keynote speaker, Dr. Mark Rosentraub, who, once again, championed a new arena and entertainment district by highlighting a few handpicked US examples—San Diego, Columbus, Indianapolis, and Los Angeles—as the sport-related urban development templates that Edmonton should follow. Rosentraub had, not incidentally, worked as a hired consultant for many of these projects—an involvement that invites skepticism about his willingness to offer objective analyses of them. As he

had done previously, Rosentraub, who had already worked as a consultant for the city of Edmonton alongside Mason, zealously promoted local aspirations to build a new arena because it would revitalize the downtown core, while suggesting that Edmonton ought to create a "mid-Western Greenwich Village."

58.   Interview, December 15, 2015.

59.   Two anonymous sources suggested that Bateman had authored the *City Shaping* report. While she declined to be interviewed for this book, her executive assistant responded via email that Bateman was not the actual author of the report and had only copyedited a version of it. In the same email, she said that Bateman didn't know who the author of the report was (personal communication, Brenda Daigneau, Executive Assistant to Margaret Bateman, February 2, 2018). We sent two follow-up emails in an attempt to determine who had asked her to oversee the report, but received no further response.

60.   Margo Goodhand, "Power 30: Edmonton's Top Movers and Shakers Are Building One of Canada's Most Exciting Cities," November 15, 2014, http://www.edmontonjournal.com/news/insight/edmonton-power-30/index.html.

61.   Yes! For Edmonton's membership included Patricia Mackenzie, a member of the ALC.

62.   Paula Simons, "New Players in the Arena Games," *Edmonton Journal*, January 14, 2011, http://edmontonjournal.com/news/local-news/new-players-in-the-arena-games.

63.   The undated report can be found online at https://www.edmonton.ca/attractions_events/documents/PDF/RosentraubReport.pdf.

64.   Mark Rosentraub, personal communication to Candice Stasynec, December 18, 2007.

65.   Arena Leadership Committee (ALC), *City Shaping: The Summary Report of the Leadership Committee for a New Sports/Entertainment Facility for Edmonton* (Edmonton, 2008), 3.

66.   ALC, *City Shaping*, 25.

67.   ALC, *City Shaping*, 3.

68.   ALC, *City Shaping*, 5.

69.   ALC, *City Shaping*, 5.

70.   ALC, *City Shaping*, 16.

71.   ALC, *City Shaping*, 18.

72.   ALC, *City Shaping*, 19.

73.   ALC, *City Shaping*, 20.

74.   Adapted from ALC, *City Shaping*, 22.

75.   ALC, *City Shaping*, 18.

76.   ALC, *City Shaping*, 18.

77.   Susan Ruttan, "Governments MVPs in Arena Game Plan: Need for Subsidies 'Highly Probable' in Proposed $450M Downtown Project," *Edmonton Journal*, March 26, 2008, A1.

78.   John MacKinnon, "Think Big: Let's Create a Landmark; A New Arena Should Be City's Yankee Stadium," *Edmonton Journal*, March 26, 2008, A1.

79.   Paula Simons, "Cut the Bull. We Know Who Will Pay—You and I, the Taxpayers," *Edmonton Journal*, March 27, 2008, B1.

80.   Simons, "Cut the Bull."

81.   Kevin Delaney and Rick Eckstein, *Public Dollars, Private Stadiums: Battles Over Building Sports Stadiums* (New Brunswick, NJ: Rutgers University Press, 2003), 34.

1. David Staples, "Public Cool to New Arena; U of A Survey Finds 50 Percent Opposes Use of Civic Funds," *Edmonton Journal*, July 20, 2008, A1.

2. Staples, "Public Cool to New Arena."

3. Scott Hennig, "Draft Arena Report Reveals New Taxes for Edmonton," *Taxpayer.com*, August 5, 2018, https://www.taxpayer.com/news-releases/draft-arena-reports-reveal-new-taxes-for-edmonton.

4. *CBC News*, "Edmonton Accused of Hiding Facts in Downtown Arena Review," August 7, 2008, http://www.cbc.ca/news/canada/edmonton/edmonton-accused-of-hiding-facts-in-downtown-arena-review-1.726646.

5. Interview, December 6, 2015.

6. We will return to this particular issue and its democratic ramifications in later chapters, but it's important to note the extent to which the city of Edmonton exerted its influence in these matters, even after the final arena agreement was signed with the Katz Group in 2013. The authors of this book, for example, submitted a FOIP request in December 2015 for the unreleased CSL and HOK reports, but were sent instead, by the office of the city clerk, identical copies of the redacted reports from the Canadian Taxpayers Federation's original FOIP request years earlier. Concerned that these reports may have been shredded—especially in light of the city's earlier refusal to release the documents—we immediately filed an appeal with the Office of the Information and Privacy Commission of Alberta to have our FOIP request reviewed.

    We also contacted councillor Mike Nickel to complain, as he had been in touch with the first author, Jay Scherer, after he had found out about our frustrations with the FOIP process. He requested to see full copies of the HOK and CSL reports from administration; we were somewhat surprised when he received full, un-redacted copies of both reports within days of his request. Though he couldn't release the documents to us, we were able to provide the Office of the Information and Privacy Commission of Alberta with indisputable evidence that the full versions of the reports did, in fact, exist and were readily accessible, despite denials. The city of Edmonton eventually confirmed that it had completed a new search and found full copies of both reports. However, while the full version of the HOK report was released to us in July 2016—8 months after our initial FOIP request—the city didn't give us the scores ranking possible arena locations. HOK's rankings were not made available to city council, either, during the early years of the arena debate.

    Likewise, the city of Edmonton continued to refuse to release an un-redacted version of the CSL report. Rather than claiming that the report no longer existed, as it had earlier, the city fell back on one of its most trusted mechanisms to block access to public information: claiming that releasing the CSL report in its entirety, a report commissioned in 2007, would be harmful to the business interests of a third party, the Edmonton Oilers (Section 16 of the FOIP Act). The city's use of Section 16 to restrict access to the report was rejected by Catherine Taylor, the senior information and privacy manager of the Office of the Information and Privacy Commission of Alberta. She made three key points in her summary of the review:

    •   *The information that was severed is at least nine years old, so is not current.*

- *Substantial changes have occurred in the economic picture in Alberta (and beyond) since 2007, so a disclosure is unlikely to create harm to the economic interest of the third party.*
- *The financial data relates to a facility owned by a public body; a public body is by definition not a third party.*

Taylor also emphasized her finding that the city of Edmonton "did not initially meet its duty as required by Section 10 of the Act by conducting an adequate search for responsive records," and that the office of the city clerk "was not able to provide me with an explanation as to why it had been unable to initially locate the two reports." We finally received the full, unredacted copy of the CSL report in October 2016.

7. CSL report, 29.
8. CSL report, 29.
9. CSL report, 26.
10. CSL report, 24.
11. CSL report, 16.
12. Over a 35-year agreement, this would result in a total of $392 million in additional profit for a new facility. See CSL, *Proposed Edmonton Arena Feasibility Study—Preliminary Draft*, 2007.
13. See CSL, *Report on the Potential New Arena in Edmonton*, 2009.
14. HOK, "Arena Site Assessment Report," February 18, 2008, 6.
15. HOK, "Arena Site Assessment," 70.
16. Interview, December 15, 2015.
17. HOK, "Arena Site Assessment," 5.
18. HOK, "Arena Site Assessment," 64.
19. HOK, "Arena Site Assessment," 5.
20. HOK, "Arena Site Assessment," 43.
21. HOK, "Arena Site Assessment," 49.
22. HOK, "Arena Site Assessment," 6.
23. HOK, "Arena Site Assessment," 52.
24. HOK, "Arena Site Assessment," 61.
25. Gordon Kent, "City Deficit Will Hit $29.7M," *Edmonton Journal*, November 14, 2008, B1.
26. Interview, December 15, 2015.
27. Scott McKeen, "Advice to Oiler Owner: Keep Arena Promises and Get a Haircut," *Edmonton Journal*, December 15, 2008, A10.
28. Dan Barnes, "New Arena for Oilers 'Imperative,' Bettman Says; NHL Boss Puts His Mouth Where His Money Isn't," *Edmonton Journal*, December 17, 2008, A1.
29. Barnes, "New Arena."
30. Interview, July 31, 2017.
31. Neil deMause and Joanna Cagan, *Field of Schemes: How the Great Stadium Swindle Turns Public Money Into Private Profit* (Lincoln and London: University of Nebraska Press, 2008), 68.
32. Gary Lamphier, "Northlands Signals Desire to Be an Even Bigger Player," *Edmonton Journal*, May 7, 2009, F1.

33. Ipsos Reid, "Three Quarters (76%) of Edmontonians 'Disagree' That City Should Provide Taxpayers' Money for A New Hockey Arena," August 20, 2009, https://www.ipsos.com/en-ca/three-quarters-76-edmontonians-disagree-city-should-provide-taxpayers-money-new-hockey-arena.

34. Gordon Kent, "New Arena 'Underway'; Team President Confirms Project Not Just Speculation," *Edmonton Journal*, September 1, 2009, A1.

35. John MacKinnon, "Much Ado About Nothing; Other Than LaForge Serving as Point Man for Katz Project, News Conference Has Little to Announce," *Edmonton Journal*, September 1, 2009, C1. See Chapter 5, note 57, for a discussion of the conference.

36. Gary Lamphier and Gordon Kent, "Billion-Dollar Makeover for Core; Oilers Owner's Arena Project Could Revitalize Downtown, Sources Say," *Edmonton Journal*, August 28, 2009, A1.

37. David Staples, "Oilers Confirm Casino Site as Best Place for New Arena; Planning Development Also Means Assembling Other Downtown Properties," *Edmonton Journal*, September 11, 2009, A3.

38. Staples, "Oilers Confirm."

39. Staples, "Oilers Confirm."

40. MacKinnon, "Much Ado About Nothing."

7 SHUT OUT

1. Interview, December 15, 2015.

2. Northlands, "Northlands Briefing Memo: A New Arena and Downtown Development for Edmonton," 2010, 1.

3. Northlands, "Northlands Briefing," 2.

4. Northlands, "Northlands Briefing," 2.

5. Interview, December 13, 2016.

6. David Staples and Gary Lamphier, "Oilers' Revenue Demands Would Shut Out Northlands; Money-Losing Team Needs All Cash Generated by Proposed Arena, President Says," *Edmonton Journal*, September 12, 2009, A1.

7. Staples and Lamphier, "Oilers' Revenue."

8. *Forbes* annual "The Business of Hockey" list can be found at forbes.com by year.

9. Interview, December 15, 2015.

10. Staples and Lamphier, "Oilers' Revenue."

11. Interview, December 12, 2017.

12. Interview, December 15, 2015.

13. Interview, January 26, 2018.

14. Gary Lamphier, "Public Cash Means Public Control," *Edmonton Journal*, September 12, 2009, A2.

15. Gary Lamphier, "Titans Square Off Over Arena Downtown," *Edmonton Journal*, September 19, 2009, E1.

16. Gary Lamphier, "Katz Group Oddly Silent as Arena Questions Pile Up; Project Appears to Lack Private-Sector Partners and Developer Interest," *Edmonton Journal*, September 26, 2009, E1.

17. Gary Lamphier, "Katz Group Fires Back Some Answers to 'Snide' Arena Questions," *Edmonton Journal*, September 29, 2009, E1.

18. Interview, September 21, 2016.

19. David Staples, "Katz Hires Pop King's Backers; Entertainment Giant AEG to Advise on New Downtown Arena Complex," *Edmonton Journal*, December 4, 2009, A1.

20. David Staples, "L.A. Arena District Revives a Downtown in Decline; AEG, an American Sports Management Company, Turned a Ghetto into a Flashy Arena District. Now AEG is Coming to Edmonton," *Edmonton Journal*, December 6, 2009, E4.

21. David Staples, "Blue Lines & Bottom Lines," *Edmonton Journal*, November 22, 2009, E1.

22. Interview, August 15, 2017.

23. David Staples, "Arena Expected to Pump Property Values; Formerly Skeptical Economists Now Find Hundreds of Millions of Dollars in Ripple Effects," *Edmonton Journal*, November 22, 2009, A1.

24. Interview, August 15, 2017.

25. Kevin Delaney and Rick Eckstein, *Public Dollars, Private Stadiums: Battles Over Building Sports Stadiums* (New Brunswick, NJ: Rutgers University Press, 2003), 38.

26. John MacKinnon, "Katz Finally Lays Cards on Table; 'Spectacular' Vision Will Spark Debate," *Edmonton Journal*, February 10, 2010, C1.

27. Bob Black to Linda Sloan, personal communication, December 19, 2009.

28. David Staples, "Former Owner Ties Oilers' Future to New Arena; Franchise Won't be Secure Unless Modern Facility Built Downtown, Cal Nichols Says," *Edmonton Journal*, December 13, 2009, A1.

29. Staples, "Former Owner."

30. Delaney and Eckstein, *Public Dollars, Private Stadiums*, 37.

31. Gordon Kent, "Arena Could Bring $1.25B in Wages; Katz Proposal Supplies 'Critical Mass' to Transform Downtown, City Agency Says," *Edmonton Journal*, December 17, 2009, A1.

32. Kent, "Arena Could Bring $1.25B in Wages."

33. John Crompton, "Economic Impact Analysis of Sports Facilities and Events: Eleven Sources of Misapplication," *Journal of Sport Management* 9, no. 1 (1995): 15.

34. Personal communication, Randy Ferguson, EEDC board chair, to Linda Sloan, March 21, 2010.

35. Personal communication, Randy Ferguson, EEDC board chair, to Linda Sloan, March 21, 2010.

36. Personal communication, Randy Ferguson, EEDC Board Chair, to Linda Sloan, March 21, 2010.

37. The EEDC report stated that the Katz Group's proposed arena development would increase Alberta's Gross Domestic Product (GDP) by $2.6 billion, while Edmonton's share of the GDP would increase by $1.8 billion. Furthermore, $1.6 billion in wages and salaries would be created in Alberta, $1.2 billion of that being in Edmonton, with 34,000 full-year jobs created in Alberta, 28,000 of those in Edmonton. Over $757 million in taxes would be generated, and total industry output would increase by over $6 billion.

38. Interview, August 15, 2017.

39. In fact, according to *Forbes*, the Oilers were also more profitable than the New Jersey Devils, Pittsburgh Penguins, Minnesota Wild, Anaheim Ducks, Colorado Avalanche, Calgary Flames, Ottawa Senators, Tampa Bay Lightning, San Jose Sharks, Washington Capitals, Carolina Hurricanes, St. Louis Blues, Buffalo Sabres, Columbus Blue Jackets,

Florida Panthers, Nashville Predators, New York Islanders, Atlanta Thrashers, and Phoenix Coyotes.

40. Joanne Ireland, "Bettman Believes New Arena Important for Rebuilding Process," *Edmonton Journal*, January 21, 2010, C4.

41. Tamara Gignac, "NHL Boss Calls for New Arena," *Calgary Herald*, January 22, 2010, B1.

42. In another classic example of the ideological work that accompanies the league strategy of planned facility obsolescence, both the Flames' ownership group and Bettman would eventually point to the improved circumstances of the Oilers after Rogers Place opened to argue that Calgary needed a new, publicly-funded arena to replace the "aging" Saddledome—opened in 1983—to ensure a level economic playing field.

43. Gordon Kent, "Don't Underestimate Public, City Manager," *Edmonton Journal*, January 23, 2010, B3.

44. David Staples, Gordon Kent and Paula Simons, "Arena Needs Katz Cash," *Edmonton Journal*, February 11, 2010, A1.

45. Staples, Kent, and Simons, "Arena Needs Katz Cash."

46. Paula Simons, "Katz Group's Sense of Entitlement Won't Get Arena Built; A Little Maturity Would Help Their Cause," *Edmonton Journal*, February 11, 2010, B1.

47. Quoted in Simons, "Katz Group's Sense of Entitlement."

48. Gordon Kent, "Arena Numbers Don't Add Up, Figures Reveal," *Edmonton Journal*, February 11, 2010, B4. 2010 municipal interest rates were used.

49. Kent, "Arena Numbers Don't Add Up."

50. Kent, "Arena Numbers Don't Add Up."

51. Staples, Kent, and Simons, "Arena Needs Katz Cash."

52. Staples, Kent, and Simons, "Arena Needs Katz Cash."

53. John MacKinnon, "Edmonton Deserves Face-to-Face with Katz; Reclusive Oilers Owner Answers Arena Questions in Video," *Edmonton Journal*, February 12, 2010, C1.

54. Gordon Kent, "Downtown Arena 'Crucial' to Oilers' Future," *Edmonton Journal*, February 21, 2010, A1.

55. Kent, "Downtown Arena."

56. Karen Kleiss, "Hoteliers, Developers Support Downtown Project; But Success in Filling New Office Towers, Hotels Contingent on Economic Recovery, They Say," *Edmonton Journal*, February 12, 2010, A2.

57. For example, see Andrew Zimbalist, *Report on Rexall Place, the Edmonton Oilers and Plans for a New Arena*, 2010.

58. Kleiss, "Hoteliers, Developers Support Downtown Project."

59. *Edmonton Journal*, "Arena Offers Rare Chance for Downtown," February 13, 2010, A18.

60. Daryl Katz, "Katz Asks Edmontonians to Hear Him Out on Downtown Arena Place," *Edmonton Journal*, February 14, 2010, A14.

61. Katz, "Katz Asks Edmontonians."

62. Jay Scherer and Michael Sam, "Policing the Cyber Agenda: New Media Technologies and Recycled Claims in a Local Stadium Debate," *Sport in Society* 13, no. 10 (2010): 1458.

63. Gordon Kent, "Mayor Suggests Ticket Tax for Arena; User-Pay System Could Help Fund New Downtown Oilers Venue," *Edmonton Journal*, February 19, 2010, A1.

64. Interview, December 20, 2017.

65. Kent, "Mayor Suggests Ticket Tax for Arena."

66. Scott McKeen, "Mayor Sends Signal to Katz City Has Expectations As Well," *Edmonton Journal*, February 19, 2010, B1.

67. *Edmonton Journal*, "Ticket Tax Will Help Sell Arena," February 19, 2010, A18.

68. Josh Wingrove, "The Puck Stops Here," April 11, 2010, https://www.theglobeandmail.com/news/national/the-puck-stops-here/article4315510/.

69. Interview, May 23, 2017.

70. *Edmonton Sun*, "Leibovici Should Recuse Herself," May 27, 2011.

71. Scott McKeen, "Leibovici Must Tread Carefully on Arena Issue; Councillor's Husband Works for Company Owned by Oilers Boss Daryl Katz," *Edmonton Journal*, February 26, 2010, B1.

72. McKeen, "Leibovici Must."

73. McKeen, "Leibovici Must."

74. Interview, October 11, 2017.

8 SHOW ME THE MONEY

1. Trish Audette, "Tory MLAs Get Tour of Rexall Place; 'There Was No Discussion About the Downtown Arena,' Danyluk Says," *Edmonton Journal*, March 25, 2010, B1.

2. Interview, September 27, 2017.

3. *CTV News*, "Poll Reveals Majority of Edmontonians Oppose Public Cash for Downtown Arena," March 22, 2010, https://edmonton.ctvnews.ca/poll-reveals-majority-of-edmontonians-oppose-public-cash-for-downtown-arena-1.494675.

4. City of Edmonton, "Description of Work," May 4, 2010, 1.

5. City of Edmonton "Description of Work."

6. *Edmonton Journal*, "Cool Talk about Hot Arena Topic," April 14, 2010, A14.

7. *Edmonton Journal*, "Cool Talk."

8. Gordon Kent, "Oilers Arena Will Cost Less Than Feared," *Edmonton Journal*, April 14, 2010, A1.

9. Kent, "Oilers Arena."

10. Gordon Kent, "Ball Gets Rolling on $1B Project; City Needs to Decide on Its Level of Commitment, Councillor Says," *Edmonton Journal*, April 20, 2010, B1.

11. Sale agreement: 104 Street Between 103 Avenue and 104 Avenue, City of Edmonton and EAD Property Holdings, February 10, 2014.

12. Paula Simons, "Approving Katz's Rezoning Application Would Be a Big Mistake; Plan is Hazy, and Rubber Stamping It Would Give Group All the Power," *Edmonton Journal*, April 20, 2010, B1.

13. Simons, "Approving Katz's Rezoning."

14. Martin Salloum, "Proposal Deserves Support: Chamber," *Edmonton Journal*, April 23, 2010, A17.

15. Gene Hochachka, "Downtown Arena Proposal Finds Support from Strange Places," *Edmonton Journal*, April 26, 2010, A17.

16. Gordon Kent and David Staples, "$1B Project Feared as 'Vacuum'; Katz Group Proposal Will 'Suck Life off the Street,' Residents' Association Says," *Edmonton Journal*, May 6, 2010, A1.

17. Gordon Kent, "Public Mostly Likes What It Sees; Drawings Unveiled for Downtown Arena Complex," *Edmonton Journal*, May 7, 2010, A1.

18. Gordon Kent, "City Eyes June Hearing on Arena; Councillors Wary of Approving Zoning Change Before Seeing Financing Details," *Edmonton Journal*, May 11, 2010, B3.

19. Kent, "City Eyes."

20. City of Edmonton, "Capital City Downtown Plan," 2010, 163.

21. Dan Barnes, "Mandel, Bettman Meet," *Edmonton Journal*, June 26, 2010, C4.

22. Kevin Delaney and Rick Eckstein, *Public Dollars, Private Stadiums: Battles Over Building Sports Stadiums* (New Brunswick, NJ: Rutgers University Press, 2003), 185.

23. Barnes, "Mandel."

24. *Sportsnet*, "Katz to Control Hamilton's Copps Coliseum," June 29, 2010, https://www.sportsnet.ca/hockey/nhl/katz-copps/.

25. Keith Gerein, "Oilers Not Part of Katz Move; Deal to Lease Hamilton Arena All about Business Expansion," *Edmonton Journal*, June 30, 2010, A1.

26. Neil deMause, "Lemieux: We Fibbed About Moving to Get Arena," August 14, 2008, http://www.fieldofschemes.com/2008/08/14/1890/lemieux-we-fibbed-about-moving-to-get-arena/.

27. Scott McKeen, "'We Are the Community,' Northlands Boss Insists; Ken Knowles Believes Group Is Misunderstood," *Edmonton Journal*, July 5, 2010, A5.

28. Interview, December 13, 2016.

29. Scott McKeen, "Katz Flips $100M Back to Arena Funding; Oilers Owner Offers Concession to City Hall, But Warns He Needs Council Decision Soon," *Edmonton Journal*, July 14, 2010, A1.

30. McKeen, "Katz Flips."

31. McKeen, "Katz Flips."

32. Rosen declined our request for an interview.

33. Scott McKeen, "Sober-Minded Arena Report Leaves Me Dizzy with Questions," *Edmonton Journal*, July 16, 2010, B1.

34. Scott McKeen, "Katz Arena Site Ranked Fourth; City Councillors Never Discussed Consultants' Report," *Edmonton Journal*, July 21, 2010, A1.

35. McKeen, "Katz Arena."

36. McKeen, "Katz Arena."

37. *Forbes* annual valuation lists and valuation breakdowns regarding NHL teams can be found by year at forbes.com.

38. Interview with Andy Huntley, December 15, 2015.

39. "Katz Group Presentation To Edmonton City Council," accessed October 29, 2011, http://revitalizedowntown.ca/kat-group-presentation-to-edmonton-city-council-july-21-2011/.

40. Don Braid, "Edmonton's Civic Surge Challenges Calgary," *Calgary Herald*, April 25, 2017, http://calgaryherald.com/news/politics/braid-edmontons-civic-surge-challenges-calgary.

41. "Katz Group Presentation."

42. "Katz Group Presentation."

43. "Katz Group Presentation."

44. "Katz Group Presentation."

45. Scott McKeen, "Airport, Arena Issues Tap Into Our Raw Emotions," *Edmonton Journal*, July 28, 2010, B1.

46. Ryan Cormier and Gordon Kent, "Oilers Owner Commits $200M To Arena Project; Team Needs Downtown Location To Survive, Council Told," *Edmonton Journal*, July 22, 2010, A2.

47. Scott McKeen, "Non-Threat Helps Focus Debate: Is Katz Really Batman, Or The Joker?," *Edmonton Journal*, July 22, 2010, A3.

48. Section 54(1) of the Procedures and Committees Bylaw 12300. A similar opportunity was not extended to a member of the public who had requested to speak on this occasion. The exclusion of popular input became commonplace as the arena debate progressed.

49. *Edmonton Journal*, "Katz Reboots Arena Debate," July 22, 2010, A18.

50. *Edmonton Journal*, "Northlands Not Key Focus," July 27, 2010, A12.

51. *Edmonton Journal*, "Katz Reboots."

52. *Edmonton Journal*, "Northlands."

9 END GAME?

1. Interview, December 15, 2015.

2. Letter from Roger Swainson to Simon Farbrother, July 16, 2010.

3. Letter from Roger Swainson to Simon Farbrother, July 16, 2010.

4. Letter from Roger Swainson to Simon Farbrother, July 16, 2010.

5. See Andrew Zimbalist, *Report on Rexall Place, the Edmonton Oilers and Plans for a New Arena*, 2010.

6. Since 1988, 30 arenas had been replaced with newer NHL/NBA facilities across North America. Of these, 15 facilities were demolished, 3 had closed or planned to close, 4 were retrofitted for different uses, and only 8 remained active (1 as a primary facility, and 7 as secondary arenas). The possibility of keeping a secondary arena for concerts was rejected because it would compete with a new facility. Sources cited in the 2009 CSL report favoured a new arena development because it was linked to the "continued revitalization of downtown." This was "preferable to the current location of Rexall Place." However, the report also noted that Rexall Place had operated successfully "as a live entertainment venue for sporting events, concerts and family shows" and that it could "continue to compete effectively for medium and large touring events." But the old facility might compete with the new arena for concerts, so this option was rejected.

   Finally, there was consideration of whether the Katz Group or Northlands ought to operate a new city-owned facility:

   > The entertainment industry insiders felt that, in general, the preferable scenario would be to have an entity not directly affiliated with the Oilers operating a new facility. Reasons for this reaction included greater booking flexibility for the facility, that a third party management company would be more likely to accommodate more events, and if public money is used to help fund the facility, the public sector should have some level of control over the operations of the facility. (CSL, *Report on the Potential New Arena in Edmonton*, 2009, 5–6.)

7. While a formal non-compete clause was never introduced, the city did grant the Katz Group the power to veto any future redevelopment of Rexall Place/city-owned land as a sport/entertainment facility. In the final version of the arena agreement, the city promised that it would not financially support nor advocate any initiative to rebuild or renovate Rexall Place for the purpose of maintaining the arena as a sports or entertainment facility.

8. The margin of error is +/-4.82 percent.

9. Interview, December 21, 2017.

10. Interview, December 21, 2017.

11. Interview, December 20, 2017.

12. Keith Gerein, "Gov't Funding for Arenas Unlikely; Health, Schools More Important Priorities, Stelmach Says," *Edmonton Journal*, September 10, 2010, A4.

13. By way of comparison, the government of Quebec had recently committed at least $175 million toward the construction of a new, $400-million arena in Quebec City, with the aim of attracting an NHL franchise. Quebec City also requested a contribution from the government of Canada, as did Edmonton. However, no federal funding was provided for an arena in either city. Quebec City and the provincial government eventually split the cost of the Videotron Centre, designed by HOK and opened in 2015. As of this book's writing, Quebec City has yet to attract an NHL franchise or secure an expansion team, and the arena remains an enormous white elephant for municipal and provincial taxpayers.

14. Ryan Cormier, "Former Journal Columnist Puts His Money Where his Mouth Is," *Edmonton Journal*, September 18, 2010, B3.

15. City of Edmonton, "Agreement Form: Strategic Communications Consulting and Support," May 29, 2012. According to the results of our FOIP submission (2017-G-0090), there was no email communication between the city of Edmonton and McKeen Communications regarding Scott McKeen's remit and the type of work he did for the downtown arena development. McKeen was then elected to council in 2013.

16. *Edmonton Journal*, "Ward 10 Forum," October 13, 2010, B3.

17. *Edmonton Journal*, "Ward 12 Forum," October 6, 2010, B3.

18. Gordon Stamp, "Mayor Stephen Mandel...Manipulating the Process From the Very Beginning," 2010.

19. Letter from David McCalla (Miller Thomson LLP) to Gordon Stamp, November 2, 2010.

20. Letter from David McCalla (Miller Thomson) to Gordon Stamp, November 30, 2010.

21. David Staples, "Arena 'Debate' Quietly Simmers on Electoral Back Burner; Mandel, Dorward Differ on Details, But Both Want Rink Downtown," *Edmonton Journal*, October 1, 2010, B1.

22. *Edmonton Journal*, "Vindication for Team Mandel," October 19, 2010, A14.

23. City of Edmonton, "A Legal Analysis of Public Participation in Decisions Regarding New Arena," December 1, 2010, 1.

24. City of Edmonton, "A Legal Analysis," 2.

25. City of Edmonton, "A Legal Analysis," 2.

26. The petition required a printed surname and signature for each signer, an address or legal description of a residence, the date of signature, the signature of a witness who "must also take an affidavit that, to the best of the person's knowledge, the signatures

witnessed are those of the persons entitled to sign the petition." See Alberta Municipal Affairs, "Petition to Your Council: Information for the General Public, Elected Officials and Municipal Officers," Government of Alberta, October 2017, 4, http://www. municipalaffairs.alberta.ca/documents/Petition%20to%20Your%20Council.pdf.

27. City of Edmonton, "A Legal Analysis," 8.

28. City of Edmonton, "A Legal Analysis," 8.

29. Kevin Maimann, "Audit Blasts Edmonton City Council's Public Engagement Process," *Edmonton Sun*, June 9, 2014, http://edmontonsun.com/2014/06/09/audit-blasts-edmonton-city-councils-public-engagement-process/ wcm/9341d49c-53e7-44cf-bf88-67767729ffe3.

30. City of Edmonton, "Amending Agreement Form: Major Downtown Development—Public Consultation and Facilitation," December 20, 2010.

31. City of Edmonton, Internal memo, March 2010.

32. Letter from Linda Cochrane to Janet Riopel, May 18, 2010.

33. Letter from Linda Cochrane to Janet Riopel, May 18, 2010.

34. City of Edmonton, Downtown Arena Consultation, August 10, 2010.

35. City of Edmonton, "Agreement Form: Major Downtown Development—Public Survey," January 25, 2011.

36. City of Edmonton, "Agreement Form."

37. Paula Simons, "Oilers' Aggressive Lobbying on Arena Project Sets Wrong Tone; Too Bad Attitude Hasn't Found Its Way onto the Ice of Late," *Edmonton Journal*, November 20, 2010, B1.

38. Simons, "Oilers' Aggressive."

39. Specifically, the five talking points were:

    1. *What's your position on building a downtown arena?*
        a. *If supportive, why?*
        b. *If not, why not?*
        c. *If conditional, why?*
    2. *If a new arena project were to proceed, what do you think is important to consider in terms of*
        a. *Design?*
        b. *Downtown connection and impact?*
        c. *Impact on surrounding communities?*
        d. *Community benefits/engagement?*
        e. *Impact on the future use of Rexall Place?*
        f. *Any other issues?*
    3. *What about using a mix of private and public funding to fund a downtown arena?*
    4. *What do you think about other possible funding sources to cover arena costs?*
        a. *Forms of user pay (e.g., a ticket tax)*
        b. *A CRL*
        c. *Funding for non-arena infrastructure from other levels of government*
        d. *Additional private investment*
        e. *Any other sources?*

40. Conal Pierse, "First Public Consultation on Arena Proposal Draws About 50," *Edmonton Journal*, November 11, 2010, B7.

41. To the question, "Do you agree that the City of Edmonton should provide taxpayers' money to build a new downtown arena?" 20 percent disagreed, while 48 percent said they strongly disagreed. To the question, "If the City of Edmonton contributes money to the construction of a new arena, do you agree or disagree that it should receive a proportionate share of the revenue?" 37 percent answered that they agreed, and 51 percent strongly agreed.

42. Board members were unable to develop and maintain the website, so a developer was employed—an ongoing and not insignificant expense.

43. Dan Barnes, "Oilers Fans Should Not Fear Relocation; Team Executives Merely Seek Arena Input in Meeting with Quebec City Mayor," *Edmonton Journal*, December 2, 2010, A1.

44. "Administration Response to Council's Questions," December 10, 2010, 4.

45. "Northlands Response—Potential Downtown Arena," December 10, 2010, 4.

46. "Administration Response," December 10, 2010, 11.

47. "Northlands Response," 4.

48. "Administration Response," 4.

49. "Administration Response," 6.

50. Interview, November 15, 2017.

51. "Katz Group Response to Council's Questions," December 10, 2010, 6.

52. "Katz Group Response," 2.

53. "Katz Group Response," 10.

54. "Katz Group Response," 8.

55. "Katz Group Response," 11.

56. "Administration Response," 8.

57. Bill Smith, "Give City Clear Arena Plan We Can Support, Ex-Mayor Bill Smith," *Edmonton Journal*, December 4, 2010, A16.

58. David Staples, "Northlands Needs to Offer Funding Ideas to Deserve Place in Future Arena; Expertise Running Facilities Won't Be Enough to Stay in Game," *Edmonton Journal*, December 11, 2010, B1.

10 THE BEAT GOES ON

1. Reports are generally released two business days before council meetings.

2. Deemed accurate to +/-3.5 percent, 19 times out of 20.

3. David Staples, "Oilers Location Agreement Is a Must," *Edmonton Journal*, January 14, 2011, A3.

4. Paula Simons, "Skepticism, Tough Questions Must Stick to Arena Debate Like Glue," *Edmonton Journal*, January 15, 2011, B1.

5. Simons, "Skepticism."

6. City Council Minutes, Item 5.4: Sports and Entertainment Facility—Information Report, "Downtown Arena—Potential Impacts," July 21, 2010, http://sirepub.edmonton.ca/sirepub/mtgviewer.aspx?meetid=447&doctype=MINUTES.

7. City of Edmonton, Update on the Potential Downtown Sports and Entertainment Facility, January 17, 2011, 3.

8. Interview, December 20, 2017.

9. City Council Minutes, Item 3.2: Update on the Potential Downtown Sports and Entertainment Facility, January 17, 2011, http://sirepub.edmonton.ca/sirepub/mtgviewer.aspx?meetid=492&doctype=MINUTES.

10. Interview, January 26, 2016.

11. Gordon Kent, "City Staff, Katz Group to Begin Talks on Arena; Deal Not Set—'Negotiations Are Just Negotiations,' Mayor Says," *Edmonton Journal*, January 18, 2011, A1.

12. Kent, "City Staff."

13. Paula Simons, "We Need More Answers Before Arena Debate Spins out of Control," *Edmonton Journal*, January 18, 2011, A5.

14. Kent, "City Staff."

15. The city of Edmonton initially refused to release the in-camera PowerPoint slides in response to our FOIP request. This decision was ultimately reversed after a lengthy appeal to the Office of the Information and Privacy Commissioner of Alberta.

16. Government of Alberta, Municipal Affairs, "In-Camera Discussions of Council," https://open.alberta.ca/publications/9781460116371.

17. Interview, December 12, 2017.

18. Interview, January 26, 2016.

19. Interview, November 15, 2017.

20. John MacKinnon, "New Arena Essential for Oilers Bettman; NHL Commissioner Reiterates Support for Katz Plan," *Edmonton Journal*, February 20, 2011, A1.

21. Gary Lamphier, "Case for New Arena No 'Slam Dunk'; Leading Analyst Says Such Plans Can Work—If Conditions Are Right," *Edmonton Journal*, February 26, 2011, E1.

22. *Forbes* estimates and NHL team valuations can be found at forbes.com by year.

23. Andrew Zimbalist, *Report on Rexall Place, the Edmonton Oilers and Plans for a New Arena*, 2010.

24. Zimbalist, *Report on Rexall Place*, 11–12.

25. Zimbalist, *Report on Rexall Place*, 13–14.

26. Mark Rosentraub, "Comments on Andrew Zimbalist's *Report on Rexall Place, the Edmonton Oilers, and Plans for a New Arena*," 2011, 7–11.

27. David Staples, "Duelling Arena Consultants Face Off; Katz Group's Guy Says Rexall Place is Cramped and Obsolete, While Northlands Side Rates it Above Average," *Edmonton Journal*, March 2, 2011, A3.

28. These latter points underscore the inherent tensions for any scholar who accepts payment for the production of commissioned research by any organization with a vested interest in the outcome, including Zimbalist himself, who has been criticized by Neil deMause on other occasions for producing reports with conclusions favourable for his clients.

29. This treatment—just like Staples' earlier misrepresentations of the work of economist Dr. Brad Humphreys—was not levelled at pro-arena sport management consultants like Mark Rosentraub, who had himself radically altered his own position over the years as he became a highly paid consultant.

30. Interview, November 12, 2015.

31. Interview, November 12, 2015.

32. The public update also provided some background information on a potential foundation model for a new arena development, the experiences of other cities, seat licensing, and corporate responsibility/community benefits—even though administration had already been conducting extensive negotiations with the Katz Group over these precise issues. These updates were, as always, supported by lengthier reports that administration had procured from Drs. Mason and Rosentraub, including one that examined the impact of various sport and entertainment districts on land values in five US cities.

33. Marianne Sorensen, *Edmonton Homeless Counts: 1999 to 2010 Trend Analysis*, December 1, 2010, 2, http://homewardtrust.ca/wp-content/uploads/2016/12/December-2010-Edmonton-Homeless-Count.pdf.

34. City of Edmonton, Update on Advancing the Downtown Arena, March 2, 2011, 3.

35. City of Edmonton, Update on Advancing the Downtown Arena, 3; emphasis added.

36. Neil Smith, *The New Urban Frontier: Gentrification and the Revanchist City* (London: Routledge, 1996).

37. Interview, November 15, 2017.

38. Interview, December 21, 2017.

39. Interview, December 12, 2017.

40. Interview with Simon Farbrother, December 21, 2017.

41. City of Edmonton, In-Camera Update on Negotiations, March 2, 2011, 26.

11 HEAD GAMES

1. David Staples, "Clarity from Council Proves New Arena is a Must," *Edmonton Journal*, March 3, 2011, B1.

2. Staples, "Clarity from Council."

3. Interview, January 26, 2018.

4. Elise Stolte, "New Arena May Offer $6.5M a Year in Taxes; Mayor Keen to See Councillors Decide by Month's End Whether to Build Downtown Facility," *Edmonton Journal*, March 3, 2011, B3.

5. Interview, November 15, 2017.

6. Staples, "Clarity From Council."

7. Letter from Roger Swainson to Simon Farbrother, April 1, 2011.

8. Letter from Roger Swainson to Simon Farbrother, April 1, 2011.

9. Gordon Kent, "Indecision Weighs Heavily on Council's Arena Stand," *Edmonton Journal*, April 5, 2011, A5.

10. John MacKinnon, "Clumsy Approach; Katz Group, City Need to Connect the Dots," *Edmonton Journal*, April 6, 2011, C1.

11. Gordon Kent, "New Arena, or No Oilers," *Edmonton Journal*, April 6, 2011, A1.

12. *Edmonton Journal*, "Put Arena in City-Building Context," April 6, 2011, A14.

13. David Staples, "Time Has Come for Council to Green-Light Arena Proposal," *Edmonton Journal*, April 6, 2011, B1.

14. Staples, "Time Has Come."

15. Staples, "Time Has Come."

16. Interview, December 20, 2017.

17. Paula Simons, "Katz Risks Public Goodwill with Ticket-Tax Stance; PR Blunder May Jeopardize Arena Negotiation," *Edmonton Journal*, April 5, 2011, A1.

18. Tom Sutherland, *Is a New Arena a Good Fit for Downtown Edmonton? Capital City Downtown Plan—Information Addendum*, presented at city council, April 6, 2011.

19. City of Edmonton, *Property and Business Tax Data—Downtown Versus City Wide, 2000 to 2010*.

20. Paula Simons, "Daft to Tie All Core Revenue Growth to Arena Project," *Edmonton Journal*, April 1, 2011, A2.

21. Letter from Gary Bettman to Simon Farbrother, April 21, 2011.

22. City of Edmonton, "Potential Downtown Arena—Alternative Funding Methods," April 6, 2011, 2.

23. City of Edmonton, In-Camera Update on Negotiations, April 6, 2011, 2.

24. Interview, May 23, 2017.

25. Interview, May 23, 2017.

26. Interview, November 15, 2017.

27. Including Ben Henderson, whose wife, Laurie Blakeman, was the MLA for Edmonton-Centre.

28. Gary Lamphier, "Arena Deal Leaves Nagging Questions," *Edmonton Journal*, April 12, 2011, D1.

29. Gordon Kent, "Northlands Vows Rexall Place Will Stay Open Despite New Arena; Venue Would Compete for Concerts, Other Events," *Edmonton Journal*, April 8, 2011, B1.

30. Sloan, personal notes, May 18, 2011.

31. Sloan, personal notes, May 18, 2011.

32. Sloan, personal notes, May 18, 2011.

33. Sloan, personal notes, May 18, 2011.

34. Sloan, personal notes, May 18, 2011.

35. Sloan, personal notes, May 18, 2011.

36. Sloan, personal notes, May 18, 2011.

37. Sloan, personal notes, May 18, 2011.

38. Sloan, personal notes, May 18, 2011.

39. Interview, November 15, 2017.

40. Sloan, personal notes, May 18, 2011.

41. Gary Lamphier, "Sloan Blasts Arena 'Manipulation'; Vote and News Conference Sprung on Councillors, Opponent Says," *Edmonton Journal*, May 21, 2011, E1.

42. Lamphier, "Sloan Blasts."

43. Lamphier, "Sloan Blasts."

44. Gordon Kent, "Council's Questions Swirl Around Katz Arena Deal; Gibbons Felt 'Pushed to the Chute' in Vote," *Edmonton Journal*, June 2, 2011, A3.

45. Gordon Kent, "City, Katz Group Reach Deal on Downtown Arena," *Edmonton Journal*, May 19, 2011, A1.

12 LOBBYING THE PROVINCE, SLAMMING NORTHLANDS

1. Terry Jones, "Time for Excitement," *Edmonton Sun*, May 20, 2011, S2.

2. *Edmonton Journal*, "Arena Deal Exciting Progress," May 20, 2011, A18.

3. An editorial in the *Edmonton Sun*, on the other hand, lambasted not just the lack of democratic transparency but the deal itself by noting that Edmonton would have the "only major municipal arena deal in Canada in which the developer has not picked up the majority of the share of cost." See, "A Bad Deal for City Ratepayers," *Edmonton Sun*, May 20, 2011, 13.

4. Letter from Stephen Mandel to Ed Stelmach, June 6, 2011.

5. David Staples, "Good Reasons for Province to Support Arena; Tax Dollars Put in Would Give a Return on Investment by Raising More Taxes," *Edmonton Journal*, July 15, 2011, A5.

6. Staples, "Good Reasons."

7. Staples, "Good Reasons."

8. Letter from Ed Stelmach to Stephen Mandel, July 26, 2011.

9. Letter from Stephen Mandel to Ed Stelmach, August 8, 2011.

10. CBC, "Katz Group Offered to Help MLAS with PR," August 5, 2011, http://www.cbc.ca/news/canada/edmonton/katz-group-offered-to-help-mlas-with-pr-1.992962.

11. Elise Stolte, "Northlands on Financial Hot Seat; Mayor Wants to See Organization's Books to Determine Its Viability," *Edmonton Journal*, July 21, 2011, A1.

12. Letter from Richard Andersen to Simon Farbrother, July 11, 2011.

13. Andrea Sands, "Katz Group, Enoch Cree Discuss Alternate Site for Arena; Veiled Threat to Move Elsewhere in the Region is Progress, City Councillor Says," *Edmonton Journal*, August 6, 2011, A3.

14. Gordon Kent, "Downtown Levy Area May Expand; Special Tax District Would Generate $1.2B for Arena, Other Improvements," *Edmonton Journal*, August 26, 2011, A1.

15. Kent, "Downtown Levy."

16. Gordon Kent, "Group Sees Downtown Boost in Tax; Special Levy Should Kick-Start Development in Central Core, Business Association Says," *Edmonton Journal*, August 27, 2011, A3.

17. Interview, November 23, 2015.

18. Interview, November 23, 2015.

19. Elise Stolte, "Arena Talks Have Cost City $1.15M; Spending on Lawyers, Consultants Moving too Fast for Some Councillors," *Edmonton Journal*, September 10, 2011, A1.

20. Stolte, "Arena Talks."

21. Gary Lamphier, "Katz Reportedly Living in Vancouver; Oilers Owner Bought Luxury Penthouse, Sources," *Edmonton Journal*, September 13, 2011, A1.

22. The Katz Group might simply have purchased all the land and provided the city of Edmonton with the option of acquiring the portion of the northern site at cost pending the finalization of the broader arena financing agreement. One could speculate that Katz was simply trying to avoid paying the attendant costs.

23. City administration advised city council that it had obtained independent appraisals of the land, but would not produce the documentation when requested by Councillor Sloan (Notes from former Councillor Linda Sloan; land title searches and historical sales data were compiled by W.W McCulloch, Linda's husband). The land owned by the city was transferred at its original purchase price, while the land owned by WAM Development Group was purchased by the city at well above its assessed value. In total, the city acquired just over 4.8 hectares of land for $57.75 million, or $11,974 million per

hectare. The amount of land used by the arena and the casino totals just 3.1 hectares. The land on which the arena is situated is owned by the city of Edmonton. The casino is located on a separate property owned by Ice District Corp., part of the Katz Group of Companies.

24. There was, in fact, a precedent for this type of arrangement: the Calgary Flames paid the Saddledome Association $20 million when they took control of the city-owned Saddledome. See David Steinhart, "Council Approves Saddledome Deal," *Calgary Herald*, March 22, 1994, A1.

25. Gordon Kent, "Mayor Expects Arena Vote by End of October; Outstanding Issues Include Land Options," *Edmonton Journal*, September 28, 2011, A3.

26. Jodie Sinnema, "Pressure Builds to OK Arena; Oilers President Urges Supporters to Lean on Council to Get Deal Done by Oct. 31," *Edmonton Journal*, October 4, 2011, A1.

27. Sinnema, "Pressure Builds."

28. Brett Wittmeier, "Northlands Denies Demanding $250M Non-Compete Clause; Figure Was Response to a Question, President Says," *Edmonton Journal*, October 5, 2011, A5.

29. Angelique Rodrigues, "Steaming Over Arena/Northlands Head, City Councillor Riled up at Messages Flying Over Decision," *Edmonton Sun*, October 5, 2011, 3.

30. Editorial, *Edmonton Sun*, "Leave the Arena Hyperbole in New York," October 9, 2011, 15.

31. We submitted a FOIP request for the October trip to New York and calculated the total cost based on invoices and receipts for airfare, accommodation and expense claims for Mandel, Farbrother and Mitsuka.

    An invitation to the meeting was not extended to Northlands, and it remained unclear how any non-compete agreement could be legitimately negotiated without all parties in attendance.

32. Interview, November 15, 2017.

33. Interview, January 26, 2016.

34. Interview, July 31, 2017.

35. Interview, December 20, 2017.

36. Interview, December 20, 2017.

37. Sloan, personal notes, October 14, 2011.

38. This option provided the Oilers with yet another tax break.

39. Gordon Kent, "Northlands Needs More Arena Info, Andersen," *Edmonton Journal*, October 19, 2011, A3.

40. Sloan, personal notes, October 14, 2011.

41. It should be noted that the answers to those questions were provided to council on October 26th, the day after the public hearing.

42. Gordon Kent, "Mayor Sees 'Reasonably Fair Deal'; Katz Drops Non-Compete Demand, Setting Stage for Final Decision on Arena," *Edmonton Journal*, October 15, 2011, A1.

43. David Staples, "Downtown Project Inches Closer to Deal; Katz Group Drops Non-Compete Demand," *Edmonton Journal*, October 15, 2011, A5.

44. Terry Jones, "Big Leap Forward/Mayor the MVP, Katz First Star in Game to Get Arena Project Back on Track," *Edmonton Sun*, October 15, 2011, S3.

45. Paula Simons, "Katz's Power Play Scores Major Concessions; Arena Deal Exempts Group From Investment and Hobbles Competition," *Edmonton Journal*, October 18, 2011, A4.

46. City of Edmonton, "Responses to Councillors' Questions," October 26, 2011, 3.

47. City of Edmonton, "Responses to Councillors' Questions," 5.

48. City of Edmonton, "Responses to Councillors' Questions," 2.

49. City of Edmonton, "Responses to Councillors' Questions," 2.

50. Cec Purves, "Report on the Downtown Arena," January 31, 2012.

51. Cec Purves, "Report on the Downtown Arena."

52. Bill Mah, "Construction Boss Backs Downtown Arena Campaign," *Edmonton Journal*, October 21, 2011, A1.

53. Mah, "Construction Boss."

54. Mah, "Construction Boss."

55. Dan Mason, "City Officials Look at the Bigger Picture—Beyond the Arena; Great Metropolises Build New Attractions to Complement Existing Ones," *Edmonton Journal*, October 25, 2011, A14.

56. Editorial, *Edmonton Journal*, "Say 'Yes' to a New Arena," October 25, 2011, A14.

57. Gary Lamphier, "New Arena Deal Bad for Taxpayers; But This Week's City Council Vote May Be a Done Deal," *Edmonton Journal*, October 25, 2011, E1.

58. Gordon Kent, "Downtown Arena Deal Might Land Today; Public Protest Mixes With Private-Sector Support of Controversial Project During Hearings," *Edmonton Journal*, October 26, 2011, A1.

59. Kent, "Downtown Arena."

60. John MacKinnon, "Battle Rages at City Hall; Public Lashes Out Over City Taking From Poor Citizens and Giving to the Richest," *Edmonton Journal*, October 26, 2011, B1.

61. Email from Bruce Saville to Linda Sloan, March 3, 2011.

62. Gordon Kent, "Game On for Downtown Arena; Oilers Could Relocate by 2015 Under Deal Touted as 'Watershed Moment,'" *Edmonton Journal*, October 27, 2011, A1.

63. Kent, "Game On."

64. Paula Simons, "Arena Land Deal Jumps to $75M; Cost of Complicated City Project with Katz Much Higher Than Expected," *Edmonton Journal*, November 1, 2011, A1.

65. It estimated that the operating income could be upwards of US$40 million, just behind the New York Rangers at US$41.4 million.

66. Jonathan Willis, "Forbes: 'Katz has Few Options,'" *Edmonton Journal*, December 1, 2011, http://edmontonjournal.com/sports/hockey/nhl/cult-of-hockey/forbes-katz-has-few-options.

13 THE ART OF THE DEAL?

1. Paula Simons, "We'll Never Know What Other Options We Might Have Had," *Edmonton Journal*, January 17, 2012, A5.

2. Cec Purves, "Arena Boosterism Won't Bolster Reckless Move by Council [Letter to the Editor]," *Edmonton Journal*, January 19, 2012, A24.

3. Including when Purves had been a prominent pro-business booster as Alderman and Mayor, supporting the construction of Northlands Coliseum and the efforts to secure an NHL hockey team for the city. See Chapter 2.

4. G.A. Phillips, "Purves Doesn't Understand [Letter to the Editor]," *Edmonton Journal*, February 1, 2012, A24.

5. Kevin Delaney and Rick Eckstein, *Public Dollars, Private Stadiums: Battles Over Building Sports Stadiums* (New Brunswick, NJ: Rutgers University Press, 2003), 48.

6. Delaney and Eckstein, *Public Dollars*, 48.

7. David Staples, "Very Bad Day for 'Grumpy Grandpas' in Edmonton Arena Debate," *Edmonton Journal*, May 17, 2012, http://edmontonjournal.com/sports/hockey/nhl/cult-of-hockey/bad-dady-for-edmontons-grumpy-grampas-in-arena-debate.

8. Staples, "Very Bad Day."

9. Personal Communication, Rick Daviss to Simon Farbrother, March 12, 2012.

10. Personal Communication, Simon Farbrother to Rick Daviss, July 11, 2012.

11. Gordon Kent, "Arena Still $35M Over Budget Report," *Edmonton Journal*, July 13, 2012, A1.

12. Kent, "Arena Still $35M Over."

13. City staff, at the time, were dispersed in five buildings. The city owned half of that office space and leased the other half (it rented 370,000 square feet downtown in the HSBC building, Scotia Place, CN Tower, City Centre West, and Churchill Manor).

14. Gordon Kent, "City Plans Office Tower Downtown; Building Could Become Biggest in Core, Realtor Speculates," *Edmonton Journal*, October 12, 2012, A3.

15. City of Edmonton, "Non-Contract: A Request for Proposal 'NFRP' No. 918593 for Lease of Downtown Office Accommodation, City of Edmonton," October 2012.

16. In its April 8, 2013 submission, for example, the developer Melcor noted that it was highly unlikely that an occupancy target of January 1, 2016 would be attainable for developers that had yet to complete building permit-ready drawings or to secure other development permits. For Melcor, the deadlines were both unreasonable and unachievable. We were unable to examine and compare the bids because of commercial sensitivity.

17. Interview, December 12, 2017.

18. Elise Stolte, "Arena 'Definitely Helped' Two Condo Projects," *Edmonton Journal*, September 20, 2012, A3.

19. Bill Mah, "Condo Project Rising Quickly," *Edmonton Journal*, September 21, 2012, D1.

20. Stolte, "Arena 'Definitely Helped.'"

21. *Edmonton Journal*, "On Arena, Let's See the Whole Ice," July 14, 2012, A22.

22. *Edmonton Journal*, "On Arena." The city of Montreal, of course, finished paying off its $1.6-billion debt for the 1976 Summer Olympic Games three decades later in 2006, and it continues to incur ongoing costs associated with the maintenance of the Olympic Stadium. See Konrad Yakabuski, "Summer Olympics: 40 years on, Quebeckers are Still Footing the Bill," August 8, 2016, https://www.theglobeandmail.com/opinion/summer-olympics-40-years-on-quebeckers-are-still-footing-the-bill/article31295801/. The facility doesn't generate much revenue, as Montreal lost the Expos and the Alouettes play in Molson Stadium.

23. Gordon Kent, "'Crap' Arena Wrong Idea, Mandel; Don't Sacrifice Quality for Short-Term Savings, Mayor Says," *Edmonton Journal*, July 18, 2012, A1.

24. Ken Barry, "Iconic New Arena Would Bolster Our Brand as Great Northern City," *Edmonton Journal*, August 28, 2012, A15.

25. Paula Simons, "Chamber Needs to Get in the Game; Business Community Not Showing Leadership on Downtown Arena," *Edmonton Journal*, September 8, 2012, A5.

26. Letter from John Karvellas to Simon Farbrother, September 11, 2012.

27. Katz and his fellow NHL owners were also trying to increase revenues through another set of arduous negotiations with the NHLPA over a new CBA before the 2012/13 hockey season. In order to control labour costs by dramatically reducing the players' share of hockey-related revenue from 57 percent to 46 percent, the NHL and its owners locked out the players in mid-September, further exposing the stark realities of the business of NHL hockey. After the cancellation of half an NHL season, a new 10-year CBA was reached in early January 2013 that included a 50–50 split of hockey-related revenue between the owners and the players. In other words, NHL owners had clawed back a substantial amount of hockey-related revenue from the players, and Katz himself now stood to make even more money. The fans were, of course, ignored in all of this, and so the lockout created an atmosphere of anger and resentment.

28. These payments had been accepted as part of the October 2011 framework worked out in New York. The Katz Group had dropped its demand for a non-compete clause with Northlands in exchange for the $2-million annual subsidy. The deal also allowed the organization to make annual lease payments instead of the up-front commitment of $100 million it had promised.

29. That the Katz Group was continuing to seek a lease extension casts more doubt on the claim that the current financing deal was unprofitable. The company wanted to ensure long-term economic stability and financial certainty by generating as high a profit margin as possible.

30. Elise Stolte, "Mayor Asks Katz to Clarify; Wants Oilers Owner to Appear at Council to Explain Position," *Edmonton Journal*, September 19, 2012, A1.

31. Stolte, "Mayor Asks Katz to Clarify."

32. John MacKinnon, "Katz 'It's Crunch Time'; Escalating Costs Could Kill Any Arena Deal, Oilers Owner says," *Edmonton Journal*, September 18, 2012, A1.

33. MacKinnon, "Katz 'It's Crunch Time.'"

34. David Staples, "'I'm Focused on Making This Deal Work'; Oilers Owner Reveals His Side of Deal to Finance New Arena," *Edmonton Journal*, September 18, 2012, A5.

35. Staples, "I'm Focused on Making This Deal."

36. Staples, MacKinnon, and Jones could have challenged Katz's interpretation and might have suggested that, even if the Oilers moved, one of the many struggling US franchises might be enticed by the strength of the Edmonton market. A relocated franchise might even pay more of its share for a new arena. Sensitive to the increasing level of opprobrium directed his way, Katz concluded his promotional interview by defending his investment in the team and his own personal role in the negotiations: "Nobody can question my good faith or my commitment." See "MacKinnon, "Katz 'It's Crunch Time.'"

37. MacKinnon, "Katz 'It's Crunch Time.'"

38. Interview, December 20, 2017.

39. Gary Lamphier, "Get Katz to Fill in Numbers; Transparency Is Key Ingredient," *Edmonton Journal*, October 2, 2012, C1.

40. The NHL had also just signed a new 10-year, $200-million television deal in the United States with NBC that would provide $6.6 million per team annually.

41. In 2011, Northlands generated $34.6 million in revenue from 46 concerts and 42 additional non-hockey events. This total could increase dramatically in a new facility.

42. Gordon Kent, "Council Cuts off Arena Talks; Mayor: 'It's Wrong to Hold Us for Ransom,'" *Edmonton Journal*, October 18, 2012, A1.

43. Interview, December 20, 2017.

44. Interview, December 21, 2017.

45. Could an alternative funding model have been developed to cover the cost of, say, a $330-million facility, roughly that of the multi-sport Air Canada Centre in Toronto? The ACC was built for $265 million in 1999; in 2012 dollars, the total would be just above $345 million. The city of Edmonton could certainly have implemented an equivalent ticket tax of $125 million, and, given the rate of downtown development, a CRL would have provided another mechanism to help pay off the arena, even if the Katz Group had decided not to proceed with its own development plans. Finally, the city of Edmonton could have followed the recommendations of the 2008 *City Shaping* report and dedicated the annual operating surplus from the new arena, as well as other sources of funding (parking, casino revenue, etc.), to help pay off its remaining debt and interest costs. Perhaps the main objection to considering this alternative model was that it meant the loss of the Katz Group's $100-million contribution to the new arena, but this contribution had already been "re-modelled" as an annual lease payment of $5.5 million.

   If it had wanted to construct a new arena on its own, the city could also have insisted that the Oilers pay more rent than $1 per year. Katz may never have agreed to these new terms, but any number of other NHL franchises might have envied such arrangements—and the profitability of the Edmonton market. Whether the NHL would have permitted them is another question. Still, the arena deal was never about producing a fiscally responsible agreement for the city of Edmonton. It had always been about the sustainability (i.e., profitability) of the Edmonton Oilers and the development of the downtown. Knowing that the downtown would continue to grow, thanks to so much other new construction, the most obvious response to the Katz Group's demands would have been to underline the current profitability of the franchise and the functionality of Rexall Place, and to invite the organization to build a new arena on its own.

46. K.C. Porteous, "'Cadillac' Arena Could be Scaled Back," *Edmonton Journal*, October 26, 2012, A23; figures in 2012 Canadian dollars.

47. David Ebner and Dawn Walton, "Billionaire Oilers Owner Katz Gave $430,000 to Alberta PCs," *The Globe and Mail*, October 24, 2012, https://www.theglobeandmail.com/news/politics/billionaire-oilers-owner-katz-gave-430000-to-alberta-pcs/article4647260/.

48. The Katz Group hedged its bets by also donating $7,500 to the opposition, the Wildrose Party. The controversy underlined the need for provincial electoral finance reform. Alberta's election-financing rules were among the weakest in the country. Unlike several other provinces, Alberta permitted corporate and union financing, and its contribution limit of $30,000 was considerably higher than the ceilings of most jurisdictions (which range from $1,100 to $15,000). Alberta also had no spending limits for election campaigns. Both the Katz Group and the government of Alberta were cleared by Elections Alberta in a subsequent investigation of the donations. The government of

Alberta has since banned campaign donations from corporations and unions, and has introduced election spending limits for parties.

49. Graham Thomson, "Katz's Donations Headache for Tories," *Edmonton Journal*, October 26, 2012, A1.

50. Jackie Larson, "Arena, Donations Flap; PCS Say They Rejected Requests from Katz, but Opposition Keeps up Pressure," *Edmonton Sun*, October 30, 2012, 7.

51. Gordon Kent and David Staples, "'One Step Forward' for Arena?; Katz Group Asks to Appear Before Council in Public Session," *Edmonton Journal*, December 11, 2012, A1.

52. Paula Simons, "Miracle Worker Required to Do Deal; Mediator Faces Uphill Battle Politically," *Edmonton Journal*, December 13, 2012, A5.

53. Simons, "Miracle Worker Required."

54. Rick McConnell, John MacKinnon, and Gary Lamphier, "Daryl Katz," *Edmonton Journal*, December 15, 2012, E1.

55. Paula Simons, "A Deal Hatched in Secret? Not so Fast...; Bettman Can't Do Deal without Council, Public," *Edmonton Journal*, January 22, 2013, A5.

56. David Staples, "Arena Deal Close, City Councillor Predicts; Council Will Pay Up to Build It Right, but Not Cheap or Ugly," *Edmonton Journal*, January 23, 2012, A5.

57. Gordon Kent, "A Deal Is Done; Construction Set to Begin Next Year As Arena Cost Grows by $30 Million," *Edmonton Journal*, January 24, 2013, A1.

58. Kent, "A Deal is Done."

59. Paula Simons, "Council's Arena Plot Line Now Waiting for No Dough; Banking of Iffy Dollars is Theatre of the Fiscally Absurd," *Edmonton Journal*, April 11, 2013, A5.

60. Interview, November 15, 2017.

61. Interview, December 21, 2017.

62. Gordon Kent, "Downtown Arena Faces Crucial Vote; Councillors Feeling the Heat from Pro-Arena Email Campaign," *Edmonton Journal*, May 8, 2013, A1.

63. Interview, November 15, 2017.

64. Don Iveson, "Final Arena Vote Rationale," May 15, 2013, https://doniveson.ca/2013/05/15/final-arena-vote-rationale/#more-1804.

65. Interview, December 20, 2017.

14 CONCLUSION

1. Bruce Kidd, "The Men's Cultural Centre," in *Sport, Men, and the Gender Order: Critical Feminist Perspectives*, eds. Michael A. Messner and Donald F. Sabo (Champaign, Illinois: Human Kinetics Books), 32.

2. Certainly, Rogers Place is popular among both women and men, and the new arena has been an improvement in many ways over the Coliseum. There's no shortage of passionate female Oilers fans in Edmonton. That said, during the 2017 playoffs, when it was estimated that 80 percent of the crowd at Rogers Place was male, a number of women's bathrooms were converted into men's facilities because of long lines, at least for fans sitting in the cheaper upper concourse section. This led to a groundswell of criticism about the poor design of Rogers Place. Following this "controversy," it was female Oilers fans who had to wait to use the washrooms. But the issue is not just about whether the facility should have more washrooms for women, but also for whom the whole thing was built.

3. Elise Stolte, "Council Wrestles with Sobering Funding Gap for Infrastructure Needs," *Edmonton Journal*, April 27, 2018, http://edmontonjournal.com/news/local-news/council-wrestles-with-sobering-funding-gap-for-infrastructure-needs.

4. Edmonton has three such mechanisms in place: the first is the Capital City Downtown CRL, which includes the new arena; the other two are in The Quarters Downtown and Belvedere.

5. City of Edmonton, 2015, Community Revitalization Levy—Forecasts (Attachment 10).

6. City of Edmonton, 2018, Capital City Downtown CRL Forecast (Attachment 4).

7. City of Edmonton, 2015, Community Revitalization Levy—Forecasts (Attachment 10).

8. City of Edmonton, 2018, Capital City Downtown CRL Forecast (Attachment 4).

9. City of Edmonton, 2015, Community Revitalization Levy—Forecasts (Attachment 10).

10. City of Edmonton, 2018, Capital City Downtown CRL Forecast (Attachment 4).

11. The impression given to the public was that the Edmonton Office Tower Project was a public project. In fact, it wasn't. The city did not own it outright, nor did it plan to. Administration proposed to council that the land be bought by the city on the Katz Group's behalf, even though the project was still up for tender, and that the city hold it tax free until it was subdivided. The city knew that its operations would not fully occupy the tower and that, ultimately, it would lease only a few floors. The lease that subsequently confirmed this arrangement was approved by a new city council formed after the 2013 civic election. The information provided by administration to the 2010–2013 city council provided some details, but never fully disclosed what the full implications and significant costs would be for the city.

12. Less than a year earlier, in exchange for $5 million from the Katz Group, council had voted, following an in-camera meeting, to drop its option to purchase space in the Edmonton Tower if the building was ever sold.

13. Rachelle Younglai, "Record Heights, Record Prices: Skyscraper for Sale in Edmonton's New Downtown," *Edmonton Journal*, February 12, 2018.

14. Details of the agreement can be found at https://www.edmonton.ca/attractions_events/rogers_place/the-agreement.aspx.

15. It should be noted that the mayor was well connected to key players in the government of Alberta in this period. After announcing that he would not seek a fourth term in 2013, Stephen Mandel was appointed Minister of Health by Premier Ed Stelmach in 2014, despite not holding a seat in the Legislative Assembly of Alberta.

16. Rick Gruneau and David Whitson, *Hockey Night in Canada: Sport, Identities and Cultural Politics* (Toronto: Garamond Press, 1993), 235.

17. John Hannigan, *Fantasy City: Pleasure and Profit in the Postmodern Metropolis* (New York: Routledge, 1995).

18. Jeremy Simes, "Building May be Vacated as Ice District Buys MacDonald Lofts," *Metro News Edmonton*, January 23, 2017, 5.

19. Graham Hicks, "Rogers Place Helping Edmonton Take Back the Night," *HicksBiz Blog*, October 22, 2016, https://www.hicksbiz.com/Home/tabid/56/entryid/548/Default.aspx.

20. Personal communication, September 15, 2017.

21. Interview, September 20, 2017.

22. Interview, October 19, 2016.

23. Interview, January 26, 2018.

24. Jim Silver, *Thin Ice: Money, Politics, and the Demise of an NHL Franchise* (Halifax: Fernwood Press, 1996), 174.

25. Interview, August 9, 2016.

26. *The Globe and Mail* did have writer Marty Klinkenberg, who favoured the new arena development, in Edmonton. He was also the author of *The McDavid Effect: Connor McDavid and the New Hope for Hockey* (Toronto: Simon & Schuster, 2016), which covered the rookie season of the Edmonton Oilers' star player, Connor McDavid—another young phenom from Ontario, just like Wayne Gretzky.

27. Karl Marx, "The Eighteenth Brumaire of Louis Bonaparte" (excerpts), in *Karl Marx: Selected Writings*, ed. L. Simon (Indianapolis: Hackett Publishing, 1994), 187–208.

28. Personal communication, September 15, 2017.

29. Interview, December 6, 2017.

30. Interview, December 6, 2015.

31. Interview, November 21, 2017.

32. Dean Mummery responded that I was not an employee in the private sector, but a tenured professor protected by academic freedom (and freedom of speech for that matter)—a level of protection not afforded to private citizens, nor indeed to scholars in every instance. Personal communication, Kerry Mummery to Jay Scherer, March 15, 2015.

33. Interview, December 6, 2015.

34. Personal communication, September 15, 2017.

35. City of Edmonton, Downtown CRL Update, November 27, 2018.

36. Elise Stolte, "Katz Group Seeks Millions of Dollars from City for Ice District Plaza," *Edmonton Journal*, June 28, 2018, http://edmontonjournal.com/business/commercial-real-estate/katz-group-seeks-millions-of-dollars-from-city-for-ice-district-plaza?utm_campaign=Echobox&utm_medium=Social&utm_source=Twitter#Echobox=1530222766.

37. Tim Querengesser, "The Station the City Doesn't Want You to Use," *Avenue Magazine Edmonton*, July 31, 2017, http://www.avenueedmonton.com/City-Life/The-Station-the-City-Doesnt-Want-You-To-Use/.

38. As per the terms of the arena agreement, the city is entitled to have free access to Rogers Place on 28 days per year for community use. However, between 2016 and 2018, the city only booked the arena for 21 days in total.

39. Paige Parsons, "'Transit Villages': Old Northlands Land Plan Would Add LRT Station, See Mixed-Use Development," *Edmonton Journal*, April 19, 2019, https://edmontonjournal.com/news/local-news/old-northlands-land-plan-would-add-lrt-station-see-mixed-use-development.

40. Howard Shubert, *Architecture on Ice: A History of the Hockey Arena* (Montreal/Kingston: McGill-Queen's University Press, 2016), 189.

41. While the city has uninterrupted access to 100 reserved parking stalls in the Edmonton Tower, it can only access the 260 unreserved parking stalls between 7:00 AM and 5:30 PM on weekdays, excluding statutory holidays.

42. Shubert, *Architecture on Ice*, 221.

43. Dave Zirin, "Sports Tax Scams Laid the Groundwork for Amazon Bidding Madness," *The Nation*, November 28, 2017, https://www.thenation.com/article/sports-tax-scams-laid-groundwork-for-amazon-bidding-madness/.

44. Interview, August 15, 2017.

EPILOGUE

1. The Saddledome was owned by the city of Calgary and originally leased to the non-profit Saddledome Foundation, which functions much like Northlands did in Edmonton. The Flames took over management of arena operations in 1996.

2. "Flames Exec Brian Burke Makes Pitch for New Arena," *CBC News*, June 6, 2014, https://www.cbc.ca/amp/1.2666469; Doug Vaessen and Tamara Elliott, "Brian Burke Says Saddledome is 'Embarrassing,' Wants New Arena," *Global News*, June 5, 2014, https://globalnews.ca/news/1376991/brian-burke-says-saddledome-is-embarrassing-wants-new-arena/. Burke once explained his approach to problems thusly: "make the first meeting as short and unpleasant as possible. Sometimes it's better to just punch the guy in the face" (quoted in Katie Baker, "How to Sell a Stadium in Six Easy Steps: Calgary Gets the High Pressure Pitch," in *Grantland*, September 2, 2015, http://grantland.com/the-triangle/how-to-sell-a-stadium-in-six-easy-steps-calgary-gets-the-high-pressure-pitch/.

3. *ESPN*, "2013–2014 NHL Attendance—National Hockey League," http://proxy.espn.com/nhl/attendance?year=2014&sort=allAvg&order=false. Calgary had estimated revenues of US$122 million, according to *Forbes*; among Canadian franchises, though, the Flames' estimated operating income of US$22.3 million was lower than all teams but the Winnipeg Jets and Ottawa Senators. See https://www.forbes.com/sites/mikeozanian/2014/11/25/the-most-valuable-teams-in-the-nhl/#2d49194d3ff5.

4. Quoted in "Brian Burke Says Calgary Needs a New Arena," *660 City News*, June 5, 2014, https://www.660citynews.com/2014/06/05/brian-burke-says-calgary-needs-a-new-arena/.

5. See, for example, Chuck Reasons, ed., *Stampede City: Power and Politics in the West* (Toronto: Between the Lines, 1984).

6. For more detail, see David Mills, "The Battle of Alberta: Entrepreneurs and the Business of Hockey in Edmonton and Calgary," *Alberta* 2 (1990): 1–25.

7. Quoted in the Calgary Flames magazine provided during an interview with Clare Rhyasen, then vice president of business and finance for the Flames, on February 21, 1989.

8. *The Globe and Mail*, January 7, 1994.

9. Quoted in D'Arcy Jenish, *The NHL: A Centennial History: 100 Years of On-Ice Action and Boardroom Battles* (Toronto: Doubleday Canada, 2013), Kindle edition, Ch. 16, loc. 6131.

10. Scott Cruickshank, "'This is a Building That Needs to Be Replaced'—Bettman on the Antiquated Saddledome," *Calgary Herald*, January 29, 2015, https://calgaryherald.com/sports/hockey/this-is-a-building-that-needs-to-be-replaced-bettman-on-the-antiquated-saddledome.

11. "Mayor Nenshi's Statement on the Flames Arena Project," *Calgary Herald*, August 18, 2015, https://calgaryherald.com/news/local-news/mayor-nenshis-statement-on-the-flames-arena-project.

12. Annalise Klingbeil, "Flames Reveal Details of $890M Downtown Arena-stadium Plan," *Calgary Herald,* August 19, 2015, http://www.edmontonjournal.com/sports/flames+reveal+details+890m+downtown+arena+stadium+plan/11299094/story.html.

13. Klingbeil, "Flames Reveal Details."

14. Deborah Yedlin, "Proposal Integral to the City's Future," *Calgary Herald*, August 19, 2015; cited in Tom Sindlinger, "Stadium Project Will Keep Calgary Vibrant," *Sindlinger,* blog, September 7, 2015, http://sindlinger.ca/Blog2015/?p=186. *Edmonton Journal* columnist Paula Simons also wrote a piece entitled, "CalgaryNEXT looks like Edmonton BEEN THERE DONE THAT," August 20, 2015, http://www.edmontonjournal.com/simons+calgarynext+looks+like+edmonton+been+there+done+that/11302424/story.html.

15. Justin Giovannetti, "An 'Ambitious' Proposal for Sports Complex in Calgary," *The Globe and Mail*, August 21, 2015, https://www.theglobeandmail.com/news/alberta/an-ambitious-proposal-for-sports-complex-in-calgary/article26060669/.

16. "National Post View: The Flames' Rotten Idea," *National Post*, August 25, 2015, https://nationalpost.com/opinion/national-post-view-the-flames-rotten-idea.

17. Scott Stinson, "Calgary Flames Proposed Arena Could Be Another Example of Why Public Funding Doesn't Equal Public Benefit," *National Post*, August 25, 2015, https://nationalpost.com/sports/hockey/nhl/calgary-flames-proposed-arena-could-be-another-example-of-why-public-funding-doesnt-equal-public-benefit.

18. Kent Wilson, "How to Think Critically about CalgaryNEXT," *FlamesNation.ca*, blog, August 24, 2015, https://flamesnation.ca/2015/08/24/how-to-think-critically-about-calgarynext/.

19. Kent Wilson, "How to Think Critically." See also "The CBA," *Why Downtown?*, September 29, 2010, for more details on the CBA and the issue of hockey-related revenue, https://whydowntown.wordpress.com/?s=CBA&submit=Search.

20. Taylor Lambert, "New Calgary Arena Proposal Nothing Short of Brazen," *National Post*, August 19, 2015. The chairman of the Flames is Murray Edwards, who chairs a merchant banking firm, Edco Financial Holdings, Canadian Natural Resources, and Ensign Energy Services. Clayton Riddell is chairman of Paramount Resources, Perpetual Energy, and Trilogy Energy. The ownership group also included Al Markin, the former chair of Canadian Natural Resources, Alvin G. Libin, who has interests in real estate, oil and gas, and financial services, and Jeff McCaig, the chairman and CEO of Trimac Transportation.

21. Justin Giovannetti, "An 'Ambitious' Proposal."

22. Trevor Howell, "Flames' $890-million CalgaryNEXT Proposal 'Not Even Half-baked,' Says Nenshi," *Calgary Herald,* November 10, 2015, https://calgaryherald.com/news/local-news/flames-890-million-calgarynext-proposal-a-half-baked-proposal-says-nenshi.

23. Eric Duhatschek, "Gary Bettman Pitches Tough Sell to Calgary for New Arena Development," *The Globe and Mail*, January 11, 2016, https://www.theglobeandmail.com/sports/hockey/gary-bettman-pitches-tough-sell-to-calgary-for-new-arena-development/article28123801/; emphasis added. While the investment is not cost-justified for the Flames ownership, it somehow is for the taxpayers of Calgary, even though, as we have noted, arenas are not good investments because they are costly to build and maintain

and remain dark on many nights of the year. That's why owners prefer that cities own them.

24. Eric Duhatschek, "Calgary Mayor Fires Back at Bettman's Support for Arena Proposal," *The Globe and Mail,* January 12, 2016, https://www.theglobeandmail.com/sports/hockey/calgary-mayor-fires-back-at-bettmans-back-of-the-napkin-arena-proposal/article28139449/.

25. Quoted in Roy MacGregor, "Calgary Mayor Nenshi Holds the Line On Arena Project," *The Globe and Mail,* January 15, 2016, https://www.theglobeandmail.com/news/national/calgarynext-mayor-nenshi-holds-the-line-on-arena-project/article28230993/.

26. *National Post,* January 15, 2016, accessed through https://www.pressreader.com/.

27. Annelise Klingbeil, "CalgaryNEXT Project on 'Pause', Focus Turns to Plan B," *Calgary Herald,* December 22, 2016, https://calgaryherald.com/news/local-news/calgarynext-project-on-pause-says-ken-king.

28. The Burke quotation comes from "Flames Could Leave Calgary Without New Hockey Arena, Team's Brian Burke Warns," *CBC Calgary,* June 7, 2017, https://www.cbc.ca/news/canada/calgary/flames-president-brian-burke-calgary-next-1.4150420.

29. Annelise Klingbeil, "CalgaryNEXT Project."

30. Melissa Gilligan, "Flames Ownership Examining 'Plan B' for CalgaryNEXT," *Global News Calgary,* June 14, 2016, https://globalnews.ca/news/2760411/flames-ownership-examining-plan-b-for-calgarynext/.

31. Annelise Klingbeil, "'CalgaryNEXT, the West Village Project, is Dead,' Says Mayor Nenshi," *Calgary Herald,* updated April 3, 2017, https://calgaryherald.com/news/local-news/calgarynext-the-west-village-project-is-dead-says-mayor-nenshi.

32. *CBC Calgary,* April 24, 2017.

33. The Burke quote and Nenshi's response are in "Flames Could Leave Calgary Without New Hockey Arena, Team's Brian Burke Warns," *CBC Calgary,* June 7, 2017, https://www.cbc.ca/news/canada/calgary/flames-president-brian-burke-calgary-next-1.4150420. Nenshi still saw no benefit in the city funding the arena fully: "Five out of the seven teams in Canada have privately owned rinks, only Edmonton and Calgary are publicly owned, and the Edmonton deal may have been right for Edmonton, where they desperately needed revitalization and construction in their downtown core, that is not the case in Calgary."

34. Carrie Tait and Allan Maki, "Calgary Flames Owner Eyes More Than Just a New Arena," *The Globe and Mail,* October 6, 2017, https://www.theglobeandmail.com/news/alberta/calgary-flames-owner-eyes-more-than-just-a-new-arena/article36521316/. The toxic nature of a meeting between the CSEC and the city is described in Carrie Tait and Allan Maki, "Politics, Personality and Passion Shape Battle Over Arena," *The Globe and Mail,* October 14, 2017, http://v1.theglobeandmail.com/servlet/GIS.Servlets.HTMLTemplate?current_row=52&tf=tgam/columnists/FullColumn.html&cf=tgam/columnists/FullColumn.cfg&configFileLoc=tgam/config&date=&dateOffset=&hub=allan Maki&title=Allan_Maki&cache_key=allanMaki&start_row=52&num_rows=1.

35. Carrie Tait and Allan Maki, "Calgary Flames Go On a Power Play Against City with Arena Proposal," *The Globe and Mail,* September 14, 2017, https://www.theglobeandmail.com/sports/hockey/calgary-flames-go-on-a-power-play-against-city-with-arena-proposal/article36255345/. It should be pointed out that the Flames were sustainable

in the Saddledome. The franchise made money—ownership simply wanted more. The team was 10th in attendance and filled to 97 percent capacity; the franchise value had increased to US$420 million, according to *Forbes*; it received TV rights money and had collected 10 expansion fees, including $16 million for Las Vegas. See Scott Stinson, "In a League Short on Sure Things, Notion the Calgary Flames Might Try to Move is Ludicrous,' *National Post,* September 18, 2017, https://nationalpost.com/sports/hockey/nhl/in-a-league-short-on-sure-things-notion-the-calgary-flames-might-try-to-move-is-ludicrous. As for the benefits to Calgary, Moshe Lander, professor of sport economics at Montreal's Concordia University, said in the *Edmonton Sun* that, "the war of words looks familiar...The data doesn't seem to show a new arena, by itself, will rejuvenate downtown or whatever particular region you place it. If there's rejuvenation already underway, if there's development already underway, then for sure an arena can help, but it just doesn't do it by itself. A new Saddledome is not going to accelerate what's already happening [in Calgary's East Village]. Not when the Saddledome, the BMO Centre and the Stampede grounds are already there." See Brian Passifiume, "'We Had That Threat at Least 3 Times': Flames Arena Battle Déjà Vu for Edmonton Councillors," *Calgary Herald,* September 17, 2017, https://calgaryherald.com/news/local-news/we-had-that-threat-i-think-at-least-3-times-flames-arena-battle-deja-vu-for-edmonton-councillors.

36. Eric Francis, "Let's Find Solution to Avoid Arena Issue that Cost Other NHL Centres," *Calgary Herald*, September 23, 2017, https://calgaryherald.com/sports/hockey/nhl/calgary-flames/city-flames-must-work-now-to-avoid-arena-issues-that-have-cost-other-nhl-centres. See also Allan Maki and Carrie Tait, "Flames, Calgary at Odds Over Arena Cost," *The Globe and Mail*, September 22, 2017, for details on the CRL, https://beta.theglobeandmail.com/sports/hockey/calgary-flames-proposal-for-new-arena/article36339341/. The authors were told in interviews with Simon Farbrother, former Edmonton city manager (December 21, 2017), and Rick Daviss of the Real Estate Branch of Financial and Corporate Services for the city of Edmonton (December 12, 2017), that Calgary would probably not get a CRL for its project because the Victoria Park area is already covered by a previous CRL.

37. Eric Francis, "Let's Find Solution." Dr. Dan Mason, professor of sport management at the University of Alberta, said that "The research shows that there actually are substantial intangible benefits" to professional sports, and cited as an example the smiles on Edmonton faces during the Oilers' playoff run in the spring of 2017. "[B]ecause in North America we work in a closed market system where the leagues artificially reduce the number of franchises and then they use cities against one another," he said, "typically the public subsidy is greater than what the intangible benefits are...[Research finds that] facilities built for professional sports teams may increase property values in nearby neighbourhoods, therefore boosting tax revenue for the city, but suggestions that job creation and tourism also benefit are generally not true." See "Economists See Little Payoff for Cities that Subsidize Pro Sports Facilities," *CBC News*, September 14, 2017. Mason, a paid consultant on the Edmonton arena project, also said, just before the Calgary municipal election: "In Edmonton, the rationale for using public money was always about relocating economic activity from one part of the city to another, to make the downtown more vibrant. In Calgary, there

isn't the same incentive, as Calgary's downtown doesn't need the same kind of boost...
This makes it much more difficult to justify the use of public funds in Calgary"; quoted
in Allan Maki and Carrie Tait, "Professor Doubts Calgary's Need to Publicly Fund New
Flames Arena," *The Globe and Mail*, October 6, 2017, https://www.theglobeandmail.
com/news/alberta/professor-doubts-calgarys-need-to-publicly-fund-new-flames-arena/
article36521301/.

38. Allan Maki and Carrie Tait, "Flames No Longer Interested in Pursuing New Calgary
     Arena," *The Globe and Mail*, September 13, 2017, https://www.theglobeandmail.
     com/sports/hockey/flames-no-longer-interested-in-pursuing-new-calgary-arena/
     article36241562/.

39. Eric Francis, "Bettman Blames Nenshi for 'No Prospect' of Getting New Flames Arena,"
     Calgary Herald, September 28, 2017, https://calgaryherald.com/sports/hockey/nhl/
     calgary-flames/bettman-blames-nenshi-for-no-prospect-of-getting-new-flames-arena.
     It's interesting that Bettman granted Francis access during this controversy. While the
     value of the Flames franchise was just 19th among all NHL teams, *Forbes* estimated it at
     US$430 million, an increase of 5 percent over 2016, despite not having a new arena.

40. Eric Francis, "Bettman Blames Nenshi." See also the *The Globe and Mail* editorial of
     September 13, 2017, "No You Really Don't Have to Subsidize an NHL Team,"
     https://www.theglobeandmail.com/opinion/editorials/globe-editorial-no-you-really-
     dont-have-to-subsidize-an-nhl-team/article36251570/.

41. "Calgary Flames CEO Says City's Arena Proposal Would Leave Team Footing the Whole
     Bill," *CBC Calgary,* September 22, 2017, https://www.cbc.ca/news/canada/calgary/
     calgary-city-council-flames-negotiations-deal-1.4291316.

42. Quoted in Howard Shubert, *Architecture on Ice: A History of the Hockey Arena (*Montreal:
     McGill-Queen's University Press, 2016), 189. The first quotation is from Michael Lischer
     of HOK Sports; the second from Rod Robbie, the architect of SkyDome, now Rogers
     Centre.

43. "'We're Just Not That Pathetic as a City': Political Panel Doubts NHL Arena Tactics Will
     Work in Calgary," *CBC Calgary,* September 29, 2017, https://www.cbc.ca/news/canada/
     calgary/calgary-political-panel-flames-nhl-bettman-arena-1.4313740.

44. "Gary Bettman Drops Gloves, Enters Calgary Election," *The Globe and Mail,* September
     28, 2017, https://www.theglobeandmail.com/opinion/editorials/globe-editorial-gary-
     bettman-drops-gloves-enters-calgary-election/article36428932/.

45. Neil deMause, on the fieldofschemes.com website, had earlier pointed out that,
     "The number of mayors who've been voted out of office for standing up to sports
     team subsidy demands remains zero"; quoted in *The Globe and Mail* editorial of
     September 13, 2017, "No You Really Don't Have to Subsidize an NHL Team," https://
     www.theglobeandmail.com/opinion/editorials/globe-editorial-no-you-really-dont-
     have-to-subsidize-an-nhl-team/article36251570/. Nenshi's victory prompted a bitter
     tweet from Sean Kelso, the Flames' director of communications and media relations:
     "I can't believe it YYC. Having @Nenshi as mayor is worse than @realDonaldTrump
     being president." See Jen Gerson, "Nenshi's Re-election is a Win for Every City
     Blackmailed by a Sports Team," in *National Post,* October 17, 2017, https://nationalpost.
     com/opinion/jen-gerson-neshis-re-election-a-win-for-every-city-blackmailed-by-
     a-sports-team. Mount Royal University political scientist Lori Williams believed

that the arena debate ignored the real issue, which was the tax loss to Calgary: "Through the whole campaign, nobody addressed the real elephant in the room—the 50 percent loss in property tax revenue from companies in the recession-ridden downtown towers." See Don Braid, "Nenshi Prevails, But There's Work to be Done," *Calgary Herald*, October 17, 2017, https://calgaryherald.com/opinion/columnists/braid-two-waves-of-supporters-crash-mid-ocean-but-do-nenshis-have-life-jackets.

46. *The Globe and Mail*, October 19, 2017. Canada's other national newspaper, the *National Post*, which includes the *Calgary Herald* and *Calgary Sun* in its chain, carried Jen Gerson's column which concluded that Nenshi's victory was "a win for every city blackmailed by a sports team." See Jen Gerson, "Nenshi's Re-election is a Win for Every City Blackmailed by a Sports Team," *National Post*, October 17, 2017, https://nationalpost.com/opinion/jen-gerson-neshis-re-election-a-win-for-every-city-blackmailed-by-a-sports-team.

47. Melissa Gilligan, "Naheed Nenshi Turns Focus to Calgary's Economic Recovery After 2017 Election Win," *Global News Calgary*, October 17, 2017, https://globalnews.ca/news/3807794/naheed-nenshi-turns-focus-to-calgarys-economic-recovery-after-2017-election-win/.

48. Chris Johnston, "Gary Bettman Turns up Heat on Ottawa, Calgary to Get Arenas Built," *Sportsnet*, November 17, 2017, http://www.sportsnet.ca/hockey/nhl/gary-bettman-turns-heat-ottawa-calgary-get-arenas-built/.

49. Eric Francis, "150 Million More Reasons for Flames Owners to Sell," *Calgary Sun*, December 12, 2017, https://calgarysun.com/sports/hockey/nhl/calgary-flames/francis-150-million-more-reasons-for-flames-owners-to-sell. Kent Wilson, in "Flames Arena Saga: Desperately Seeking Leverage by Invoking Houston," effectively demolished Francis' screed and the threat of Calgary relocating. See the December 17, 2017 issue of *The Athletic*, https://theathletic.com/182400/2017/12/12/flames-arena-saga-desperately-seeking-leverage-by-invoking-houston/.

50. *The Globe and Mail*, October 13, 2018. See also Justin Giovannetti, "Province of Alberta Leaves Calgary, Ottawa with 2026 Olympics Tab," *The Globe and Mail*, October 13, 2017, https://www.theglobeandmail.com/canada/article-province-of-alberta-leaves-calgary-ottawa-with-2026-olympics-tab/.

51. *Calgary Herald*, November 16, 2018. See also Giovannetti, "Province of Alberta."

52. *The Globe and Mail*, October 13, 2018. See also Justin Giovannetti, "Province of Alberta." An analysis by University of Calgary economics professor Trevor Tombe concluded that the economic benefits of a mega-event like the Olympics are not as great as the boosters suggest; see Carrie Tait, "Hosting Olympics in Calgary Could Threaten Canadian Economy, Report Says," *The Globe and Mail*, November 17, 2017, https://www.theglobeandmail.com/news/alberta/hosting-olympics-in-calgary-could-threaten-canadian-economy-report-says/article37023435/. See also Jen Gerson, "On Calgary's Olympic Bid, Economists Say Run Away—Fast," *National Post*, November 19, 2017, https://nationalpost.com/news/canada/jen-gerson-on-calgarys-olympic-bid-economists-say-run-away-fast.

53. Calgary Municipal Land Corporation (CMLC), "Rivers District Master Plan," 2018, http://www.calgarymlc.ca/riversdistrictmasterplan#rivers-district-intro.

54. Meghan Potkins, "Arena Talks Back on Track? Councillor Moves to Revive Negotiations With the Flames," *Calgary Herald*, April 29, 2018, https://calgaryherald.com/news/local-news/councillor-hopes-to-resurrect-talks-with-flames-for-new-arena.

55. Rick Bell, "NHL Arena Talk, City Wants Flames Back to the Table," *Calgary Sun*, April 25, 2018, https://calgarysun.com/opinion/columnists/bell-nhl-arena-talks-city-wants-flames-back-to-the-table.

56. Scott Dippel, "Calgary Flames Ask for Media Blackout as Caveat for Resuming Arena Talks with City," CBC *Calgary News*, June 19, 2018, https://www.cbc.ca/news/canada/calgary/calgary-city-council-arena-flames-1.4713493.

57. "Calgary City Council Invites Flames Back to Table to Talk New Arena," *Canadian Press*, October 9, 2018, https://www.sportsnet.ca/hockey/nhl/calgary-city-council-invites-flames-back-table-talk-new-arena/.

58. Justin Giovannetti and James Keller, "Calgary Voters Reject City's Pursuit of 2026 Olympic Bid," *The Globe and Mail*, November 14, 2018, https://www.theglobeandmail.com/canada/alberta/article-calgary-voters-reject-citys-pursuit-of-2026-winter-olympics/.

59. Eric Francis, "Calgary's 'No' Vote a Squandered Opportunity for a City in Need," November 14, 2018, https://www.sportsnet.ca/olympics/calgarys-no-vote-squandered-opportunity-city-need/.

60. Donna Spencer, "Calgary City Council to Once Again Discuss Getting a New Home for Flames," *The Globe and Mail*, January 25, 2019, https://www.theglobeandmail.com/sports/hockey/article-calgary-city-council-to-once-again-discuss-getting-a-new-home-for/.

61. Meghan Potkins, "Council Approves More Than $1.5B in Major Capital Projects, Including An Arena," *Calgary Herald*, updated March 7, 2019, https://calgaryherald.com/news/local-news/council-approves-more-than-1-5b-for-major-capital-projects-including-arena. It is interesting to note that Mark Rosentraub, professor of sport management and policy, and Simon Farbrother, former Edmonton city manager, were both involved in the Calgary process as paid consultants because of their familiarity with the deal for Rogers Place in Edmonton. See Meghan Potkins, "'We Were Going to Make Mistakes'; Council Vote Hints at Fault Lines in Arena Negotiations," *Calgary Herald*, March 1, 2019, https://calgaryherald.com/news/local-news/we-were-going-to-make-mistakes-council-vote-hints-at-fault-lines-on-arena-negotiations. Kent Wilson raised important concerns about the arena deal in his article "Four Questions That Need Viable Answers Before Calgary Moves Ahead On a New Arena Deal," *The Athletic*, March 11, 2019, https://calgaryherald.com/news/local-news/we-were-going-to-make-mistakes-council-vote-hints-at-fault-lines-on-arena-negotiations.

62. Sarah Rieger, "City of Calgary, Flames Agree to 50–50 Split on Proposed $550M Deal for New Arena," CBC *News*, July 22, 2019, https://www.cbc.ca/news/canada/calgary/calgary-proposed-arena-deal-1.5220867?fbclid=IwAR0_srgf_hTW6n92hz911WddPP5YsRfHDH-1AHhcjycjvVdsajKGlvOhkMo. See also Megan Potkins, "Calgarians Have Six Days to Weigh In on $550-Million Arena Deal," *Calgary Herald*, July 22, 2019, https://calgaryherald.com/news/local-news/council-could-vote-on-arena-deal-as-early-as-next-week.

63. Rieger, "City of Calgary, Flames Agree to 50–50 Split"; Potkins, "Calgarians Have Six Days to Weigh In."

64. Rieger, "City of Calgary, Flames Agree to 50–50 Split"; Potkins, "Calgarians Have Six Days to Weigh In."

65. Potkins, "Calgarians Have Six Days to Weigh In."

66. Rieger, "City of Calgary, Flames Agree to 50–50 Split."

67. Rieger, "City of Calgary, Flames Agree to 50–50 Split."

68. Megan Potkins, "'Public Money is Being Used for Public Good': Council Votes to Spend $275 Million on New Flames Arena," *Calgary Herald*, updated July 31, 2019, https://calgaryherald.com/news/local-news/live-council-could-decide-fate-of-arena-deal-today.

69. Don Braid, "Council Finds a Backbone, City Gets an Arena," *Calgary Herald*, updated July 31, 2019, https://calgaryherald.com/opinion/columnists/braid-council-finds-a-backbone-city-gets-an-arena.

70. Scott Cruickshank, "Amid Controversy, Calgary—Finally—Gets Approval for its New Rink," *The Athletic*, July 31, 2019, https://theathletic.com/1107552/2019/07/31/amid-controversy-calgary-finally-gets-approval-for-its-new-rink/.

71. Jeff Davison, "The Time is Now for the Event Centre," *Calgary Herald*, July 29, 2019, https://calgaryherald.com/opinion/columnists/davison-the-time-is-now-for-the-event-centre. See also, from the Calgary Chamber of Commerce, "Opinion: Investment in Event Centre is an Investment in the Future," in *Calgary Herald*, July 26, 2019, https://calgaryherald.com/opinion/columnists/opinion-investment-in-event-centre-is-an-investment-in-the-future. And an op-ed from several prominent Calgarians, "Opinion: Calgary Needs New Arena to Reinvigorate the Economy and its Spirit," in *Calgary Herald*, July 30, 2019, https://calgaryherald.com/opinion/columnists/opinion-calgary-needs-new-arena-to-reinvigorate-the-economy-and-its-spirit.

72. Robson Fletcher, "Why Calgary 'Will Not be Making Money' From the Arena Deal—But That's Not the Only Consideration," *CBC News*, July 23, 2019, https://www.cbc.ca/news/canada/calgary/calgary-arena-deal-financial-loss-gain-intangible-benefits-1.5221881; Sammy Hudes, "'A Lot of Asterisks': Benefits for City in Arena Deal Not What They Seem, Economists Say," *Calgary Herald*, July 23, 2019, https://calgaryherald.com/news/local-news/a-lot-of-asterisks-benefits-for-city-in-arena-deal-not-what-they-seem-economists-say. See also Moshe Lander's comments in Hudes' piece about the benefits of the deal; it is largely the cost of keeping the Flames in Calgary. For more, see Justin Giovannetti, "Calgary Council to Vote on Flames Arena," *The Globe and Mail*, July 29, 2019, https://www.theglobeandmail.com/canada/alberta/article-calgary-council-to-vote-on-flames-arena/; Duane Bratt, "Calgary's New Arena Deal Was Driven by Politics, Not Economics," *The Globe and Mail*, July 31, 2019, https://www.theglobeandmail.com/opinion/article-calgarys-new-arena-deal-was-driven-by-politics-not-economics/.

73. Cruickshank, "Amid Controversy, Calgary—Finally—Gets Approval."

74. Donna Spencer, "Calgary City Council Approves Arena Deal with NHL's Flames," *The Globe and Mail*, July 30, 2019, https://www.theglobeandmail.com/canada/alberta/article-calgary-city-council-approves-arena-deal-with-nhls-flames/.

75. Potkins, "'Public Money is Being Used for Public Good.'"

76. Braid, "Council Finds a Backbone, City Gets an Arena."

77. Cruickshank, "Amid Controversy, Calgary—Finally—Gets Approval."

78. Amanda Stephenson, "Flames Ownership Poised to Take on New Role as Real Estate Developer," in *Calgary Herald*, July 25, 2019, https://calgaryherald.com/business/

local-business/flames-ownership-poised-to-take-on-new-role-as-real-estate-developer. See also Patrick Johnston, "The Canucks Built Their Arena All by Themselves, So Why Can't The Flames?" in *The Province*, July 26, 2019, https://theprovince.com/sports/hockey/nhl/vancouver-canucks/patrick-johnston-the-canucks-built-their-arena-all-by-themselves-so-why-cant-the-flames.

79. Marty Klinkenberg, "After Years of Stunted Talks, Calgary May Be Ready to Build a New Hockey Arena," *The Globe and Mail*, July 21, 2019, https://www.theglobeandmail.com/sports/hockey/article-after-years-of-stunted-talks-calgary-may-be-ready-to-build-a-new/.

80. Bruce Garrioch, "NHL Commissioner Gary Bettman Says Ottawa Senators Need a New Home," *Ottawa Sun*, November 10, 2017, https://ottawasun.com/sports/hockey/nhl/ottawa-senators/bettman-says-the-senators-need-a-new-home.

81. Lisa Wallace, "Sens Owner Melnyk's Relocation Talk Puts Chill On NHL 100 Festivities," *CBC Sports*, December 15, 2017, https://ottawasun.com/sports/hockey/nhl/ottawa-senators/bettman-says-the-senators-need-a-new-home. In an effort to improve his bottom line, Melnyk cut the Senators' office staff and since the end of the 2017–18 season has had several of the team's high-priced players—Erik Karlsson, Mike Hoffman, Matt Duchene, Ryan Dzingel, and Mark Stone—traded to other teams.

82. Melnyk was quoted in Wayne Scanlon, "Melnyk Back to Stirring Pot on LeBreton Flats," *Ottawa Citizen,* April 13, 2018, https://ottawacitizen.com/news/local-news/melnyk-back-to-stirring-pot-on-lebreton-flats.

83. All quotations from John Willing, "NCC, RendezVous have agreed in principle on LeBreton Flats," *Ottawa Citizen*, January 25, 2018, https://ottawacitizen.com/news/local-news/ncc-rendezvous-have-agreement-in-principle-on-lebreton-flats.

84. Watson was quoted in Joanne Chianello, "Senators Asked City to Pay for Arena, Mayor Says," *CBC News*, November 29, 2018, https://www.cbc.ca/news/canada/ottawa/senators-ask-city-pay-arena-mayor-1.4923338.

85. Both quotations from John Willing, "Ottawa Senators Owner Eugene Melnyk Suing Partners Over 'Failed' Downtown NHL Arena Bid," *Ottawa Citizen*, updated November 24, 2018, https://ottawacitizen.com/news/local-news/eugene-melnyk-suing-john-ruddy-and-trinity-over-failed-joint-venture-at-lebreton-flats. For a detailed examination of these developments, see Adrian Humphreys and Barbara Shecter, "Field of Broken Dreams: The Inside Story of How Ottawa's $4B Landmark Development Deal Fell to Pieces," *National Post*, November 23, 2018, https://nationalpost.com/news/canada/field-of-broken-dreams-eugene-melnyk-files-lawsuit-against-partners-in-failing-4b-ottawa-development-project.

86. Ian Mendes, "Melnyk Now Willing to Play in a Building He Doesn't Own," *TSN.ca*, December 19, 2018, https://www.tsn.ca/melnyk-now-willing-to-play-in-a-building-he-doesn-t-own-1.1228850. See also *Edmonton Journal*, December 18, 2018.

87. Zack Spedden, "NHL Could Get Involved in Ottawa Senators Arena Situation," *Arena Digest,* December 5, 2018, https://arenadigest.com/2018/12/05/nhl-get-involved-ottawa-senators-arena-situation/.

88. Adrian Humphreys and Barbara Shecter, "Field of Broken Dreams: The Inside Story of How Ottawa's $4B Landmark Development Deal Fell to Pieces," *National Post*, November 23, 2018, https://nationalpost.com/news/canada/field-of-broken-dreams-eugene-melnyk-files-lawsuit-against-partners-in-failing-4b-ottawa-development-project.

89. James Bagnall, "The NCC's Next Steps After RendezVous LeBreton's Demise," *Ottawa Citizen*, updated March 2, 2019, https://ottawacitizen.com/business/local-business/bagnall-the-nccs-next-steps-after-rendezvous-lebretons-demise.

90. James Bagnall, "Does Ottawa Senators Owner Eugene Melnyk Have a Case of Edmonton Envy?" *Ottawa Citizen,* January 24, 2019, https://ottawacitizen.com/news/local-news/bagnall-does-ottawa-senators-owner-eugene-melnyk-have-a-case-of-edmonton-envy. Gary Bettman has at least reassured Senators fans that the Ottawa franchise will not be moved. See "Bettman Denies Possibility of Sens Moving; Is Confident in Melnyk," *TSN*, March 6, 2019, https://www.tsn.ca/bettman-denies-possibility-of-sens-moving-is-confident-in-melnyk-1.1268794.

BIBLIOGRAPHY

BOOKS AND ARTICLES

Artibise, Alan F.J. "Boosterism and the Development of Prairie Cities, 1871–1913." In *Town and City: Aspects of Western Canadian Urban Development*, edited by Alan F.J. Artibise, 209–35. Regina: Canadian Plains Research Centre, 1981.

Betke, Carl. "The Original City of Edmonton: A Derivative Prairie Urban Community." In *Town and City: Aspects of Western Canadian Urban Development*, edited by Alan F.J. Artibise, 329–36. Regina: Canadian Plains Research Centre, University of Regina, 1981.

———. "Sports Promotion in the Western Canadian City: The Example of Early Edmonton." *Urban History Review* XII (1983): 47–56.

———. "Winter Sports in the Early Urban Environment of Prairie Canada." In *Winter Sports in the West*, edited by Elise A. Corbet and Anthony W. Rasporich, 52–68. Calgary: University of Calgary, 1990.

Bliss, Michael. *A Living Profit: Studies in the Social History of Canadian Business, 1883–1911*. Toronto: McClelland & Stewart, 1974.

Cashman, Tony. *The Edmonton Story: The Life and Times of Edmonton, Alberta*. Edmonton: Institute of Applied Art, 1956.

———. *The Best Edmonton Stories*. Edmonton: Hurtig Publishers, 1976.

———. *Edmonton Exhibition: The First Hundred Years*. Edmonton: Edmonton Exhibition Association, 1979.

Coates, Dennis, and Brad Humphreys. "Do Economists Reach a Conclusion on Subsidies for Sports Franchises, Stadiums, and Mega-Events?" *Econ Journal Watch* 5, no. 3 (2008): 294–315.

———. "The Effect of Professional Sports on Earnings and Employment in the Services and Retail Sectors in U.S. Cities." *Regional Science and Urban Economics* 33 (2003): 175–98.

Coleman, Charles L. *The Trail of the Stanley Cup*. Vol. 1: 1826–1926. Dubuque: National Hockey League, 1966.

Conacher, Brian. *As the Puck Turns: A Personal Journey through the World of Hockey*. Mississauga: John Wiley & Sons Canada, 2007.

Crompton, John. "Economic Impact Analysis of Sports Facilities and Events: Eleven Sources of Misapplication." *Journal of Sport Management* 9, no. 1 (1995): 14–35.

Delaney, Kevin, and Rick Eckstein. *Public Dollars, Private Stadiums: Battles Over Building Sports Stadiums*. New Brunswick, New Jersey: Rutgers University Press, 2003.

deMause, Neil, and Joanna Cagan. *Field of Schemes: How the Great Stadium Swindle Turns Public Money Into Private Profit*. Lincoln and London: University of Nebraska Press, 2008.

Ducey, Brant E. *The Rajah of Renfrew*. Edmonton: University of Alberta Press, 1998.

Dys, Hans J. *Gut Instinct: The Life and Times of Dr. Charles Allard*. Edmonton: Camary Holdings, 2010.

Euchner, Charles C. *Playing the Field: Why Sports Teams Move and Cities Fight to Keep Them*. Baltimore and London: Johns Hopkins University Press, 1994.

Florida, Richard. *The Rise of the Creative Class*. New York: Basic Books, 2002

———. "The Never-Ending Stadium Boondoggle." CityLab, September 10, 2015. https://www.citylab.com/equity/2015/09/the-never-ending-stadium-boondoggle/403666/.

———. *The New Urban Crisis: How Our Cities Are Increasing Inequality, Deepening Segregation, and Failing the Middle Class—And What We Can Do about It*. New York: Basic Books, 2017.

Gilpin, John F. *Edmonton: Gateway to the North. An Illustrated History*. Edmonton: Windsor Publications, 1984.

Goldblatt, David. *The Game of Our Lives: The English Premier League and the Making of Modern Britain*. New York: Nation Books, 2014.

Granzow, Kara, and Amber Dean. "Revanchism in the Canadian West: Gentrification and Resettlement in a Prairie City." *Topia: Canadian Journal of Cultural Studies* 18 (2007): 89–106.

Grescoe, Paul, and David Cruise. *The Money Rustlers: Millionaires of the New West*. Markham: Penguin Books Canada, 1985.

Gruneau, Richard, and David Whitson. *Hockey Night in Canada: Sport, Identities and Cultural Politics*. Toronto: Garamond Press, 1993.

Hall, M. Ann. *The Grads Are Playing Tonight!* Edmonton: University of Alberta Press, 2011.

Hannigan, John. *Fantasy City: Pleasure and Profit in the Postmodern Metropolis*. New York: Routledge, 1995.

Hardy, Stephen. "Two-Way Hockey: Selling Canada's Game in North America, 1875–1935." In *Playing for Change: The Continuing Struggle for Sport and Recreation*, edited by Russell Field, 198–228. Toronto: University of Toronto Press, 2015.

Howell, Colin. *Blood, Sweat, and Cheers: Sport and the Making of Modern Canada*. Toronto: University of Toronto Press, 2001.

Humphreys, Brad R., and Li Zhou. "Sports Facilities, Agglomeration, and Public Subsidies." *Regional Science and Urban Economics* 54 (2015): 60–73.

Hunter, Bill (with Bob Weber). *Wild Bill: Bill Hunter's Legendary 65 Years in Canadian Sport*. Calgary: Johnson Gorman Publishers, 2000.

Hunter, Douglas. *The Glory Barons: The Saga of the Edmonton Oilers*. Toronto: Viking, 1999.

Ipsos Reid. "Three Quarters (76%) of Edmontonians 'Disagree' That City Should Provide Taxpayers' Money for a New Hockey Arena." Accessed August 28, 2009. https://www.

ipsos.com/en-ca/three-quarters-76-edmontonians-disagree-city-should-provide-taxpayers-money-new-hockey-arena.

Iveson, Don. "Final Arena Vote Rationale." Accessed May 23, 2013. https://doniveson.ca/2013/05/15/final-arena-vote-rationale/#more-1804.

Jenish, D'Arcy. *The NHL: A Centennial History: 100 Years of On-Ice Action and Boardroom Battles.* Toronto: Doubleday Canada, 2013.

———. *The Stanley Cup: A Hundred Years of Hockey at Its Best.* Toronto: McClelland & Stewart, 1992.

Kidd, Bruce. "The Men's Cultural Center." In *Sport, Men, and the Gender Order: Critical Feminist Perspectives*, edited by Michael A. Messner and Donald F. Sabo, 31–43. Champaign, Ill: Human Kinetics Books, 1990.

———. *The Struggle for Canadian Sport.* Toronto: University of Toronto Press, 1996.

Kidd, Bruce, and John Macfarlane. *The Death of Hockey.* Toronto: New Press, 1972.

Klinkenberg, Marty. *The McDavid Effect: Connor McDavid and the New Hope for Hockey.* Toronto: Simon & Schuster, 2016.

Leo, Christopher. "Global Change and Local Politics: Economic Decline and the Local Regime in Edmonton." *Journal of Urban Affairs* 17, no 3 (1995): 277–300.

Leonard, David, John E. McIsaac, and Sheilagh Jameson. *A Builder of the Northwest: The Life and Times of Richard Secord, 1860–1935.* Edmonton: Richard Y. Secord, 1981.

Lightbody, James. *City Politics, Canada.* Peterborough: Broadview Press, 2006.

———. "Edmonton." In *City Politics in Canada*, edited by Warren Magnusson and Andrew Sancton, 255–90. Toronto: University of Toronto Press, 1983.

Long, Judith Grant. "Full Count: The Real Cost of Public Funding for Major League Sports Facilities." *Journal of Sports Economics* 6 (2005): 119–43.

———. *Public/Private Partnerships for Major League Sports Facilities.* New York: Routledge, 2013.

Lorenz, Stacy. "A Lively Interest on the Prairies: Western Canada, the Mass Media, and a 'World of Sport,' 1870–1939." *Journal of Sport History* 27 (2000): 195–227.

MacGregor, James Grierson. *Edmonton: A History.* Edmonton: Hurtig Publishers, 1975.

Marx, Karl. "The Eighteenth Brumaire of Louis Bonaparte" (excerpts). In *Karl Marx: Selected Writings*, edited by L. Simon, 187–208. Indianapolis: Hackett Publishing, 1994.

Mason, Dan. *Sports Development Projects: Current and Proposed in North America.* Report prepared for the city of Edmonton, 2007.

McConnell, Terry, and J'Lyn Nye, with Peter Pocklington. *I'd Trade Him Again: On Gretzky, Politics and the Pursuit of the Perfect Deal.* Bolton: Fenn Publishing, 2009.

McKinley, Michael. *Hockey: A People's History.* Toronto: McClelland & Stewart, 2006.

———. *Putting a Roof on Winter: Hockey's Rise from Sport to Spectacle.* Vancouver: Greystone Books, 2000.

Mills, David. "100 Years of Sports." In *Alberta: A State of Mind*, edited by Sydney Sharpe, Roger Gibbins, James H. Marsh, and Heather Bala Edwards, 197–231. Toronto: Key Porter Books, 2005.

———. "The Battle of Alberta: Entrepreneurs and the Business of Hockey in Edmonton and Calgary." *Alberta* 2 (1990): 1–25.

———. "The Blue Line and the Bottom Line: Entrepreneurs and the Business of Hockey, 1927–90." In *The Business of Professional Sports*, edited by Paul D. Staudohar and James A. Mangan, 175–202. Urbana: University of Illinois Press, 1991.

———. "Peter Pocklington and the Business of Hockey." In *Edmonton: The Life of a City*, edited by Bob Hesketh and Frances Swyripa, 306–15. Edmonton: NeWest Publishers, 1995.

———. "The Visible Hand and the Management of Hockey." In *Method and Methodology in Sport and Cultural History*, edited by Kevin B. Wamsley, 244–80. Dubuque: A Times Mirror Higher Education Group, 1995.

Morrow, Don, and Kevin B. Wamsley. *Sport in Canada: A History*. Don Mills: Oxford University Press, 2013.

Mott, Morris. "The British Protestant Pioneers and the Establishment of Manly Sports in Manitoba, 1870–1886." *Journal of Sport History* 7 (1980): 25–36.

Newman, Peter C. *The Acquisitors: The Canadian Establishment*, vol. 2. Toronto: McClelland & Stewart, 1981.

O'Riordan, Terence. "The 'Puck-Eaters': Hockey as a Unifying Community Experience in Edmonton and Strathcona, 1894–1905." *Alberta History* 49, no. 2 (2001): 2–11.

Proudfoot, Shannon. "Long-Time Listener, First-Time Caller." In *Best Canadian Sports Writing*, edited by Stacey May Fowles and Pasha Malla, 29–37. Toronto: ECW Press, 2017.

Quirk, James, and Rodney D. Fort. *Pay Dirt: The Business of Professional Team Sports*. Princeton: Princeton University Press, 1992.

Richler, Mordecai. "King of the New Canada." *New York Times Magazine*. September 29, 1985. https://www.nytimes.com/1985/09/29/magazine/king-of-the-new-canada.html.

Rosentraub, Mark S. *Major League Losers: The Real Cost of Sports and Who's Paying For It*. New York: Basic Books, 1999.

———. *Major League Winners: Using Sports and Cultural Centers as Tools for Economic Development*. Boca Raton, FL: CRC Press, 2009.

Ross, James Andrew. "Hockey Capital: Commerce, Culture, and the National Hockey League, 1917–1967." PhD diss., University of Western Ontario, 2008.

Roxborough, Henry. *The Stanley Cup Story*. Toronto: The Ryerson Press, 1964.

Sandor, Stephen. *The Battle of Alberta: A Century of Hockey's Greatest Rivalry*. Edmonton: Heritage House, 2005.

Scherer, Jay, and Judy Davidson. "Promoting the 'Arriviste' City: Producing Neoliberal Urban Identity and Communities of Consumption During the Edmonton Oilers' 2006 Playoff Campaign." *International Review For the Sociology of Sport* 46, no. 2 (2011): 157–80.

Scherer, Jay, and Steven J. Jackson. "From Corporate Welfare to National Interest: Newspaper Analysis of the Public Subsidization of NHL Hockey Debate in Canada." *Sociology of Sport Journal* 21 (2004): 36–60.

Scherer, Jay, and Michael Sam. "Policing the Cyber Agenda: New Media Technologies and Recycled Claims in a Local Stadium Debate." *Sport in Society* 13, no. 10 (2010): 1469–85.

Short, John. "The Edmonton Oilers: A History." In *Positive Power: The Story of the Edmonton Oilers*, edited by William F. Dowbiggin, 82–96. Edmonton: Executive Sport Publications, 1982.

Shubert, Howard. *Architecture on Ice: A History of the Hockey Arena*. Montreal: McGill-Queens University Press, 2016.

Silver, Jim. *Thin Ice: Money, Politics, and the Demise of an NHL Franchise*. Halifax: Fernwood Press, 1996.

Smith, Neil. *The New Urban Frontier: Gentrification and the Revanchist City*. London: Routledge, 1996.

Sorensen, Marianne. *Edmonton Homeless Counts: 1999 to 2010 Trend Analysis*. December 1, 2010. http://homewardtrust.ca/wp-content/uploads/2016/12/December-2010-Edmonton-Homeless-Count.pdf.

Stamp, Gordon. "Mayor Stephen Mandel...Manipulating the Process From the Very Beginning." Election Pamphet, 2010.

Staudohar, Paul. *The Sports Industry and Collective Bargaining*. Ithaca: Cornell University Press, 1986.

Taft, Kevin. *Democracy Derailed: A Breakdown of Government Accountability in Alberta and How to Get It Back on Track*. Red Deer: Red Deer Press, 2007.

———. *Follow the Money: Where is Alberta's Wealth Going?* Calgary: Detselig Enterprises, 2012.

Turchansky, Ray. *Edmonton Oilers Hockey Club: Celebrating 25 Years in the Heartland of Hockey*. Edmonton: Edmonton Journal Group, 2003.

Voisey, Paul. "Boosting the Small Prairie Town, 1904–1931: An Example from Southern Alberta." In *Town and City: Aspects of Western Canadian Urban Development*, edited by Alan F.J. Artibise, 201–35. Regina: Canadian Plains Research Centre and University of Regina, 1981.

———. "Unsolved Mysteries of Edmonton's Growth." In *Edmonton: The Life of a City*, edited by Bob Hesketh and Frances Swyripa, 316–35. Edmonton: NeWest Publishers, 1995.

Wall, Karen L. *Game Plan: A Social History of Sport in Alberta*. Edmonton: University of Alberta Press, 2012.

Whitson, David. "Hockey and Canadian Popular Culture: The Making and Remaking of Identities." In *Method and Methodology in Sport and Cultural History*, edited by K.B. Wamsley, 188–202. Dubuque: Brown & Benchmark Publishers, 1995.

Whitson, David, and Richard Gruneau. "Introduction." In *Artificial Ice: Hockey, Culture, and Commerce*, edited by David Whitson and Richard Gruneau, 1–25. Toronto: Garamond Press, 2006.

Whitson, David, and Donald Macintosh. "Becoming a World-Class City: Hallmark Events and Sport Franchises in the Growth Strategies of Western Canadian Cities." *Sociology of Sport Journal* 10 (1993): 221–40.

Willes, Ed. *The Rebel League: The Short and Unruly Life of the World Hockey Association*. Toronto: McClelland & Stewart, 2004.

Wong, John. "From Rat Portage to Kenora: The Death of a (Big-Time) Hockey Dream." *Journal of Sport History* 33 (2006): 175–91.

Zimbalist, Andrew. *The Bottom Line: Observations and Arguments in the Sports Business*. Philadelphia: Temple University Press, 2006.

MUNICIPAL REPORTS AND OFFICIAL DOCUMENTS

The municipal reports and official documents listed are either not accessible, do not have further information regarding where to find them, were obtained by FOIP requests, and/or are from Linda McCulloch's (then Linda Sloan) documents and notes from the period when she was councillor (2004 to 2013).

"Administration Response to Council's Questions." December 10, 2010.

Alberta Municipal Affairs, "Petition to Your Council: Information for the General Public, Elected Officials and Municipal Officers." Government of Alberta, October 2017. http://www.municipalaffairs.alberta.ca/documents/Petition%20to%20Your%20Council.pdf.

Arena Leadership Committee. *City Shaping: The Summary Report of the Leadership Committee for a new Sports/Entertainment Facility for Edmonton.* Edmonton, 2008.

———. *City Shaping: Confidential Draft Report of the Leadership Committee for a new Sports/Entertainment Facility for Edmonton.* Edmonton, 2007.

Calgary Municipal Land Corporation (CMLC). "Rivers District Master Plan." April 2018. http://www.calgarymlc.ca/riversdistrictmasterplan#rivers-district-intro.

City of Edmonton. "Agreement Form: Major Downtown Development—Public Survey." January 25, 2011.

———. "Agreement Form: New Edmonton Arena." September 21, 2006.

———. "Agreement Form: Strategic Communications Consulting and Support." May 29, 2012.

———. *Alternative Locations of Proposed Sports Arena to Replace the Edmonton Gardens: A Report Prepared for the Special Projects Committee of City Council and the Board of Directors, Edmonton Exhibition Association.* Edmonton: Urban Renewal Section, City Planning Department, 1964.

———. "Amending Agreement Form: Major Downtown Development—Public Consultation and Facilitation." December 20, 2010.

———. *Capital City Downtown Plan.* Adopted by the City of Edmonton, April 30, 1997. https://issuu.com/aesdl/docs/edmonton__alta.__-_1997_-_capital_c.

———. "Capital City Downtown Plan." 2010.

———. *A Coliseum, Trade Centre or Domed Stadium for Edmonton.* Edmonton: Planning Department, 1968.

———. "Description of Work." May 4, 2010.

———. Downtown Arena Consultation. August 10, 2010.

———. In-Camera Update on Negotiations. March 2, 2011.

———. In-Camera Update on Negotiations. April 6, 2011.

———. Internal memo. March 2010.

———. "A Legal Analysis of Public Participation in Decisions Regarding New Arena." December 1, 2010, 1.

———. "Non-Contract: A Request for Proposal 'NFRP' No. 918593 for Lease of Downtown Office Accommodation, City of Edmonton." October 2012.

———. *Northlands Area Redevelopment Plan (1990).* Edmonton: City of Edmonton Planning & Development, 2003.

———. "Potential Downtown Arena—Alternative Funding Methods." April 6, 2011.

———. "Responses to Councillors' Questions." October 27, 2011.

———. Update on the Potential Downtown Sports and Entertainment Facility. January 17, 2011.

———. *The Urban Renewal Concept Report: Central Business District.* Edmonton: Urban Renewal Division, Planning Department, 1967.

City of Edmonton Planning Department. *General Plan for the City of Edmonton: Part I: The Problem.* Edmonton: City of Edmonton, 1963.

———. *General Plan for the City of Edmonton: Part X: Downtown Edmonton*. Edmonton: City of Edmonton, 1963.

Cobb, Russell. "Retrofutures: Edmonton's Omniplex; Part 1." January 26, 2015. http:// citymuseumedmonton.ca/2015/01/26/retrofuture-edmontons-omniplex-part-1/.

———. "Retrofutures: Edmonton's Omniplex; Part 2." January 26, 2015. http:// citymuseumedmonton.ca/2015/01/26/retrofuture-edmontons-omniplex-part-2/.

———. "Recap: Retrofutures—Edmonton's Omniplex Debate." http://blog.mastermaq. ca/2014/12/17/recap-retrofutures-edmontons-omniplex-debate/.

Conventions, Sports & Leisure International (CSL). *Proposed Edmonton Arena Feasibility Study—Preliminary Draft*. 2007.

———. *Report on the Potential New Arena in Edmonton*. 2009.

Economic Development Edmonton (EDE). *Economic Impact of the Edmonton Oilers in the Edmonton, Alberta Capital Region, 1996–1997*. Edmonton: EDE, 1998.

Hellmuth, Obata & Kassabaum (HOK). "Arena Site Assessment Report." February 18, 2008.

———. *Rexall Renovation Study*. 2007.

Income Tax Act (Canada) R.S.C. 1985 (5th Supp), c.1 (the "Act"), 67.1 (1) Expenses for food, etc. [or entertainment]. https://laws-lois.justice.gc.ca/eng/acts/I-3.3/section-67.1.html.

"Katz Group Presentation To Edmonton City Council." Accessed October 29, 2010. http:// revitalizedowntown.ca/kat-group-presentation-to-edmonton-city-council-july-21-2011/.

"Katz Group Response to Council's Questions." December 10, 2010.

Mason, Dan. *Sports Development Projects: Current and Proposed in North America*. 2007.

Northlands. "Northlands Briefing Memo: A New Arena and Downtown Development for Edmonton." 2010.

"Northlands Response—Potential Downtown Arena." December 10, 2010.

Purves, Cecil. "Report on the Downtown Arena." January 31, 2012.

Rosentraub, Mark S. "Sports Facilities, A New Arena in Edmonton, And The Opportunities for Development and A City's Image: Lessons from Successful Experiences." Research paper commissioned by city of Edmonton, circa 2007, undated. https://www. edmonton.ca/attractions_events/documents/PDF/RosentraubReport.pdf.

———. "Comments on Andrew Zimbalist's *Report on Rexall Place, the Edmonton Oilers, and Plans for a New Arena*." 2011.

Rosentraub, Mark, and Dan Mason. *A New Arena-Anchored Development in Edmonton: A Confluence of Public and Private Needs*. Research paper commissioned by city of Edmonton, March 2010.

Sutherland, Tom. *Is a New Arena a Good Fit for Downtown Edmonton? Capital City Downtown Plan—Information Addendum*. Edmonton: Dialog, 2011.

Zimbalist, Andrew. *Report on Rexall Place, the Edmonton Oilers and Plans for a New Arena*, 2010.

INTERVIEWS

Anderson, Bryan (former Edmonton city councillor), September 27, 2017.

Bouma, Jerry (Northlands), October 25, 2016.

Caterina, Tony (Edmonton city councillor), November 15, 2017.

Daviss, Rick (executive director, Downtown Arena Project), December 12, 2017.

deMause, Neil (journalist), November 17, 2017.

Diotte, Kerry (former Edmonton city councillor), January 26, 2016.

Farbrother, Simon (former Edmonton city manager), December 21, 2017.

Fawcett, Max (journalist), August 9, 2016.

Gibbons, Ed (former Edmonton city councillor), October 11, 2017.

Grabia, Andy (hockey blogger), December 6, 2017.

Griffiths, Doug (former Minister of Alberta Municipal Affairs), November 23, 2015.

Griwkowsky, Fish (journalist), September 15, 2017.

Hennig, Scott (Canadian Taxpayers Federation), December 6, 2015.

Humphreys, Brad (sports economist), August 15 and October 12, 2017.

Huntley, Andy (Northlands), December 15, 2015.

Kent, Gordon (journalist), September 20, 2017.

Knowles, Ken (Northlands), December 13, 2016.

LaForge, Patrick (former president of the Edmonton Oilers), March 7, 2018.

Lamphier, Gary (journalist), September 21, 2016.

Leibovici, Karen (former Edmonton city councillor), May 23, 2017.

MacKinnon, John (journalist), September 20, 2017.

Mandel, Stephen (former mayor of Edmonton), December 20, 2017.

Maurer, Al (former Edmonton city manager), July 31, 2017.

McKeen, Scott (journalist and Edmonton city councillor), February 10, 2018.

Pocklington, Peter (former Oilers owner), October 11, 1988.

Purves, Cecil (former mayor of Edmonton), April 5, 2016.

Reimer, Jan (former mayor of Edmonton), February 20, 2018.

Rhyasen, Clare (former vice president of business and finance, Calgary Flames), February 21, 1989.

Simons, Paula (journalist), January 11, 2018.

Staples, David (journalist), January 26, 2018.

Williams, Mimi (community activist, Edmonton), November 21, 2017.

Zimbalist, Andrew (economist), November 12, 2015.

WEBSITES

The Battle of Alberta. http://battleofalberta.blogspot.com

BuildTheArena.com. http://www.buildthearena.com

Edmonton Maps. https://maps.edmonton.ca

ESPN. https://espn.com.

Field of Schemes. http://www.fieldofschemes.com

FlamesNation. https://flamesnation.ca

HicksBiz. http://www.hicksbiz.com

Huffington Post Alberta. https://www.huffingtonpost.ca/alberta/

Taxpayer.com. https://www.taxpayer.com

Why Downtown? https://whydowntown.wordpress.com

MAGAZINES AND NEWSPAPERS

Alberta Report	*Edmonton Sun*	*Macleans*
Alberta Venture	*Financial Post*	*The National Post*
Calgary Herald	*Financial World Magazine*	(Toronto)
Calgary Sun	*Forbes Magazine*	*Ottawa Citizen*
Edmonton Bulletin	*The Globe and Mail*	*Pacific Standard*
Edmonton Journal	(Toronto)	*Sports Illustrated*
Edmonton Metro	*The Hockey News*	*Washington Times*

INDEX

438